ZAGAT®

Chicago
Restaurants
2008/09

Including
Milwaukee

LOCAL EDITORS
Alice Van Housen and Ann Christenson
STAFF EDITOR
Allison Lynn

Published and distributed by
Zagat Survey, LLC
4 Columbus Circle
New York, NY 10019
T: 212.977.6000
E: chicago@zagat.com
www.zagat.com

ACKNOWLEDGMENTS

We thank Bill Rice, Brenda, Earl and Matthew Shapiro, Laura Levy Shatkin, Steven Shukow and Tom Van Housen, as well as the following members of our staff: Caitlin Eichelberger (assistant editor), Stacey Slate (editorial assistant), Sean Beachell, Maryanne Bertollo, Amy Cao, Sandy Cheng, Reni Chin, Larry Cohn, Deirdre Donovan, Alison Flick, Jeff Freier, Roy Jacob, Natalie Lebert, Mike Liao, Dave Makulec, Andre Pilette, Kimberly Rosado, Becky Ruthenburg, Liz Borod Wright, Sharon Yates, Anna Zappia and Kyle Zolner.

Contents

About This Survey

Here are the results of our **2008/09 Chicago Restaurants Survey,** covering 1,089 eateries in the Chicago area and Milwaukee. Like all of our guides, this one is based on the collective opinions of thousands of local consumers. Ratings have been updated throughout. We have retained a prior year's review for some places that have had no significant factual or ratings changes.

WHO PARTICIPATED: Input from 5,370 frequent diners forms the basis for the ratings and reviews in this guide (their comments are shown in quotation marks within the reviews). Of these surveyors, 44% are women, 56% men; the breakdown by age is 8% in their 20s; 24%, 30s; 23%, 40s; 26%, 50s; and 19%, 60s or above. Collectively they bring roughly 861,000 annual meals worth of experience to this Survey. We sincerely thank each of these participants – this book is really "theirs."

HELPFUL LISTS: Whether you're looking for a celebratory meal, a hot scene or a bargain bite, our top lists and indexes help you find exactly the right place. See Most Popular (page 7), Key Newcomers (page 9), Top Ratings (pages 10–15) and Best Buys (page 16). Milwaukee top lists start on page 225. We've also provided 41 handy indexes.

OUR EDITORS: Special thanks go to our local editors, Alice Van Housen, a freelance writer and editor; and Ann Christenson, the dining critic for *Milwaukee Magazine.*

ABOUT ZAGAT: This marks our 29th year reporting on the shared experiences of consumers like you. What started in 1979 as a hobby involving 200 of our friends has come a long way. Today we have well over 300,000 surveyors and now cover dining, entertaining, golf, hotels, movies, music, nightlife, resorts, shopping, spas, theater and tourist attractions worldwide.

SHARE YOUR OPINION: We invite you to join any of our upcoming surveys – just register at **ZAGAT.com,** where you can rate and review establishments year-round. Each participant will receive a free copy of the resulting guide when published.

AVAILABILITY: Zagat guides are available in all major bookstores as well as on **ZAGAT.com, ZAGAT.mobi** (for web-enabled mobile phones) and **ZAGAT TO GO** (for smartphones). The latter two products allow you to contact many thousands of establishments with just one click.

FEEDBACK: There is always room for improvement, thus we invite your comments and suggestions about any aspect of our performance. Did we get anything wrong? We really need your input! Just contact us at **chicago@zagat.com.**

New York, NY
June 26, 2008

Nina and Tim

Nina and Tim Zagat

What's New

This year was dominated by fresh debuts from familiar faces, tempting 81% of Chi-Towners to dine out as much as or more than they did two years ago. Up next, a rich roster of top toques is eyeing the Windy City.

HOT OPENINGS: Takashi Yagihashi launched his eponymous eatery in the former Scylla space, Art Smith's TABLE fifty-two became one of the city's toughest reservations to book, Bob Djahanguiri and Roland Liccioni debuted Old Town Brasserie Market, the Moto team opened Otom and Park 52 brought high-profile restaurateur Jerry Kleiner to Hyde Park. In Trump Tower, Sixteen served up swanky supping, while in the West Suburbs, Gaetano Di Benedetto pleased fans of his former La Piazza by returning with Gaetano's.

THIN (AND SMALL) IS IN: When a thin-crust purveyor, Spacca Napoli, nabs the No. 1 pizza rating, you know the flatbread revolution is here to stay. A Mano, La Madia, Purgatory Pizza and Union Pizzeria all got in the game, and Tocco, FoLLia's wood-fired sequel, was getting set to open at press time. Meanwhile, smaller bites are a hit as Shochu introduced an Americanized izakaya concept and Mercat a la Planxa premiered Jose Garces' Barcelona-inspired nibbles.

LOOKING FORWARD: Scheduled debuts include the Lettuce/Laurent Gras seafooder L.20; Marcus Samuelsson's small-plater C-House; ex-Avenues star Graham Elliot Bowles' eponymous River North New American; and Coco Pazzo chef Tony Priolo's Piccolo Sogno. Also upcoming are Jackson Park Grill, the long-delayed steakhouse from Jason Paskewitz; Jacky Pluton's return with brasserie Haussmann; and Province, Randy Zweiban's Latin-inspired New American. Finally, get ready for a haute invasion: super-chefs Terrance Brennan, Alain Ducasse, Todd English, Gordon Ramsay and Joël Robuchon are in varying stages of setting up – from rumor to lease signing – Chicago shops.

FINAL BOWS: As Schwa closed and reopened, other venerable venues had less fortunate fates. Among others, we said goodbye to: Allen's, Kevin, Le Français, Mas, Meritage, Salbute and Timo.

MILWAUKEE HOLDS ITS OWN: Staying true to its reputation for valuing quality over novelty, longtime high-caliber classics Sanford and Lake Park Bistro (and Lake Park's offspring, Bacchus) rose to the top of the Most Popular list. New arrivals included the sophisticated but affordable Meritage, sassy Southern comforter Maxie's and cosmopolitan Hinterland Erie Street Gastropub.

KEEPING TABS: While the average Chicago dinner tallies $35.17, just above the national average of $33.80, that's not stopping the city's fine diners. In fact, 54% would be willing to pay more for meals that are organic and 57% would pay extra for sustainably raised or procured fare, so expect to see those trends rise in the future.

Chicago, IL
Milwaukee, WI
June 26, 2008

Alice Van Housen
Ann Christenson

Ratings & Symbols

Zagat Top Spot	Name	Symbols	Cuisine	Zagat Ratings			
				FOOD	DECOR	SERVICE	COST

Area, Address & Contact

Ⓩ **Tim & Nina's** ◗ *Pizza*   ▽ 23 | 9 | 13 | $15

Hyde Park | 456 E. Chicago Ave. (Division St.) | 312-555-3867 | www.zagat.com

Review, surveyor comments in quotes

Hordes of "unkempt" U of C students have discovered this cafeteria-style "24/7 dive", which "single-handedly" started the "deep-dish sushi pizza craze" that's "sweeping the Windy City like a lake-effect storm"; "try the eel-pepperoni-wasabi-mozzarella or Osaka-Napolitano pies" – "they're to die for" – but bring patience, since "T & N never heard of training servers."

Ratings

Food, Decor and **Service** are rated on the Zagat 0 to 30 scale.

0	–	9	poor to fair
10	–	15	fair to good
16	–	19	good to very good
20	–	25	very good to excellent
26	–	30	extraordinary to perfection
	▽		low response | less reliable

Cost reflects our surveyors' average estimate of the price of a dinner with one drink and tip and is a benchmark only. Lunch is usually 25% less.

For **newcomers** or survey **write-ins** listed without ratings, the price range is indicated as follows:

I	$25 and below
M	$26 to $40
E	$41 to $65
VE	$66 or more

Symbols

Ⓩ	Zagat Top Spot (highest ratings, popularity and importance)
◗	serves after 11 PM
Ⓢ	closed on Sunday
Ⓜ	closed on Monday
⊄	no credit cards accepted

Maps

Index maps show restaurants with the highest Food ratings in those areas.

Most Popular

These places are plotted on the map at the back of the book.

1 Wildfire | *Steak*	**21** Mon Ami Gabi | *French*
2 Frontera Grill | *Mexican*	**22** Chicago Chop House | *Steak*
3 Tru | *French*	**23** Shaw's Crab House | *Seafood*
4 Charlie Trotter's | *American*	**24** Capital Grille | *Steak*
5 Gibsons | *Steak*	**25** Heaven on Seven | *Cajun/Creole*
6 Morton's | *Steak*	**26** NoMI | *French*
7 Alinea | *American*	**27** P.F. Chang's | *Chinese*
8 Joe's Seafood | *Seafood/Steak*	**28** Weber Grill | *BBQ*
9 Topolobampo | *Mexican*	**29** Blackbird | *American*
10 Everest | *French*	**30** Les Nomades | *French*
11 Lou Malnati's | *Pizza*	**31** Nick's Fishmarket | *Seafood*
12 Francesca's | *Italian*	**32** Coco Pazzo | *Italian*
13 mk | *American*	**33** Gene & Georgetti | *Steak*
14 Maggiano's | *Italian*	**34** North Pond | *American*
15 McCormick/Schmick's | *Sea*	**35** Palm, The | *Steak*
16 Spiaggia | *Italian*	**36** Café Spiaggia | *Italian*
17 Catch 35 | *Seafood*	**37** Bob Chinn's | *Seafood*
18 Giordano's | *Pizza*	**38** Spring* | *American/Seafood*
19 Cheesecake Factory | *American*	**39** Trattoria No. 10* | *Italian*
20 Rosebud, The | *Italian*	**40** Pappadeaux | *Seafood*

It's obvious that many of the above restaurants are among the Chicago area's most expensive, but if popularity were calibrated to price, we suspect that a number of other restaurants would join their ranks. Thus, we have added a list of 80 Best Buys on page 16.

---

* Indicates a tie with restaurant above

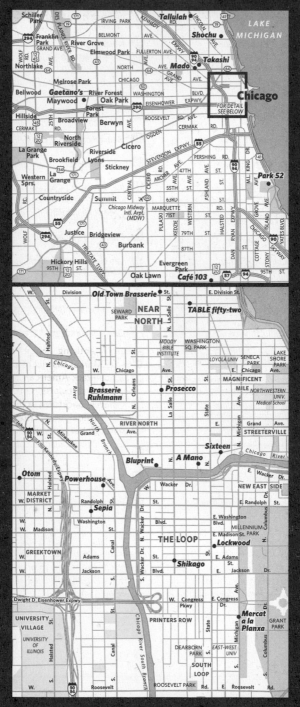

KEY NEWCOMERS

Schiller Park
Franklin Park
Northlake
River Grove
Elmwood Park
Tallulah
Shochu
LAKE MICHIGAN
Takashi
Mado
Melrose Park
Bellwood
Gaetano's
River Forest
Maywood
Oak Park
Forest Park
Hillside
Broadview
Berwyn
North Riverside
La Grange Park
Riverside
Lyons
Brookfield
Stickney
Western Sprs.
La Grange
Cicero
Chicago
FOR DETAIL SEE BELOW
Countryside
Summit
Chicago Midway Intl. Arpt. (MDW)
Park 52
Justice
Bridgeview
Burbank
Hickory Hills
Evergreen Park
Oak Lawn
Café 103

Old Town Brasserie
E. Division St.
NEAR NORTH
TABLE fifty-two
SEWARD PARK
MOODY BIBLE INSTITUTE
WASHINGTON SQ. PARK
LOYOLA UNIV
SENECA PARK
LAKE SHORE PARK
Brasserie Ruhlmann
Prosecco
MAGNIFICENT MILE
NORTHWESTERN UNIV. Medical School
RIVER NORTH
STREETERVILLE
Otom
Bluprint
A Mano
Sixteen
NEW EAST SIDE
Powerhouse
MARKET W. DISTRICT
Sepia
Wacker Dr.
THE LOOP
MILLENNIUM PARK
Lockwood
GREEKTOWN
Shikago
UNIVERSITY VILLAGE
UNIVERSITY OF ILLINOIS
PRINTERS ROW
Mercat a la Planxa
GRANT PARK
EAST-WEST UNIV
DEARBORN PARK
SOUTH LOOP
ROOSEVELT PARK

Key Newcomers

Our editors' take on some of the year's main new arrivals. See page 210 for a full list.

A Mano	*Italian*	Park 52	*American*
Bluprint	*American*	Powerhouse	*American*
Brasserie Ruhlmann	*French*	Prosecco	*Italian*
Café 103	*American*	Sepia	*American*
Gaetano's	*Italian*	Shikago	*Asian*
Lockwood	*American*	Shochu	*Amer./Japanese*
mado	*Italian/Mediterranean*	Sixteen	*American*
Mercat a la Planxa	*Spanish*	TABLE fifty-two	*American*
Old Town Brasserie	*French*	Takashi	*American/French*
Otom	*American*	Tallulah	*American*

The year to come should prove to be equally enticing. A number of spin-offs are in the works, including **Olo** (the Market District offshoot of Isabella's Estiatorio), **Perennial** (a Lincoln Park American bistro from the BOKA team) and an unnamed South Loop Lula spin-off. **The Bristol,** an affordable, artisanal New American in Bucktown, is the upcoming baby of Rick Tramonto protégé Chris Pendal; and **Mana Food Bar,** from part of the sushi wabi team, will mix global genres into modern vegetarian cuisine in the Division Street Corridor.

Top Food Ratings

Excludes places with low votes.

29 Alinea | *American*
Tallgrass | *French*

28 Carlos' | *French*
Les Nomades | *French*
Topolobampo | *Mexican*
Vie | *American*
Le Titi de Paris | *French*
Niche | *American*

27 Tru | *French*
Spring | *American/Seafood*
Charlie Trotter's | *American*
Everest | *French*
Seasons | *American*
Arun's | *Thai*
Blackbird | *American*
Spiaggia | *Italian*
Hot Doug's | *Hot Dogs*
Frontera Grill | *Mexican*
Avec | *Mediterranean*

26 sushi wabi | *Japanese*
Va Pensiero | *Italian*

mk | *American*
a tavola | *Italian*
Michael | *French*
Joe's Seafood | *Seafood/Steak*
Riccardo Trattoria | *Italian*
Barrington Country | *French*
M. Henry | *American*
Oceanique | *French/Seafood*
NoMI | *French*
1776 | *American*
Lao | *Chinese*
Lula | *Eclectic*
Green Zebra | *Vegetarian*
Gabriel's | *French/Italian*
Morton's | *Steak*

25 Tango Sur | *Argentinean*
Meiji | *Japanese*
Agami | *Japanese*
Avenues | *American*
Courtright's* | *American*
North Pond | *American*

BY CUISINE

AMERICAN (NEW)
29 Alinea
28 Vie
Niche
27 Spring
Charlie Trotter's

AMERICAN (TRAD.)
24 Kuma's Corner
TABLE fifty-two
Lawry's
Bongo Room
Hot Chocolate

ASIAN (MISC.)
25 Le Lan
Shanghai Terrace
23 Karma
22 Opera
21 Stir Crazy

BARBECUE
24 Smoque BBQ
23 Fat Willy's
22 Twin Anchors
Carson's Ribs
Robinson's Ribs

CAJUN/CREOLE
21 Pappadeaux
Wishbone
Heaven on Seven
20 Davis St. Fish
Dixie Kitchen

CHINESE
26 Lao
22 Evergreen
Happy Chef
Emperor's Choice
21 Phoenix

COFFEE SHOP/DINER
23 Manny's
Glenn's Diner
Original Pancake/Walker Bros.
22 Orange
Milk & Honey

ECLECTIC
26 Lula
25 Moto
24 Tweet
23 Aria
Twist

FRENCH

29 Tallgrass
28 Carlos'
   Les Nomades
   Le Titi de Paris
27 Tru

FRENCH (BISTRO)

26 Barrington Country
25 Retro Bistro
   D & J Bistro
24 Bistro Campagne
   Le Bouchon

GREEK

23 Artopolis
22 Santorini
   Parthenon
   Greek Islands
   Roditys

HOT DOGS/BURGERS

27 Hot Doug's
22 Superdawg
21 Al's #1 Beef
   Gold Coast Dogs
20 Wiener's Circle

INDIAN

24 India House
23 Marigold
22 Tiffin
   Indian Garden
   Mt. Everest

ITALIAN

27 Spiaggia
26 Va Pensiero
   a tavola
   Riccardo Trattoria
25 Mia Francesca

JAPANESE

26 sushi wabi
25 Meiji
   Agami
   Mirai Sushi
   Yoshi's Café

MEDITERRANEAN

27 Avec
25 Isabella's
24 Pita Inn
23 Artopolis
   Café des Architectes

MEXICAN

28 Topolobampo
27 Frontera Grill
25 Dorado
24 Cafe 28
   Salpicón

MIDDLE EASTERN

24 Noon-O-Kabab
   Pita Inn
23 Maza
22 Turquoise
21 Tizi Melloul

NUEVO LATINO

23 Nacional 27
22 Cuatro
   DeLaCosta
   Carnivale
21 Vermilion

PIZZA

24 Spacca Napoli
   Lou Malnati's
23 La Gondola
   Piece
22 Bricks

SEAFOOD

27 Spring
26 Joe's Seafood
   Oceanique
24 Catch 35
   Tramonto's

SMALL PLATES

27 Avec
26 Green Zebra
24 BOKA
23 Maza
21 Quartino

SPANISH/TAPAS

24 Mesón Sabika/Tapas
   Valencia
23 La Tasca
   Twist
22 Café Iberico
   Cafe Ba-Ba-Reeba!

STEAKHOUSES

26 Joe's Seafood
   Morton's
25 Tango Sur
   Ruth's Chris
   Gibsons

THAI

VEGETARIAN

BY SPECIAL FEATURE

BREAKFAST

BRUNCH

BUSINESS DINING

CHILD-FRIENDLY

HOTEL DINING

LATE DINING

MEET FOR A DRINK

NEWCOMERS (RATED)

PEOPLE-WATCHING

WINNING WINE LISTS

WORTH A TRIP

BY LOCATION

ANDERSONVILLE/ EDGEWATER

26 M. Henry
24 Francesca's
23 Anteprima
   Hopleaf
22 Ethiopian Diamond

BUCKTOWN

25 Coast Sushi
24 Café Absinthe
   Le Bouchon
   Hot Chocolate
23 Irazu

CHINATOWN

26 Lao
22 Penang
   Evergreen
   Happy Chef
   Emperor's Choice

GOLD COAST

27 Seasons
   Spiaggia
26 NoMI
   Morton's
25 Gibsons

GREEKTOWN

23 Artopolis
22 Santorini
   Parthenon
   Greek Island
   Roditys

LAKEVIEW

25 Tango Sur
   sola
   Yoshi's Café
   Mia Francesca
24 HB Home Bistro

LINCOLN PARK

29 Alinea
27 Charlie Trotter's
26 Riccardo Trattoria
25 North Pond
24 Tsuki

LINCOLN SQUARE/ UPTOWN

25 Agami
   Dorado
24 Thai Pastry
   Bistro Campagne
   Tweet

LITTLE ITALY

24 Francesca's
23 Chez Joël
22 Tuscany
   RoSal's Kitchen
   Rosebud

LOOP

27 Everest
   Avec
26 Morton's
24 Catch 35
   N9ne

MARKET DISTRICT

26 sushi wabi
25 Moto
   one sixtyblue
23 FoLLia
   Otom*

RIVER NORTH

28 Topolobampo
27 Frontera Grill
26 Joe's Seafood
25 Avenues
   Le Lan

STREETERVILLE

28 Les Nomades
27 Tru
25 Capital Grille
24 Volare
   Cité

SUBURBS

29 Tallgrass
28 Carlos'
   Vie
   Le Titi de Paris
   Niche

WEST LOOP

27 Blackbird
25 Meiji
23 May St. Market
   La Sardine
22 Coalfire Pizza

WICKER PARK

27 Spring
25 Mirai Sushi
24 Francesca's
   Bongo Room
   Bob San

Top Decor Ratings

| 28 | NoMI |
| | Alinea |

26	Tru
	North Pond
	Spiaggia
	Seasons
	Alhambra
	Room 21*
	Carnivale
	Shanghai Terrace
	Tramonto's
	Everest
	Japonais
	Niche
	SushiSamba rio
	Karma

25	Sepia
	Signature Room
	Les Nomades
	RL

Brasserie Ruhlmann
Lobby, The
Marché*
Zealous*
DeLaCosta
N9ne
Tallgrass
Cité
Courtright's
TABLE fifty-two
Charlie Trotter's
Finley's Grill
Carlos'

24	Lovells of Lake Forest
	Le Titi de Paris
	Avenues
	Le Colonial
	Hachi's Kitchen
	Opera
	Va Pensiero

OUTDOORS

Flatwater
Fulton's
Green Dolphin St.
Japonais
Mesón Sabika

Park Grill
Puck's at MCA
Room 21
Shanghai Terrace
SushiSamba rio

ROMANCE

Bistro Campagne
Brasserie Ruhlmann
DeLaCosta
Drawing Room/Le Passage
Everest

Le Colonial
Nacional 27
Pops for Champagne
Prosecco
Tizi Melloul

ROOMS

Alinea
Carnivale
Lockwood
Mercat a la Planxa
NoMI

North Pond
RL
Sepia
Shanghai Terrace
Spiaggia

VIEWS

Cité
Courtright's
Everest
NoMI
Park Grill

Riva
Signature Room
Sixteen
Spiaggia
Zed 451

Top Service Ratings

29 Alinea
Tallgrass

28 Niche

27 Seasons
Les Nomades
Everest
Tru
Charlie Trotter's
Avenues
Carlos'*
Le Titi de Paris

26 Shanghai Terrace
Arun's
Spiaggia
Moto
NoMI
Gabriel's

25 Michael
Topolobampo
Seasons Café

Spring
Va Pensiero
Otom
Vie*

24 Fogo de Chão
North Pond
Retro Bistro
mk
Capital Grille
TABLE fifty-two
1776
Courtright's
Joe's Seafood
a tavola
Lawry's
Ritz-Carlton Café
Blackbird
Froggy's
Morton's
one sixtyblue

Best Buys

In order of Bang for the Buck rating.

1. Potbelly Sandwich
2. Superdawg
3. Hot Doug's
4. Hannah's Bretzel
5. Margie's Candies
6. fRedhots
7. Gold Coast Dogs
8. Pita Inn
9. Wiener's Circle
10. Al's #1 Beef
11. Mr. Beef
12. Julius Meinl
13. M. Henry
14. Victory's Banner
15. Original Pancake/Walker Bros.
16. Aladdin's Eatery
17. Pompei Bakery
18. Irazu
19. Yolk
20. Milk & Honey
21. Lou Mitchell's
22. Penny's Noodle
23. Artopolis
24. Billy Goat Tavern
25. Russell's BBQ
26. Kuma's Corner
27. Nookies
28. Thai Pastry
29. Icosium Kafe
30. Art of Pizza
31. Smoque BBQ
32. Ann Sather
33. Poag Mahone's
34. Tweet
35. Breakfast Club
36. Eleven City Diner
37. Orange
38. Bongo Room
39. Chicago Diner
40. Duke of Perth

OTHER GOOD VALUES

African Harambee
Al Primo Canto
Andies
Army & Lou's
Babylon Eatery
Backstage Bistro
Bagel, The
Bandera
Chataigne
C.J.'s Eatery
Depot Diner
Dining Room/Kendall College
El Presidente
erwin
Flat Top Grill
Francesca's
Glenn's Diner
Hema's Kitchen
Ina's
Jerry's
Joy Yee's
La Brochette
Las Tablas
LuLu's Dim Sum
Maiz
Old Jerusalem
Parrot Cage
Pasta Palazzo
Pomegranate
Reza's
Riques
Silver Seafood
Stanley's
Stir Crazy
Tango Sur
Tempo
Tre Kronor
Tufano's
Uncommon Ground
West Town Tavern

CHICAGO
RESTAURANT
DIRECTORY

	FOOD	DECOR	SERVICE	COST

Adelle's *American* — 24 | 21 | 24 | $42

Wheaton | 1060 College Ave. (bet. President St. & Stoddard Ave.) | 630-784-8015 | www.adelles.com

A "find" in the Western Suburbs, this "steady performer" delivers "American-sized portions" of "homestyle" New American "with an upscale flair", "good wine deals" and live music on Thursdays; the "romantic" interior features a "fireplace in the background", while outdoors you'll find "great courtyard" seating "when it's warm."

Adesso *Italian* — 18 | 16 | 17 | $25

Lakeview | 3332 N. Broadway St. (bet. Buckingham Pl. & W. Aldine Ave.) | 773-868-1516 | www.eatadesso.com

"Italian bistro food" that's "decent for the price" brings boosters to this "tiny" Boys Town BYO for a "simple lunch, quick bite or to meet friends" (or make new ones at two communal tables); "spotty service" and "minimalistic" decor discourage some, but even those who mark it merely "average" assess it higher in summer when "you can dine outdoors" and "the boys walking by are hot"; N.B. scores do not reflect a recent chef and owner change.

Adobo Grill *Mexican* — 21 | 19 | 20 | $33

Old Town | 1610 N. Wells St. (North Ave.) | 312-266-7999
Wicker Park | 2005 W. Division St. (Damen Ave.) | 773-252-9990
NEW **Lombard** | Shops on Butterfield | 356 Yorktown Shopping Ctr. (S. Fairfield Ave.) | 630-627-9990
www.adobogrill.com

Pleased patrons of this "midscale Mexican" trio praise the "quality" fare with "bold flavors" and "a nice variety of Latin specialties" ("don't look for tacos or burritos"); the "party atmosphere", "especially on weekends", is "fun" to some, "noisy" to others, and while the "killer" "custom-made guacamole", "potent margaritas" and "impressive tequila list" are widely praised, banditos bemoan that they "seem to be the standouts."

NEW **African Harambee** *African* — ▽ 18 | 10 | 20 | $25

Rogers Park | 7537 N. Clark St. (Howard St.) | 773-764-2200

This Rogers Park newcomer offers a "good beginner's guide to African food" with "more variety" than a strictly Ethiopian restaurant and a choice of flatware or fingers, though hotheads hint the offerings "could be spicier"; a "friendly owner", honey wine and beer from the featured continent are additional assets, but the "decor is unfortunately not on par with the food."

Agami ● *Japanese* — 25 | 24 | 20 | $41

Uptown | 4712 N. Broadway St. (Leland Ave.) | 773-506-1854 | www.agamisushi.com

The "outrageous" "LSD-trip" decor rates almost as high as the "innovative maki" and "fresh, flavorful" fish (and "excellent cooked dishes too") at this "hip" Japanese "with a nightclub twist"; with a "helpful staff", it's "surprisingly upscale for its [Uptown] location", and partyers peg it as "perfect before or after a show at the Riv or Aragon" – in part due to its "creative" signature aloe and pear martinis.

	FOOD	DECOR	SERVICE	COST

Aigre Doux *American*   24 | 21 | 21 | $59

River North | 230 W. Kinzie St. (bet. N. Franklin & Wells Sts.) | 312-329-9400 | www.aigredouxchicago.com

"Inventive" but "not over-the-top" New American cuisine has the "pretty people" packing into this "upbeat", slightly "pricey" River Norther for "knockout dishes" and "incredible desserts"; the "contemporary loft" space "replete with hanging bulbs" can get "unspeakably (as it were) loud", and some aver the "overworked" service "needs improvement" – but consensus calls it "more sweet than sour."

NEW Ai Sushi Lounge ● *Japanese*   21 | 22 | 19 | $40

River North | 358 W. Ontario St. (Orleans St.) | 312-335-9888 | www.aichicago.us

This "hip, stylish" River North Japanese "brings something new" to the former Kizoku space – including "blowfish in season" (from one of the few licensed fugu chefs in the U.S.) and "fresh, inventive maki and sashimi"; service is deemed "above average" while the outlay is either "pricey" or "reasonable", depending on your budget.

Akai Hana *Japanese*   21 | 13 | 18 | $26

Wilmette | 3223 W. Lake Ave. (Skokie Blvd.) | 847-251-0384 | www.akaihanasushi.com

North Suburban sushi stalwarts "crowd" this "reliable", "family-friendly" Japanese in Wilmette that "keeps it simple" via "solid" "bargain"-priced fare in a "low-key" "strip-mall location" with a staff that "means well"; snipers see it "getting tired", though, saying the service is "mixed" and the "decor could use a tweak."

Aladdin's Eatery *Mideastern*   21 | 14 | 17 | $14

Lincoln Park | 614 W. Diversey Pkwy. (Clark St.) | 773-327-6300 | www.aladdinseatery.com

"Simple, tasty ethnic fast food" such as "soul-warming soups", a "quick pita or shawarma" and other "low-priced Middle Eastern dishes" satisfies surveyors who seek out this Lincoln Park "staple" that also offers "good smoothies"; even middle-of-the-roaders who mark it "nothing special" admit it's "dependable" for a "cheap date."

A La Turka *Turkish*   20 | 20 | 20 | $27

Lakeview | 3134 N. Lincoln Ave. (Belmont Ave.) | 773-935-6447 | www.alaturkachicago.com

"Savor the flavors" of "Turkey without leaving Chicago" at this "funky", "dim" Lakeview lair, where the "authentic" food is "tasty" and "well prepared", the "Zorba-like owner is charming" and the "beautiful belly dancers" (Thursday–Sunday nights) are "amazing"; it adds up to "a fun evening of Turkish food, culture and atmosphere" "at a reasonable price."

⧫ Alhambra Palace Restaurant *Mideastern*   13 | 26 | 12 | $37

Market District | 1240 W. Randolph St. (bet. Elizabeth St. & Racine Ave.) | 312-666-9555 | www.alhambrapalacerestaurant.com

Offering an "exotic experience without the airfare", this massive Market District Middle Eastern is "high on the entertainment factor" thanks to its "opulent" "Casbah" decor and "great people-watching", belly dancing, flamenco, bands and other attractions; most are less amused by the food ("mediocre", "overpriced") and "spotty" service, but optimists theorize that they're "still learning."

Ⓩ Alinea Ⓜ *American* `29` `28` `29` `$195`

Lincoln Park | 1723 N. Halsted St. (bet. North Ave. & Willow St.) | 312-867-0110 | www.alinearestaurant.com

"Visionary" chef Grant Achatz is "back in full swing" after a much-publicized health scare and offers an "adventure in amazement" at this Lincoln Park "gastronomic theater for all five senses", rated No. 1 for Food in Chicago (and maybe "the world") thanks to "delicate", "witty" New American dishes (some "come with instructions" and "creative tableware") exhibiting "staggering" "innovation"; a "flawless", "surprisingly unpretentious" staff (ranked No. 1 for Service), "thoughtful wine pairings" and "quiet, minimalist" surroundings are more reasons why "anyone who cares about food" "must visit" – just brace for "astronomically expensive" tabs.

NEW Al Primo Canto Ⓜ *Brazilian/Italian* `-` `-` `-` `M`

Northwest Side | 5414 W. Devon Ave. (Central Ave.) | 773-631-0100 | www.alprimocanto.com

If you want a "different type of restaurant", try this "thoughtful, civilized" Northwest Side churrascaria that puts Brazilian-Italian *galetto* (rotisserie chicken) on a prix fixe menu of "delicious" food that "just keeps coming" (now you can also order à la carte); "neat surroundings" and "good service" also net nods.

Al's #1 Italian Beef *Sandwiches* `21` `8` `15` `$10`

River North | 169 W. Ontario St. (Wells St.) | 312-943-3222 ◑
Little Italy | 1079 W. Taylor St. (Aberdeen St.) | 312-226-4017 🗷🖘
Evanston | 622 Davis St. (Chicago Ave.) | 847-424-9704
Lincolnwood | Lincolnwood Town Ctr. | 3333 W. Touhy Ave. (McCormick Blvd.) | 847-673-2333
Addison | 1600 W. Lake St. (bet. Lombard & Rohlwing Rds.) | 630-773-4599
Niles | 5948 W. Touhy Ave. (N. Lehigh Ave.) | 847-647-1577
Park Ridge | 33 S. Northwest Hwy. (bet. Euclid & Prospect Aves.) | 847-318-7700
Chicago Heights | 551 W. 14th St. (Division St.) | 708-748-2333
Oak Lawn | 10276 S. Harlem Ave. (103rd St.) | 708-636-2333
Tinley Park | 7132 183rd St. (Harlem Ave.) | 708-444-2333
www.alsbeef.com
Additional locations throughout the Chicago area

"Are your cholesterol and sodium dangerously low?" – then visit this "quintessential" "Chicago legend", a "cheap-eats" chain spun off from the 1938 "Taylor Street original" that's cheered for Italian beef "sandwiches so juicy there's no neat way to eat them" (plus "delicious burgers and sausages, and even better fries"); "lacking" service and "nonexistent" decor don't deter the "crowds", though some who swear the kitchen's "getting a little skimpy on the meat" say they "don't get why it calls itself #1."

	FOOD	DECOR	SERVICE	COST

NEW A Mano *Italian* — 21 | 19 | 20 | $40

River North | 335 N. Dearborn St. (bet. Kinzie St. & Wacker Dr.) | 312-629-3500 | www.amanochicago.com

The Bin 36 creators turn out "flavorful" seasonal sustenance alongside Brian Duncan's "great wine by the glass list" at this River North Italian that's prime for a "night out with friends" or a date that "won't break the bank"; the "airy lower-level room" with an "open kitchen" strikes some as a "cool" "blend of rustic and modern", others as an "upscale cafeteria", and surveyors are similarly split on the service ("excellent" vs. "uncoordinated").

Amber Cafe ⑤ *American* — 24 | 21 | 21 | $47

Westmont | 13 N. Cass Ave. (Burlington Ave.) | 630-515-8080 | www.ambercafe.net

Western Suburban locals feel "lucky" to have this "excellent" "seasonal" New American "gem" in Westmont with "a real downtown feel", "inviting atmosphere" and "well-priced wine list", even if some suppers call the experience "pricey for the quality"; P.S. the "beautiful" enclosed patio is "a nice place to sit out in the summer."

American Girl Place Cafe *American* — 13 | 23 | 21 | $27

Gold Coast | American Girl Pl. | 111 E. Chicago Ave. (Michigan Ave.) | 312-943-9400 | www.americangirlplace.com

"Your daughter/granddaughter/niece will remember forever" her meal at this Gold Coast "little girls' heaven", even if some find it "expensive" for "ok" American food that cynics claim "even the dolls would reject"; but those toys get their own "adorable seats and table settings", and service is "efficient", causing grown-ups to concede the "show is very well done"; N.B. a fall '08 move is planned to Water Tower Place.

Andies *Mediterranean/Mideastern* — 19 | 15 | 18 | $22

Andersonville | 5253 N. Clark St. (Berwyn Ave.) | 773-784-8616
Ravenswood | 1467 W. Montrose Ave. (Greenview Ave.) | 773-348-0654 Ⓜ
www.andiesres.com

"Good-size portions" of "fresh, flavorful" Med–Middle Eastern cuisine (including "many vegetarian options") are "a great value" at these "reliable" "casual" "standbys" that regularly draw "crowds"; a few raters cite uneven service and food, but "solid" sums it up for most; N.B. the Andersonville location serves a brunch buffet and is open later than Ravenswood.

Angelina Ristorante *Italian* — 21 | 19 | 19 | $32

Lakeview | 3561 N. Broadway St (Addison St.) | 773-935-5933

Within the "cozy neighborhood" confines of this "romantic" "little storefront" in Lakeview, "surprisingly authentic" Southern Italian fare is offered at "reasonable prices" along with "earnest" "service by the adorable Boys Town set"; indifferent types label it "average", but most aver Sunday "champagne brunch is a great deal."

	FOOD	DECOR	SERVICE	COST

Anna Maria Pasteria Ⓜ *Italian*   23 | 17 | 21 | $28

Ravenswood | 4400 N. Clark St. (Montrose Ave.) | 773-506-2662 |
www.annamariapasteria.com

"Comforting Italian cuisine" including "fresh homemade pasta" and
"many vegetarian dishes" earns *amici* for this "welcoming, family-
owned" trattoria that's a "favorite for locals" in Ravenswood, "without the downtown price tag"; the atmosphere is "fairly upscale", and
there's seasonal sidewalk dining.

Ann Sather *American/Swedish*   20 | 14 | 19 | $17

Andersonville | 5207 N. Clark St. (Foster Ave.) | 773-271-6677
Lakeview | 909 W. Belmont Ave. (Roscoe St.) | 773-348-2378

Ann Sather Café *American/Swedish*

Lakeview | 3411 N. Broadway St. (Roscoe St.) | 773-305-0024
Lakeview | 3416 N. Southport Ave. (W. Roscoe St.) | 773-404-4475
www.annsather.com

"Cherished" for their "fabulous" "colossal cinnamon rolls", this
"family-friendly" string of breakfast-and-lunch cafes hands out
"huge portions" of Swedish and American classics at "value" prices;
sure, a few Ann-tis label it "lackluster" and the decor gets middling
scores (at least the "new and improved" West Belmont Avenue location "no longer looks like a funeral home"), but most say it's "good
for what it is with no pretense to be anything more"; P.S. expect
"long lines for brunch."

Anteprima *Italian*   23 | 19 | 22 | $39

Andersonville | 5316 N. Clark St. (bet. Berwyn & Summerdale Aves.) |
773-506-9990 | www.anteprimachicago.com

"Popular with the Northside hipoisie", this Andersonville Italian
packs 'em in for "authentic", "hearty" fare at "reasonable" prices,
"wine by the quartino" and bottle, and "enthusiastic service"; while
the "crowds" make its "homey-yet-sophisticated" room "extrem-
emly loud", the patio is "nice and quiet in summer" and most are re-
lieved that "they now take reservations."

Antico Posto *Italian*   22 | 20 | 21 | $31

Oak Brook | Oakbrook Ctr. Mall | 118 Oakbrook Ctr. (Rte. 83) |
630-586-9200 | www.leye.com

Boosters boom *"buono!"* for this "cute", "classy" and "relaxing"
West Suburban Italian "tucked away in Oakbrook Center", where an
"attentive staff" delivers "fresh, delicious" fare from a "varied
menu" paired with "a wine list for all occasions"; add in the "great,
tiny dollar desserts", and, all in all, it's "better than expected from
a mall restaurant."

Arco de Cuchilleros Ⓜ *Spanish*   18 | 14 | 16 | $27

Lakeview | 3445 N. Halsted St. (Cornelia Ave.) | 773-296-6046

Amigos of this "overlooked" Spanish spot "hidden" "in the heart of
Boys Town" enjoy sampling its 40-plus menu of "reliably delicious",
"cheap tapas" along with "sangria on the patio" (there's also a small
Iberian wine list); opposers, though, point to what they call "uninteresting" edibles, "sketchy service" and "cramped quarters."

	FOOD	DECOR	SERVICE	COST

Aria *American/Eclectic*

23 | 22 | 22 | $52

Loop | Fairmont Chicago Hotel | 200 N. Columbus Dr. (bet. Wacker Dr. & Randolph St.) | 312-444-9494 | www.ariachicago.com

Friends of this New American–Eclectic eatery in the Fairmont Chicago Hotel maintain that its "menu is like a trip around the world", its wine list is "well thought out" and its "service has improved" of late; the "posh" Loop location is set up for "sleek comfort", with "space between you and your dining neighbors", and "the bar is good for cozy dessert and drinks"; N.B. they offer a children's menu and have added a sushi bar.

Army & Lou's *Southern*

▽ 24 | 18 | 20 | $25

Far South Side | 422 E. 75th St. (Martin Luther King Dr.) | 773-483-3100 | www.armyandlous.com

A "mecca" for "real soul food", this Far South Sider has been serving up a Southern "blast from the past" since 1945 – "breakfast is yummy but so is everything else", including what adherents call "the best fried chicken ever" and signature peach cobbler; live jazz on Fridays and a monthly Sunday buffet help make it "worth the trip", though some feel the decor could use an "overhaul."

Art of Pizza, The *Pizza*

21 | 5 | 15 | $13

Lakeview | 3033 N. Ashland Ave. (Nelson St.) | 773-327-5600

This Lakeview storefront's "really good, genuine deep-dish pizza" and "can't-be-beat" "by-the-slice prices" win mostly praise from raters who also laud its "courteous" if "rushed" counter service; still, a few dissenters claim it "doesn't live up to its name", and given the "nothing special" atmosphere even fans "recommend carryout" or delivery.

Artopolis Bakery, Cafe & Agora ❶ *Greek/Mediterranean*

23 | 19 | 19 | $18

Greektown | 306 S. Halsted St. (Jackson Blvd.) | 312-559-9000 | www.artopolischicago.com

All-day dining on Greek-Med goodies like "unbelievable artopitas" (Hellenic calzones) and "wonderful pastries" makes this "informal", inexpensive Greektown cafe a "refreshing change from its *opa!* neighbors" ("no flaming food"); with "friendly" service, it's "great" for lunch or "late-night drinks, dessert or a light nosh", especially in summer "when the windows along Halsted are opened."

ⓩ Arun's Ⓜ *Thai*

27 | 22 | 26 | $93

Northwest Side | 4156 N. Kedzie Ave. (bet. Irving Park Rd. & Montrose Ave.) | 773-539-1909 | www.arunsthai.com

"There are no menus" at Arun Sampanthavivat's "peaceful", top-scoring Thai – instead, this Northwest Side standout offers an "original", "unbelievably artistic" 12-course prix fixe feast "fit for royalty" (with "royal prices" to match) backed by an "exceptional wine list" and "polite, efficient service" that "accommodates" spice-level preferences (peaking at "surface-of-the-sun hot"); diehards insist the "strange location" and somewhat "sterile dining room" "do not detract" from this "special" experience.

	FOOD	DECOR	SERVICE	COST

☑ a tavola ☒ *Italian* | 26 | 19 | 24 | $45

Ukrainian Village | 2148 W. Chicago Ave. (bet. Hoyne Ave. & Leavitt St.) | 773-276-7567 | www.atavolachicago.com

Chef-owner Daniel Bocik's "superb craftsmanship" satisfies supporters of this Ukrainian Village Northern Italian serving "simple", "elegant" fare in a "grown-up", "conversation-friendly" atmosphere; the servers "know their stuff" – no wonder the "tiny" space is "always full" ("get reservations"); P.S. "the patio is a great spot in the summer."

Athena ◗ *Greek* | 19 | 19 | 19 | $28

Greektown | 212 S. Halsted St. (Adams St.) | 312-655-0000

"The prices are right" at this "family-oriented" Greektown "standard" with a "nice staff" serving "tasty", "basic" Greek cooking; fans fawn over the "fabulous garden" in summer (not to mention "winter indoors by the fireplaces"), but critics crow that the "crowds seem to overlook" faults with the fare just "for a chance to dine" "alfresco."

Atwater's *American/French* | ▽ 21 | 21 | 21 | $59

Geneva | Herrington Inn | 15 S. River Ln. (State St.) | 630-208-7433 | www.herringtoninn.com

"Classy", "intimate" surroundings and "wonderful" (if "pricey") New American–New French fare is served by a "helpful staff" at this West Suburban spot in the Herrington Inn; there's a "great view" of the Fox River, a fireplace in winter and outdoor dining in summer.

Atwood Cafe *American* | 21 | 24 | 21 | $38

Loop | Hotel Burnham | 1 W. Washington St. (State St.) | 312-368-1900 | www.atwoodcafe.com

The "upscale" Traditional American "home cooking" is "obscenely portioned" at this "relaxed" "art deco" spot in the "stunning" Hotel Burnham, making it a "choice Loop locale for theatergoers"; "cheerful" service is a plus, but while some like the "fun" mix of seats, others wish they'd level it out ("my couch was at least six inches lower than my companion's chair"); P.S. eat outside and "enjoy shopper-watching."

Aurelio's Pizza *Pizza* | 21 | 14 | 18 | $17

Loop | Holiday Inn | 506 W. Harrison St. (Canal St.) | 312-994-2000

Addison | Centennial Plaza | 1455 W. Lake St. (Lombard Rd.) | 630-889-9560

Chicago Heights | 1545 Western Ave. (south of Lincoln Hwy./14th St.) | 708-481-5040

Homewood | 18162 Harwood Ave. (183rd St.) | 708-798-8050

South Holland | 601 E. 170th St. (Cottage Grove Ave.) | 708-333-0310

Orland Park | Aurelio's Plaza | 11329 W. 143rd St. (Wolf Rd.) | 708-873-4448

Palos Heights | 6543 W. 127th St. (Ridgeland Ave.) | 708-389-5170

Tinley Park | 15901 Oak Park Ave. (Rte. 6) | 708-429-4600

Downers Grove | 940 Warren Ave. (Highland Ave.) | 630-810-0078

Oak Brook | 17 W. 711 Roosevelt Rd. (Summit Rd.) | 630-629-3200 www.aureliospizza.com

Additional locations throughout the Chicago area

Supporters salivate for the "different", "delicious thin-crust" pies with "sweet tomato sauce" and the "great antipasto salad" at these "favorite" "suburban staples"; traditionalists are true to the family-owned Homewood location (the others are franchises) with its "old-fashioned pizza-parlor decor", saying it offers "the best" chow in the chain (in-the-know "regulars ask for theirs cooked in the old oven").

☑ Avec ● *Mediterranean* `27 | 20 | 22 | $43`

Loop | 615 W. Randolph St. (Jefferson St.) | 312-377-2002 | www.avecrestaurant.com

Blackbird's "great-value" West Loop wine bar spin-off is "as close to Europe as you can get in Chicago", "succeeding on all levels" thanks to Koren Grieveson's "hearty, high-class" Mediterranean small and large plates, an "expansive" vino list and "knowledgeable servers"; a "pretty" crowd keeps the "super-cool", "cedar closet"–esque digs "noisy" and full of "verve", though the "communal seating" "can leave you needing a chiropractor"; P.S. there's no reserving, so you may "have to wait, standing up, for an hour."

Avenue M ● *American* `21 | 23 | 19 | $57`

River West | 695 N. Milwaukee Ave. (Huron St.) | 312-243-1133 | www.avenue-m.com

This "cool" River West New American steakhouse is in step with the current culinary vogue for "simpler food and lots of meat"; boosters find it "interesting enough for foodies" and praise the "boisterous bar", "romantic" patio and live jazz on Thursdays, but a few fault-finders cite "little imagination" and "uneven service" that doesn't match the "fine-dining price tag"; N.B. the Food score does not reflect a post-Survey chef change.

☑ Avenues ⓈⓂ *American* `25 | 24 | 27 | $105`

River North | Peninsula Hotel | 108 E. Superior St. (Michigan Ave.) | 312-573-6754 | www.peninsula.com

"Quiet and elegant", this River North "hotel restaurant for people who hate hotel restaurants" has turned New American with the post-Survey departure of chef Graham Elliot Bowles and arrival of Alinea/Trio alum Curtis Duffy (brunch is history too); "sparkling service" makes every guest "feel like a celebrity", and though a few find it "ultraexpensive" and "stuffy", it's hard to argue with the "vintage champagne cart" and "incredible views"; N.B. jackets suggested.

Azucar Ⓜ *Spanish* `▽ 23 | 19 | 20 | $30`

Logan Square | 2647 N. Kedzie Ave. (bet. Milwaukee & Diversy Aves.) | 773-486-6464 | www.azucartapasrestaurant.com

Expect "nontraditional" Spanish tapas and "delightful drinks" at this "unpretentious", "witty", no-reserving "addition to Logan Square", situated in a "sweet location across from the train station" and staying open until 2 AM on weekends; service can be "uneven", and the space is "tiny", making the outdoor patio a "terrific" option.

Babylon Eatery *Mideastern* `▽ 20 | 9 | 13 | $13`

Bucktown | 2023 N. Damen Ave. (McLean Ave.) | 773-342-7482

"Huge servings" of "cheap" Middle Eastern kebabs (try the "juicy", "perfectly spiced" chicken), shawarma and hummus draw diners to this "very casual", "reliable" Bucktown BYO; the "no frills" ambiance is decidedly "not special", so many opt for "delivery or takeout" that's "perfect for a weeknight."

Bacchanalia ∌ *Italian*　　　　∇ 24 | 17 | 24 | $28

Southwest Side | 2413 S. Oakley Ave. (bet. 24th & 25th Sts.) | 773-254-6555 | www.bacchanaliachicago.com

"Simple" Northern *Italiano* fare "done very well" is served by staffers who "seem like relatives" at this "quaint" Heart of Italy haunt that's "like Italian restaurants used to be" (the "decor hasn't changed" for "almost 30 years"); family-style portions ensure "you'll get enough food to have a second meal at home", and while the "no–credit-card policy is an inconvenience", "they do have an ATM machine."

BackStage Bistro 🗷 Ⓜ *American*　　∇ 22 | 15 | 18 | $36

River North | Illinois Institute of Art | 350 N. Orleans St. (bet. W. Kinzie St. & W. Upper Wacker Dr.) | 312-475-6920

This "test kitchen" for the Illinois Institute of Art's culinary school in River North concocts "well-prepared foods served by future chefs" who favor "interesting", "high-end" New American preps that are "superb when you consider the cost"; the "students work very hard to please", and you can "observe class" from the "cafe" setting; N.B. they close for seasonal breaks.

Bagel, The *Deli*　　　　　　19 | 11 | 17 | $17

Lakeview | 3107 N. Broadway St. (Belmont Ave.) | 773-477-0300
Skokie | Westfield Shoppingtown | 4999 Old Orchard Ctr. (Old Orchard Rd.) | 847-677-0100
www.bagelrestaurant.com

"If you're having a knish fit", consider this pair of "old-time delis" in Skokie and Lakeview for "big portions" of "nosh-worthy fare" such as "softball-size matzo balls" and "mish-mash soup" that "should be served with a snorkel"; fans find comfort in "decor and clientele reminiscent of Miami Beach in the '50s" and even service that ranges from "friendly" to "crabby", but grouches "can't figure out why" these "greasy spoons are so popular."

NEW **Balanced Kitchen, The** Ⓜ *American*　　– | – | – | I

Northwest Side | 6263 N. McCormick Rd. (bet. Devon & Lincoln Aves.) | 773-463-1085 | www.gfreev.com

A serious commitment to organic and sustainable ingredients drives this gluten-free, vegan Northwest Sider offering inexpensive New American fare like watermelon-radish 'ravioli'; set in a bright white space with a stark modern look and eco-friendly details like sustainable bamboo, recycled glass and resin panels, it serves lunch on weekdays (with retail and carryout till 7 PM) and a six-course brunch on weekends; N.B. no alcohol service.

Ballo *Italian*　　　　　　20 | 17 | 19 | $33

River North | 445 N. Dearborn St. (Illinois St.) | 312-832-7700 | www.rosebudrestaurants.com

Contributors converge on the "partylike atmosphere" at Alex Dana's (Rosebud) "flashy" River North ristorante, complete with "disco ball", "loud music" and "mob movies playing on plasma TVs"; whether the "hearty", "old-fashioned Italian" eats are "surprisingly good" or "nothing to rave about", the scene "hot" or "cheesy", and the service "friendly" or "in-your-face" – maybe because "you can't hear your waiter" – are your call.

Bandera *American*　　　22 | 20 | 21 | $33

Streeterville | 535 N. Michigan Ave., 2nd fl. (bet. Grand Ave. & Ohio St.) | 312-644-3524 | www.hillstone.com

The "sinful" Southwestern-style American "favorites" are "simple and fresh" at this "reliable", "down-to-earth home-cooking haven" in Streeterville; service may sometimes be "lacking", but the "cozy" atmosphere with a fireplace "attracts families", while the "jet set" files in for nightly jazz accompanied by "wonderful margaritas and mojitos" – "to impress a date, request a window table" "overlooking Michigan Avenue."

Bank Lane Bistro ⬛ *American*　　23 | 20 | 22 | $50

Lake Forest | 670 N. Bank Ln. (bet. Deerpath Rd. & Market Sq.) | 847-234-8802 | www.banklanebistro.com

This "upstairs, upscale" sibling of South Gate Cafe boasts an "innovative" New American menu backed by a wine list offering "offbeat surprises" and staff that "tries hard"; in winter, the "civilized", "romantic" setting is "cozy", and in summer, its "enclosed porch" offers views "overlooking Market Square"– just know that what some locals call "reasonable for Lake Forest", others deem "expensive."

NEW Bank Restaurant & Bar *American*　▽ 15 | 23 | 13 | $35

Wheaton | 121 W. Front St. (bet. Hale & Main Sts.) | 630-665-2265 | www.thebankwheaton.com

"Wheaton needed a good restaurant", but surveyors aren't certain yet whether to "invest" in this novice New American–Eclectic "hot spot" across from the train station, where Patrick Cassata's menu strikes some as "interesting" while others wish it were "more creative"; ratings suggest the "food and service need to work themselves up a notch" to compete with the "classy, comfortable" "old bank decor."

Bar Louie ● *Pub Food*　　　15 | 14 | 16 | $21

River North | 226 W. Chicago Ave. (Franklin St.) | 312-337-3313
Wrigleyville | 3545 N. Clark St. (Addison St.) | 773-296-2500
Bucktown | 1704 N. Damen Ave. (Wabansia Ave.) | 773-645-7500
Hyde Park | 5500 S. Shore Dr. (55th St.) | 773-363-5300
Printer's Row | 47 W. Polk St. (Dearborn St.) | 312-347-0000
Little Italy | 1321 W. Taylor St. (Ashland Ave.) | 312-633-9393
NEW Market District | 741 W. Randolph St. (Halsted St.) | 312-474-0700
Evanston | 1520 Sherman Ave. (Grove St.) | 847-733-8300
Naperville | 22 E. Chicago Ave. (Washington St.) | 630-983-1600
Oak Park | 1122 Lake St. (Harlem Ave.) | 708-725-3300
www.barlouieamerica.com
Additional locations throughout the Chicago area

Barflies befriend this bevy of "casual" Traditional Americans as "pit stops" for "meeting friends", "ogling" others, enjoying "late-night dining" or just "hanging and watching a game" while snarfing an "interesting" "variety" of "good" "pub food" along with a "great beer selection"; still, skeptics swat at the "noisy" "chain"-sters' "uneven offerings" and "inconsistent service at the various locations."

☑ Barrington Country Bistro ⑤ *French* 26 | 20 | 24 | $45

Barrington | Foundry Shopping Ctr. | 700 W. Northwest Hwy. (Hart Rd.) | 847-842-1300 | www.barringtoncountrybistro.com

This "approachable" Northwest Suburban "classic" woos diners with "outstanding" "country French cuisine and comfort" in a "quaint" setting in a shopping center; a "knowledgeable", "friendly staff", "super wine list", "great soufflés" and prices that do "not break the wallet" help keep the "tight" tables "busy at lunch and dinner."

Basil Leaf Café *Italian* 21 | 17 | 21 | $27

Lincoln Park | 2465 N. Clark St. (Fullerton Pkwy.) | 773-935-3388 | www.basilleaf.com

"Reliable" Northern Italian "comfort food" lures Lincoln Parkers to this "pleasant" "neighborhood spot", which recently relocated across the street and tripled in size by merging with Sage; they've added a full spirits selection, and fans of the former "romantic" "outdoor seating" should appreciate its new quieter alfresco area – but they still don't take reservations; N.B. scores do not reflect the move or menu/wine list expansion.

NEW BBOP Lounge ⑤ Ⓜ *Korean* - | - | - | M

Old Town | 1507 N. Sedgwick St. (Blackhawk St.) | 312-981-1775

Traditional Korean cookery inhabits Old Town's onetime Heat space, which has been redone with a clean, modern feel (blond wood, a wall of polished stones) and a grill bar; generous accompaniments add to the value of the already-reasonable pricing – as does the BYO policy.

Bella Bacino's *Italian* 20 | 14 | 17 | $22

Loop | 118 S. Clinton St. (Adams St.) | 312-876-1188 ⑤
Loop | 75 E. Wacker Dr. (N. Upper Michigan Ave.) | 312-263-2350
Lincoln Park | 2204 N. Lincoln Ave. (Webster Ave.) | 773-472-7400
La Grange | 36 S. La Grange Rd. (Harris Ave.) | 708-352-8882 Ⓜ
www.bellabacinos.com

Touters say "take the kids or grandkids" to these family-owned outposts for "very good pizzas both thick and thin" ("the deep-dish spinach will make you forget how much you love pepperoni"), plus pasta, salads and other "solid Italian food" in a "casual atmosphere"; maybe "service can be sloppy", but they do offer "quick delivery."

Bella Notte *Italian* 22 | 16 | 19 | $34

West Loop | 1374 W. Grand Ave. (Noble St.) | 312-733-5136 | www.bellanottechicago.com

"Head west on Grand" to this "friendly", "family-run" "favorite" if you fancy "huge portions" of "old-school Chicago Italian" ("great seafood pasta dishes", and the "stuffed bone-in filet is the bomb"); the "convivial" West Loop "neighborhood" mileu is "flashier" than its "homey" former quarters (next door).

Benihana *Japanese/Steak* `20` `18` `22` `$35`

Wheeling | 150 N. Milwaukee Ave. (Dundee Rd.) | 847-465-6021
Schaumburg | 1200 E. Higgins Rd. (Meacham Rd.) | 847-995-8201
Lombard | 747 E. Butterfield Rd. (Meyers Rd.) | 630-571-4440
www.benihana.com

"Dinner and a show" take on new meaning at this "entertaining" Japanese steakhouse chain, the "original teppanyaki experience" complete with "acrobatic", "knife-flipping" chefs who "slice and dice" your meal tableside; party-poopers protest "bland" grub, "hokey" theatrics and "chop-chop" service, noting that "if you go without kids", it helps to "drink a lot."

Ben Pao *Chinese* `21` `22` `20` `$32`

River North | 52 W. Illinois St. (Dearborn St.) | 312-222-1888 | www.benpao.com

"Pillars and waterfalls" in a "glamorous" setting "put you in a mood for an exotic meal" at this "trendy" Lettuce Entertain You Chinese-"themed palace" in River North, where supporters savor "surprising twists" on Asian food, with "innovative preparations" of "fresh ingredients"; antis, however, take aim at what they call an "Americanized" and "expensive" experience.

Berghoff Cafe ⊠ *German* `19` `18` `17` `$26`

Loop | 17 W. Adams St. (bet. Dearborn & State Sts.) | 312-427-7399 | www.theberghoff.com

Berghoff Cafe O'Hare *German*

O'Hare Area | O'Hare Int'l Airport | Concourse C (I-190) | 773-601-9180
Though this Loop "institution" is now open only for weekday lunch, locals still laud the "old-style German food" such as "classic sandwiches", "creative seafood dishes and salads" and "better desserts" – even if it's "pricey for self-serve"; nostalgists sigh "oh woe, gone are the days of ritual humiliation" at the hands of "grumpy old waiters" who "gave the place its character"; P.S. the airport outpost is a "particularly great option for O'Hare dining and drinking."

NEW Between Boutique

Cafe & Lounge ◑ Ⓜ *Eclectic*

Wicker Park | 1324 N. Milwaukee Ave. (Paulina St.) | 773-292-0585 | www.betweenchicago.com

This loungey Wicker Park Eclectic with a long-winded name serves what you might call 'medium plates' – i.e. scaled-up sharing dishes – in a rose-hued Cupid's bordello setting with plush furniture and fringe curtains; its swirling stuccolike walls are actually made of acoustic material, which helps absorb the sounds of wooing-and-cooing as well as the downtempo background music.

Bice Ristorante *Italian* `22` `20` `20` `$47`

Streeterville | 158 E. Ontario St. (bet. Michigan Ave. & St. Clair St.) | 312-664-1474 | www.bice.ws

"Trendy and lively", this upmarket Northern Italian chain "without the chain feel" was born in Milan in 1926 and now boasts "nicely decorated" global satellites, including this "pricey" Streeterville outpost; "snooty service" seems to be its weak link (they "only treat you well if you're a regular"), but the dining's "consistently good."

Big Bowl *Asian*

19 | 18 | 18 | $23

River North | 60 E. Ohio St. (Rush St.) | 312-951-1888
Gold Coast | 6 E. Cedar St. (State St.) | 312-640-8888
Lincolnshire | 215 Parkway Dr. (Milwaukee Ave.) | 847-808-8880
Schaumburg | 1950 E. Higgins Rd. (Rte. 53) | 847-517-8881
www.bigbowl.com

There's "always a good warm bowl" at these "standby" "stir-fry" sibs from the Lettuce Entertain You "empire" where the "light and tasty" Asian fare at "decent prices" includes a "compose-it-yourself" "wok bar"; ok, some find it "franchisey" with "inauthentic" eats and "uneven service", but the "boisterous", "family-friendly" feel is "fun" and the "homemade ginger ale" scores a solid strike; N.B. a recent earth-friendly evolution includes bamboo uniforms and no bottled water.

NEW Big Jones 🅢 Ⓜ *Southern*

- | - | - | M

Andersonville | 5347 N. Clark St. (bet. Balmoral & Summerdale Aves.) | 773-275-5725

Those jonesing for comfort food coastal Southern-style can dig in at this midpriced Andersonville arrival whose menu sails from New Orleans to the Carolina Low Country and beyond with dishes featuring crawfish and gator sausage; brunch, afternoon tea and dinner are served in a comfy-yet-refined setting with quaint blue chairs and lots of windows; N.B. libations include local brews and classic Dixie elixirs.

Bijan's Bistro ☽ *American*

18 | 15 | 17 | $27

River North | 663 N. State St. (Erie St.) | 312-202-1904 | www.bijansbistro.com

River North's "local crowd" appreciates this neighborhood "drop-in place" for "good-value", "homestyle" New American "bistro cooking" that's especially appealing "after the many nearby bars and clubs close" (the kitchen stays open till at least 3:30 AM daily); those who deem the eats "average" (if "consistent") tease that it's "for late-night creatures only", since "everything tastes great" in the wee hours.

Billy Goat Tavern *American*

15 | 11 | 14 | $12

Loop | 309 W. Washington St. (Franklin St.) | 312-899-1873 🅢⊄
Loop | 330 S. Wells St. (Van Buren St.) | 312-554-0297 🅢⊄
River North | Chicago Mart Plaza | 350 N. Orleans St. (W. Kinzie St.) | 312-464-1045
River North | 430 N. Lower Michigan Ave. (Illinois St.) | 312-222-1525 ☽⊄
Streeterville | Navy Pier | 700 E. Grand Ave. (Lake Shore Dr.) | 312-670-8789
O'Hare Area | O'Hare Field Terminal 1 | Concourse C (I-190) | 773-462-9368
West Loop | 1535 W. Madison St. (Ogden Ave.) | 312-733-9132 ⊄
www.billygoattavern.com

Among this herd of Traditional American "joints", the original "shrine" "down in the belly of the el" is a "dingy" "icon" with a "storied past" ("home of the Cubs curse") offering a "salt-of-the-earth Chicago-style" experience famed for "paper-thin" "cheezborgers" and "lousy" service; still, shrinking violets who keep "waiting for the grill man to press a hamburger patty in his armpit" say your "time and money are better spent renting a video of the *Saturday Night Live* skit."

Bin 36 *American/French*   20 | 20 | 21 | $40
River North | 339 N. Dearborn St. (Kinzie St.) | 312-755-9463 | www.bin36.com

Bin Wine Café *American/French*
Wicker Park | 1559 N. Milwaukee Ave. (Damen Ave.) | 773-486-2233 | www.binwinecafe.com

Oenophiles can opt for the "wine flights", "cheese bar", snacks, dinner or merely drinks at this "flexible"-format, "airy" (vs. "sterile") New American–French River Norther, or check out its "casual", and to some "more inviting", Wicker Park "baby" sister, where the pours are paired with "seasonal" bistro fare; both are perhaps "pricey" considering they "can be great or just good", and know that the original is "noisy" with generally "knowledgeable" service that "varies" with the "crowds."

Birch River Grill *American*   – | – | – | M
Arlington Heights | Doubletree Hotel Chicago-Arlington Heights | 75 W. Algonquin Rd. (Arlington Heights Rd.) | 847-427-4242

This "comfortable", "welcoming" kitchen churns out midpriced Traditional American eats like Yankee pot roast and meatloaf that are "good", "especially for a restaurant attached to a hotel"; the North Suburban digs resemble a "Colorado mountain lodge" tricked out in birch logs and leather, complete with a working fireplace; N.B. it serves breakfast, lunch and dinner.

Bistro Campagne *French*   24 | 22 | 22 | $42
Lincoln Square | 4518 N. Lincoln Ave. (bet. Sunnyside & Wilson Aves.) | 773-271-6100 | www.bistrocampagne.com

Michael Altenberg's "authentic", "market-driven" French bistro fare made from "sustainably farmed" ingredients, plus an "awesome beer list" (especially "if you are a Belgian ale fan") draw devotees to this "reasonably priced" "darling" in Lincoln Square; the "informal" but "professional" service can be "good or average", and sardined surveyors wish they "would not stuff everyone in so tight" – though there is a "beautiful" outdoor garden with a private-dining cottage.

Bistro Monet Ⓜ *French*   ∇ 23 | 18 | 24 | $43
Glen Ellyn | 462 N. Park Blvd. (bet. Crescent Blvd. & Duane St.) | 630-469-4002

"Small" and "charming", this Glen Ellyn bistro earns enthusiasm for serving both "traditional" and "modern" French fare created by a "hands-on chef" who "really cares about the product" and also "respects vegetarian cuisine"; a "nice staff" manages the "pleasant", wood-paneled space that's appropriately decorated with Monet reproductions.

	FOOD	DECOR	SERVICE	COST

Bistro 110 *French*

20 | 19 | 20 | $41

Gold Coast | 110 E. Pearson St. (bet. Michigan Ave. & Rush St.) | 312-266-3110 | www.bistro110restaurant.com

"Hearty" "French bistro classics" "shine" at this "lively" Gold Coast "mainstay of the Mag Mile", a shopper and "tourist haven" that also delivers a "Dixieland jazz Sunday brunch"; the jaded may jab at "tables on top of each other", "inconsistent" service and "average" fare at "Parisian prices", yet it draws "heavy crowds", so regulars "know to get reservations."

Bistro 22 *French*
(fka Bistro Kirkou)

22 | 19 | 21 | $42

Lake Zurich | 500 Ela Rd. (Maple Ave.) | 847-438-0200 | www.bistro-22.com

Under new ownership, Lake Zurich's former Bistro Kirkou has well-wishers labeling it a "little bit of Chicago dining in the 'burbs" thanks to the "quality" of its "somewhat inventive" French menu and "warm", "intimate" atmosphere ("especially if you snag one of the tables in front of the fireplace"); regardless, a smattering of skeptics deem it merely "decent."

Bistrot Margot *French*

21 | 19 | 20 | $37

Old Town | 1437 N. Wells St. (bet. North Ave. & Schiller St.) | 312-587-3660 | www.bistrotmargot.com

"Authentic French bistro food" "done well" is the draw at this "romantic", "unpretentious" eatery, causing one devotee to exclaim, "Old Town residents are lucky to have this as their neighborhood place", even if the high "noise level" and "close tables" make it "conversation-challenging"; P.S. check out the outdoor seats and "great" Saturday–Sunday brunch.

Bistrot Zinc *French*

20 | 20 | 20 | $35

Gold Coast | 1131 N. State St. (bet. Cedar & Elm Sts.) | 312-337-1131 | www.bistrotzinc.com

"Your classic neighborhood bistro" is a "quiet getaway" just "a few paces from the hubbub of Rush Street", where the "good take on standard" French food and "charming atmosphere" (including an "authentic zinc bar") serve up "a little bit of Paris in the Gold Coast"; P.S. contributors compliment the "outstanding child-friendly weekend brunch."

☑ Blackbird ☒ *American*

27 | 22 | 24 | $64

West Loop | 619 W. Randolph St. (bet. Desplaines & Jefferson Sts.) | 312-715-0708 | www.blackbirdrestaurant.com

Paul Kahan and Mike Sheerin's "exceptional, seasonal" cuisine "sings", "releasing the inner spirit" of every ingredient at their West Loop New American that's "still in top form" after 10 years; other assets include a "superb wine list", "attentive, personable service" and "hip", "minimalist", "not-for-romantics" decor that "makes the food the star" – just know that it's "pricey" and one diner's "lively" is another's "deafening", as "beautiful people" and "enthusiastic foodies" chatter away at "tight tables."

	FOOD	DECOR	SERVICE	COST

Blind Faith Café *Vegetarian*

| 21 | 15 | 19 | $20 |

Evanston | 525 Dempster St. (Chicago Ave.) | 847-328-6875 |
www.blindfaithcafe.com

Evanston's "child-friendly" "venerable vegetarian veteran keeps on keepin' on" (since 1979) with "global flavors" (that are even "satisfying" to "meat eaters"), "great vegan options" and service that's "generally very good for a half-hippie place"; though buzzkills brand it "bland", to most it's a "brunch favorite" with "baked goods to die for", and "feels just like Berkeley" right down to the "very granola" "Birkenstock" crowd.

Blu Coral *Japanese*

| 22 | 20 | 20 | $38 |

Wicker Park | 1265 N. Milwaukee Ave. (bet. Ashland Ave. & Paulina St.) |
773-252-2020 | www.blucoralchicago.com

"Fresh fish is abundant" at this "loungey but comfortable" Wicker Park Japanese (occupying a "weird spot next to the Jewel") laying out "large pieces of sushi" and "innovative" maki; eaters earmark it an "enjoyable experience" unless you find the "hip", "dark" decor and "techno music" "annoying", and a few feel it's "comparatively expensive."

🆕 Bluebird, The ● *American*

| 19 | 21 | 19 | $29 |

Bucktown | 1749 N. Damen Ave. (Willow St.) | 773-486-2473 |
www.bluebirdchicago.com

Bucktown's "swank", "intimate" New American "addition" to the "neighborhood" scene from the Webster Wine Bar folks is a "true gastropub", churning out "hearty, interesting" (if "uneven") small plates; a smattering say service can be "lacking", but imbibers admire the "amazing range of specialty beers" and "modestly priced wine selection"; N.B. it also offers late service, a fireplace and WiFi – but not reservations.

Blue Water Grill *American/Seafood*

| 23 | 23 | 20 | $49 |

River North | 520 N. Dearborn St. (Grand Ave.) | 312-777-1400 |
www.brguestrestaurants.com

Fin-fans swim to this "stylish", "handsome" River North seafooder (part of a "NY-based chain") for its "creative", "inspiring" New American menu that includes "unusual sushi options" alongside "classic fish fare", as well as a "great Sunday brunch"; if foes cite "inconsistent" food and "spotty service" that "come with a price tag", that doesn't faze the "eye-candy" types who fill the "dark, sleek" dining room and "very chic bar area."

🆕 Bluprint *American*

| 22 | 22 | 21 | $41 |

River North | Merchandise Mart | 222 Merchandise Mart Plz. (Wells St.) |
312-410-9800 | www.bluprintchicago.com

"As chic as the design shops in the Merchandise Mart", this freshman New American located inside that River North destination is "very much needed" say adherents of its "fresh approach" to classic dishes; the shopper traffic and prix fixe lunch explain why the "calming", "slick" interior is usually "crowded by day, quiet at dinner."

	FOOD	DECOR	SERVICE	COST

Bob Chinn's Crab House *Seafood* 22 | 12 | 18 | $37

Wheeling | 393 S. Milwaukee Ave. (Dundee Rd.) | 847-520-3633 |
www.bobchinns.com

"You ain't had fish till you've taken it on the Chinn" cheer champions of
this North Shore seafood "factory" where the "daily delivery" is
posted "on the bulletin board" and "really good mai tais come in take-
home cups"; the "dated" "dining-hall" decor doesn't dissuade "loud"
"crowds" from forming "lines like at Disneyland on a really bad day",
and jaded jurists jab at its "undistinguished" "expensive entrees"
and warn that after "you wait forever to get seated", "they can't wait
to get you out" (so "go at lunch" – "same menu, lower prices").

Bob San 🅿 *Japanese* 24 | 18 | 18 | $36

Wicker Park | 1805 W. Division St. (Wood St.) | 773-235-8888 |
www.bob-san.com

Bob Bee's "hip but relaxed" sister to Sushi Naniwa scores with "excellent", "creative" Japanese "cooked and raw fish" and generally
"good service" offered amid a "real", "funky" Wicker Park "neighborhood vibe"; it's peopled with "singles" and "couples", many of
who enjoy the outdoor dining option that's "great in summer."

Bogart's Charhouse *Steak* 20 | 17 | 18 | $36

Homewood | 18225 Dixie Hwy. (183rd St.) | 708-798-2000
Tinley Park | 17344 Oak Park Ave. (bet. North & 171st Sts.) |
708-532-5592 Ⓜ

"The first thing you see is the meat cooler and BBQs flaring" at these
similar but separately owned South and Southwest Suburban steakhouses praised by "Humphrey Bogart fans" for purveying "great
steaks for the price" within an "atmosphere that puts you right in the
middle of Casablanca"; pickier eaters pronounce the pair "pleasant"
and a "good choice if you're in the neighborhood", but "not worth
a special trip."

BOKA *American* 24 | 22 | 23 | $53

Lincoln Park | 1729 N. Halsted St. (North Ave.) | 312-337-6070 |
www.bokachicago.com

"Talented" new chef and "Charlie Trotter alum" Giuseppe Tentori
puts out "subtle, inventive" food in "artistic presentations" matched
by a "very good wine list" at this "romantic" Lincoln Park New
American "small-plates" specialist; an "intelligent staff" caters to
the "theater and twentysomething crowd" in a "loungey", "contemporary" milieu that includes "two patios, one outdoors and one
tented" – in short, this "winner" is "worth" the "expensive" price.

Bongo Room *American* 24 | 16 | 17 | $19

Wicker Park | 1470 N. Milwaukee Ave. (Honore St.) |
773-489-0690
South Loop | 1152 S. Wabash Ave. (Roosevelt Rd.) | 312-291-0100
Delighted drummers who "dream about" the "interesting pancake
options" arrive "early to get a seat" for the "indulgent" weekend
brunch (they don't serve dinner) at this "Wicker Park standard" with
a "varied and delicious" Traditional American menu that's "worth

every penny and calorie" – "if you don't want to wait an hour" try the "great" South Loop location; that said, savory sorts warn that much of the menu is "sugar overkill."

Bonsoiree ⊠ Ⓜ *American/French* — | — | — | M

Logan Square | 2728 W. Armitage Ave. (Fairfield Ave.) | 773-486-7511 | www.bon-soiree.com

The surprises at this petite Logan Square spot don't end with its big New American and New French flavors – it also has affordable prix fixe options and a bargain-enhancing BYO policy, plus invitation-only "underground" Saturday nights featuring a special tasting menu (sign up on the website); the low-key, candlelit setting is augmented by a small seasonal patio.

Boston Blackies *Burgers* 19 | 13 | 16 | $20

Loop | 120 S. Riverside Plaza (bet. Adams & Monroe Sts.) | 312-382-0700 ⊠
Streeterville | 164 E. Grand Ave. (St. Clair St.) | 312-938-8700
Deerfield | 405 Lake Cook Rd. (Rte. 43) | 847-418-3400
Glencoe | Hubbard Woods Plaza | 73 Green Bay Rd. (Scott Ave.) | 847-242-9400
Arlington Heights | 222 E. Algonquin Rd. (Tonne Dr.) | 847-952-4700 ◖
www.bostonblackies.com

"Basic", "affordable" Traditional American "tavern food" like "legendary" "juicy" burgers is the "thing to go for" at this cadre of "crowded", "comfortable" city and suburban "standbys" where beef eaters don't seem to mind the "dated" "diner" decor; grumps grouse "they do not take reservations" so "you may have to wait for a seat", and service can be "fast", "timely" or "slow" depending on the day.

Brasserie Jo *French* 22 | 21 | 21 | $42

River North | 59 W. Hubbard St. (bet. Clark & Dearborn Sts.) | 312-595-0800 | www.brasseriejo.com

"The Frenchiness is obvious" at Lettuce Entertain You's "unpretentious" "hardy perennial" in River North where the "well-priced", "reliable", "authentic fare" exhibits an Alsatian accent that also translates to the "wonderful wine list" (there's a "fantastic beer selection" too); "helpful" service haunts the "oversized", "boisterous" space that comes complete with a "zinc bar" and "dog-friendly patio dining", so it's a "safe bet" for a "date night", "business lunch" or "group" outing.

Ⓩ NEW Brasserie Ruhlmann 21 | 25 | 20 | $59
Steakhouse *French/Steak*

River North | 500 W. Superior St. (Kingsbury St.) | 312-494-1900 | www.brasserieruhlmannch.com

Its "exquisite art deco dining room with a mirrored bar" is the star at this "noisy" River North "hot spot for the stiletto crowd"; its "appropriately Americanized French" brasserie offerings and steakhouse fare include an "excellent raw bar" and "well-thought-out Franco wine list", though some cite "consistency problems" like service that swings from "professional" to "striving toward mediocre", and penny-pinchers pan prices as "pretty high for the genre."

	FOOD	DECOR	SERVICE	COST

Brazzaz *Brazilian/Steak* | 22 | 20 | 22 | $54 |

River North | 539 N. Dearborn St. (Grand Ave.) | 312-595-9000 | www.brazzaz.com

Among River North's "several Brazilian meat markets", this *riodizio* scores with carnivores craving "tons" of "good grilled" beef, lamb and seafood accompanied by an "interesting salad bar"; still, surveyors cross swords over service that's either "accommodating" or "inattentive" and debate whether it's "too much money and too much food" or a "good bang for your buck if you're hungry."

Breakfast Club, The *American* | 20 | 12 | 17 | $16 |

West Loop | 1381 W. Hubbard St. (Noble St.) | 312-666-2372 | www.chicagobreakfastclub.com

"The 'morning after' crowd" makes its way to this "cramped" "breakfast nook" "hidden down by the rail tracks" in West Town for "tasty" American "diner-style food" served amid "homey" "pink decor" that reminds some of "eating at grandma's"; N.B. name notwithstanding, lunch is also served seven days a week.

Bricks *Pizza* | 22 | 14 | 18 | $20 |

Lincoln Park | 1909 N. Lincoln Ave. (Wisconsin St.) | 312-255-0851 | www.brickspetaluma.com

"As underground as its underground location", this Lincoln Park parlor serves "gourmet" "thin-crust pizzas" in a "groovy" atmosphere with "fun servers", "reasonable pricing" and a "strong beer" list; the "cavernous" confines are "cozy" and "relaxed" to some, "dark" and "dank" to others.

NEW Brio Tuscan Grille *Italian* | 21 | 22 | 20 | $34 |

Lombard | The Shops on Butterfield | 330 Yorktown Ctr. (Butterfield Rd.) | 630-424-1515 | www.brioitalian.com

This Lombard link in an "up-and-coming" Italian chain features "reasonably priced", "well-prepared" meals that manage to "bring Tuscany near home" ("nothing beats their flatbread"); just ignore its "uneven" service – the "airy", villalike setting is transporting enough to make you feel like you're "not eating with the masses."

Broadway Cellars *American* | 21 | 18 | 20 | $33 |

Edgewater | 5900 N. Broadway (Rosedale Ave.) | 773-944-1208 | www.broadwaycellars.net

"Huge portions" of "solid", "somewhat trendy" New American eats, a "commitment to wine" (and the "ability to pick one's own flight"), "comfortable" conditions and "friendly staff" have turned this Edgewater eatery into a "reliable" "neighborhood spot"; cellar-dwellers suggest the "amazing prix fixe dinner on Thursday nights" and "outdoor seating in the summer."

Bruna's Ristorante *Italian* | 23 | 14 | 22 | $33 |

Southwest Side | 2424 S. Oakley Ave. (24th Pl.) | 773-254-5550

Opened in 1933, this "homey", "family-run" Heart of Italy "favorite" is "as old as the school gets" when it comes to "real Italian food from real Italians"; "the din can get to you on weekends", but during the week "it's like being at your best buddy's mom's house" with "good quality" and "large portions" at a "great value" – so "*mangia!*"; N.B. they offer valet parking on weekends.

Buona Terra Ristorante Ⓜ *Italian* | 23 | 16 | 20 | $30

Logan Square | 2535 N. California Ave. (Logan Blvd.) | 773-289-3800 | www.buona-terra.com

"Good-value" Northern Italian "comfort food" backed by a Cal-Ital wine list and seasonal garden qualify this "casual", "dependable" "neighborhood" trattoria as a "find in the heart of Logan Square"; "extremely nice hosts" offer a warm welcome, and regulars note the "Thursday night prix fixe is the best bang for your buck."

Butterfly Sushi Bar & Thai Cuisine *Japanese/Thai* | 21 | 15 | 19 | $26

West Loop | 1156 W. Grand Ave. (bet. May St. & Racine Ave.) | 312-563-5555

The "combination of fun atmosphere", "fresh" sushi, an "excellent selection" of Japanese and Thai items and "fast service" makes this West Loop BYO a prime place for a "cheap" "night out"; fans who are aflutter over the "huge portions" don't seem to mind that the vibe can be "a bit loud" and "seating is tight."

Cab's Wine Bar Bistro *American* | 22 | 18 | 21 | $41

Glen Ellyn | 430 N. Main St. (Duane St.) | 630-942-9463 | www.cabsbistro.com

"Solid" New American cuisine "well prepared" by a chef "with an eye for taste and beauty" and served within an "elegant yet cozy" setting by an "unpretentious staff" (that "makes great wine picks") has confreres calling a cab and heading for this "welcoming" West Suburban "find"; N.B. periodic wine dinners are an added draw.

Café Absinthe *American* | 24 | 20 | 21 | $45

Bucktown | 1954 W. North Ave. (Damen Ave.) | 773-278-4488 | www.cafeabsinthechicago.com

"Creative", "diverse" seasonal New American fare and a "very good wine selection" make the heart grow fonder for aficionados of this "old favorite", who aver it's "aging gracefully" in its "secret" ("entrance through the alley") Bucktown/Wicker Park digs; "decadence meets urban chic" within the "minimalist setting" replete with "rustic brick walls" and an "open kitchen", but even converts caution it can be "loud."

Cafe Ba-Ba-Reeba! *Spanish* | 22 | 19 | 19 | $31

Lincoln Park | 2024 N. Halsted St. (Armitage Ave.) | 773-935-5000 | www.cafebabareeba.com

One of the "city's first tapas bars" is "still going strong" In Lincoln Park thanks to the "impressive variety" of "tasty" Spanish small plates (a "value" or "overpriced" depending on who's grazing), "festive atmosphere", "flavored sangrias" and "lovely" "summertime patio"; nags note the noshes are not the "real" thing, the "decor needs a pick-me-up" and "service can be sporadic", perhaps since

FOOD | DECOR | SERVICE | COST

it's "always packed" – expect a "twentysomething" crowd, a big "din" and "long waits on weekends."

Café Bernard *French*
19 | 14 | 19 | $37

Lincoln Park | 2100 N. Halsted St. (Dickens Ave.) | 773-871-2100 | www.cafebernard.com

Francophiles "feel at home" at this "solid", "understated" Lincoln Park "old-timer" where they're cheered by the "unpretentious" "charm" and "good value" French bistro meals accompanied by "old-world service"; *contraire*-ians, however, contend it "seems tired", citing "uneven food" and "dreary decor"; P.S. its attached sibling – the "mellow", "intimate" Red Rooster wine bar and cafe – is a "gem."

Café Bionda *Italian*
22 | 18 | 20 | $35

NEW **Wicker Park** | 1467 N. Milwaukee Ave. (bet. Evergreen Ave. & Honore St.) | 773-342-2100
South Loop | 1924 S. State St. (Archer Ave.) | 312-326-9800
www.cafebionda.com

Champions of "no-nonsense" "Chicago Italian" cheer that these South Loop and Wicker Park sibs "smack you in the face" with "monster portions, lively atmosphere, rich flavors and stiff drinks" in a "retro", "urban-style setting"; faint-praisers label it "totally adequate", but "lounge areas" and "easy parking" are bonuses.

Cafe Bolero *Cuban*
20 | 15 | 18 | $24

Bucktown | 2252 N. Western Ave. (bet. Belden Ave. & Lyndale St.) | 773-227-9000 | www.cafebolero.com

"Down-to-earth Cuban cooking" and 40 varieties of rum delight denizens of this "cozy", "no-frills" Bucktown *cucina*; "what it lacks in decor it makes up for" with its "inexpensive", "homestyle staples" and "friendly staff", plus on Tuesdays and Thursdays there's "live music to give you a flavor of [island] life"; P.S. "nice outdoor seating" too.

Cafe Central Ⓜ *French*
23 | 17 | 23 | $39

Highland Park | 455 Central Ave. (bet. Linden & St. Johns Aves.) | 847-266-7878 | www.cafecentral.net

Make for this "small, intimate" "medium-priced Carlos'" spin-off if you crave "creative", "hearty [French] bistro fare" complemented by a "colorful room and staff" (owner "Debbie [Nieto] makes you feel right at home"); most cafe-goers consider it a "top-notch choice for semi-elegant" North Shore "neighborhood" dining, though a contingent claims it can be "crowded and noisy, uncomfortable" – in other words "authentically Parisian"; P.S. "summertime means south-facing tables under umbrellas" on the sidewalk.

Café des Architectes *French/Mediterranean*
23 | 23 | 21 | $43

Gold Coast | Sofitel Chicago Water Tower | 20 E. Chestnut St. (Wabash Ave.) | 312-324-4063 | www.sofitel.com

"Stylish" and "modern", this New French-Med hotel restaurant "professionally" proffers "artistic" "classic" meals including an "impressive lunch" and "fantastic brunch" (which some say stack up "better than dinner") "right in the middle of the Gold Coast shopping district"; if it's "surprisingly uncrowded", perhaps that's because it gets "lost" in the Sofitel Chicago Water Tower and tariffs are on the "pricey side"; P.S. you can "eat outside in warmer weather."

Café Iberico ● *Spanish* | 22 | 15 | 17 | $26

River North | 739 N. LaSalle Dr. (bet. Chicago Ave. & Superior St.) | 312-573-1510 | www.cafeiberico.com

As "hectic" as a "train station", this "raucous" River North Spaniard delivers with "delectable" tapas that are "terrific" for groups and "grazers" who don't mind the "crushing" "two-hour" waits (no reservations on weekends) that are made "quite bearable" by "top-notch" "pitchers of sangria"; eager "locals" and "Gen-Y kids" forgive the "spotty" service and "sparse" atmosphere, since an evening here is a "value"; N.B. the Decor score may not reflect a recent update.

Café la Cave *Continental* | 20 | 23 | 23 | $58

Des Plaines | 2777 Mannheim Rd. (bet. Higgins Rd. & Touhy Ave.) | 847-827-7818 | www.cafelacaverestaurant.com

This "elegant" "hideout" that's conveniently "near the airport" is so "romantic" it "feels like being in a mountain cave" say sentimentalists who dub the "pricey" Continental fare "delicious"; less-satisfied sorts remain unconvinced: "overrated", "needs to move out of the 1970s."

Café le Coq Ⓜ *French* | 23 | 21 | 22 | $40

Oak Park | 734 Lake St. (Oak Park Ave.) | 708-848-2233

It "feels like a bistro in Paris", right "down to the service" say *amis* of this "dependable" Oak Park "find" with "nice wines" and "affordable prices"; its "highly recommended" prix fixe options are a "bargain", and the "pleasant" decor is perfect for a "special evening"; N.B. there's sidewalk seating too.

Cafe Matou Ⓜ *French* | 23 | 19 | 22 | $43

Bucktown | 1846 N. Milwaukee Ave. (bet. Leavitt St. & Oakley Ave.) | 773-384-8911 | www.cafematou.com

Feline friends of this "funky", "out-of-the-way" Bucktown "neighborhood winner", whose name means 'tom cat', "purr" over chef-owner Charlie Socher's "consistently interesting and well-prepared" "classic French" preps with "sublime sauces" from a "menu that changes often", not to mention the "lovely wine selection"; even so, a litter of catty commenters contends service goes "south" on "off nights."

NEW Café 103 ⓈⓂ *American/Eclectic* | – | – | – | E

Far South Side | 1909 W. 103rd St. (Walden Pkwy.) | 773-238-5115 | www.cafe103.com

"Finally, a great restaurant on the [Far] South Side" is one early take on this diminutive BYO; expect a New American–Eclectic menu crafted from local and regional ingredients and served in an upscale white-tablecloth ambiance.

Cafe Pyrenees Ⓜ *French* | 23 | 19 | 23 | $40

Libertyville | Adler Square Shopping Plaza | 1762 N. Milwaukee Ave. (Buckley Rd./Rte. 137) | 847-362-2233 | www.cafepyrenees.com

"Classic, well-done" French "bistro food" at "reasonable prices" is accompanied by "efficient service" and "personal" attention "from the owner" at this "unpretentious" North Suburban "gem"; the experience is "better than its location ["nestled in a strip mall"] would imply" aver admirers who appreciate the "amazing values for lunch."

Café Selmarie American
22 | 18 | 19 | $22

Lincoln Square | 4729 N. Lincoln Ave. (Lawrence Ave.) | 773-989-5595 | www.cafeselmarie.com

The "European mood" is "so authentic you want to pay in euros" at this "kid-friendly" "neighborhood treasure" and "dessert oasis" tableing "tasty meals" of New American "comfort foods" (eager eaters "get up early" for its "champion of breakfasts"); the location "on the fountain park in Lincoln Square" provides "perfect people-watching", and "summer nights are magic" on the "charming" patio.

Café Spiaggia Italian
25 | 23 | 24 | $54

Gold Coast | 980 N. Michigan Ave., 2nd fl. (Oak St.) | 312-280-2750 | www.cafespiaggia.com

"City chic meets casual dining" at this "jeans-friendly" Gold Coast "escape for the shopping cognoscenti" that serves "wonderful" "Spiaggia-quality" Italian (the siblings "share the same kitchen") plus pizza and sandwiches; a "well-trained staff", "smashing views" and the ability to "get in and out quickly" are added incentives, though wallet-watchers warn even if the tabs add up to a "fraction of the cost" of its "big brother", they're still "expensive" – especially considering the "crowded" seating.

Cafe 28 Cuban/Mexican
24 | 19 | 20 | $32

North Center/St. Ben's | 1800-1806 W. Irving Park Rd. (Ravenswood Ave.) | 773-528-2883 | www.cafe28.org

This North Center "hidden gem under the el" issues "mouthwatering" Cuban and Mexican meals "at a reasonable price", paired with "fresh sangria", "outstanding mojitos" and other "Latin-inspired cocktails"; "don't let the word 'cafe' fool you", it's "upscale, yet relaxed" and quite large, though "no reservations means" the "wait on weekends" can be "unbearable" and the quarters "noisy" (yet still "awesome" for a date or brunch).

Caliterra Bar & Grille American/Italian
22 | 21 | 22 | $52

Streeterville | Wyndham Chicago | 633 N. St. Clair St. (Erie St.) | 312-274-4444 | www.wyndham.com

A "pleasant surprise" awaits voyagers who venture to this Streeterville venue with a "refined, distinctive menu" of "spot-on", "wine-friendly" New American–Italian cuisine and one of the city's "best cheese carts"; supporters surmise "some of the locals think it's just a 'hotel dining room' and miss out on a great experience", asserting "if it weren't hidden on the second floor [of the Wyndham Chicago] it would be packed every night."

Campagnola Italian
23 | 19 | 20 | $44

Evanston | 815 Chicago Ave. (Washington St.) | 847-475-6100 | www.campagnolarestaurant.com

"Combinations of organic and wholesome ingredients" make for "creative, interesting" fare at this "friendly" "outpost for unique

FOOD | DECOR | SERVICE | COST

Italian dining", an "upscale" "North Shore treasure" where a "thoughtful wine selection" and "service with a delicate touch" are offered in a "cozy", "understated atmosphere"; P.S. its "outdoor dining is a welcome treat in warmer months."

Cape Cod Room *Seafood* 22 | 21 | 22 | $58

Streeterville | Drake Hotel | 140 E. Walton Pl. (Michigan Ave.) | 312-787-2200 | www.thedrakehotel.com

The seas part for this "clubby" Streeterville seafood "standby" "with a maritime theme", "a welcome anachronism in food and service style" if you're a "sucker" for "Bookbinder soup" "served with a side of sherry" and "Dover sole deboned as it should be"; critics, however, crab that this "classic" is "coasting", snapping "service is not their strong point" and quipping "the only thing that has changed in [75] years is the prices"; N.B. the Decor score does not reflect a post-Survey updating.

☒ Capital Grille, The *Steak* 25 | 24 | 24 | $61

Streeterville | 633 N. Saint Clair St. (Ontario St.) | 312-337-9400
Lombard | 87 Yorktown Shopping Ctr. (Highland Ave.) | 630-627-9800
www.thecapitalgrille.com

"Everything a steakhouse ought to be", this decidedly "upscale" chain with links in Lombard, Streeterville and Milwaukee's Downtown lures "buttoned-down" "power" players with its "flavorful", "artfully presented" chops; the "low-lit, dark-wood" digs and "attentive" service are "ideal for a special occasion or a business dinner", and though the bill can be "way expensive", "you get what you pay for."

☒ Carlos' *French* 28 | 25 | 27 | $89

Highland Park | 429 Temple Ave. (Waukegan Ave.) | 847-432-0770 | www.carlos-restaurant.com

Carlos and Debbie Nieto's "venerable" North Suburban Highland Park "dining institution" – long an "incubator for many top chefs in the region" – has faithful followers fawning over its "outstanding" New French fare, "attentive" service and "astounding" wine list that's "biased toward France"; it may be "very expensive" and, to some, a soupçon "pretentious", but the majority ranks it a "romantic" "classic", "perfect for anniversaries, birthdays, Valentine's Day" or any "special occasion"; N.B. jackets required.

Carlos & Carlos Ⓜ *Italian* ▽ 23 | 22 | 23 | $33

Arlington Heights | 115 W. Campbell St. (Vail Ave.) | 847-259-5227 | www.carlosandcarlosinc.com

"Ciao bella!" cheer champions of this returning favorite (once in Bucktown, now in the Northwest Suburbs) as they keep coming back for its "varied and ambitious" Northern Italian fare (with some French flavors) and "fair-priced wine list"; its "elegant", "cozy" bistro confines are "convenient for the Metropolis Performing Arts Center", and an "accommodating" staff rounds out the picture.

	FOOD	DECOR	SERVICE	COST

Carlucci *Italian*

21 | 20 | 21 | $39

Rosemont | Riverway Complex | 6111 N. River Rd. (Higgins Rd.) |
847-518-0990
Downers Grove | 1801 Butterfield Rd. (I-355) | 630-512-0990
www.carluccirestaurant.com

These separately owned suburban "standbys" welcome with "well-balanced menus" ("more than just pasta and red sauce") of "uncommonly good" Northern Italian fare "at a great price", proffered in a "bustling", sometimes "loud", atmosphere; voters aver they're "on an upswing" in all departments (its Service score is up three points since the last Survey); P.S. the Rosemont branch is "among the better eats near O'Hare."

Carmichael's Chicago Steak House ● *Steak*

21 | 18 | 18 | $44

West Loop | 1052 W. Monroe St. (bet. Aberdeen & Morgan Sts.) |
312-433-0025 | www.carmichaelsteakhouse.com

This West Loop "carnivore's paradise" pleases most with its "traditional" steakhouse sustenance (including "salads that would feed a small army"), "friendly chef", "warm" ambiance, absence of "attitude" and "free valet parking"; to boot, "shuttle" service to United Center makes it "great" "before a Bulls game."

Carmine's ● *Italian*

21 | 19 | 20 | $41

Gold Coast | 1043 N. Rush St. (bet. Bellevue Pl. & Cedar St.) |
312-988-7676 | www.rosebudrestaurants.com

To allies, this gregarious Gold Coast offshoot of the Rosebud family tree is a "hot spot" for "gargantuan" heaps of "honest-to-goodness Italian" "pasta and other delights" delivered in a "hopping" house where frequent "entertainment is a plus" – enjoy "brilliant live piano" within or "eat outside to watch all the action" on Rush Street; even antis who argue that the food is "not fabulous" and the prices are "above average" grant it's "good for tourists."

☑ Carnivale *Nuevo Latino*

22 | 26 | 20 | $43

Loop | 702 W. Fulton Market (Halsted St.) | 312-850-5005 |
www.carnivalechicago.com

"It's a party all the time" at Jerry Kleiner's "enormous", "over-the-top" Loop "see-and-be-seen"-ster that's fueled by "great people-watching, a fun bar scene", "riotous decor", "large, fabulous drinks" and "tasty if not transcendent" Nuevo Latino flavors that come at a slightly "expensive" price; the "throbbing din" discourages diners who find the "energy" more "frenetic" than "lively" ("carnivale or circus?"), but "festive" sorts don't seem deterred.

Carson's Ribs *BBQ*

22 | 14 | 18 | $32

River North | 612 N. Wells St. (Ontario St.) | 312-280-9200
Deerfield | 200 Waukegan Rd. (bet. Deerfield & Lake Cook Rds.) |
847-374-8500
www.ribs.com

Feasters "dive into their food" at these "supper club"-ish "favorites" for "dang good" BBQ ("chewy" ribs, "delicious" "garbage salad" and "free chopped liver") at a "fair dollar value"; maybe service swings from "old-fashioned" to "indifferent" and dissenters regard them as "relics", but most have no complaints, especially given the "recent makeover" of the River Norther and "beautiful" new patio with fireplace in Deerfield; N.B. reservations for groups of six or more only.

☑ Catch 35 *Seafood* | 24 | 21 | 22 | $47 |

Loop | Leo Burnett Bldg. | 35 W. Wacker Dr. (bet. Dearborn & State Sts.) | 312-346-3500
Naperville | 35 S. Washington St. (bet. Benton & Van Buren Aves.) | 630-717-3500
www.catch35.com

Finatics looking to catch "beautifully presented", "Asian-influenced" "fresh fish" and a "balanced wine list" head for these "fine-dining" seafood "favorites"; the Loop locale has the "feel of a high-powered businessman's restaurant" (it's "popular" with the "lunch crowd" and after-work eaters who favor the "live music"), while Naperville boasts an "open atmosphere"; still, doubters find them "somewhat pricey" with occasional "average" service.

NEW Cellar Bistro, The ☑ *Eclectic* | - | - | - | M |

Wheaton | 132 N. Hale St. (Wesley St.) | 630-653-6299
Eclectic "vegetarian-friendly" "small plates" at affordable prices "make dinner fun" at this "comfortable", "cozy" bistro and wine bar with a focus on "organic ingredients, wines and beers"; supporters who say the candlelit atmosphere feels like it could be in the city wonder "am I really still in Wheaton?"

Chalkboard *American* | 22 | 20 | 21 | $42 |

Lakeview | 4343 N. Lincoln Ave. (bet. Montrose & Pensacola Aves.) | 773-477-7144 | www.chalkboardrestaurant.com

"The handwriting (menu) is on the wall, and the reward is on your plate" say fans of this "adorable" "white-tablecloth" Lakeview "storefront" where chef Gil Langlois "seeks out small farmers and boutique wineries" for his "mostly organic" New American menu that changes nearly daily ("you can't go wrong with the fried chicken" or "mac 'n' cheese"); the staff is "gracious" to boot, but while most are charmed, an unenthused few "don't see what all the fuss is about."

NEW Chant ◑ *Asian* | ▽ 16 | 24 | 17 | $26 |

Hyde Park | 1509 E. 53rd St. (bet. Harper & Lake Park Aves.) | 773-324-1999 | www.chantchicago.com

"Trendy" decor, a "lively" vibe and "Asian comfort food" "for those who prefer a small-plates approach" (plus some big plates too) make this "casual" eatery a "nice addition" to the "Hyde Park dining scene"; however, a minority names it "nothing special" and warns it's "still working out" the service.

☑ Charlie Trotter's ☑Ⓜ *American* | 27 | 25 | 27 | $142 |

Lincoln Park | 816 W. Armitage Ave. (Halsted St.) | 773-248-6228 | www.charlietrotters.com

Lincoln Park's jackets-required "nirvana on Armitage" showcases the "boundless imagination" of its namesake "master chef" and his

FOOD | DECOR | SERVICE | COST

"daring" prix fixe seasonal American menus, which are "perfectly paired" with a 1,800-bottle wine list and served by a "highly trained", "gracious" staff in "quiet" environs; though querulous types quibble it's "no longer the novelty it once was" and balk at the "pretentious" air and "essence-of-expense-account" prices, supporters swear that this "world-class" "landmark" is "still the gold standard"; P.S. "the kitchen table is a must" for a "special night out."

Châtaigne ⊠ *Eclectic/French*   - | - | - | M
(fka CHIC Cafe)

Near North | Cooking & Hospitality Institute of Chicago | 361 W. Chestnut St. (Orleans St.) | 312-873-2032 | www.chic.edu

Enjoy a "blue-jeans evening with business-suit food" at this Near North "gem" (formerly CHIC Cafe) staffed by the Cooking & Hospitality Institute's "friendly" "future chefs", who concoct "imaginative" New French–Eclectic prix fixe menus; if the "earnest" service can come with "a glitch", "bargain-hunters" insist the gentle tabs make up for it; N.B. the schedule is based on the school's curriculum.

⊠ Cheesecake Factory *American*   19 | 19 | 18 | $27

Streeterville | John Hancock Ctr. | 875 N. Michigan Ave. (bet. Chestnut St. & Delaware Pl.) | 312-337-1101 ◗

Lincolnshire | Lincolnshire Commons | 930 Milwaukee Ave. (W. Aptakisic Rd.) | 847-955-2350

Skokie | Westfield Shoppingtown | 374 Old Orchard Shopping Ctr. (Skokie Blvd.) | 847-329-8077

Schaumburg | Woodfield Shopping Ctr. | 53 Woodfield Rd. (Golf Rd.) | 847-619-1090

Oak Brook | Oakbrook Center Mall | 2020 Spring Rd. (bet. Harger Rd. & 22nd St.) | 630-573-1800

www.thecheesecakefactory.com

The menu's "mammoth" – and "so are the crowds" – at this "family-pleasing" chain where the "endless" American options arrive in "colossal" portions ("they give you so much there's no room" for their "heavenly" namesake desserts); despite "ordinary" settings, "spotty" staffing and "commotion", these "well-oiled machines" are so "busy" that they're best accessed "off-hours" to avoid a "long wait."

Chef's Station ⓜ *American*   22 | 18 | 22 | $43

Evanston | Davis Street Metro Station | 915 Davis St. (Church St.) | 847-570-9821 | www.chefs-station.com

Commenters commute to this haute Evanston hideaway boasting a "surprisingly creative contemporary menu" for "great-quality" New American (with French accents) dining with an "excellent wine list" (the "prix fixe meal with wine flight is a terrific value"); less enthusiastic eaters equivocate over "uneven service" and "whimsical" decor, but all agree you can "have a lovely summer" meal on the patio.

Chens *Chinese/Japanese*   20 | 17 | 18 | $25

Wrigleyville | 3506 N. Clark St. (Addison St.) | 773-549-9100 | www.chenschicago.com

Regulars "highly recommend" this "cool", "soothing" Wrigleyville hybrid of "refined" Chinese-Japanese cuisine delivering "classic faves" (like "General Tsao's chicken") and "passable sushi" amid an atmosphere of "subdued elegance"; "low-fat options" cheer the waistline-conscious as well.

Chez Joël ⓜ *French*

23 | 19 | 21 | $44

Little Italy | 1119 W. Taylor St. (Racine Ave.) | 312-226-6479 | www.chezjoelbistro.com

"France comes to Little Italy and triumphs" testify touters of this "surprise" French find featuring "fresh", "quality bistro dining" "in the middle of the spaghetti belt"; the "small" space is "cute" and "comfortable" – especially the "beautiful backyard patio" – and regulars are "thankful" that "it's not that well known."

🇿 Chicago Chop House *Steak*

25 | 20 | 24 | $56

River North | 60 W. Ontario St. (bet. Clark & Dearborn Sts.) | 312-787-7100 | www.chicagochophouse.com

"Beef is king" at this "jammed" River North steakery that's "as much a Chicago icon as Sandburg and Frank's song", serving "masculine-sized" meat that "makes you want to lick your chops", plus an "impressive" 600-bottle wine list; its "old Chicago townhouse" confines include a "piano bar" and "pictures of gangsters", and insiders insist if you find the "coolly professional service" "pushy", "just give it right back to them"; P.S. dinner includes salad and potatoes, which may make it "more reasonably priced than its competitors."

Chicago Diner, The *Diner*

21 | 13 | 20 | $18

Lakeview | 3411 N. Halsted St. (Roscoe St.) | 773-935-6696 | www.veggiediner.com

Lakeview's "retro" "veggie" diner delights with "lots of options" that include "fresh and tasty" "comfort food", "vegan" vittles and "milk-shakes to die for", causing convinced carnivores to cry "you won't miss the meat"; the vibe evokes a "hippie" hang with "groovy" servers, making it a "reliable" "standby for health-food people."

Chicago Firehouse *American*

22 | 22 | 22 | $45

South Loop | 1401 S. Michigan Ave. (14th St.) | 312-786-1401 | www.chicagofirehouse.com

Rising ratings support boosters who say "there's a reason this restaurant was popular even before the neighborhood boomed" – credit its "solid", "properly prepared" Traditional American "comfort food with an upscale flair", "excellent side dishes" and "welcoming" service; set in a "historic, restored" South Loop firehouse, it also boasts a "great bar" and "wonderful" back garden.

Chicago Pizza & Oven Grinder Co. ⊅ *Pizza*

22 | 15 | 19 | $21

Lincoln Park | 2121 N. Clark St. (bet. Dickens & Webster Aves.) | 773-248-2570 | www.chicagopizzaandovengrinder.com

"There are long lines for a reason" at this Lincoln Park "landmark" and "great old family place", "a true Chicago original" to pie-*sani* who praise its "awesome pizza pot pies", "gigantic salads", "out-of-this-world grinders" and a host who "never forgets where you are in the wait order"; even fans, though, "wish they'd take reservations"

FOOD DECOR SERVICE COST

and find the "cash-only policy" "slightly irritating", while idealists insist the "unique" signature dish is merely "masquerading" as 'za and "claustrophobes" criticize its "catacombs"-like setting.

Chief O'Neill's Pub Food

17 | 19 | 18 | $24

Northwest Side | 3471 N. Elston Ave. (Addison St.) | 773-583-3066 | www.chiefoneillspub.com

Eire-ophiles say you'll "swear you were in Ireland" at this Northwest Side "corner bar" that dishes out "hearty", "nicely executed pub grub", a "great selection of whiskey" and brews and "cheerful service"; it's "all about tradition", from the imported "wood-and-tin ceiling" to one of the "best beer gardens in the city"; N.B. visit on the weekend for live music jams.

China Grill Asian

20 | 21 | 19 | $48

Loop | Hard Rock Hotel | 230 N. Michigan Ave. (Lake St.) | 312-334-6700 | www.chinagrillmgt.com

"It's a scene" at this "splashy", "high-class chain" outpost in the Loop's Hard Rock Hotel, where the "big portions" of "trendy, tasty" Asian dishes are "meant for sharing"; still, some supporters who "love the food" think it's "overpriced" "for what it is", while others note that it can be "way too loud" for conversation.

Chinn's 34th St. Fishery Seafood

22 | 12 | 19 | $38

Lisle | 3011 W. Ogden Ave. (bet. Fender Ave. & Naper Blvd.) | 630-637-1777 | www.chinns-fishery.com

"Cousin of the famous Bob Chinn's" ("but without the long waits"), this "low-key family seafood spot" in Lisle is "still serving up tasty", "incredibly fresh" fish – and displaying "documentation of today's-catch flights in the foyer" – along with notorious mai tais that "take the edge off the subpar", "cafeteria-style" ambiance.

Cinners Chili Parlour & Cocktail Lounge ⌼Ⓜ American

- | - | - | I

Lincoln Square | 4757 N. Talman Ave. (Lawrence Ave.) | 773-654-1624 | www.cinners.net

Lincoln Square locals will all become cinners if this budget-friendly den has its way – it tempts with Cincinnati-style chili (thinner than Texas-style) served every which way, from inside muffins to atop fries to "5-Way" (with spaghetti, shredded Cheddar, onions, red beans and oyster crackers); the red-and-black-themed space comes complete with a red cement bar dispensing crazy cocktails.

Cité American

24 | 25 | 22 | $74

Streeterville | Lake Point Tower | 505 N. Lake Shore Dr., 70th fl. (Navy Pier) | 312-644-4050 | www.citechicago.com

This sky-high, jackets-suggested Streeterville 30-year-old provides an "excellent" "360-degree" view from "atop Lake Point Tower", rendering it "great for special occasions" (if "too expensive for regularity"), complete with "terrific presentations" of New American fare and a "tuxedoed staff"; even those who deem the dining merely "decent" admit that the "view makes it taste better"; N.B. brunch is served.

	FOOD	DECOR	SERVICE	COST

NEW C.J.'s Eatery M *Eclectic* — | — | — | I

Humboldt Park | 3839 W. Grand Ave. (Avers Ave.) | 773-292-0990 | www.cjs-eatery.com

In Humboldt Park, this corner storefront serves bargain Eclectic fare with a Southern accent amid casual neighborhood environs adorned with splashes of bright artwork; BYO or indulge in nonalcoholic beverages like blueberry lemonade.

Clubhouse, The *American* 20 | 22 | 20 | $37

Oak Brook | Oakbrook Center Mall | 298 Oakbrook Ctr. (Rte. 83) | 630-472-0600 | www.theclubhouse.com

Fans figure this "hip but dignified" Traditional American clubhouse in Oak Brook's mall is "a fun place to meet for martinis" "after work", a "power lunch", a "fine Sunday brunch" or a "special meal" of "fantastic sandwiches, sizzling steaks" and desserts "bigger than your head" – but duffers dis it as an "overpriced", "noisy" "suburban" "pickup place"; P.S. there's a "large outdoor dining area."

Club Lucky *Italian* 19 | 17 | 19 | $28

Bucktown | 1824 W. Wabansia Ave. (bet. Honore & Wood Sts.) | 773-227-2300 | www.clubluckychicago.com

Boasters for this "lively" Bucktown "local favorite" "smack dab in a residential neighborhood" swear its "large servings" of Southern Italian "comfort food", "romantic" "retro atmosphere", "all-ages clientele", "great" "hefty martinis" and "attentive service" amount to "an offer you can't refuse"; P.S. "outdoor dining is a plus in nice weather."

Coalfire Pizza M *Pizza* 22 | 12 | 15 | $17

West Loop | 1321 W. Grand Ave. (bet. Ada & Elizabeth Sts.) | 312-226-2625 | www.coalfirechicago.com

"Fired-up" fans of "New Haven" "thin-crust" come to this "cute", "crowded" West Loop "neighborhood" BYO for the "addictive" pizza "with char on the crust" ("cooked in an actual coal-fired oven"); hesitators hint it's "hit-or-miss", but "when it's a hit, it's out of the ballpark" – just "don't expect good service" or anything but "plain" decor.

Coast Sushi Bar ☻ *Japanese* 25 | 21 | 20 | $32

Bucktown | 2045 N. Damen Ave. (bet. Dickens & McLean Aves.) | 773-235-5775 | www.coastsushibar.com

South Coast *Japanese*
NEW South Loop | 1700 S. Michigan Ave. (bet. 16th & 18th Sts.) | 312-662-1700

This "sleek", "trendy" Bucktown Japanese entices an "eclectic mix of folks" with its "outstanding" "signature rolls" ("try the fresh wasabi"), "sashimi that melts in your mouth" and "non-sushi entrees"; the BYO policy helps "keep the cost reasonable", which may be why "there is always a crowd swarming" – so "go early" and "make sure to have a reservation", or hit up the new South Loop spin-off, which is "still somewhat unknown."

	FOOD	DECOR	SERVICE	COST

Coco Pazzo *Italian* | 25 | 22 | 23 | $50 |

River North | 300 W. Hubbard St. (Franklin St.) | 312-836-0900 |
www.cocopazzochicago.com

"Fresh, flavorful ingredients" and "perfect homemade pastas" are the
hallmark of this "hip", "exquisite" Nothern Italian "perennial winner" that brings Tuscany to River North; an all-Italy wine list features
"some out-of-the-ordinary choices", and "quality service" reigns
over the "warm", "sophisticated" "retro-warehouse setting" outfitted with "wood beams and exposed brick" – as for cost, some praise
"fair prices for the quality", others consign it to the "expense account" category; N.B. the Food score may not reflect a chef change.

Coco Pazzo Café *Italian* | 23 | 19 | 20 | $38 |

Streeterville | Red Roof Inn | 636 N. St. Clair St. (Ontario St.) |
312-664-2777 | www.cocopazzocafe.com

"One block off the Mag Mile" in Streeterville, this "great city neighborhood restaurant" is "ever-popular" for its "high-quality"
Northern Italian output at a "better value" than its "fancier" parent
in River North; there's also a "good midpriced wine list", and alfresco addicts appreciate the "nice outdoor seating for people-
watching"; P.S. "who would have thought – in a Red Roof Inn?"

Convito Café & Market *French/Italian* | 16 | 17 | 16 | $32 |

Wilmette | Plaza del Lago | 1515 Sheridan Rd. (bet. 10th St. &
Westerfield Dr.) | 847-251-3654 | www.convitocafeandmarket.com

The "marriage of Betise and Convito" spawned this Wilmette "grocery that grew a dining room" and "seems to be working well" ac-
cording to supporters, offering a "variety" of French-Italian fare
(including "great Sunday brunch selections") in a "pleasant", "improved location"; contrarians claim the combo may have "taken the
worst from each", but the patio is a "reason to go."

Coobah ●Ⓜ *Filipino/Nuevo Latino* | 20 | 21 | 17 | $33 |

Lakeview | 3423 N. Southport Ave. (bet. Newport Ave. & Roscoe St.) |
773-528-2220 | www.coobah.com

"Swank and exotic", this Lakeview "date spot" is considered "a full-
flavored experience" by "the mid- to late-twentysomething" crowd
that frequents it for "tasty" Nuevo Latino–Filipino fusion fare, "fun
drinks" and "loud music" – but more staid surveyors say "the atmosphere is better than the food" and cite "service issues"; P.S. "the
outdoor seating is great for people-watching."

copperblue Ⓜ *French/Mediterranean* | 21 | 20 | 21 | $55 |

Streeterville | Lake Point Tower | 580 E. Illinois St. (Navy Pier) |
312-527-1200 | www.copperbluechicago.com

A small, "inventive" New French–Med menu makes "good use of local produce" and other seasonal and organic ingredients at this "upscale", "intimate" Streeterville spot with a "limited" but
"reasonable" Euro wine list; the "sedate setting" is home to "attentive service", but it's still "not well known" due to a location "in the
middle of everything yet still hard to find" – the ground floor of Lake
Point Tower, to be precise.

	FOOD	DECOR	SERVICE	COST

Cordis Brothers Supper Club M *American* ▽ 20 | 17 | 19 | $45

Lakeview | 1625 W. Irving Park Rd. (Paulina St.) | 773-935-1000 | www.cordisbrothers.com

"Relish trays and martinis", a "limited" "meat-heavy" menu of "honest" Traditional American eats and an "affordable wine list" lure Lakeview loyalists to this "neighborhood joint"; maybe a few find it "undistinguished", but "nice people" staff the "old-time supper club" setting, and there's live jazz on Wednesdays.

Costa's *Greek* 22 | 19 | 21 | $32

Greektown | 340 S. Halsted St. (Van Buren St.) | 312-263-9700
Oakbrook Terrace | 1 S. 130 Summit Ave. (Roosevelt Rd.) | 630-620-1100
www.costasdining.com

"Zorba would be proud" of the "great, authentic" Greek dishes, "old-world service" and "comfortable" quarters at these Greektown and West Suburban "standbys", even if they're "pricier" and "more formal" than most in the genre; N.B. Oakbrook Terrace has piano entertainment on most weekends, and a roaring fireplace in winter.

Côtes du Rhône M *French* 18 | 11 | 14 | $37

Edgewater | 5424 N. Broadway St. (bet. Balmoral & Catalpa Aves.) | 773-293-2683

This candlelit Edgewater BYO proffers "consistent" French bistro dining" at "reasonable prices", but service can be "uneven" and while some find the atmosphere "romantic", others argue it's "almost nonexistent" and so "dark" you "can barely see the food."

Courtright's M *American* 25 | 25 | 24 | $58

Willow Springs | 8989 S. Archer Ave. (Willow Springs Rd.) | 708-839-8000 | www.courtrights.com

A "beautiful wooded setting" complete "with deer roaming" meets "exquisite" seasonal New American cooking ("can't resist their tasting menus") at this "romantic", "refined-dining" "standout" in the Southwest Suburbs; "attentive" service and one of the "best wine selections around" (25,000 bottles) seal the deal; N.B. the Food score may not reflect a recent chef change.

Cousin's *Mediterranean* 19 | 16 | 17 | $22

Lakeview | 2833 N. Broadway St. (Clark St.) | 773-880-0063

"Fresh", "satisfying", "authentic" Turkish eats and a "relaxing" environment with "cushioned" "floor seating for the limber" appeal to adherents of this "vegetarian-friendly" Med spot in Lakeview; cranky cousins complain it "lacks consistency", service can be "slow" and the atmosphere needs "beefing-up", but most agree it's "priced right"; N.B. no relation to Cousin's Incredible Vitality raw-food specialist on the Northwest Side.

Crofton on Wells Z *American* 25 | 19 | 23 | $59

River North | 535 N. Wells St. (bet. Grand Ave. & Ohio St.) | 312-755-1790 | www.croftononwells.com

"Fine dining without pretense" describes Suzy Crofton's "expensive-but-worth-it" River North "oasis" where the "sophisticated, subtle"

New American cookery is "prepared with high quality", "locally grown" "ingredients" and matched by a "fabulous wine list" featuring "many good small producers"; a "discreetly attentive", "well-informed staff" works the "simply decorated", "sedate" space that pickier sorts describe as "BYOA: bring your own atmosphere."

Cru Café & Wine Bar ● *American*   17 | 19 | 19 | $34

Gold Coast | 25 E. Delaware Pl. (bet. N. State St. & N. Wabash Ave.) | 312-337-4001 | www.cruwinebar.com

The "primary attraction" at Debbie Sharpe's recently remodeled Gold Coast getaway is its "diverse" (400-bottle, 50 by-the-glass), "more-than-respectable" wine list, not the "high-class" New American snack fare that "doesn't always come together" (the "olive-and-cheese flights" are a good bet); locals complain it's "not as cozy as before" – but there's still the "fireplace on a cold winter night" and "people-watching" on the sidewalk "in the summer."

Crust *Pizza*   21 | 17 | 19 | $26

Wicker Park | 2056 W. Division St. (Hoyne Ave.) | 773-235-5511 | www.crustchicago.com

"Unique" "brick-oven" flatbreads and "fresh" salads lure crowds to Michael Altenberg's "hip", "certified-organic" Wicker Park pizzeria with an "interesting beer list", "alfresco dining" and "fabulous cocktails"; on the flip side, service may "leave something to be desired", and crusty commenters claim that considering the "hype", the noshing is "not as special as expected" – plus it's "a bit spendy" "for what it is."

Cuatro *Nuevo Latino*   22 | 20 | 21 | $40

South Loop | 2030 S. Wabash Ave. (21st St.) | 312-842-8856 | www.cuatro-chicago.com

"Spicy, sassy" and "hip" describe this Nuevo Latino spot serving "inventive", "delectable" fare alongside "strong drinks" brought by a "good-humored" staff; Latin lovers also praise the "diversity of clientele" and the DJ and "live bands on certain nights" that "add to the festive environment", labeling it an "exciting" "addition to the South Loop"; N.B. Sunday brunch, sidewalk seating and late service (2 AM Friday-Saturday) are pluses.

NEW Cucina Paradiso *Italian*   ∇ 25 | 21 | 23 | $28

Oak Park | 814 North Blvd. (Oak Park Ave.) | 708-848-3434 | www.cucinaoakpark.com

Regulars who "really missed" this "lovely" "Oak Park favorite" when "it was closed after a fire" are "delighted" that it's reopened with, once again, "really, really good Italian food" from an "extensively updated menu" that blends "traditional" and "creative dishes" (including "great specials"); since it's now fully remodeled, expect to dine in a whimsical, "beautiful new room."

Custom House *American*   25 | 24 | 24 | $62

Printer's Row | Hotel Blake | 500 S. Dearborn St. (Congress Pkwy.) | 312-523-0200 | www.customhouse.cc

Chef Shawn McClain's New American "meat emporium" is "one of those rare glamorous see-and-be-seen places where the food is terrific" thanks to "fresh seasonal ingredients and refined flavor combinations" that well match the "impressive wine selection"; it's situated in Printer's Row, an area "that doesn't have a lot of great restaurants", so locals love to linger in the "delightfully warm", "classy" confines with service that's "timely" and "knowledgeable"; P.S. it's especially "great on an expense account."

Cyrano's Bistrot & Wine Bar *French* 21 | 18 | 19 | $38

River North | 546 N. Wells St. (Ohio St.) | 312-467-0546 | www.cyranosbistrot.com

"Personable" chef-owner Didier Durand "takes a great deal of pride in this restaurant and it shows" in the "fine", "authentic" bistro fare, "good wine recommendations", "romantic atmosphere" and "reasonable prices" (the "prix fixe is always a great deal") – all aspects of a "French country experience" right in River North; P.S. pet people "love" the "dog-friendly" sidewalk cafe.

D & J Bistro Ⓜ *French* 25 | 21 | 23 | $42

Lake Zurich | First Bank Plaza Ctr. | 466 S. Rand Rd./Rte. 12 (Rte. 22) | 847-438-8001 | www.dj-bistro.com

This "little" Northwest Suburban "strip-mall" joint evokes "Montmartre in Lake Zurich, sans the cobblestones" but with "honest", "high-quality" French bistro fare "served without attitude" at a "fraction of the cost of Downtown"; "they like their clientele and it shows", and the decor is "inviting" – the "only drawback is the noise level when full", which is often, so reservations are suggested.

Dave's Italian Kitchen *Italian* 17 | 12 | 17 | $20

Evanston | 1635 Chicago Ave., downstairs (bet. Church & Davis Sts.) | 847-864-6000 | www.davesik.com

Despite "long waiting times", diehards submit this is "still one of the [Evanston] area's best bargains" for "large portions" of Southern "Italian just like mom used to make" and "wine bargains" in a "loud" "basement" "zoo"; others who "don't understand why this place is so popular" opine that the "ordinary-to-bland" offerings are only for "impoverished" "NU students" or those "too lazy to boil water at home."

David Burke's Primehouse *Steak* 24 | 23 | 23 | $69

River North | The James Chicago Hotel | 616 N. Rush St. (Ontario St.) | 312-660-6000 | www.brguestrestaurants.com

Aficionados of "tender" "aged [prime] beef the way it should be" ("the restaurant has its own bull; how can you beat that?") also offer accolades for the "wonderful tableside Caesar" and "creative desserts" at David Burke's "trendy, modern" New American steakhouse in River North; nitpickers, however, say service can be somewhat "lacking for a restaurant of this level" and with such "expense-account" prices; N.B. brunch is served both Saturday and Sunday.

David's Bistro Ⓩ Ⓜ *American/French* ▽ 23 | 17 | 21 | $43

Des Plaines | Wolf Plaza | 623 N. Wolf Rd. (Central Ave.) | 847-803-3233 | www.davidsbistro.com

"Tucked into a [Northwest] Suburban strip mall", this "reasonably priced" "little bistro"-that-could conjures compliments for its New

American–French slate "with some Cajun thrown in"; the setting is "warm" and "comfortable", despite being "without much atmosphere", and a "friendly, knowledgeable staff" helps "keep this a neighborhood joy" for "casual-fine dining"; N.B. paintings by David himself are on display and for sale.

Davis Street Fishmarket *Seafood*   20 | 16 | 18 | $36

Evanston | 501 Davis St. (Hinman Ave.) | 847-869-3474
NEW **Schaumburg** | 1383 Meacham Rd. (Golf Rd.) |
847-969-1200
www.davisstreetfishmarket.com

"Catch dinner here and you'll be hooked" claim converts to the "very good", "all-around-honest" seafood (the "oyster bar is a plus") at this "Evanston fixture" and its Northwest Suburban Schaumburg schoolmate; some grouse that the original is "not the same old funky fishmarket" after its recent "upscale" "makeover", but most "welcome" the change, even if it "made prices higher" and service can still be "erratic."

de cero ☒ *Mexican*   22 | 18 | 17 | $33

Market District | 814 W. Randolph St. (bet. Green & Halsted Sts.) |
312-455-8114 | www.decerotaqueria.com

Muchachos meet at this "tapas-style" Market District taqueria for a "fun alternative to traditional Mexican fare", with "many inventive fillings" of "fresh ingredients" for the "tasty tacos" and "delicious drinks" served in a "hip" yet "rustic environment" with a side of "loud music"; iffier inputters indicate "inattentive service", but that doesn't keep the place from getting frequently "crowded."

Dee's *Asian*   19 | 17 | 19 | $28

Lincoln Park | 1114 W. Armitage Ave. (Seminary Ave.) | 773-477-1500 |
www.deesrestaurant.com

Loyalists love this Lincoln Parker for its "wide selection of Asian favorites" (Mandarin, Sichuan, sushi) served in a "cozy" "neighborhood" atmosphere with a "great garden for outside dining" – not to mention "hands-on, ever-present owner Dee" Kang, who always "sees to customers' needs"; still, querulous quills question the quality and value of what they call "inconsistent" output that's "considerably more expensive" than in Chinatown.

DeLaCosta *Nuevo Latino*   22 | 25 | 19 | $54

Streeterville | 465 E. Illinois St. (bet. Lake Shore Dr. & McClurg Ct.) |
312-464-1700 | www.delacostachicago.com

It's a "party" "for grown-ups" at chef Douglas Rodriguez's "posh", "trendy" "little bit of Miami" in Streeterville, an "expensive" "hot spot for both dining and lounging" where the decor seems to be taken "straight out of a Tim Burton movie"; the "flavorful", "original" Nuevo Latino menu is backed by "popsicle drinks that rock", "beautiful people galore" and open-air seating on the river, though a sector of surveyors sees it as "more scene than substance" and notes "nothing's consistent except the noise level."

	FOOD	DECOR	SERVICE	COST

Deleece *Eclectic*
20 | 16 | 19 | $31

Lakeview | 4004 N. Southport Ave. (Irving Park Rd.) | 773-325-1710 | www.deleece.com

Regulars rank this Lakeview Eclectic a "neighborhood gem" for its "scrumptious", "interesting global menu", "fantastic [weekend] brunch" and a "cozy feel" abetted by "exposed brick and candles on each table", as well as touting the Monday–Tuesday prix fixe as a "great deal"; P.S. "summer on the sidewalk patio is a treat."

Del Rio ⊠ *Italian*
22 | 16 | 23 | $38

Highwood | 228 Green Bay Rd. (Rte. 22) | 847-432-4608

"Very tasty" if "not gourmet" Northern Italian "red-sauce" profferings nudge nostalgic sorts toward this North Shore "family"-friendly "blast from the past", boasting a "great heritage" and "killer" "wine cellar"; overseen by "warm people" and a "staff that's been there forever", it's still a "favorite", though modernists moan the "chef needs to be reminded it's not 1960"; N.B. they don't take reservations.

Depot American Diner, The *Diner*
- | - | - | I

Far West | 5840 W. Roosevelt Rd. (S. Austin Blvd.) | 773-261-8422

Blue-plate specials and WiFi meet at this "friendly diner next to a CTA bus turnaround" in the Far West, where nonstop blues are the background for "delightful surprises" from the affordable Traditional American menu, all "made with imagination and loving care"; ravers recommend the "open-face turkey" or "pot roast sand-wich", and add there's a "great breakfast" too.

Devon Seafood Grill *Seafood*
21 | 21 | 20 | $43

River North | 39 E. Chicago Ave. (Wabash Ave.) | 312-440-8660 | www.devonseafood.com

The River North branch of this Philly-spawned seafood group is a "solid performer" satisfying with "fresh and tasty" "fish dishes", a "happening happy hour" and "good service"; some call the "spacious basement" dining room "relaxed" and "sleek" while others label it "strange" (giving higher marks to the "welcoming" above-ground bar area), and a minority labels the "pricey" fodder "nothing special."

Dine *American*
▽ 15 | 17 | 17 | $41

West Loop | Crowne Plaza Chicago Metro Hotel | 733 W. Madison St. (Halsted St.) | 312-602-2100 | www.dinerestaurant.com

Dine-rs reckon it's the "1950s" at this West Loop destination in the Crowne Plaza Chicago Metro Hotel where the "appealing" American "comfort food" "on steroids" (not literally) includes pork chops and mac 'n' cheese; some say "service can be uneven", and if you find it "a little expensive", try the "bar specials"; N.B. there's patio seating.

Dining Room at Kendall College, The ⊠ *French*
▽ 24 | 20 | 23 | $41

Near West | Kendall College | 900 N. North Branch St. (Halsted St.) | 312-752-2328 | www.kendall.edu

"Some of the dishes are great, others get an 'E for effort'" at this Near West "training restaurant" where Kendall College's "student chefs" prepare "great value" New French fare; its "earnest" servers "aim to please", and the "surprisingly pleasant room" ("much glitzier than its old digs") boasts a "killer" "skyline view", new chef's table and "three-course prix fixe lunch" that's an "unbeatable" bargain.

Dinotto Ristorante *Italian*   21 | 18 | 19 | $34
Old Town | 215 W. North Ave. (Wells St.) | 312-202-0302 | www.dinotto.com

"Tasty" "everyday" eats greet goers to this "great neighborhood Italian", an Old Town "standby" with "reliably good service"; it's a "convenient" stop "before catching a movie across the street", and the "romantic setting" is "nice" for a "date night" – especially the prime "courtyard" patio (with its own bar) that's "like eating in a piazza in Italy"; a minority of *mangia*-ers, however, marks it "middle of the pack."

Di Pescara *Italian/Seafood*   21 | 18 | 19 | $36
Northbrook | Northbrook Court Shopping Ctr. | 2124 Northbrook Ct. (Lake Cook Rd.) | 847-498-4321 | www.leye.com

In Northbrook Court, this "Italian seafooder from the Lettuce group" is a "solid choice" for "people-watching" over "reasonably priced fresh fish" and pastas paired with Alpana Singh's wine program (her "A-list" choices are a "deal") in a "sophisticated" if somewhat "bare" and "noisy" "white-tablecloth" setting; but the lure is lost on a minority that reports "mediocre" meals and "spotty" service during peak times, when there's often a "wait, even with reservations."

NEW Distinctive Cork 🅂Ⓜ *American*   ∇ 22 | 24 | 22 | $35
Naperville | 192 W. Gartner Rd. (Washington St.) | 630-753-9463 | www.distinctivecork.com

This West Suburban wine bar "shouldn't be shunned for its strip-mall location" say advocates of its "great" "by-the-glass" offerings (though perhaps the list "could use some more reserve selections") and "sophisticated" American food that includes plates of "interesting cheeses and meats" and "tiny hamburgers"; the staff is "helpful", and there's live music on Thursdays–Sundays, so it's popular for a "date night or girl's night out."

Dixie Kitchen &   20 | 18 | 18 | $20
Bait Shop *Cajun/Southern*
Hyde Park | 5225 S. Harper Ave. (53rd St.) | 773-363-4943
Evanston | 825 Church St. (Benson Ave.) | 847-733-9030
Lansing | 2352 E. 172nd St. (Torrence Ave.) | 708-474-1378
www.dixiekitchenchicago.com

"Put some South in your mouth" at this "charming", "fun-as-cow-tipping" city and suburban trio "serving" "solid", "stick-to-your-ribs" Southern-Cajun cooking ("staples like fried green tomatoes, po' boys, étouffée and gumbo") to "a diverse clientele" of Dixie chicks and Dicks; the "rustic decor" is "contrived but cute", and the vittles are a "value."

	FOOD	DECOR	SERVICE	COST

Don Juan's *Mexican* | 21 | 14 | 18 | $27 |

Edison Park | 6730 N. Northwest Hwy. (bet. Devon & Ozark Aves.) | 773-775-6438

Coming up on 25 years, Edison Park's "friendly", "family-owned" "oasis" is famous for meting out "good-quality" seasonal Mexican meals that range "from simple tacos to gourmet dishes" (though it's maybe "not as creative as in prior days"); drinkers delight in the "legendary margaritas", 60-plus tequilas and "small but good wine list", and everyone's on board with its "reasonable prices."

Don Roth's Blackhawk *Seafood/Steak* | 23 | 20 | 23 | $43 |

Wheeling | 61 N. Milwaukee Ave. (Dundee Rd.) | 847-537-5800 | www.donroths.com

Nearing 30 years in a "comfortable" North Suburban location (after moving from its 1920 original), this "solid" surf 'n' turfer harboring "top-notch prime rib and Boston scrod" is "still 'spinning' a great salad" in "small", "conversation-friendly" dining rooms staffed by "old-fashioned, attentive" servers; "jazz-era nostalgia" and two fire-places round out the decor, and while portions are "huge", penny-pinchers say that doesn't justify the prices "going up."

Dorado *French/Mexican* | 25 | 16 | 23 | $31 |

Lincoln Square | 2301 W. Foster Ave. (bet. Claremont & Oakley Aves.) | 773-561-3780 | www.doradorestaurant.com

"Complexity and comfort combine" on the "innovative menu" of "ex-cellent modern Mexican" fare "with French influences" ("tasty duck nachos" and a "scrumptious chocolate chimichanga dessert") at this "unpretentious" Lincoln Square "winner" in a simple "storefront you might pass by"; if "ambiance is lacking", at least there's an "ex-hibition kitchen that's fun to watch", plus the "service is responsive" and "BYO makes it a great dining deal."

Drake Bros.' Steakhouse *Seafood/Steak* | 20 | 19 | 20 | $60 |

Streeterville | Drake Hotel | 140 E. Walton St. (Michigan Ave.) | 312-932-4626 | www.thedrakehotel.com

"Tourists and locals" traffic this "nonchain alternative" meat 'n' sea-fooder in Streeterville's Drake Hotel for its "good but not great steak", fish and "non-red meats as well", and laud the "consistent" service and lake view; still, some lament that it's "very expensive", except on Tuesdays, when the beef is "two for the price of one, plus one penny."

NEW Drawing Room at Le Passage, The Ⓜ *American* | – | – | – | M |

Gold Coast | 937 N. Rush St. (bet. Oak & Walton Sts.) | 312-255-0022 | www.lepassage.com

Shawn McClain (Spring, Green Zebra) concocts a tipple-tailored roster of New American small plates for this moderately priced Gold Coast 'culinary cocktail lounge' set in a chic subterranean space adorned with cushy chairs and natural textures; libations spiked with the likes of rosemary syrup and fresh-grated ginger can be mixed tableside from rolling carts to fuel grazers and preeners into the wee hours (open till 5 AM Saturdays).

	FOOD	DECOR	SERVICE	COST

Duke of Perth *Scottish*   21 | 17 | 19 | $19

Lakeview | 2913 N. Clark St. (Oakdale Ave.) | 773-477-1741 | www.dukeofperth.com

"Wonderfully friendly" with an "authentic" British comfort-food menu (on Wednesdays and Fridays, "all-you-can-eat fish 'n' chips is a must"), this "cozy" Lakeview Scottish pub also features the "finest selection of single-malt scotch around", plus "drafts" and "hard cider" "from across the pond" poured by "animated bartenders"; another "big plus: no TV, no jukebox", just "great conversation", or for privacy, pick the "patio in summer, tucked away in the back."

Ed Debevic's *Diner*   13 | 18 | 17 | $19

River North | 640 N. Wells St. (Ontario St.) | 312-664-1707
Lombard | Yorktown Shopping Ctr. | 157 Yorktown Shopping Ctr. (bet. Butterfield Rd. & 22nd St.) | 630-495-1700
www.eddebevics.com

Diners who are "feeling snarky" "trade insults" with the "smart-aleck staff" at this "campy" River North and West Suburban diner duo, "fun places" for a "'50s" "drive-in-type experience" of "fair-to-good" burgers and milkshakes and a side of "obnoxious-by-design service"; more staid surveyors sidestep the "sass" and "so-so" sustenance, though, hinting it's "had its moment" and wondering "why would anyone" "line up to be treated" "like a private in the army"?

Edelweiss *German*   22 | 22 | 23 | $31

Norridge | 7650 W. Irving Park Rd. (bet. Cumberland & Harlem Aves.) | 708-452-6040 | www.edelweissdining.com

"Plentiful portions" of "hearty", "traditional" German fare and over 100 "great beers" make this a "*gemütlichkeit*" "classic", serving the Northwest Suburbs since 1971; the "old-time" atmosphere is enhanced by "friendly" service, a fireplace and "live music" on weekends, and for midday munchers it's "open for lunch."

Edwardo's Natural Pizza *Pizza*   20 | 11 | 15 | $18

Gold Coast | 1212 N. Dearborn St. (Division St.) | 312-337-4490
Lincoln Park | 2662 N. Halsted St. (bet. Schubert & Wrightwood Aves.) | 773-871-3400
Hyde Park | 1321 E. 57th St. (Kimbark Ave.) | 773-241-7960
South Loop | 521 S. Dearborn St. (bet. Congress Pkwy. & Harrison St.) | 312-939-3366
Skokie | 9300 Skokie Blvd. (Gross Point Rd.) | 847-674-0008
Wheeling | 401 E. Dundee Rd. (Milwaukee Ave.) | 847-520-0666
Oak Park | 6831 North Ave. (Grove Ave.) | 708-524-2400
www.edwardos.com

"Man, what a great pie" moan memoirists about this widespread chain whose "natural" pizzas, "whether stuffed or thin", are topped with "fresh-tasting sauce" and ingredients such as "ambrosial spinach" and "great pesto"; the locations may "not be much in the way of decor or service" but they "still deliver the box of pizza some people dream of" (though others opine they're "good but not the best"); P.S. the lunch specials are perfect "for people on the go."

	FOOD	DECOR	SERVICE	COST

EJ's Place *Italian/Steak* `20` `15` `19` `$49`

Skokie | 10027 Skokie Blvd. (Old Orchard Rd.) | 847-933-9800 | www.ejsplaceskokie.com

Earning enthusiasm for its "expensive, quality [prime] meat" and other more "reasonably priced" Northern Italian dishes, this North Suburban steakhouse "relative of Gene and Georgetti" features "uniformly above-average" food in a "faux Wisconsin lodge" locale that's "great if you like real wood-burning fire-places"; knockers note the "knowledgeable service" can "seem stretched", though, adding that for the cost you "might as well make the trek" Downtown.

Eleven City Diner *Diner* `19` `19` `18` `$18`

South Loop | 1112 S. Wabash Ave. (11th St.) | 312-212-1112 | www.elevencitydiner.com

Diehards disagree about whether this "upscale" but "relaxed" South Looper is more "diner" or "deli" and whether the "owner" is "friendly" or "rude", but they're nearly unanimous in digging the "all-day" breakfast, "homemade soups", "huge sandwiches" "piled high with meats" and "soda fountain" "favorites", plus "full cocktail service and an excellent import beer list"; just know that "service is spotty" and "brunch lines are long."

El Nandu *Argentinean* `19` `15` `18` `$26`

Logan Square | 2731 W. Fullerton Ave. (California Ave.) | 773-278-0900

This "hidden treasure" located in Logan Square is "fun" for "wonderful Argentinean fare" including "huge steaks", "empan-adas that burst with flavor" and "tasty sangria", all of which is served in "authentic, cozy" environs; P.S. there's also "live entertainment on weekends."

El Presidente ● *Mexican* `15` `6` `14` `$15`

Lincoln Park | 2558 N. Ashland Ave. (Wrightwood Ave.) | 773-525-7938

Feeders "from all walks of life" favor this "divey" 24/7 BYO "neigh-borhood hangout" on the western fringe of Lincoln Park for its "cheap" if "mediocre" Mexican chow; despite "cafeteria lighting and generic decor", there's "pretty good service" and entertaining "sightseeing, especially after 2 AM"; P.S. regulars relate that "its real strength is breakfast."

Emilio's Sunflower Bistro Ⓜ *American* `24` `22` `22` `$41`

La Grange | 30 S. La Grange Rd. (Harris Ave.) | 708-588-9890 | www.sunflowerbistro.com

A "cozy bistro feel" and "ambitious" seasonal New American plates "with fresh organic ingredients" win friends for this "se-rene" West Suburban "sibling" of the Emilio's tapas empire (though "wholly unrelated" in concept); the "teeny" bar area "in the back" pours "good" "'tinis", the "charming" chef/co-owner's artwork decorates the walls and if the servers could "use some polish", at least they're "knowledgeable."

	FOOD	DECOR	SERVICE	COST

Emilio's Tapas *Spanish* | 22 | 18 | 20 | $32 |

Lincoln Park | 444 W. Fullerton Pkwy. (Clark St.) | 773-327-5100
Hillside | 4100 Roosevelt Rd. (Mannheim Rd.) | 708-547-7177

Emilio's Tapas La Rioja *Spanish*

Wheaton | 230 W. Front St. (Wheaton Ave.) | 630-653-7177

Emilio's Tapas Sol y Nieve *Spanish*

Streeterville | 215 E. Ohio St. (St. Clair St.) | 312-467-7177
www.emiliostapas.com

Emilio Gervilla's "casual" Spanish "socializing and grazing" spots sate with a "diversity" of "authentic" tapas and "creative specials" accompanied by "multiple varieties of sangria", a "great wine list" and "interesting selection of sherries" poured by a "well-trained" staff; the locations, which vary in noise and crowd levels, all have their loyalists, though grumps groan "to get full here, you'll need to spend plenty."

Emperor's Choice ● *Chinese* | 22 | 12 | 16 | $26 |

Chinatown | 2238 S. Wentworth Ave. (Cermak Rd.) | 312-225-8800
The "excellent Chinese food" is "fit for royalty" and can be "authentic if desired" – including some "dishes that can be frightening for the casual newcomer" – or "cooked more for the American taste" at this Chinatown "seafood heaven" that serves until midnight six nights a week, 11 PM on Sundays; the "predictable" decor may not be every emperor's choice, however (though the saltwater tank containing "live fish is cool").

Enoteca Piattini Ⓜ *Italian* | 18 | 17 | 18 | $27 |

Lincoln Park | 934 W. Webster Ave. (bet. Bissell St. & Sheffield Ave.) | 773-935-8466 | www.enotecapiattini.net
This "quaint", "family-owned and -operated" "neighborhood wine bar" in Lincoln Park specializes in "quality" Southern Italian "small-plates" cuisine plus "good-value" larger plates, along with a "huge selection of wines by the glass"; surly sorts report "drab" decor and "spacey" service, but a majority maintains the experience is "pleasantly surprising", especially in summer when the sidewalk tables are a "delight."

Entourage on American Lane *American* | 22 | 24 | 21 | $47 |

Schaumburg | 1301 American Ln. (bet. Meacham Rd. & National Pkwy.) | 847-995-9400 | www.entourageventures.com
Head to this sprawling Northwest Suburban Traditional American for "elegant dining in a beautiful setting" with two fireplaces and "Hummers and other large SUVs filling the parking lot"; service may be "spotty", and though there's "not a lot of creativity" on the steakhouse-slanted slate, it all rates "quite good", perhaps peaking with the "high-quality Sunday brunch" and "great bar experience"; P.S. economists "enjoy lunch more than dinner, due to the cost."

Erba *Italian* | 20 | 18 | 20 | $33 |

Lincoln Square | 4520 N. Lincoln Ave. (Sunnyside Ave.) | 773-989-4200 | www.eaterba.com
It's "tough to decide" among the "better-than-average" Northern Italian dishes made with herbs from the kitchen garden at this "re-

laxing and romantic" ristorante, a "nice addition to the Lincoln Square food scene" set in a "hip, minimalist room"; in nice weather "sit outside, which is lovely", and though they "don't take reservations, you can call ahead to put your name on the list."

Erie Cafe *Italian/Steak*

22 | 18 | 22 | $50

River North | 536 W. Erie St. (Kingsbury St.) | 312-266-2300 | www.eriecafe.com

"Take the boys for a power lunch" or dinner at this "real Italian steakhouse", a Gene & Georgetti descendent in River North, where "meat and fish in the best Chicago tradition" (including "elephantine prime rib") are delivered with "no-nonsense service" amid "good old-fashioned-joint" atmo complete with a "great river location" (the terrace seating is a "hidden treasure"); still, some offput outsiders opine that the output is "overpriced for the area."

erwin, an american cafe & bar Ⓜ *American*

22 | 20 | 22 | $37

Lakeview | 2925 N. Halsted St. (Oakdale Ave.) | 773-528-7200 | www.erwincafe.com

Aficionados of Erwin Drechsler's "homey" yet "urban" Lakeview "neighborhood standby" affirm it's "always a good choice" for a monthly changing menu of New American dishes ("some unusual, some standard, all well prepared"), an "out-of-the-ordinary brunch" and an "extensive, excellent wine list"; the "relaxed", "intimate" room is "conversation-friendly" and decorated with a "whimsical mural that makes great Chicago references"; P.S. wallet-watchers appreciate that it's a "good value."

Essence of India *Indian*

21 | 15 | 17 | $24

Lincoln Square | 4601 N. Lincoln Ave. (Wilson Ave.) | 773-506-0002 | www.essenceofindiachicago.com

Gourmands go to this "good place to experiment with Indian cuisine" that's "convenient to all that Lincoln Square has to offer" and harbors "helpful servers" (and a liquor license); a portion of Punjab proponents purports that the provisions are "pricey", though, and opts for the "drive to Devon" instead; N.B. a lunch buffet is served on Fridays and Saturdays.

Ethiopian Diamond *Ethiopian*

22 | 14 | 21 | $21

Edgewater | 6120 N. Broadway St. (Glenlake Ave.) | 773-338-6100 | www.ethiopiandiamond.com

"Who needs silverware when you have fingers and injera?" wonder those who feel it's "worth the trek north" for this Edgewater eatery's "authentic, cheap and yummy" Ethiopian eats in "family-friendly" "pleasant surroundings"; there's a one-man jazz band on Friday nights, and while service is "helpful and patient", it can also be "slow."

☑ Everest 🅂 Ⓜ *French*

27 | 26 | 27 | $100

Loop | One Financial Pl. | 440 S. LaSalle St., 40th fl. (Congress Pkwy.) | 312-663-8920 | www.everestrestaurant.com

Ascend to the "top of the mountain" for a "heavenly view" at Jean Joho's Loop showcase boasting "phenomenal", "high-end" New

French–Alsatian cuisine and a "mind-blowing" 1,700-bottle wine list that includes a "good choice of half bottles" and selections from Germany and Alsace; the "swank new interior" is presided over by a "first-rate" staff, and while a few modernists maintain it's "stuffy" and "no fun", partialists proclaim this "peak experience" "well worth" the "high-in-the-sky prices"; N.B. jackets suggested.

Evergreen ◗ Chinese
22 | 12 | 18 | $22

Chinatown | 2411 S. Wentworth Ave. (24th St.) | 312-225-8898

The "interesting", "authentic" Cantonese-Mandarin cooking is "always good" at this "bustling" "comfort-food" classic "at a quiet end of Chinatown"; it's "affordable" too, so most munchers overlook that the decor "could use some updating."

NEW Exposure Tapas Supper Club ⓜ Eclectic
▽ 18 | 23 | 19 | $35

South Loop | 1315 S. Wabash Ave. (13th St.) | 312-662-1060 | www.exposuretapas.com

"Original" options of "not-exactly-traditional" Eclectic tapas make this "classy" South Loop lair a prime place for a "first date" or "night out with friends"; even those who feel the service needs work and the fare is "overpriced" concede it's "still new", ergo they "should be able to correct these minor flaws in the future."

NEW Fat Cat American
18 | 20 | 16 | $21

Uptown | 4840 N. Broadway St. (Lawrence Ave.) | 773-506-3100 | www.fatcatbar.com

A "rockin'", "energetic" atmosphere sets the stage for "innovative [American] comfort food" at this "good local" Uptown "pub" that also offers "unique beers" and "inventive, reasonable" drink specials; there's an "art deco bar", patio dining, billiard table and plenty of "plasma TV screens with 'what game do you want to watch' hospitality from the staff"; N.B. children are discouraged overall and unwelcome after 7 PM.

Fat Willy's Rib Shack BBQ/Southern
23 | 11 | 17 | $21

Logan Square | 2416 W. Schubert Ave. (Western Ave.) | 773-782-1800 | www.fatwillysribshack.com

"Everything is homemade and tasty" at this "family-friendly" Logan Square Southern setup serving "sweet and smoky" "BBQ the way it should be", with "lots of meat choices", including "tender ribs" with "tangy sauce", plus "heart attack–worthy macaroni and cheese", "more soups and salads than you'd think" and "awesome desserts"; true, its decor is merely "decent", but at least it's "comfortable (and convenient for takeout)."

Feast American
21 | 18 | 18 | $26

Bucktown | 1616 N. Damen Ave. (North Ave.) | 773-772-7100 | www.feastrestaurant.com

You can "always count on" chef Debra Sharpe's "creative" New American comfort food at this "above-average" "Bucktown standard" with "staying power"; "outdoor seating" on the "see-and-be-

"seen" summer patio is "delightful", the interior "homey" and it's a "good value both in food and wine pricing", even if a passel of partakers "prefer brunch to dinner" and note that service can be "slow and unconnected."

Fiddlehead Café *American* 19 | 17 | 20 | $36

Lincoln Square | 4600 N. Lincoln Ave. (Wilson Ave.) | 773-751-1500 | www.fiddleheadcafe.com

Expect an "exceptionally friendly" staff, "especially interesting" roster of wines and "tasty" array of "American bistro cuisine" at this "pleasant", "upscale neighborhood option" in Lincoln Square; a few fiddlers find the decor "rather bland" and evaluate the experience as "expensive" for everyday eating, though most sing the "quiet" space's praise.

NEW Fifty/50, The ●🖼Ⓜ *American* – | – | – | M

Wicker Park | 2047 W. Division St. (bet. Damen & Hoyne Aves.) | 773-489-5050 | www.thefifty50.com

Joe's Seafood veterans sired this upscale Wicker Park sports bar (complete with sports-figure investors and memorabilia) serving Traditional American comfort food and beer-based cocktails in the tri-level former Bravo Tapas space; the revamped design features earth tones, comfy booths, a loungier basement with plasma TVs and expanded outdoor seating; N.B. lunch is served Friday–Sunday, and the kitchen's open till 1 AM nightly.

Filippo's *Italian* 22 | 16 | 22 | $30

Lincoln Park | 2211 N. Clybourn Ave. (Webster Ave.) | 773-528-2211 | www.filipposristorante.com

Patrons are *positivo* over this "basic Italian" respite "from the hectic Lincoln Park area" (and recommended for "after the movies") proffering "top-notch pasta", veal chops, risotto and other "reliably well-prepared plates"; its "warm" space is overseen by service that makes partialists "feel at home every time" they go.

Finley's Grill Room ● *American* 22 | 25 | 21 | $32

Downers Grove | 3131 Finley Rd. (Branding Ln.) | 630-964-3131 | www.finleysgrillroom.com

Stepping into this West Suburban site is "like going to a Wisconsin supper club" from the '70s, complete with "very good" Traditional American "comfort food", a "spacious bar", "entertainment on weekends" and two fireplaces; "friendly service" and "large portions" at "reasonable prices" add to the allure.

Fiorentino's Cucina Italiana *Italian* ∇ 22 | 18 | 19 | $36

Lakeview | 2901 N. Ashland Ave. (George St.) | 773-244-3026 | www.fiorentinoscucina.com

This Lakeview "find" is a "cut above the rest at this price point" thanks to its "delicious", "prepared-to-order" Southern Italian sustenance served by a "friendly staff" in "cozy" conditions (with "very close" tables); holdouts, however, hint at "hit-or-miss" meals and a sometimes less-than-congenial owner; N.B. outdoor seating is a seasonal option.

	FOOD	DECOR	SERVICE	COST

545 North *American*
20 | 17 | 18 | $41

Libertyville | 545 N. Milwaukee Ave. (Lake St.) | 847-247-8700 | www.545north.com

Locals label this North Suburban New American "refreshing" for its "creative yet not overly complicated dishes" served in a "stylish, modern" milieu – or, in summer, in the "wonderful outdoor seating" area with a fire pit; look for "lots of activity at the bar on weekends" along with live music (Thursday–Saturday), and be aware that the quality of the service often "depends on how busy they are."

Five O'Clock Steakhouse Ⓜ *Steak*
23 | 18 | 21 | $50

Fox River Grove | 1050 Northwest Hwy. (Kelsey Rd.) | 847-516-2900 | www.fiveoclocksteakhouse.com

See review in Milwaukee Directory.

Flat Top Grill *Asian*
19 | 15 | 17 | $20

Lakeview | 3200 N. Southport Ave. (Belmont Ave.) | 773-665-8100
Old Town | 319 W. North Ave. (Orleans St.) | 312-787-7676
Market District | 1000 W. Washington Blvd. (Carpenter St.) | 312-829-4800
Evanston | 707 Church St. (bet. Orrington & Sherman Aves.) | 847-570-0100
NEW **Lombard** | Shops on Butterfield | 305 Yorktown Ctr. (S. Highland Ave.) | 630-652-3700
Oak Park | 726 Lake St. (Oak Park Ave.) | 708-358-8200
www.flattopgrill.com

"If you're not full and happy when you leave it's your own fault" say fans of this "young, fun" chain of "do-it-yourself" all-you-can-eat Asian stir-fries, "solid cheap eateries" where "you choose your own ingredients" from a "great variety of fresh" fare; then again, those lacking "culinary can-do" may end up with "not the best outcome", but most find this "interesting experience" a "novel" "alternative to typical dining."

Flatwater Ⓩ *Eclectic*
15 | 22 | 13 | $35

River North | 321 N. Clark St. (bet. Kinzie St. & Wacker Dr.) | 312-644-0283 | www.flatwater.us

A "fantastic" "waterside" setting "for a date" or "people-watching" with a "patio in summer" and "fireplace in winter" draws "crowds of beautiful people" to this Eclectic River North redo of the old Sorriso; those for whom it falls flat advise "get a drink and watch the river, skip the food", which they call "overpriced", "pedestrian" and served by a "not-so-knowledgeable" staff.

Fleming's Prime
Steakhouse & Wine Bar *Steak*
22 | 22 | 22 | $57

Lincolnshire | Lincolnshire Commons | 960 Milwaukee Ave. (Rte. 33) | 847-793-0333 | www.flemingssteakhouse.com

"Not as stuffy" as the competition, this "inviting" chophouse chain with branches in Lincolnshire and Brookfield purveys "classic" steaks and sides in "clubby" digs conducive to both "business and romance"; "low-profile" service and "excellent wines by the glass" take it up a notch, but since "everything's à la carte", expect "high-end" tabs.

Flight *Eclectic* | 19 | 20 | 18 | $39 |

Glenview | 1820 Tower Dr. (Patriot Blvd.) | 847-729-9463 |
www.flightwinebar.com

Frequent fliers land at this "hip", "friendly" North Suburban
"quickie" to "nosh and drink with friends" on Eclectic American and
"Asian-influenced" small-plates eats in a "sophisticated wine bar"
setting that also features an "interesting selection of wines and presentation of flights"; grumps ground it as "too trendy and too expensive for what you get."

Flo Ⓜ *American* | 22 | 17 | 18 | $22 |

West Town | 1434 W. Chicago Ave. (bet. Bishop & Noble Sts.) |
312-243-0477 | www.eatatflo.com

A flo-tilla of fans favors this "arty", "off-the-beaten-track" West
Towner that "caters to the twentysomething pierced crowd" with
American "cheap eats", including "great Southwestern" fare (the
"Frito pie is a must"), and a "standing-room-only" Sunday brunch –
"go midweek to avoid the crowds."

Ⓩ Fogo de Chão *Brazilian/Steak* | 25 | 20 | 24 | $58 |

River North | 661 N. La Salle Dr. (Erie St.) | 312-932-9330 |
www.fogodechao.com

At this "paradise for Atkins diet-lovers", a Brazilian churrascaria
chain with a River North link, "wonderful" "skewer-wielding"
staffers roll out "ridiculous volumes" of all-you-can-eat meats
that sate folks seeking to "embrace their inner caveperson"; the
"meal-in-itself" salad bar is equally "tasty", and the drinks sure
"pack a punch", just be careful and "pace yourself" to avoid the
inevitable "protein swoon."

FoLLia *Italian* | 23 | 21 | 20 | $52 |

Market District | 953 W. Fulton St. (Morgan St.) | 312-243-2888 |
www.folliachicago.com

Though "you wouldn't expect to find" it "amongst the 18-
wheelers" and warehouses, this "hip" "jewel" makes its home in
the Market District, where its "very tasty" Northern Italian cooking includes "marvelous" "little pizzas" from a "wood-fired
oven"; you can also choose from a "good selection of wines", and
a "beautiful staff" enhances the "minimalist" "Milano decor" –
even if opponents peg it as "pricey"; a sequel, called Tocco, is
in the works.

Fonda del Mar *Mexican/Seafood* | 24 | 16 | 21 | $30 |

Logan Square | 3749 W. Fullerton Ave. (Ridgeway Ave.) |
773-489-3748

Compadres give "four stars" to this casual Logan Square Mexican's
"first-rate" "creative seafood combinations" (you "can definitely see
the Frontera influences"), "reasonable prices", "genuinely pleasant
servers" and acquisition of a "much-needed liquor license"; the "colorful, vibrant room" strikes some as a "joy", though others find it
"overwhelmingly orange" and prefer the "outdoor summer seating"
that's a "sea of tranquility."

	FOOD	DECOR	SERVICE	COST

foodlife *Eclectic* | 16 | 12 | 11 | $17 |

Streeterville | Water Tower Pl. | 835 N. Michigan Ave. (bet. Chestnut & Pearson Sts.) | 312-335-3663 | www.leye.com

Thirteen kitchens issue an Eclectic mix of eats that includes "every kind of ethnic and comfort food" "for the health nut to the trencherman" at this food court in Streeterville's Water Tower Place that's a "notch above" the norm; it's "fast" for when you need to "drop while you shop" (especially "for families of picky eaters"), though snarky shoppers say this "glorified cafeteria" is "overpriced" for a "self-serve concept" and can be as "frenetic as *MTV News*."

Fornetto Mei *Chinese/Italian* ▽ 21 | 17 | 19 | $41 |

Gold Coast | The Whitehall Hotel | 107 E. Delaware Pl. (bet. Michigan Ave. & Rush St.) | 312-573-6300 | www.thewhitehallhotel.com

Named for its "wood-burning pizza oven", this "friendly", "intimate" Gold Coast "boutique hotel" restaurant delivers a hybrid of Northern Italian and Chinese chow with a "generous selection of wines by the glass" in "an elegant but not stuffy dining room" – plus "a glassed-in porch with views of a pretty street scene"; adventurers affirm the "fusion" fare is a "neat surprise" but others complain the "strange menu makes it difficult to decide what to eat."

1492 Tapas Bar *Spanish* | 19 | 18 | 19 | $32 |

River North | 42 E. Superior St. (Wabash Ave.) | 312-867-1492 | www.1492tapasbar.com

Some explorers find this Spanish small-plates purveyor "tucked" away in a "quaint" River North "brownstone" with "lots of levels" to be a "sophisticated", "romantic" destination for "quality" tapas and "yummy sangria" – minus the "loud post-college crowd" of its competitors; still, others chart a course elsewhere, citing "slow service" and an "unimaginative", "overpriced" menu; N.B. the occasional Flamenco dancers on weekend nights are "a lot of fun."

Z Francesca's Amici *Italian* | 24 | 20 | 22 | $34 |

Elmhurst | 174 N. York St. (2nd St.) | 630-279-7970

Z Francesca's Bryn Mawr *Italian*

Edgewater | 1039 W. Bryn Mawr Ave. (Kenmore Ave.) | 773-506-9261

Z Francesca's by the River *Italian*

St. Charles | 200 S. 2nd St. (Illinois St.) | 630-587-8221

Z Francesca's Campagna *Italian*

West Dundee | 127 W. Main St. (2nd St.) | 847-844-7099

Z Francesca's Famiglia *Italian*

Barrington | Cook Street Plaza | 100 E. Station St. (Hough St.) | 847-277-1027

Z Francesca's Fiore *Italian*

Forest Park | 7407 Madison St. (Harlem Ave.) | 708-771-3063

Z Francesca's Forno *Italian*

Wicker Park | 1576 N. Milwaukee Ave. (North Ave.) | 773-770-0184

Z Francesca's Intimo *Italian*

Lake Forest | 293 E. Illinois Rd. (Western Ave.) | 847-735-9235

FOOD   DECOR   SERVICE   COST

(continued)

Z Francesca's on Taylor *Italian*
Little Italy | 1400 W. Taylor St. (Loomis St.) | 312-829-2828

Z La Sorella di Francesca *Italian*
Naperville | 18 W. Jefferson Ave. (bet. Main & Washington Sts.) | 630-961-2706
www.miafrancesca.com
Additional locations throughout the Chicago area

"Consistently" "scrumptious" Northern Italian "with an upscale touch", and "at reasonable prices", is the hallmark of this ever-extending family of "rustic, homey" city and suburban eateries, where the frequently "changing menu" makes "everything a special"; peripatetic patrons purport "service can vary" "across locations", however, and ambiance ranges from "romantic" to "ear-splitting", as some branches make "great use of space" whereas others have "tables on top of each other."

Francesco's Hole in the Wall ⊘ *Italian*   25 | 14 | 21 | $32
Northbrook | 254 Skokie Blvd. (bet. Dundee & Lake Cook Rds.) | 847-272-0155

"Those in-the-know" go to this "local" North Suburban "treasure" where the "old-fashioned" Southern Italian "menu is on the wall", "everything is wonderful" and the "robust portions" are prime for "family-style enjoyment"; it may be a "less-than-private experience" ("if only they took reservations and added an inch between tables"), but willing "sardines" say "squeeze me in"; P.S. "no credit cards!"

NEW Frankie's Scaloppine &   - | - | - | M
Fifth Floor Pizzeria *Pizza*
Gold Coast | 900 Shops, The | 900 N. Michigan Ave., 5th fl. (Walton Ave.) | 312-266-2500 | www.leye.com

Tucci Benucch took a final bow to make way for this Lettuce Entertain You Italian duo, divided into two distinctive dining concepts; the first serves up scaloppine everything (salmon, chicken, calamari, portobello) with salads and antipasti in an upscale-rustic setting, while the more casual pizzeria specializing in classic and Sardinian-style pies offers takeout, patio seating and mall parking validation.

Frasca Pizzeria & Wine Bar *Pizza*   19 | 19 | 19 | $24
Lakeview | 3358 N. Paulina St. (Lincoln Ave.) | 773-248-5222 | www.frascapizzeria.com

"Unique" "thin-crust" "wood-oven" pies, "good apps and salads", a "surprisingly extensive cheese selection" and "wine flights" draw Lakeview locals to this "high-end pizza joint" with a "family-friendly, hipster" vibe; though some say it's "not up to par", there's "outdoor seating", plus vino and food "specials on various nights."

fRedhots & Fries *Hot Dogs*   18 | 10 | 18 | $9
Glenview | 1707 Chestnut Ave. (bet. Monroe Ave. & Waukegan Rd.) | 847-657-9200

"Warm hellos" welcome folks to this North Shore "hole-in-the-wall" offering "yummy", "imaginative versions" of the Chicago frank "made by someone who cares", plus "Belgian frites served in a paper cone" with "awesome" dipping sauces; expect "typical hot dog stand decor", and know that a few critics contend it shows "nowhere near the inventiveness or quality" of its "gourmet" aspirations.

Froggy's French Cafe ☒ *French/Seafood* | 23 | 17 | 24 | $47

Highwood | 306 Green Bay Rd. (Highwood Ave.) | 847-433-7080 | www.froggyscatering.com

This "longtime" "favorite" (since 1980) offers "old-fashioned" French plates ("heavy and creamy but delicious") and signature seafood dishes, all presented by an "amiable" staff in "comfortable" if "typical" environs; drawing an "older crowd", it's a "great alternative to snobby bistros" say *amis* who label it the "best bet in Highwood", especially if you opt for the "multicourse fixed-price menu."

☑ Frontera Grill ☒Ⓜ *Mexican* | 27 | 22 | 23 | $43

River North | 445 N. Clark St. (bet. Hubbard & Illinois Sts.) | 312-661-1434 | www.fronterakitchens.com

"Master of his kitchen" Rick Bayless concocts "authentic regional" Mexican "flavors that jump off the plate" ("even the usual choices have an unusual spin") at this River North "classic" where the "mouthwatering margaritas are shaken tableside"; it's more "noisy", "festive" and "affordable" than sibling Topolobampo, though several suppers cite surprisingly "slow", even "surly" service, perhaps because it's "so crowded" and only takes limited reservations; P.S. "Saturday brunch is divine."

Fulton's on the River *Seafood/Steak* | 19 | 21 | 18 | $48

River North | 315 N. La Salle Dr. (Wacker Dr.) | 312-822-0100 | www.fultonsontheriver.com

Cousin to Fulton's Crab House at Florida's Disney World, this "huge", "contemporary" "expense-account seafooder" and steakhouse is a "reliable" "find for on-the-river dining" in River North; hooked honchos hail the "big", "diverse menu" of "fresh fish" and "prime steaks" and the "magnificent view", while holdouts hint that the "service isn't what you'd expect for the price and the ambiance."

☑ Gabriel's ☒Ⓜ *French/Italian* | 26 | 22 | 26 | $67

Highwood | 310 Green Bay Rd. (Highwood Ave.) | 847-433-0031 | www.egabriels.com

"Gabe is back!" gloat grateful gourmands now that namesake Gabriel Viti has returned to both the kitchen and dining room of this "traditional" "fine-dining" destination in Highwood, where his "excellently prepared" New French–Italian cuisine is "presented by well-versed servers"; still, a few antis aver the service is "stuffy" and the experience a "little tired", though no one's grousing about the "wonderful" 1,400-bottle wine list.

NEW Gaetano's ☒Ⓜ *Italian* | - | - | - | M

Forest Park | 7636 Madison St. (bet. Ashland & Lathrop Aves.) | 708-366-4010 | www.gaetanos.us

Chef-owner Gaetano Di Benedetto goes back to the future at his eponymous Forest Park eatery where the intimate atmosphere channels a pre-expansion La Piazza (his popular former kitchen, now closed) via a casual-yet-elegant dining room decorated in earth tones and framed art; the 'Italian fusion' menu crossbreeds regions and is enhanced by a wood-burning oven, seasonal ingredients and modestly priced, mostly Italian wines.

Gage, The *American*

21 | 21 | 19 | $37

Loop | 24 S. Michigan Ave. (Madison St.) | 312-372-4243 | www.thegagechicago.com

This "stylish" Loop gastropub that's "convenient to Millennium Park" and the museums "stands out" with New American meals ranging from "burgers to more sophisticated fare", paired with an "impressive" range of beers, ales and "signature drinks" – so expect a "good happy-hour scene" in the "pubby" setting with a 50-ft. mahogany bar and "tin ceilings"; grudging graders gauge it "high-end bar food at fine-dining prices" and can't handle the "unbearable noise levels."

Gale Street Inn *American*

21 | 16 | 21 | $32

Jefferson Park | 4914 N. Milwaukee Ave. (Lawrence Ave.) | 773-725-1300 | www.galestreet.com

Mundelein | 935 Diamond Lake Rd. (Rte. 45) | 847-566-1090 | www.galest.com Ⓜ

"The supper clubs of old" live on in these "comfy" "neighborhood institutions" – a "perennial Northwest Side establishment across from the Jefferson Park el stop" and a younger Mundelein location – that are separately owned but serve a similar, "fairly priced" Traditional American menu of "rocking ribs" and other "plain, simple" offerings; the "uninspired", though, report "uneventful meals", advising "do not go out of your way."

Gaylord Fine Indian Cuisine *Indian*

21 | 17 | 18 | $30

Schaumburg | 555 Mall Dr. (Higgins Rd.) | 847-619-3300 | www.gaylordindia.net

Curry cravers "keep coming back" to this "upscale" Northwest Suburban Indian for "quality" selections like "very good tandoori" and "Thali plates" delivered by "respectful" waiters in "white-tablecloth" surroundings; the "phenomenal lunch buffet" is an added "bonus", though bargain-hunters who feel the fare is only "fair" find it "pricey"; N.B. at press time, their former River North location was closed, awaiting a move to a new Gold Coast address.

Geja's Cafe *Fondue*

22 | 23 | 23 | $50

Lincoln Park | 340 W. Armitage Ave. (bet. Clark St. & Lincoln Ave.) | 773-281-9101 | www.gejascafe.com

Dippers dig the "delicious decadence" involved in this Lincoln Parker's "old-school" (since 1971) fondue, an "interactive" experience best shared with "friends" or an "über-romantic" "date" (the "carved" wood interior is "very dark"); nightly flamenco guitar and an "excellent wine list" with 50 by-the-glass pours put most in a good mood, though a few frown it's "rather expensive" and "you will come out smelling like pilot fuel"; N.B. no children under age 10.

Gene & Georgetti ● ☒ *Steak* 24 | 16 | 21 | $59

River North | 500 N. Franklin St. (Illinois St.) | 312-527-3718 |
www.geneandgeorgetti.com

This "quintessential Chicago" chophouse draws loyal fans to River
North for "real steaks", "great garbage salad" and "terrific spumoni"
consumed "where the pols and press meet to eat" amid "decor that
feels like the '40s; coddled "regulars" claim the "gruff waiters are
part of the charm", though outsiders opine the staff is "overly busy
caressing" the cognoscenti while "others go unattended", and peg
this "dinosaur" as "past its prime."

☑ Gibsons Bar & Steakhouse ● *Steak* 25 | 20 | 23 | $63

Gold Coast | 1028 N. Rush St. (Bellevue Pl.) | 312-266-8999
Rosemont | Doubletree Hotel | 5464 N. River Rd. (bet. Balmoral &
Bryn Mawr Aves.) | 847-928-9900
www.gibsonssteakhouse.com

"Bigger is better" at this "primal", "popular" Gold Coast purveyor of
a porterhouse that "should have its own zip code", "jumbo drinks"
and sweets "so large you need a forklift"; service is "professional"
and its "packed" piano bar is a "spectacle" ("see the old men with
their nieces", "cougars on the prowl" and "local celebs") – just expect "expense-account" prices and frequent "waits", "even if you
have reservations"; P.S. the Rosemont rerun is a "welcome respite
near the airport."

Gio *Italian* 20 | 18 | 19 | $31

Evanston | 1631 Chicago Ave. (bet. Church & Davis Sts.) | 847-869-3900 |
www.giorestaurant.com

"Excellent wood-fired pizza" from the brick oven behind the bar, plus
"good salads" (even a "salad pizza" that's "a winner"), daily pasta
and "fish specials", and an "above-average, affordable wine selection" lure Evanston locals to this "unpretentious" Northern Italian
charmer "where you can actually talk" most times – though it "can
get loud when near capacity"; P.S. it's also "priced very well."

Gioco *Italian* 24 | 22 | 21 | $41

South Loop | 1312 S. Wabash Ave. (13th St.) | 312-939-3870 |
www.gioco-chicago.com

Scores are up across the board for this South Loop "neighborhood
favorite" that's "not your typical Italian" thanks to its "great rustic"
fare, "fresh ingredients" and "cute" former "speakeasy" setting with
"exposed brick", an "open kitchen", "good vibe" and "knowing service"; if you want to avoid the "noise" and bustle, "Sunday brunch
is an undiscovered treat"; N.B. the Food score does not reflect a
recent chef change.

☑ Giordano's *Pizza* 21 | 14 | 16 | $20

Loop | 135 E. Lake St. (Upper Michigan Ave.) | 312-616-1200
Loop | 223 W. Jackson Blvd. (Franklin St.) | 312-583-9400
Loop | 310 W. Randolph St. (Franklin St.) | 312-201-1441
River North | 730 N. Rush St. (Superior St.) | 312-951-0747 ●
Lakeview | 1040 W. Belmont Ave. (Kenmore Ave.) | 773-327-1200

(continued)
Giordano's
Edison Park | 5927 W. Irving Park Rd. (Austin Ave.) | 773-736-5553
Northwest Side | 2855 N. Milwaukee Ave. (Wolfram St.) | 773-862-4200
Southwest Side | 5159 S. Pulaski Rd. (Archer Ave.) | 773-582-7676 ◗
Southwest Side | 6314 S. Cicero Ave. (63rd St.) | 773-585-6100
Greektown | 815 W. Van Buren St. (Halsted St.) | 312-421-1221
www.giordanos.com
Additional locations throughout the Chicago area

Surveyors are split over whether you should opt for the "ooey gooey" stuffed 'za or "skip the pan and go for the thin" at these "no-frills", "family-friendly" Italians/"pizza joints" where the "just serviceable" "service and decor are irrelevant"; some say hit "one of the franchises for the same pie without the wait" involved at the River North flagship, others chide that the "chain locations can be inconsistent."

Glenn's Diner and Seafood House *Diner* | 23 | 16 | 22 | $24 |
Ravenswood | 1820 W. Montrose Ave. (Honore St.) | 773-506-1720 | www.glennsdiner.com

The "blackboard fish specials" feature "excellent fresh catches daily" at this "casual" Ravenswood "haunt" where Traditional American "upscale diner food" meets a "great staff"; its "bright, cheery" ("not romantic") digs are among the "best" around for a "chilled-out breakfast or dinner with friends" "at a low price" – so it's no surprise surveyors ask "why didn't I hear about this place sooner?"

Gold Coast Dogs *Hot Dogs* | 21 | 8 | 14 | $9 |
Loop | 159 N. Wabash Ave. (bet. Lake & Randolph Sts.) | 312-917-1677
Loop | Union Station | 225 S. Canal St. (Jackson Blvd.) | 312-258-8585
Rogers Park | 2349 W. Howard St. (Western Ave.) | 773-338-0900
O'Hare Area | O'Hare Int'l Airport | Terminal 3 | 773-462-9942
O'Hare Area | O'Hare Int'l Airport | Terminal 5 | 773-462-0125 ◗
Ravenswood | 1429 W. Montrose Ave. (Clark St.) | 773-472-3600
Southwest Side | Midway Int'l Airport | 5700 S. Cicero Ave. (55th St.) | 773-735-6789 ◗
Glenview | Glen Town Center | 1845 Tower Dr. (Patriot Blvd.) | 847-724-0123

"Drunk or sober", fans say "arf!" to this litter of "no-atmosphere", "counter-service" hot dog stands supplying "one helluva" "quintessential Chicago dog" plus "awesome cheese fries"; naysayers neuter this pack, though, vaunting "better versions" of these vittles elsewhere.

Goose Island Brewing Co. *Pub Food* | 16 | 15 | 17 | $21 |
Wrigleyville | 3535 N. Clark St. (Addison St.) | 773-832-9040
Lincoln Park | 1800 N. Clybourn Ave. (Sheffield Ave.) | 312-915-0071
www.gooseisland.com

"You won't find better microbreweries in Chicago" than this "fun", "family-friendly" Lincoln Park–Wrigleyville pair pouring "delicious beers", available in "flights" and "growlers to go"; the "upscale" Traditional American "pub food" ("with some beer in it") comes in second to the suds, though the "Stilton burger is an awesome choice", but "let's be honest – you didn't really come here for the food, did you?" N.B. the Lincoln Parker will be closing at the end of 2008.

Gordon Biersch Brewery
Restaurant *American*

20 | 18 | 17 | $26

Bolingbrook | Promenade Bolingbrook | 639 E. Boughton Rd. (Preston Dr.) | 630-739-6036 | www.gordonbiersch.com

"Beer is the star" of this "upbeat" brewpub chain with a Bolingbrook branch where the "pretty standard" American grub plays second fiddle to the suds (though aficionados say its "to-die-for garlic fries" are the thing to order); the "too loud" decibel levels don't seem to faze its "rollicking" "frat-boy" following.

Grace O'Malley's *Pub Food*

18 | 15 | 15 | $23

South Loop | 1416 S. Michigan Ave. (14th St.) | 312-588-1800 | www.graceomalleychicago.com

"Where the civilized people tailgate before Bears games", this South Loop pub purveys "traditional" tavern fare like "great burgers" and "good sandwiches" on "yummy pretzel buns" in a "cute", "kid-friendly" atmosphere; "spotty service" is an issue, and cynics snub it for being not as Irish as its name suggests; N.B. brunch buffet is served on weekends.

Grand Lux Cafe *Eclectic*

19 | 20 | 18 | $29

River North | 600 N. Michigan Ave. (Ontario St.) | 312-276-2500 | www.grandluxcafe.com

"Basically an upscale Cheesecake Factory" "with many of the same items" – and "just as crammed as its sister" spot – this "boisterous" River North pack-'em-in purveyor proffers an "insanely diverse" Eclectic menu ("fabulous Asian nachos") with an emphasis on "oversized everything" amid "opulent", "over-the-top" surroundings (the "rotunda" room provides a "sensational view" of Boul Mich); bashers, though, brand it as "big hype on Michigan Avenue" that's "not bad if you don't mind" "formula" feeding, "crowds with lots of children and strollers", and "medium lux service."

Greek Islands *Greek*

22 | 19 | 21 | $30

Greektown | 200 S. Halsted St. (Adams St.) | 312-782-9855 ◗
Lombard | 300 E. 22nd St. (Highland Ave.) | 630-932-4545
www.greekislands.net

You'll get "no pretensions", "just the classics" at this "noisy", "huge" Greektowner and it's Lombard offshoot, with "wonderful local color", "abundant portions" and service that's "accommodating to cranky children, picky eaters and large-party mayhem"; prices are "inexpensive", especially if you "go family-style", but prepare to be "herded in and out without much ceremony", and tipsters who tag it as "touristy" wish the staff would "ease up on the whole *opa!*" thing.

Green Dolphin Street Ⓜ *American*

19 | 22 | 19 | $47

Lincoln Park | 2200 N. Ashland Ave. (Webster Ave.) | 773-395-0066 | www.jazzitup.com

Whether you "go for the live jazz" (and "stay for a bite") or for the "well-prepared and -presented" New American dining (and "stay for the great live music"), raters reckon this "romantic" Lincoln Parker with supper-club decor will "surprise" you; a faction feels it's "overpriced" and "disappointing", but fans insist it's a "cool place to go", especially in summer when there's dining "alfresco near the river."

Green Door Tavern *Pub Food* | 15 | 17 | 16 | $21 |
River North | 678 N. Orleans St. (Huron St.) | 312-664-5496
"You'll be walking crooked before your first drink" at this River North "haunt", a "landmark" with "leaning walls", "local charisma" and a circa-1921 speakeasy in the basement; it represents a "fast-disappearing Chicago-type bar/restaurant" (it's "now surrounded by million-dollar condos"), with "fun decor" that will "keep your eyes busy for hours" and help you overlook the "simple" – some say "so-so" – Traditional American "grub."

Green Zebra *Vegetarian* | 26 | 23 | 24 | $52 |
West Town | 1460 W. Chicago Ave. (Greenview Ave.) | 312-243-7100 | www.greenzebrachicago.com
It's "veggie heaven" at Shawn McClain's "ultrahip" West Town vegetarian (with a bit of fish) where the "pricey-but-worth-it" seasonal small plates are "so good and innovative, the absence of meat becomes an afterthought"; the "Zen-like experience" includes a "down-to-earth" staff, "wine list beautifully matched with the cuisine" and "inventive specialty cocktails and nonalcoholic beverages", though even devotees declare that the "haute" green eats are "not for everyone"; N.B. they now serve brunch.

Grill on the Alley, The *American* | 20 | 18 | 20 | $47 |
Streeterville | Westin Hotel | 909 N. Michigan Ave. (Delaware Pl.) | 312-255-9009 | www.thegrill.com
A "varied menu" of "very good" Traditional American vittles in an "old-fashioned", "formal bar-and-grill" setting satisfies Streeterville steakhouse-seekers, especially given that it's "superior for a hotel" venue and "always a safe bet for getting a table"; still, critical correspondents "who have been to the real Grill on the Alley in Beverly Hills" are "not thrilled" by what they consider "average" meals at "Michigan Avenue prices."

Grillroom, The *Steak* | 18 | 17 | 18 | $40 |
Loop | 33 W. Monroe St. (bet. Dearborn & State Sts.) | 312-960-0000 | www.restaurants-america.com
"When you're looking to take lunch up a notch", or for a "pre-show, pre-symphony spot", supporters suggest this "well-located" Loop venue where the "reliable" if "nothing-fancy" "steakhouse fare" comes with an "excellent variety of salads" and "specials showing more of a seasonal flair", all in a "classic wood-finish" locale; despite this, diners who deem it "decidedly average" yawn "you sit in a room, and apparently the food is grilled, and there's not much more to it than that."

Gruppo di Amici Ⓜ *Pizza* | ∇ 21 | 20 | 22 | $26 |
Rogers Park | 1508 W. Jarvis Ave. (Greenview Ave.) | 773-508-5565 | www.gruppodiamici.com
"Roman-style pizza from a true wood-burning oven" and a "limited [Italian] menu" (the "daily specials are always tasty") are matched by

a "short", "well-selected" and "reasonably priced" wine and beer list at this Rogers Park pie palace; with its "nice" outdoor seating and Sunday brunch, regulars call it a "neighborhood home-away-from-home."

Gulliver's Pizzeria & Restaurant *Pizza*

▬ | ▬ | ▬ | I

Rogers Park | 2727 W. Howard St. (California Ave.) | 773-338-2166

"Passable pizza" and "very eccentric decorating" distinguish this "kitschy", "congenial" Rogers Park parlor and "deep-dish" pioneer that's been filling up since 1965 – though new owners are making big changes, including selling off the "weird antique-y decor"; service can be "slow", and there's "an ample bar and outdoor garden seating."

Habana Libre *Cuban*

▽ 21 | 12 | 18 | $20

West Town | 1440 W. Chicago Ave. (bet. Bishop St. & Greenview Ave.) | 312-243-3303

"Everything is smothered in garlic" at this West Town BYO Cuban "hole-in-the-wall" where the "authentic apps", "fantastic empanadas" and must-try coconut flan come at a "great price"; "service is a little slow", though, so you may want to bring an "opener" for your bottle rather than "waiting forever to be uncorked."

Hachi's Kitchen *Japanese*

24 | 24 | 23 | $31

Logan Square | 2521 N. California Ave. (bet. Logan Blvd. & Fullerton St.) | 773-276-8080 | www.hachiskitchen.com

Logan Square locals "love" the "postmodern ambiance" and "terrific" midpriced sushi at this "cool" "sister restaurant to Sai Café" serving a similar Japanese menu; "welcoming" owners and outdoor seating help define it as "definitely a keeper" for everything from delivery to a "special night out."

Hackney's *American*

18 | 13 | 18 | $20

Printer's Row | 733 S. Dearborn St. (bet. Harrison & Polk Sts.) | 312-461-1116
Glenview | 1241 Harms Rd. (Lake Ave.) | 847-724-5577
Glenview | 1514 E. Lake Ave. (bet. Sunset Ridge & Waukegan Rds.) | 847-724-7171
Wheeling | 241 S. Milwaukee Ave. (Dundee Rd.) | 847-537-2100
Lake Zurich | 880 N. Old Rand Rd. (Rand Rd.) | 847-438-2103
Palos Park | 9550 W. 123rd St. (La Grange Rd.) | 708-448-8300
www.hackneys.net

For "a heaping helping of nostalgia", surveyors say these suburban American "time warps" (or the newer Printer's Row location) are "still the place to go" thanks to "great greasy burgers" on "black bread soaked by the juice" plus "that onion loaf thing" that's "to die for – probably literally"; some surmise the "service can be iffy", though, and hint these "hackneyed" hamburger haunts are "living on past laurels."

Hai Yen *Chinese/Vietnamese*

20 | 13 | 14 | $21

Lincoln Park | 2723 N. Clark St. (Diversey Pkwy.) | 773-868-4888
Uptown | 1055 W. Argyle St. (B'way) | 773-561-4077
www.haiyenrestaurant.com

This "hidden jewel on Argyle" and its newer Clark Street sibling offer a "large selection" of "flavorful" Mandarin Chinese and Vietnamese vittles that prove you can "dine on a budget" "without sacrificing food quality"; traditionalists tout the "Uptown location as superior", saying the Lincoln Parker is "toned down for American tastes", even if it's a "huge step up" in the decor category.

Half Shell ⊟ *Seafood* 22 | 7 | 14 | $31

Lincoln Park | 676 W. Diversey Pkwy. (bet. Clark & Orchard Sts.) | 773-549-1773

"If there is such a thing as a seafood greasy spoon, this is it" declare devotees of this "no-frills" Lincoln Park "relic" with "great personality" (the "surly staff adds charm") and "dumpy decor" ("try to sit outside"); it's "changed little" over the past 40 years, which is fine with a-fish-ionados who pant over its "cheap and fresh" aquatic eats; P.S. "they don't take plastic" or reservations.

Hamburger Mary's *Burgers* 16 | 16 | 16 | $19

Andersonville | 5400 N. Clark St. (Balmoral Ave.) | 773-784-6969 | www.hamburgermaryschicago.com

"Serviceable hamburgers", fries and other "typical American food" (plus a "deep-fried Twinkie that should probably be outlawed") come with "snazzy cocktails" and a "side of kitsch" at this "sassy", "affordable and quick" Andersonville chain link; its "campy staff" serves amid an environment that's both "family" and "gay-friendly", and there's "karaoke and drag shows" upstairs in "Mary's attic" (so "grab your pumps, purse" "and boa").

Hannah's Bretzel ⊠ *Sandwiches* 23 | 15 | 18 | $11

Loop | 180 W. Washington St. (bet. N. La Salle & Wells Sts.) | 312-621-1111
Loop | Illinois Center | 233 N. Michigan Ave. (S. Water St.) | 312-621-1111
www.hannahsbretzel.com

Among the "healthier places to eat in the Loop", this "high-end fast-food" duo doles out "fresh and delicious organic sandwiches" on "homemade" "pretzel bread" along with "amazing" chocolates; sure, it's "on the pricey side", but the "extra dollar or two" is well "worth it" for such "high quality"; P.S. "Michigan Avenue has long communal tables", but "Washington Street is cramped and better for takeout."

Happy Chef Dim Sum House ◑ *Chinese* 22 | 5 | 13 | $16

Chinatown | 2164 S. Archer Ave. (Cermak Rd.) | 312-808-3689

"Everything comes out fresh and fast" at this "spartan", "authentic" Chinatown dim sum spot where the "seafood is particularly good" and prices are "amazingly cheap"; lunch and "late-night" (till 2 AM) eats are especially popular, and expect "waits" "on weekends during peak times."

Hard Rock Cafe ◑ *American* 12 | 19 | 14 | $25

River North | 63 W. Ontario St. (bet. Clark & Dearborn Sts.) | 312-943-2252 | www.hardrock.com

The "awesome" "memorabilia on the walls" is "why you go" to this 22-year-old "chain" member that's "full of spirit" (and "loud music") and serves up "average" American eats that appeal to "kids" and "tourists"; rock critics call it a "T-shirt factory" where the "bland food" is "a sideline" and the service "slow", quipping that they'll "just drop off the out-of-town relatives next time."

Harry Caray's *Italian/Steak* 20 | 20 | 19 | $40

River North | 33 W. Kinzie St. (Dearborn St.) | 312-828-0966
Rosemont | O'Hare International Ctr. | 10233 W. Higgins Rd. (Mannheim Rd.) | 847-699-1200
NEW **Lombard** | 70 Yorktown Shopping Ctr. (Butterfield Rd.) | 630-953-3400

Harry Caray's Seventh Inning Stretch *Italian/Steak*

Southwest Side | Midway Int'l Airport | 5757 S. Cicero Ave. (55th St.) | 773-948-6300
www.harrycarays.com

"Baseball buffs" bet on this triple play of "classic", "sporty" steakhouses (plus a Midway Airport oasis) that are "dedicated to Chicago's legendary announcer" and "sure to enthrall any true Cubs fan"; the "huge portions" of "properly prepared" "Sunday-dinner Italian fare" are "not a home run, but a solid double", and while service can be "so-so", the "memorabilia" compensates.

Harvest *American* ▽ 24 | 20 | 24 | $52

St. Charles | Pheasant Run Resort | 4051 E. Main St. (Pheasant Run) | 630-524-5080 | www.pheasantrun.com

Harvesters "highly recommend" this "inviting" West Suburban New American in the Pheasant Run Resort serving "interesting seasonal selections" and "homemade" bread and desserts; the "infused martinis" are poured by "friendly bartenders" as "professional" servers work the "boutiquelike but refreshing" room.

HB Home Bistro M *American* 24 | 17 | 23 | $32

Lakeview | 3404 N. Halsted St. (Roscoe St.) | 773-661-0299 | www.homebistrochicago.com

"Passionate" chef-owner Joncarl Lachman "takes enormous pride" in his "awesome", "creative" New American cooking, turning out "big, tasty dinners" and "outstanding" Sunday brunch at this "small storefront" BYO in Boys Town; "reasonable prices" and "personable" personnel make it a "favorite of locals", who know the "Wednesday prix fixe is a steal."

Heartland Cafe *Eclectic/Vegetarian* 17 | 14 | 15 | $18

Rogers Park | Heartland Bldg. | 7000 N. Glenwood Ave. (Lunt Ave.) | 773-465-8005 | www.heartlandcafe.com

For 32 years, this "earthy-crunchy" Rogers Park "health-food" "haven" has been "where the hippies go" for "great beer", "live bands" and poetry, and "good, hearty" Eclectic and vegetarian eats served with "optimism" (plus some of "the best outdoor seating" in town) – but eaters with images of "everyone wearing tye-dye" say the "slacker" staff is too "laid-back" and "wish the food were better"; P.S. there's a "fabulous general store" on-site.

Z **Heaven on Seven** *Cajun/Creole* 21 | 17 | 18 | $25

Loop | Garland Bldg. | 111 N. Wabash Ave., 7th fl. (Washington Blvd.) | 312-263-6443 S ⊄

	FOOD	DECOR	SERVICE	COST

(continued)

Heaven on Seven

River North | 600 N. Michigan Ave., 2nd fl. (bet. Ohio & Ontario Sts.) | 312-280-7774

Naperville | 224 S. Main St. (bet. Jackson & Jefferson Aves.) | 630-717-0777

www.heavenonseven.com

"Get your New Orleans fix" at this moderately priced spice specialist where the Cajun-Creole cooking comes alongside "every single bottle of hot sauce on the market" ("if you like it when smoke comes out of your ears, this is the place"); it's "Mardi Gras all year long" in the "loud" digs – though purists posit the ambiance at the spin-offs is "never going to be the same" as at the "cash-only" Loop original; "inconsistent" service and "hordes of tourists" also draw knocks.

Hecky's Barbecue *BBQ*   21 | 5 | 15 | $17

Evanston | 1902 Green Bay Rd. (Emerson St.) | 847-492-1182

Hecky's of Chicago *BBQ*

Near West | 1234 N. Halsted St. (Division St.) | 312-377-7427

www.heckys.com

"Leave the fancy duds at home" and head for this Evanston "institution" earning a "thumbs-up" for its "true BBQ" flavors, including "some of the best ribs" around, with "tangy, tasty sauce" – not to mention "authentic, mouthwatering Southern-style fried chicken"; some tipsters prefer "takeout" due to the "nonexistent ambiance", and traditionalists tout the original as "better than the [Near West] Chicago" sequel.

Hema's Kitchen *Indian*   21 | 11 | 14 | $20

Lincoln Park | 2411 N. Clark St. (Fullerton Pkwy.) | 773-529-1705

West Rogers Park | 6406 N. Oakley Ave. (W. Devon Ave.) | 773-338-1627

www.hemaskitchen.net

"Wonderful", "offbeat dishes" of "succulent" Indian cuisine made from "fresh ingredients" and "available at all spice levels" appeal to allegiants of this "favorite" "Devon-area choice", who sometimes "miss seeing Mama Hema around since she now divides her time between two restaurants" (and is planning a third); Lincoln Park locals sense their spin-off is "not as appealing" as its sister spot – but "very little ambiance" and "crazy-slow" service seem to be constants; P.S. both are BYO and "good for vegetarians."

Hemmingway's Bistro *American/French*   ∇ 20 | 19 | 21 | $38

Oak Park | The Write Inn | 211 N. Oak Park Ave. (Ontario St.) | 708-524-0806 | www.hemmingwaysbistro.com

Feasters "feel welcome" at this West Suburban "neighborhood hangout" "hidden" in the old Write Inn with "simple" but "interesting" Traditional American and French bistro dishes doled out alongside an "excellent wine list"; the "cozy" setting also appeals ("I'm not having an affair but if I were, it would be here"), though the less-impressed find the package "nothing to write home about"; N.B. there's live jazz at Sunday brunch and on Wednesday nights.

	FOOD	DECOR	SERVICE	COST

NEW Holy Mackerel!
American Fish House *Seafood*

| 19 | 21 | 19 | $44 |

Lombard | Yorktown Ctr. | 70 Yorktown Shopping Ctr. (Butterfield Rd.) | 630-953-3444 | www.harrycarays.com

"Surprisingly good" seafood, "fresh lobster" and the fact that "they allow you to order off the Harry Caray steakhouse menu" (the sibs "share a kitchen") win fans for this fish spot in Lombard's "tony new Westin"; the "beautifully decorated" rooms sport a "pleasant", "unassuming nautical theme", but bargain-hunters who find the tabs "pricey" hoot "holy wallets!"

Honey 1 BBQ ☑ *BBQ*

| 19 | 5 | 18 | $18 |

Bucktown | 2241 N. Western Ave. (Lyndale St.) | 773-227-5130 | www.honey1bbq.com

There's a "wonderful taste and texture" to the ribs at this "laid-back" Bucktown barbecue BYO courtesy of the owner's hard work "slaving over an open wood-burning oven"; so "who cares about the service or decor?" ask acolytes who come for the "honest" fare "at an honest price" and outnumber the holdouts who harp it's "hit-or-miss – amazing when it's on and forgettable when it's not."

Hop Häus ◐ *Burgers*

| 18 | 15 | 15 | $21 |

River North | 646 N. Franklin St. (Erie St.) | 312-467-4287

"So many burger choices, so little time" fret fans of this "nothing-fancy" "new venture in [River North's] old Leona's space" where the "exotic" patties include "kangaroo, bison, wild boar and ostrich to name a few"; even those who knock "super-spotty" service admire the "clever and hilarious" photos on the wall and anoint it an "ultimate beer 'n' sports" spot with "good specialty" brews.

Hopleaf *Belgian*

| 23 | 17 | 17 | $26 |

Andersonville | 5148 N. Clark St. (Foster Ave.) | 773-334-9851 | www.hopleaf.com

The city's "most authentic Belgian spot" attracts "diners of all kinds" with its "European-type gastropub" menu, "bargain" "moules frites to die for" and "insane" selection of beers "served in the correct glassware"; there's a "fireplace in winter and outdoor patio in summer", and the "beautified bohemian" Andersonville interior includes a "crowded, jovial" 21-and-over-only barroom – just expect "long lines on weekends."

Hot Chocolate ☑ *American*

| 24 | 21 | 20 | $34 |

Bucktown | 1747 N. Damen Ave. (Wabansia Ave.) | 773-489-1747 | www.hotchocolatechicago.com

"Chocoholics" will "go here in a heartbeat" for the "scrumptious" sweets from dessert diva Mindy Segal (ex mk), "definitely the high point" of this "trendy", "crowded" Bucktowner; that said, "the savory side" of its "limited but interesting" American "comfort-food" menu "is no slouch either", and even the "chocolaty decor" is rich – but wallet-watchers warn so are the comestibles' "high prices."

	FOOD	DECOR	SERVICE	COST

☑ Hot Doug's ⊠🗗 *Hot Dogs* | 27 | 13 | 21 | $11 |

Northwest Side | 3324 N. California Ave. (Roscoe St.) | 773-279-9550 | www.hotdougs.com

This Northwest Side "temple" – the highest-scoring hot dog stand in the history of the Chicago Survey – is lorded over by "rebel-with-a-clue" Doug Sohn, whose "affordable gourmet" "encased meats" include "elk, pheasant, gator" and "cranberry-infused buffalo", plus there are "duck fat fries" on Fridays and Saturdays; lazy pups lament "lines around the block" (though they "move at an amazing clip") to get into the "intentionally schlocky" "Elvis-and-sausage–themed" space, which closes at 4 PM daily; N.B. no credit cards.

Hot Tamales *Mexican* | 21 | 13 | 18 | $23 |

Highland Park | 493 Central Ave. (St. John Ave.) | 847-433-4070 | www.hottamales4u.com

"The atmosphere is loud but the cuisine is louder" at this "crowded" no-reserving North Shore family "favorite" for "delicious", "creative" (some say "inauthentic") "made-to-order" Mexican such as "duck tacos from heaven" and a "wonderful salmon burrito"; the "non-romantic atmosphere" "will hurry your meal along" – unless you nab a spot in the "outdoor dining" area, the "hottest seat in town."

Hugo's Frog Bar & Fish House ◑ *Seafood* | 23 | 19 | 21 | $49 |

Gold Coast | 1024 N. Rush St. (bet. Bellevue Pl. & Oak St.) | 312-640-0999
Naperville | Main Street Promenade Bldg. | 55 S. Main St. (bet. Benton & Van Buren Aves.) | 630-548-3764
www.hugosfrogbar.com

These local Gold Coast and Naperville seafood "scenes" with "noisy", "active bars" and "consistently good" fish also offer the same "classic service", steaks and "prices" as sibling/neighbor Gibsons Steakhouse; some diners complain that the "dense" dining rooms with a "country-club feel" are "too crowded, every night", however the hordes keep on coming, so "if you don't have a reservation, bring a novel"; P.S. weekday lunch is an "outstanding value."

Icosium Kafe *African* | 19 | 13 | 17 | $16 |

Andersonville | 5200 N. Clark St. (Foster Ave.) | 773-271-5233 | www.icosiumkafe.com

"Sweet or savory crêpes" for breakfast, lunch or dinner, plus "excellent salads" and other "cheap", "high-quality" eats make up the African-Algerian menu at this Andersonville storefront; it's BYO and a "family favorite" with fresh-squeezed juices, so don't be dissuaded by the "mismatched exterior" or no-reservations policy.

Il Covo *Italian* | ▽ 20 | 20 | 20 | $39 |

Bucktown | 2152 N. Damen Ave. (Webster Ave.) | 773-862-5555 | www.ilcovochicago.com

"Affordable" Italian in "huge" portions with "nice plating details" and a "varied wine list" appeal to Bucktown "neighborhood"-ers who consider this "cute place" "a real find"; the space is "roomy" and the waiters "enthusiastic" to boot; N.B. a recent chef change may not be reflected in the Food score.

	FOOD	DECOR	SERVICE	COST

NEW Il Fiasco *Italian* — 19 | 18 | 19 | $30

Andersonville | 5101 N. Clark St. (Carmen Ave.) | 773-769-9700 | www.ilfiascochicago.com

"Solid" Italian fare including "yummy pasta", "thin-crust pizza" and "some unique dishes" come at a "nice price point for Andersonville" in this "cozy" space where "service is mostly friendly and efficient" and the "pictures on the wall come from the owners' travels in Italy"; a few report "mediocre" meals, but they're outvoted; N.B. a recent chef change is not reflected in the Food score.

Il Mulino New York *Italian* — 24 | 23 | 23 | $70

Gold Coast | 1150 N. Dearborn St. (bet. Division & Elm Sts.) | 312-440-8888 | www.ilmulinonewyork.com

While this "over-the-top" Italian in the Gold Coast's Biggs mansion "hasn't become the legend that the NY version is", fans find the food "approachable" yet "ethereal" (including the "many complimentary antipasti") and the "warm" setting (with nine working fireplaces) suited to a "special occasion" or to "impress" "your best client"; antis aver the "fawning" staff can be "marginally over-attentive" and aren't buying the "attitude" – especially since it's "pricey beyond belief."

Ina's *American* — 22 | 16 | 21 | $23

West Loop | 1235 W. Randolph St. (Elizabeth St.) | 312-226-8227 | www.breakfastqueen.com

"Lovely Ina" the "breakfast queen" lures lunchers and suppers too into her "unpretentious" West Loop haunt for "melt-in-your-mouth" pancakes, "amazing" fried chicken and other "down-home" American eats; "free parking", "fair prices" and "warm service" have pleased patrons proclaiming "in the absence of my mother, Ina's is best."

India House *Indian* — 24 | 18 | 20 | $29

River North | 59 W. Grand Ave. (bet. Clark & Dearborn Sts.) | 312-645-9500
Buffalo Grove | Buffalo Grove Town Ctr. | 228-230 McHenry Rd. (Lake Cook Rd.) | 847-520-5569
Schaumburg | 1521 W. Schaumburg Rd. (Springinsguth Rd.) | 847-895-5501 Ⓜ
Oak Brook | 2809 Butterfield Rd. (Meyers Rd.) | 630-472-1500 Ⓢ Ⓜ
www.indiahousechicago.com

Chicago's "best Indian" fare can be found at this foursome that thrives thanks to "generous portions" of "fantastic", "fresh, authentic" "standards" for both "those who like spicy" and "novices" too; even contributors who consider it "a bit pricey" think the "extensive" lunch buffets are "an affordable delight", and raters out of River North range are grateful for the "convenient suburban locations."

Indian Garden, The *Indian* — 22 | 13 | 18 | $24

Streeterville | 247 E. Ontario St., 2nd fl. (Fairbanks Ct.) | 312-280-4910
West Rogers Park | 2546 W. Devon Ave. (Rockwell St.) | 773-338-2929
Schaumburg | 855 E. Schaumburg Rd. (Plum Grove Rd.) | 847-524-3007
www.indiangardenchicago.com

"Feel the subcontinent" at these separately owned Indian eateries where "delicious breads, authentic dishes" and "veggie foods" are

	FOOD	DECOR	SERVICE	COST

"above average" (and "a little more expensive"); service is generally "gracious" and the "buffet during the week is one heck of a deal"; P.S. the former Westmont location is no longer part of the chain.

Indie Cafe *Japanese/Thai*   ▽ 23 | 17 | 22 | $19

Edgewater | 5951 N. Broadway St. (bet. Elmdale & Thorndale Aves.) | 773-561-5577 | www.indiecafe.us

Gourmands who "can't get enough" of this "cheap" "neighborhood" Edgewater BYO credit its "great mix" of "Japanese/sushi and Thai foods", "friendly staff" and tiny, "cute" confines that get "crowded on weekends" (when they don't take reservations); small spenders love the "cheap" lunch specials that "can't be beat."

Irazu ☒⇎ *Costa Rican*   23 | 8 | 17 | $14

Bucktown | 1865 N. Milwaukee Ave. (Western Ave.) | 773-252-5687 | www.irazuchicago.com

"Nice", "earnest" people run this "still-relatively hidden gem", a "small" BYO "with big food" in the form of "consistently fresh", "genuine" Costa Rican cuisine (and some Mex) with "lots of vegetarian choices" – and "don't miss the tropical-fruit-and-oatmeal shakes"; it's "a hole-in-the-wall for sure" ("so basic it's hip"), but there's a "busy, Latin vibe", and "bargain"-hunters bask in "prices that make you think they don't know Bucktown has gentrified."

Irish Oak Restaurant & Pub *Pub Food*   ▽ 19 | 19 | 19 | $18

Wrigleyville | 3511 N. Clark St. (Addison St.) | 773-935-6669 | www.irishoak.com

"More than just a cheap imitation", this Wrigleyville watering hole with "true Irish character" is like "a visit to the Emerald Isle without leaving the city", delighting denizens with "pub-style" "comfort food" including "great burgers" and "fantastic fish 'n' chips" paired with "a perfect pour of Guinness" "at the correct temperature"; P.S. the "decor was actually imported from Erin" in crates.

Isabella's Estiatorio Ⓜ *Mediterranean*   25 | 22 | 23 | $45

Geneva | 330 W. State St. (4th St.) | 630-845-8624 | www.isabellasgeneva.com

"Exquisite" seasonal Mediterranean cuisine (with predominantly organic ingredients), "knowledgeable servers", "wonderful decor" and a "good wine list" amount to an "excellent dining experience in [West Suburban] Geneva", even if it is "a little pricey"; though the noise level inside can be "conversation unfriendly", the "outdoor patio" is a "perfect place to enjoy the food."

Itto Sushi ◗☒ *Japanese*   23 | 14 | 23 | $31

Lincoln Park | 2616 N. Halsted St. (Wrightwood Ave.) | 773-871-1800 | www.ittosushi.com

"Fresh, no-frills sushi" and "authentic" Japanese plates "prepared expertly" are the assets at this "very reliable" and "warm family-run restaurant" in Lincoln Park that has "been around for more than two decades"; the atmosphere may be sparse, but it's a "great value" and "service is very good"; N.B. they offer seasonal patio seating.

	FOOD	DECOR	SERVICE	COST

NEW Jack Rabbit *Southwestern* — | — | — | M
(fka Brioso)

Lincoln Square | 4603 N. Lincoln Ave. (Wilson Ave.) | 773-989-9000 |
www.eatjackrabbit.com

The cozy neighborhood setting with colorful tables and blue-tiled
bar remains, but the midpriced menu at Lincoln Square's former
Brioso has morphed into a Southwestern bistro mix – happily, regulars are still likely to find many former favorites alongside the requi-
site sangria, margaritas and mojitos.

Jack's on Halsted *American* 21 | 20 | 20 | $36

Lakeview | 3201 N. Halsted St. (Belmont Ave.) | 773-244-9191 |
www.jackjonesrestaurants.com

A crowd of "gays and straights, older and younger, men and women"
gather at this "upscale yet relaxed" New American bistro that combines "creative" "comfort food", "flavored martinis" and "terrific
people-watching" in a "beautiful" Lakeview space ("sit near the windows and watch the world of Belmont and Halsted pass by"); still, a
faction of foodies flags it as "a bit pricey" and "hit-or-miss."

Jacky's Bistro *American/French* 24 | 20 | 21 | $46

Evanston | 2545 Prairie Ave. (Central St.) | 847-733-0899 |
www.jackysbistro.com

New American meets "hearty French" in the near North Suburbs at
this "cozy place to linger over a good meal" "in a bistro setting" with
an "impressive wine list" and "excellent service"; lauders label it "a
sure bet", but other jurists are jaded by its "always crowded (and not
in a good way)" conditions – not to mention the "city prices."

J. Alexander's *American* 20 | 19 | 19 | $31

Lincoln Park | 1832 N. Clybourn Ave. (bet. Willow & Wisconsin Sts.) |
773-435-1018
Northbrook | 4077 Lake Cook Rd. (bet. I-294 & Sanders Rd.) |
847-564-3093
Oak Brook | 1410 16th St. (Rte. 83) | 630-573-8180
www.jalexanders.com

Chums of this Traditional American chain champion its "hearty"
"grown-up" "comfort food" offered in a "spacious", "conversation-
friendly" "steakhouse atmosphere" with consistently "solid service", "comfortable seating" and "no hype", cheering "your dollar is
well spent" for a "date" or a "family meal – without going over the
top"; still, some dissatisfied chowhounds are "unimpressed" with
what they find to be "formula" fare, especially "in a city of excellent
independent dining" options.

Jane's *American/Eclectic* 21 | 19 | 20 | $30

Bucktown | 1655 W. Cortland St. (Paulina St.) | 773-862-5263 |
www.janesrestaurant.com

It's "cozy but alive" "with good vibes" at this "adorable", "crowded"
"place for a date", "for girls to catch up or for a family brunch" that's
"tucked away" on a Bucktown "residential street"; the New
American–Eclectic edibles include "some unique takes on comfort

food" and "plenty of grazing for vegetarians", and "now that they've expanded, the waits aren't so bad" – plus, as always, it's "nice to enjoy dining outside in warm weather."

☑ Japonais *Japanese* | 24 | 26 | 21 | $59 |

River North | 600 W. Chicago Ave. (Larrabee St.) | 312-822-9600 | www.japonaischicago.com

"Watch the stars (movie and celestial)", at this "super-sleek", "ultratrendy" River North Japanese that's "still one of the buzziest places in town", serving "expensive but excellent" "innovative" cooked food and sushi in a "seductive" setting with "techno surround-sound"; doubters, however, don't like "paying for the pretentious atmosphere" ("be sure to bring your ego") and say the "knowledgeable" servers sway between "personable" and "arrogant"; P.S. "downstairs along the river" is among the "best lounges" in the city.

NEW Jerry's *Sandwiches* | 20 | 17 | 14 | $18 |

Wicker Park | 1938 W. Division St. (Winchester Ave.) | 773-235-1006 | www.jerryssandwiches.com

Expect a menu so "overwhelming" it can "make your head hurt" at this Wicker Park sandwich shop where the "smashing" variety includes "vegetarian selections", a kids' menu and "amazing" beer list; the "fireplace and rustic utensil chandeliers make it cozy", though "sub-par service" has Dagwoods declaring "if they replaced their staff with nice, upbeat folks, they'd have me there for every meal"; N.B. it has sidewalk seating and serves till 2 AM on Friday and Saturday.

Jilly's Cafe Ⓜ *American/French* | 24 | 19 | 22 | $43 |

Evanston | 2614 Green Bay Rd. (Central St.) | 847-869-7636 | www.jillyscafe.com

"Romantics" frequent this "tiny" New American–New French "treasure" in the near North Suburbs for "high-quality food and service" amid "charming" country inn surroundings that feel "cozy and familiar, even if it's your first visit"; claustrophobes caution "go on a slow night", though, or you'll find yourself "listening to three conversations at once" in the "crowded" setting; P.S. "Sunday brunch is a great buy."

Jin Ju Ⓜ *Korean* | 21 | 18 | 20 | $32 |

Andersonville | 5203 N. Clark St. (Foster Ave.) | 773-334-6377 | www.jinjuchicago.com

The "fresh and creative" "upscale Korean food with a twist" at this Andersonville spot may be "a bit pricey" for the genre, but it comes with "great style" and "hip, dark" ambiance that "makes even a bad date tolerable"; even those who generally "eschew trendy ethnic-tini drinks" swear that "their soju concoctions hit the spot" – which is part of why it's "noisy" and "packed on weekends" with "pretty people."

☑ Joe's Seafood, | 26 | 21 | 24 | $59 |
Prime Steak & Stone Crab *Seafood/Steak*

River North | 60 E. Grand Ave. (Rush St.) | 312-379-5637 | www.joesstonecrabchicago.com

Lettuce Entertain You's "classy", "crazy-popular" River North surf 'n' turfer takes its name from the legendary Miami fishhouse and in-

FOOD | DECOR | SERVICE | COST

deed serves fresh "stone crab in season" (otherwise it's frozen) along with "simple" seafood, "superb steaks" and "standout Key lime pie"; the "1940s"-esque, "old boys' club" atmo includes a "festive bar", generally "friendly and professional" service and "expense-account" prices – so prepare to "crack open your wallet when they crack you some claws."

John's Place ⓜ American   17 | 14 | 17 | $20

Lincoln Park | 1200 W. Webster Ave. (Racine Ave.) | 773-525-6670 | www.johnsplace.com

"Homey-hip" and "family-friendly", this Lincoln Park "neighborhood haunt" is regarded as "reliable" for "solid, basic American food" with an "excellent kids' menu"; while some commenters veto it as a "veritable babypalooza", moderates maintain it's "much more enjoyable now that one room is for adults" and the other for families with kids – except at "crowded weekend brunch"; N.B. a Roscoe Village location is in the works.

Joy Yee's Noodle Shop Asian   22 | 11 | 15 | $17

Chinatown | 2139 S. China Pl. (Archer Ave.) | 312-328-0001
South Loop | 1335 S. Halsted St. (bet. W. Liberty & Maxwell Sts.) | 312-997-2128
Evanston | 521 Davis St. (Chicago Ave.) | 847-733-1900
Naperville | 1163 E. Ogden Ave. (Iroquois Ave.) | 630-579-6800
www.joyyee.com

"Good food, lots of it and fast" describes this quartet purveying "cheap", "fresh, well-spiced" Asian eats, "flavorful" bubble teas and "smoothies par excellence"; they're "not exactly highbrow" (and "such a scene for students and singles, you won't be able to carry on a conversation") and the decor is "either minimalist by intent or sparse by accident", though the new South Loop and remodeled Evanston branches are more "attractive"; N.B. BYO only, no reservations.

Julius Meinl Café Austrian   22 | 21 | 18 | $15

Lakeview | 3601 N. Southport Ave. (Addison St.) | 773-868-1857 | www.meinl.com

"Attention is paid to every last detail" at this "civilized" Lakeview coffeehouse, a "truly Austrian cafe experience" where patrons polish off "pastries to die for", "crave"-worthy salads and soups, "the best coffee in this country" and a "ridiculous selection of teas" "served on silver platters"; there's occasional "live music" in the "fancy European dining room" – small wonder "it's become a favorite spot (if you can get a seat)"; N.B. a Lincoln Square location is in the works.

Kabul House ⓜ Afghan   21 | 14 | 20 | $19

Skokie | 3320 Dempster St. (McCormick Blvd.) | 847-763-9930 | www.kabulhouse.com

For "an excellent intro to an unusual cuisine", try this North Suburban "gem" where "authentic" Afghani fare (including "mouth-watering vegetarian entrees") is "humbly prepared and served" in "modest surroundings" by a staff that "values your business"; it's also a "good place to take kids with an adventurous palate", and though there's "no alcohol", you can BYO; N.B. they're planning a move to new digs several blocks west on Dempster Street.

Kamehachi *Japanese*
22 | 18 | 19 | $35

Streeterville | 240 E. Ontario St. (bet. Fairbanks Ct. & St. Clair St.) | 312-587-0600

Old Town | 1400 N. Wells St. (Schiller St.) | 312-664-3663 ◑

Northbrook | Village Green Shopping Ctr. | 1320 Shermer Rd. (Waukegan Rd.) | 847-562-0064

www.kamehachi.com

Raters rely on this "traditional Japanese" clan for "fresh sushi" and "really good non-sushi" sustenance in settings that vary by venue (the Old Town location has a "nice garden in the summer"); perhaps it's "not innovative", but it's certainly dependable – though hedgers who hint it "has not kept up" in the raw-fish race bemoan "bite-sized portions" and "hit-or-miss" help.

Kansaku *Japanese*
▽ 22 | 21 | 17 | $34

Evanston | 1514 Sherman Ave. (Grove St.) | 847-864-4386

"Well-done" "nouveau sushi", "innovative drinks" and a "large cold sake selection" draw an "'in' crowd" to this Evanston Japanese; it has a "city feel", "open kitchen", "good music" and sidewalk seating – though marginalists maintain "nothing is memorable."

Kan Zaman *Lebanese*
▽ 20 | 15 | 17 | $21

River North | 617 N. Wells St. (Ontario St.) | 312-751-9600 | www.kanzamanchicago.com

"Yummy", "interesting" Lebanese food (including a "great veggie platter"), as well as comfortable "booths" and "coveted pillow couches" – plus "the sounds and sights of belly dancing" on Fridays and Saturdays – combine to make this River North BYO an exotic "good time."

☑ Karma *Asian*
23 | 26 | 21 | $37

Mundelein | Crowne Plaza Hotel | 510 E. Il. Rte. 83 (Rte. 45) | 847-970-6900 | www.karmachicago.com

"You feel like you're no longer in the 'burbs" muse Mundelein locals who favor this "fantastic urban find in an otherwise boring landscape of suburban chain restaurants"; the "subtle" and "creative" Asian fare is served in "minimalist", "ethereal" (despite its hotel milieu) surroundings, all adding up to an "impressive spot to entertain"; P.S. "the lounge is good too."

Karyn's Cooked *Vegetarian*
21 | 19 | 20 | $25

River North | 738 N. Wells St. (Superior St.) | 312-587-1050

Karyn's Fresh Corner *Vegetarian*

Lincoln Park | 1901 N. Halsted St. (Armitage Ave.) | 312-255-1590

www.karynraw.com

An "ethnic mix" of "satisfying", "flavorful" dishes that are "great if you are vegan, good if you are vegetarian, fine if you are neither" (but maybe not "if you are a real carnivore") is on offer at this "elegant" River Norther where the waiters "gladly explain all that's unfamiliar"; its 'Fresh' "raw foodie" counterpart in Lincoln Park sends out "very adventurous cuisine" that ranges from "amazing" to "weird."

Katsu Japanese ⓜ *Japanese* | 24 | 16 | 23 | $49 |
Northwest Side | 2651 W. Peterson Ave. (California Ave.) | 773-784-3383

"Authentic", "wonderful sushi and sashimi", a "good sampling of hot foods" and "so-friendly" owners lure a "loyal clientele" who label this Northwest Side Japanese "one of the best", just "don't be put off by the out-of-the-way location"; though enthusiasts earmark it as "expensive and worth every penny", some pronounce it "overpriced."

Kaze Sushi *Japanese* | 23 | 19 | 22 | $44 |
Roscoe Village | 2032 W. Roscoe St. (Seeley Ave.) | 773-327-4860 | www.kazesushi.com

It's all about "Japanese food for the adventurous palate" at this "glamorous" (if "too precious" to some) Roscoe Village haunt that's "one of the most unusual sushi spots" around thanks to its "surprising, sophisticated soups" and "inventive" nigiri with "specialized sauces" (the "chef's menu is the way to go"); those who find it "very expensive" should try the "Tuesday night prix fixe."

Keefer's ⓩ *American* | 24 | 22 | 22 | $60 |
River North | 20 W. Kinzie St. (Dearborn St.) | 312-467-9525 | www.keefersrestaurant.com

"Known for its excellent steaks but offering great food in all categories", including "wonderful seafood", River North's "Keefer's is a keeper" to coveters of its "contemporary American" "urban"-"chic" setting, "attentive staff" and "great happy-hour grown-up bar scene" with "fishbowl-sized martinis"; challengers who lack "expense accounts" complain about the "steep prices", though, suggesting you "try it for lunch", as the tariff is "easier to handle."

KiKi's Bistro ⓩ *French* | 23 | 20 | 22 | $46 |
Near North | 900 N. Franklin St. (Locust St.) | 312-335-5454 | www.kikisbistro.com

Take a "mini-trip to France" inside this "convivial", "off-the-beaten-path" Near North "darling" with "authentic" French country cuisine, "lots of character" and "affordable wines"; its "older crowd" is catered to by appropriately "Gallic", "hospitable" service – so while naggers nitpick that there's "no pizzazz", the tables are "rather close" and the decibels "deafening" during dinner, regulars keep coming back for an "old-reliable" experience.

Kinzie Chophouse *Steak* | 20 | 18 | 21 | $48 |
River North | 400 N. Wells St. (Kinzie St.) | 312-822-0191 | www.kinziechophouse.com

"Under the radar" in River North, this "red-blooded steakhouse" is a "cozy little corner place with lots of regulars" who tout is as "tried-and-true", with "very tasty" steaks and chops served in a "friendly" setting that's not as "glitzy" or "plastic" as some competitors' (and "a good choice for lunch if you're near the Mart"); still, wallet-watchers might go more often if they "cut the portions and prices in half."

	FOOD	DECOR	SERVICE	COST

Kit Kat Lounge & Supper Club ⏺Ⓜ *Eclectic*
15 | 18 | 15 | $36

Wrigleyville | 3700 N. Halsted St. (Waveland Ave.) | 773-525-1111 | www.kitkatchicago.com

This Boys Town boîte "intrigues" with a "supper-club feel", "phenomenal drink menu" and "drag queens belting out" celeb impersonations – it's all about the "entertainment and humor with a side of [Eclectic] food" (served till 2 AM); some shrinking violets say the "shrieking bachelorette parties have begun to wear thin, and so has the service."

Kitsch'n on Roscoe *Eclectic*
16 | 18 | 16 | $19

Roscoe Village | 2005 W. Roscoe St. (Damen Ave.) | 773-248-7372

Kitsch'n River North *Eclectic*
River North | 600 W. Chicago Ave. (Larrabee St.) | 312-644-1500 www.kitschn.com

"Nineteen seventies kitsch reigns" at these "popular" "family restaurants" and "brunch spots" where "the decor is tacky" (lava lamps, lunchboxes) "but that's the point"; the "reasonably priced" Eclectic "home cooking with a modernized take" includes "coconut-encrusted pancakes" and "Twinkie tiramisu" that have some surveyors at hello, but others complain that the "items sound better than they taste" and the "quirky staff" "can disappear at times for no reason"; P.S. River North is "way roomier than the Roscoe Village location."

Klay Oven *Indian*
21 | 15 | 18 | $32

River North | 414 N. Orleans St. (Hubbard St.) | 312-527-3999 | www.klayovenrestaurant.com

"Good, basic Indian" fare that's "fresh" and "beautifully served" makes this "serene" River Norther a "solid" choice for city dwellers; it may not be "as authentic as the places on Devon", but its "quiet" ambiance is "upscale", the "buffet lunch is a deal" and it's "great for pickup" too.

Koi *Asian*
20 | 22 | 19 | $33

Evanston | 624 Davis St. (bet. Chicago & Orrington Aves.) | 847-866-6969 | www.koievanston.com

To gourmands who get this "upscale Chinese-sushi" hybrid as "a great addition to the Evanston dining scene", there's gold in the Asian fare, "excellent drink list including rare and delicious teas" and "hip" "yet elegant" environs with a "welcoming fireplace"; on the flip side, disheartened diners wish the "expensive", "inconsistent food" and sometimes "inattentive staff" "lived up to the style."

Koryo Ⓜ *Korean*
▽ 19 | 20 | 20 | $28

Lakeview | 2936 N. Broadway St. (bet. Oakdale & Wellington Aves.) | 773-477-8510

"Friendly and gracious" folks await at Lakeview's "trendy" Korean "joint" with a "spare", "stylish" if "'80s" atmosphere and "solid dishes" served with beer, wine and Korean liquor; it might "not be the best" but it's "accessible" for your "bibimbop fix" and especially appealing to "non-native diners wanting an intro into the cuisine."

	FOOD	DECOR	SERVICE	COST

Kroll's *American* | 14 | 15 | 16 | $19 |

South Loop | 1736 S. Michigan Ave. (18th St.) | 312-235-1400 | www.krolls-chicago.com

Get some "Green Bay love" at this South Loop branch of the Wisconsin "classic", bringing "solid" American "sports-bar food", plenty of flat-screen TVs and "reasonable prices" to the "heart of Bears country"; most "come here with friends to watch the games" while snacking on "beer and cheese curds", since the "specialty items such as butter burgers and chicken and dumpling soup" can be "underwhelming."

Kuma's Corner ◐ *American* | 24 | 15 | 21 | $19 |

Logan Square | 2900 W. Belmont Ave. (Francisco Ave.) | 773-604-8769 | www.kumascorner.com

It may look like a "dressed-up" "heavy metal" "dive bar", but this Logan Square American "doesn't serve your average eats" – instead, expect "excellent mussels" and "some of the best" burgers "loaded up" with "classic and original toppings"; the "sexy, tattooed staff" "knows its stuff", especially when it comes to the "great beer selection" poured amid "rocker/biker" decor complete with "blaring" music; P.S. hit the patio in summer "to chillax with friends."

Kuni's *Japanese* | 21 | 13 | 18 | $32 |

Evanston | 511-A Main St. (bet. Chicago & Hinman Aves.) | 847-328-2004

"Fresh" "traditional" raw fin fare with "few extravagant combinations" ("if you like your sushi with cream cheese, go elsewhere"), plus "straightforward" Japanese "classics" make up the "reasonably priced" menu at this Evanston "hidden gem"; surveyors are split over the service ("spectacular" vs. "standoffish"), but aren't deterred by atmosphere that may be "more befitting of a diner"; N.B. the bar serves only beer, wine and sake, and reservations are for six or more only.

La Bocca della Verità *Italian* | 20 | 14 | 19 | $31 |

Lincoln Square | 4618 N. Lincoln Ave. (bet. Lawrence & Wilson Aves.) | 773-784-6222 | www.laboccachicago.com

A "quaint" "neighborhood Italian" with "family character", this Lincoln Square spot has adherents who admire its "simple, delicious" fare and "homey atmosphere", saying it "will bring you back to that last Roman holiday"; a chorus of antis, though, claims that it's "overrated" and "nothing special" – though fresh air fiends find that the "outdoor dining is comfortable."

NEW La Brochette *Mideastern/Moroccan* | – | – | – | I |

Wicker Park | 1401 N. Ashland Ave. (Blackhawk St.) | 773-276-5650

Bargain-priced Moroccan-Mideastern skewers and a smattering of Eclectic dishes are served all day at this cozy, corner Wicker Park African cafe; its space, which last housed Stevie B's, has been remodeled with ochre and jewel tones, fabric-draped windows and an open kitchen.

	FOOD	DECOR	SERVICE	COST

La Cantina ☒ *Italian/Seafood* `21` `19` `23` `$30`

Loop | Italian Vill. | 71 W. Monroe St. (bet. Clark & Dearborn Sts.) | 312-332-7005 | www.lacantina-chicago.com

This "dark and dependable" "Loop favorite" is part of the Italian Village complex and sets out Northern Italian eats with "excellent fish preparations" accompanied by a 1,400-bottle wine list; surveyors debate whether the "basement" "hideout" is "outdated" or "intimate", and a few brand it "basically a lunch place for the lawyers and their accomplices" or "to meet people for cocktails and appetizers."

La Casa de Isaac *Mexican* `22` `15` `21` `$22`

Highland Park | 431 Temple Ave. (Waukeegan Ave.) | 847-433-5550 | www.lacasadeisaac.com

It may have an "interesting concept" – religious Jews running a Mexican restaurant" (so there's "no pork" and they're "closed Friday night through early Saturday evening") – but what truly draws North Suburbanites to this "noisy", "homey" hangout is the "carefully prepared" "fresh" fare such as "fish tacos to die for" and "great margaritas"; the "servers try really hard to please", and it's a good "value", with sidewalk seating in summer.

NEW La Cocina de Frida *Mexican* `-` `-` `-` `I`

Andersonville | 5403 N. Clark St. (Balmoral Ave.) | 773-271-1907 | www.lacocinadefrida.com

Sisters with a thing for Frida Kahlo helm this devotional Andersonville Mexican serving fresh, inexpensive fare (including some of Frida's favorites and a tamale of the day) in a funky storefront setting painted brown, pink and orange; there's also full bar service (emphasis on margaritas and tequilas), brunch and seasonal outdoor dining.

La Crêperie Ⓜ *French* `21` `17` `20` `$23`

Lakeview | 2845 N. Clark St. (bet. Diversey Pkwy. & Surf St.) | 773-528-9050 | www.lacreperieusa.com

This "quaint" "standard" in Lakeview features "value"-priced "sweet and savory crêpes" and "classic French selections" served by a "charming staff" in "two tiny" rooms and a patio that's a "little oasis"; raters rank it "really nice for when granny visits", "a date – gay or straight", "hangover mornings" or "after a movie at Century Mall."

La Cucina di Donatella *Italian* ▽ `24` `17` `22` `$33`

Rogers Park | 2221 W. Howard St. (Ridge Blvd.) | 773-262-6533

The namesake chef-owner is "passionate about pasta", and "her roots in Roman cuisine show" at this "tiny, well-run" Rogers Park BYO respite where the "great-value" "imaginatively prepared" cuisine is "not your typical Italian"; the pace is "relaxed", and if "the room is rather dull, the food makes up for it" (as does the "outside cafe in summer").

La Donna *Italian* `19` `17` `18` `$30`

Andersonville | 5146 N. Clark St. (Foster Ave.) | 773-561-9400 | www.ladonnarestaurantchicago.com

Amici announce it's "always crowded and for good reason" at this Andersonville "neighborhood" ristorante cooking a "combination of

FOOD | DECOR | SERVICE | COST

authentic Italian dishes" and some "with creative touches" ("oh, the pumpkin ravioli!") in a "casual-romantic" setting "with floor-to-ceiling windows"; conflicted consumers mark it "middle of the pack", though.

La Fonda Latino Ⓜ *Colombian*   ∇ 24 | 17 | 19 | $26

Andersonville | 5350 N. Broadway St. (Balmoral Ave.) | 773-271-3935
Andersonvillagers are "fond" of the "excellent", "interesting" Colombian cuisine and "all the right Latin standards" at this "welcoming" way-station where the "tasty drinks" include a "must-have sangria"; though the "decor could be warmed up a bit", assets include sidewalk seating, "decent prices" and a "wonderful lunch buffet."

La Gondola *Italian*   23 | 11 | 19 | $27

Lakeview | Wellington Plaza | 2914 N. Ashland Ave. (Wellington Ave.) | 773-248-4433 | www.lagondolachicago.com
Coming up on 25 years in Lakeview, this "storefront" Italian that's "tucked into a strip mall" (ergo "easy parking") hands out "huge servings" of "surprisingly good", "inexpensive" "basic" nosh and "some of the best thin-crust pizza" around; though the servings are "huge", the space is "tiny", so "make reservations" or "get it to go and make a pig of yourself in the privacy of your own home."

Lalo's *Mexican*   17 | 17 | 18 | $23

River North | 500 N. LaSalle St. (Illinois St.) | 312-329-0030
Lincoln Park | 1960 N. Clybourn Ave. (bet. Clifton Ave. & Cortland St.) | 773-880-5256
Des Plaines | 1535 Ellinwood Ave. (bet. Lee & Pearson Sts.) | 847-296-1535
Far South Side | 4126 W. 26th St. (Kedvale Ave.) | 773-762-1505
Southwest Side | Midway Int'l Airport | 5757 S. Cicero Ave. (55th St.) | 773-838-1604
Glenview | 1432 Waukegan Rd. (Lake Ave.) | 847-832-1388
Schaumburg | 425 S. Roselle Rd. (bet. Schaumburg Rd. & Weathersfield Way) | 847-891-0911
Berwyn | 3011 S. Harlem Ave. (31st St.) | 708-484-9411
Oak Park | 804 S. Oak Park Ave. (Rte. 290) | 708-386-3386
www.lalos.com
A "good variety" of "solid", "Americanized Mexican food served in a fun party atmosphere" with "powerful" "fishbowl" "margaritas" and "mariachi" music (at some sites) is enough for frequenters of this family of "kid-friendly" cantinas; still, some say "skip it" due to "subpar" sustenance without "much flair or flavor", while other "disappointed" diners deem them "not authentic."

NEW La Madia ◗ *Italian*   22 | 21 | 20 | $30

River North | 59 W. Grand Ave. (bet. Clark & Dearborn Sts.) | 312-329-0400 | www.dinelamadia.com
Pie-*sani* "pair pizzas with wines by the glass" at this "ultracool", "modern" River North Italian entrant into the "wood-fired" "thin-crust" market, pleasing with a "somewhat limited" menu of "crunchy" seasonal pies topped with "up-to-the-minute ingredients"; it's a prime spot for lunch, a "date night" and going "out with friends", though the penny-wise peg it as "pricey" for the category.

	FOOD	DECOR	SERVICE	COST

Landmark *American* — 21 | 20 | 18 | $45

Lincoln Park | 1633 N. Halsted St. (North Ave.) | 312-587-1600 |
www.landmarkgrill.net

"Be ready for a scene and a half" at this "cool", "midpriced" Lincoln
Park New American set in a "funky, multilevel interior" where "hipster" and pre/post-theater "crowds" converge "for a full dinner,
quick bite in the lounge" or "rockin'" vibe "after 10"; fogeys frown on
having to "practice your smug expression in front of a mirror to fit in"
and bemoan the need to "shout at your companions over the lobster
club", given the "loud" acoustics.

L'anne 🖼 Ⓜ *French/Vietnamese* — ▽ 21 | 17 | 16 | $44

Wheaton | 221 W. Front St. (bet. Hale St. & Wheaton Ave.) | 630-260-1234
A "unique", "inventive menu" of Vietnamese-focused French-Asian
fusion fare fans the flames for followers of this "quaint" West
Suburban supplier of a "city dining experience", which for critics can
include portions that "are small in comparison to the prices" and
"spotty service"; N.B. a pianist tickles the ivories on weekend nights.

Ⓩ Lao Beijing *Chinese* — 26 | 11 | 16 | $20

NEW **Chinatown** | Chinatown Mall | 2138 S. Archer Ave. (China Pl.) |
312-881-0168 | www.tonygourmetgroup.com

Ⓩ Lao Sze Chuan *Chinese*

Chinatown | 2172 S. Archer Ave. (Princeton Ave.) | 312-326-5040 ●
Downers Grove | 1331 W. Ogden Ave. (Main St.) | 630-663-0303
www.laoszechuan.com

"Low prices" and lots of "spices" enhance "awesome", "authentic"
regional Chinese fare from "menus as long as *Gone with the Wind*"
(though insiders say "stick to the real", un-Americanized offerings)
at theses otherwise "standard" "no-frills" sibs in Chinatown and
Downers Grove; the spaces are "crowded but lively", and on weekends there can be a "long wait"; N.B. alcohol service varies by location.

La Peña Ⓜ *S American* — ▽ 18 | 15 | 20 | $27

Northwest Side | 4212 N. Milwaukee Ave. (Montrose Ave.) |
773-545-7022 | www.lapenachicago.com

Dig into a "nice variety" of "delicious, different" South American
dishes like "quality" "Ecuadorian tamales", "humitas" and "great
ceviche" that go for "good prices" at this "friendly" Northwest Sider;
the "festive atmosphere" includes live entertainment like DJs,
"karaoke and bands", and they make a mean tropical margarita.

La Petite Amelia *French* — 20 | 18 | 19 | $38

Evanston | 618 Church St. (bet. Chicago & Orrington Aves.) |
847-328-3333 | www.lapetiteamelia.com

Confreres of this "lovely", "tiny" Evanston bistro and its "friendly",
"well-informed staff" enthuse over the "extensive seasonal menu"
of "classic" "*très* French" fare with a "high-quality wine list" – and
most "don't mind the cost", since they "can see where the money's
going, and it's all good"; a few *contraires*, however, consider it "ordinary" and "overpriced", except on Monday–Thursdsay nights, when
the prix fixe is a "real deal."

la petite folie Ⓜ *French*

23 | 19 | 21 | $43

Hyde Park | Hyde Park Shopping Ctr, | 1504 E. 55th St. (Lake Park Blvd.) | 773-493-1394 | www.lapetitefolie.com

"Hyde Park's sole claim to fine dining" rests with this "fancy" Classic French "surprise" "hidden" "in a strip mall", serving "top-notch traditional" cuisine with a "criminally cheap wine collection" in its "lush Parisian rooms"; even surveyors who sense the "service is not as professional as the food" agree the experience is of "generally high quality", and the "early-bird prix fixe" dinner and "lunches are a fantastic value."

La Sardine Ⓩ *French*

23 | 20 | 22 | $47

West Loop | 111 N. Carpenter St. (bet. Randolph St. & Washington Blvd.) | 312-421-2800 | www.lasardine.com

"Well-executed *classique* French" bistro fare packs 'em into this "delightful" West Looper that's "perfect for a Paris-style lunch or dinner" but with "better service" – plus it's "not as frenetic as" its tiny sister, Le Bouchon (though it can be just as "noisy when busy"); P.S. the penny-wise praise the "half-price wine nights on Mondays" and "Tuesday night prix fixe (a steal)."

La Scarola *Italian*

23 | 14 | 19 | $37

River West | 721 W. Grand Ave. (bet. Halsted St. & Milwaukee Ave.) | 312-243-1740 | www.lascarola.com

"Consistently one of the best medium-range" Italian ristoranti around, this "crowded", "bustling" River Wester features "excellent", "no-nonsense" "comfort food" (kudos for the heaps of "fresh pastas"); enthusiasts insist that if you "eat there more than once they treat you like family", even if some critics don't dig being "packed in" to the "storefront" space.

Las Palmas *Mexican*

22 | 18 | 20 | $25

Bucktown | 1835 W. North Ave. (Honore St.) | 773-289-4991
Buffalo Grove | 86 W. Dundee Rd. (Old Buffalo Grove Rd.) | 847-520-8222

"Branch out beyond the obvious taco-enchilada dishes and you'll be rewarded" at this Bucktown and Buffalo Grove duo where the "gourmet" Mexican fare features "fresh and flavorful ingredients" matched with "generous margaritas" and a side of "great hospitality"; N.B. there are a slew of more-casual suburban siblings.

Las Tablas *Colombian/Steak*

20 | 17 | 18 | $26

Lakeview | 2942 N. Lincoln Ave. (Wellington Ave.) | 773-871-2414
Northwest Side | 4920 W. Irving Park Rd. (Cicero Ave.) | 773-202-0999
www.lastablas.com

"Tasty steak, chicken" and "grilled seafood" ("not many veggie options") "served on wooden *tablas*" tempt touters who also champion the "cheap" prices at these Lincoln Park and Northwest Side Colombian steakhouses (both now have liquor licenses); though the "slow" service causes consternation, the "ambiance is great for a large group", they serve weekend brunch and Irving Park Road has outdoor dining.

	FOOD	DECOR	SERVICE	COST

La Tache *French* — 22 | 21 | 20 | $39

Andersonville | 1475 W. Balmoral Ave. (bet. Clark St. & Glenwood Ave.) | 773-334-7168

Andersonville has adopted this "popular hideout" for "solid" "traditional French" bistro plates and other dishes with "creative twists"; it's "a great deal for Sunday brunch", especially "outside when summer finally finds Chicago", but a few gourmets grade it "good but not spectacular", while others maintain that the "service could be better."

La Tasca *Spanish* — 23 | 21 | 21 | $32

Arlington Heights | 25 W. Davis St. (Vail Ave.) | 847-398-2400 | www.latascatapas.com

Respondents pick this Spanish purveyor in the Northwest Suburbs for its "great variety of options" in the small-plates department (though "full entrees are available" as well), plus "killer sangrias"; the "fun", "friendly" setting makes it a "great place to go with friends" or "kids" – or even "to have a romantic evening" with that special someone.

La Vita *Italian* — ∇ 22 | 18 | 22 | $29

Little Italy | 1359 W. Taylor St. (Loomis St.) | 312-491-1414 | www.lavitarestaurant.com

This "neighborhood" "favorite" in the "heart of Little Italy" gives "great satisfaction" with "classic" Northern Italian cuisine that "holds its own among the greats on Taylor Street"; service also earns kudos, and there's a "rooftop deck in the summer."

Lawry's The Prime Rib *Steak* — 24 | 22 | 24 | $52

River North | 100 E. Ontario St. (Rush St.) | 312-787-5000 | www.lawrysonline.com

"Nostalgia helps nourish the palate" at this "reliable" River North "throwback" where "mouthwatering prime rib" is "carved-to-order tableside" and paired with "traditional" trimmings and "delicious" "spinning salad"; the "gorgeous" "old-world dining room" feels like "your grandma's, if your grandma was a Rockefeller", and times are slowly changing: they "now hire male staffers, and the females no longer have to wear coffee filters on their heads!"

Le Bouchon ☒ *French* — 24 | 19 | 20 | $39

Bucktown | 1958 N. Damen Ave. (Armitage Ave.) | 773-862-6600 | www.lebouchonofchicago.com

Bistro junkies "just can't get enough of" this "lively, authentic" Bucktown "institution" that "attracts well-mannered diners" looking for "solid" "country French" "favorites" – "some of the best" around – from Jean Claude Poilevey's kitchen; no wonder so many put up with "interminable waits for a table" in "noisy", "closetlike" confines, and service that swings from "wonderful" to "grumpy."

Le Colonial *Vietnamese* — 23 | 24 | 21 | $49

Gold Coast | 937 N. Rush St. (bet. Oak & Walton Sts.) | 312-255-0088 | www.lecolonialchicago.com

"If your date's not impressed, it's you, not the place" say romantics entranced by this Gold Coaster that evokes a "sexy" "movie set" of "old

Saigon" and serves "bright, modern" French-influenced Vietnamese; a cadre of critics calls the fare "inconsistent" and "overpriced" and the service "spotty", but most laud the bi-level "escape" – there's "exotic sophistication downstairs" with "white tablecloths", "palm trees and overhead fans", and a "laid-back lounge upstairs."

Le Lan ⚅ Asian/French

25 | 22 | 23 | $61

River North | 749 N. Clark St. (Chicago Ave.) | 312-280-9100 | www.lelanrestaurant.com

"Contemporary" French-Asian flavors "explode in your mouth" at this "sexy-chic" "fine"-dining space in River North, where executive chef and "Charlie Trotter alum" Bill Kim has "expanded the fusion menu beyond Vietnamese" and offers "great pairings of wine by the glass"; consensus says sometimes the "service does not measure up", and value-minded voters suggest pursuing the pre-theater and "Tuesday night dinner specials", since otherwise it can be "a little pricey."

Lem's BBQ ◑⇎ BBQ

▽ 25 | 7 | 16 | $17

Far South Side | 311 E. 75th St. (bet. Calumet & Prairie Aves.) | 773-994-2428

Since 1968, some of the "most original and best" BBQ around has issued from this Far South Side "stand" where you can "taste the love" in every "tangy rib"; just don't expect actual service, as this "carry-out" classic "doesn't have a dining area"; N.B. they're open till 2 AM nightly, closed Tuesdays.

Leonardo's Ristorante Ⓜ Italian

▽ 21 | 20 | 20 | $34

Andersonville | 5657 N. Clark St. (Hollywood Ave.) | 773-561-5028

This "relaxing", "undiscovered" Andersonville "neighborhood" "favorite" delivers "large portions" of "really good" Northern Italian dishes in a "quiet", "classy" setting that's "better inside than it looks from the outside"; a few warn, however, that the fare can be "too checkered-tablecloth for the prices."

Le P'tit Paris Continental/French

▽ 24 | 19 | 22 | $50

Streeterville | 260 E. Chestnut St. (Dewitt Pl.) | 312-787-8260

Traditionalists tout this "romantic", candlelit Streeterville "hideaway" for its "very good" Continental and French fare, "quiet", "old-fashioned" (some say a bit "stuffy") ambiance and "nice service" that offers "right-on-the-money wine suggestions"; given its "little" space, reservations are encouraged; N.B. the Food score may not reflect a recent chef change.

ⓩ Les Nomades ⚅Ⓜ French

28 | 25 | 27 | $100

Streeterville | 222 E. Ontario St. (bet. Fairbanks Ct. & St. Clair St.) | 312-649-9010 | www.lesnomades.net

This 30-year-old "oasis" of "good taste" delivers "top-notch", "high-end" "modern French" fare alongside an "excellent" France-heavy wine list (including a "good half-bottle selection") served in a "staid" Streeterville "townhouse setting" with a "real wood fireplace" and "beautiful flowers" ("ask to be upstairs"); some find the "polished" service "haughty" and note the experience "comes at a price", but fans feel it's "worth every penny"; P.S. "jackets are required, not just suggested."

Z Le Titi de Paris Ⓜ *French* | 28 | 24 | 27 | $65
Arlington Heights | 1015 W. Dundee Rd. (Kennicott Ave.) | 847-506-0222 | www.letitideparis.com
Four years into their ownership, Michael and Susan Maddox "continue the tradition" at this longtime Northwest Suburban "temple" of "exceptional" New French fare that's "not as fancy" as it used to be (though the "robust sauces and desserts" evoke "old Paris"); the staff remains "courteous and pleasant" ("gone are the silver haired servers"), a "knowledgeable sommelier" oversees the "excellent" wine list and while the tabs are still "pricey", it's "not pretentious" – just a "great place to celebrate."

Le Vichyssois Ⓜ *French* | ▽ 27 | 20 | 23 | $57
Lakemoor | 220 Rand Rd. (2 mi. west of Rte. 12) | 815-385-8221 | www.levichyssois.com
Stepping inside Bernard Cretier's "charming" Northwest Suburban "bastion" of "old school" French cuisine is "like walking back in time" thanks to the "great sauces" (which are sold in the restaurant) and *"très, très bon"* "traditional" *nourriture*; city-dwellers proclaim it's "worth the long drive occasionally" for a "romantic" evening or "special celebration."

NEW Libertine
Gastropub & Lounge 🅱Ⓜ *American* | - | - | - | M
Lincoln Park | 1615 N. Clybourn Ave. (North Ave.) | 312-654-1782 | www.libertinechicago.com
This bi-level Lincoln Park gastropub lures loungers and late-nighters with creative New American fare paired with a solid mix of draft, craft and Belgian beers and served in a decadent, clubby setting accented by gargoyles, fleurs de lis and multiple TVs (some hidden behind artwork); there's an upstairs lounge with cushy seating, a second bar and the occasional DJ for dancing.

Z Lobby, The ❶ *Continental/Seafood* | 24 | 25 | 23 | $57
River North | Peninsula Hotel | 108 E. Superior St., 5th fl. (bet. Michigan Ave. & Rush St.) | 312-573-6760 | www.peninsula.com
"A treat if you want to feel posh", this "highly civilized" River North refuge in the Peninsula Hotel serves Continental and seafood selections (and Sunday brunch) in an "opulent" room "filled with natural light"; lobbyists "love" the "afternoon high tea", "chocolate bar" buffet on Fridays and Saturdays, and "live jazz" on weekend "nights", noting it's "hard to imagine that this isn't [the hotel's] fancy restaurant."

NEW Lockwood *American* | - | - | - | E
Loop | Palmer House Hilton | 17 E. Monroe St. (bet. State St. & Wabash Ave.) | 312-917-3404 | www.lockwoodrestaurant.com
Part of a multimillion-dollar renovation, this high-end New American revives the dining scene at the Loop's venerable Palmer House Hilton, serving business breakfasts (à la carte or buffet), power lunches and elegant dinners; the sleek lobby setting exudes

| | FOOD | DECOR | SERVICE | COST |

☑ Lou Malnati's Pizzeria *Pizza*

| 24 | 14 | 18 | $19 |

River North | 439 N. Wells St. (Hubbard St.) | 312-828-9800
Lincoln Park | 958 W. Wrightwood Ave. (Lincoln Ave.) | 773-832-4030
Southwest Side | 3859 W. Ogden Ave. (Cermak Rd.) | 773-762-0800
Evanston | 1850 Sherman Ave. (University Pl.) | 847-328-5400
Lincolnwood | 6649 N. Lincoln Ave. (bet. Devon & Pratt Aves.) |
847-673-0800
Buffalo Grove | 85 S. Buffalo Grove Rd. (Lake Cook Rd.) | 847-215-7100
Elk Grove Village | 1050 E. Higgins Rd. (bet. Arlington Heights &
Busse Rds.) | 847-439-2000
Schaumburg | 1 S. Roselle Rd. (Schaumburg Rd.) | 847-985-1525
Naperville | 131 W. Jefferson Ave. (Washington St.) | 630-717-0700
Naperville | 2879 W. 95th St. (Rte. 59) | 630-904-4222
www.loumalnatis.com
Additional locations throughout the Chicago area

"Order a thin crust as an appetizer, a deep dish for the main course"
and the "chocolate chip cookie pizza" for dessert at this "iconic"
longtime chain that some say still slices up the "best old-fashioned
Chicago pizza" ("what they serve during football games in heaven")
despite being edged off its pedestal by the artisanal 'za craze; "service is friendly", and though settings range from "sports bar–like" to
"tired", impatient pie-lovers don't mind, since they "get takeout" to
avoid the "always long wait" for a table.

Lou Mitchell's *Diner*

| 21 | 12 | 20 | $16 |

Loop | 565 W. Jackson Blvd. (Jefferson St.) | 312-939-3111 ⊭
O'Hare Area | O'Hare Int'l Airport | Terminal 5 | 773-601-8989 ●
www.loumitchellsrestaurant.com

"Welcome to the City of Big Shoulders" at this "landmark" West
Loop coffee shop serving a "great" American breakfast still "in the
skillet" as well as other "honest diner food" from the crack of dawn
to midafternoon; the retro setting is "kitschy", the "veteran servers
can be insulting" and the "cash-only [policy] is a pain" – and "prepare to wait in line" (with free "doughnut holes and Milk Duds to
nosh on"); N.B. the airport outpost is a quick take-out station.

Lovells of Lake Forest *American*

| 22 | 24 | 23 | $56 |

Lake Forest | 915 S. Waukegan Rd. (Everett Rd.) | 847-234-8013 |
www.lovellsoflakeforest.com

"Classic elegance" is enhanced by "Apollo 13 artifacts" at this North
Suburbanite where service that's "attentive without being stifling"
shepherds "very good" New American meals to the "business" and
"country club" crowd; grumps, however, ground it as "stiff" and "not
yet top-tier", with "well-prepared but not surprising" sustenance at
"downtown prices" – yet even contrarians concede the "cozy" downstairs bar is "relaxing" for "an after-dinner drink and live entertainment" on weekends; P.S. on some nights, the chef-owner's father,
astronaut Jim Lovell, "greets guests."

Lucia Ristorante 🅱 *Italian* ▽ 23 | 16 | 20 | $28

Wicker Park | 1825 W. North Ave. (Honore St.) | 773-292-9700

An "interesting combination of deli and eatery", this Wicker Park BYO is a "fun place to go with friends" for "delicious" Italian fare; the "friendly" service includes attention from the "hands-on owner", and it's "great for a quick lunch" as the counter "up front makes the best sandwiches in the neighborhood."

Lula *Eclectic* 26 | 17 | 20 | $28

Logan Square | 2537-41 N. Kedzie Blvd. (bet. Fullerton Ave. & Logan Blvd.) | 773-489-9554 | www.lulacafe.com

"Hipsters, retirees, yuppies and tourists all mix" with the "heavily tattooed and pierced staff" at this "arty", "upscale"-"casual" Logan Square "insider" that dishes out "sophisticated" Eclectic eats with an emphasis on "market-driven produce" (and includes "vegetarian" vittles and "weekday brunch"); the digs are "funky" and some say "overcrowded", and the "no-reservations" policy results in "long lines"; N.B. a South Loop sequel is in the works.

LuLu's Dim Sum & Then Sum *Pan-Asian* 19 | 14 | 17 | $20

Evanston | 804 Davis St. (Sherman Ave.) | 847-869-4343 | www.lulusdimsum.com

For a fix of "very good Americanized" Pan-Asian small plates, "soups and noodle dishes that never disappoint", "Northwestern students" and others "who don't want a big bill" descend upon this Evanston "hangout" offering a "fantastic array" of foods amid "fun decor using everything from wild colors to funky art to Godzilla figurines"; purists, however, pan the provender as a "pale imitation" of the original fare.

Luna Caprese 🅼 *Italian* ▽ 26 | 17 | 21 | $30

Lincoln Park | 2239 N. Clybourn Ave. (bet. Greenview & Webster Aves.) | 773-281-4825 | www.lunacaprese.com

A "sweet, cozy date spot" in Lincoln Park, this "undiscovered gem" serves a "diverse menu" of "wonderful" Southern Italian sustenance, including "housemade pastas", along with "well-priced wines"; adding to the warm "welcome" of its "hospitable chef-owner" is the "wonderful aroma" of its "quaint" setting, which just might make "you feel like you're in an Italian home."

Lupita's 🅼 *Mexican* 19 | 14 | 20 | $23

Evanston | 700 Main St. (Custer Ave.) | 847-328-2255 | www.lupitasmexicanrestaurant.com

Diners divide over this midpriced North Suburban Mexican mainstay, with pros presenting it as "upscale" "fine dining" with "authentic", "creative" choices that "aren't your everyday" offerings plus "wonderful margaritas", while cons say it's "just ok in a pinch"; the "simple" decor wins few raves, though all agree that it's run by "lovely people."

LuxBar ◑ *American* 19 | 18 | 18 | $32

Gold Coast | 18 E. Bellevue Pl. (Rush St.) | 312-642-3400 | www.luxbar.com

"For the young, successful" "super-tight jeans" and "busy power-lunch crowds", this casual Gold Coaster (a member of Gibsons family, "without the wallet-breaking cost") is a "swanky little cocktail" "hot spot" where "tasty staffers" serve "pretty decent" "upscale" American "bar food" in a "noisy", "upbeat city atmosphere"; conversely, some contributors criticize it as conceptually confused, i.e. "trying to be down-home, trendy and a neighborhood spot all in one."

L. Woods Tap & Pine Lodge *American*   20 | 19 | 19 | $30

Lincolnwood | 7110 N. Lincoln Ave. (Kostner Ave.) | 847-677-3350 | www.lwoodsrestaurant.com

"Consistently good, standard" Traditional "Americana fare" feeds fans of this "comfy" "rib, steak, burger and bar joint" with a "woodsy" "Wisconsin"-esque "cabin look" located "halfway between the North 'burbs and the city"; maybe there's "no surprises", but that's fine with most; P.S. when faced with the "sometimes long wait", regulars report "the take-out [store] is a viable alternative."

NEW Macarena *Eclectic*   - | - | - | M

Naperville | Naper West Plaza | 618 Rte. 59 S. (bet. 111th & 119th Sts.) | 630-420-8995 | www.macarenatapas.com

Chef John Borras, who studied under Ferran Adrià at El Bulli, combines Eclectic molecular-gastronomy concoctions (whimsies like tins of mango 'caviar') and traditional tapas at this romantic, mid-priced West Suburbanite; the strip-mall space is done in red, black and earth tones with faux-finished walls and a small bar.

NEW Macello *Italian*   ∇ 19 | 21 | 16 | $34

Market District | 1235 W. Lake St. (bet. Elizabeth St. & Racine Ave.) | 312-850-9870

"Meat-cooler" chic meets "bordello" style at this Market District Italian in a former butchery with "great glass globes hanging from the ceiling"; its "broad, well-priced menu" includes "tasty pizzas" and "neighborhood" fare that's "ok at times, great at others", served by a staff that "can seem a little overwhelmed."

NEW mado ⊠ Ⓜ *Italian/Mediterranean*   - | - | - | M

Bucktown | 1647 N. Milwaukee Ave. (Concord Pl.) | 773-342-2340

This Bucktown Italian-Mediterranean run by a husband and wife offers simple, reasonably priced dishes focusing on local and sustainable ingredients – highlights include house-cured charcuterie, housemade pastas, wood-fired and rotisserie meats and lunch panini; the funky/rustic, green-minded setting boasts blackboard menus on exposed-brick walls and a reclaimed farmhouse table for communal dining.

Ⓩ Maggiano's Little Italy *Italian*   21 | 19 | 20 | $32

River North | 516 N. Clark St. (Grand Ave.) | 312-644-7700
Skokie | Westfield Shoppingtown | 175 Old Orchard Ctr. (bet. Golf & Old Orchard Rds.) | 847-933-9555
Schaumburg | 1901 E. Woodfield Rd. (Rte. 53) | 847-240-5600
Oak Brook | Oakbrook Center Mall | 240 Oakbrook Ctr. (Rte. 83) | 630-368-0300
www.maggianos.com

You almost "expect to see Sinatra walk in behind you" at this "1940s-esque" checkered-tablecloth chain where "monster portions" of "red-sauce" Italiana are dished out in "enjoyably hectic" surroundings; some dub it a "mixed bag", citing a "mass-production" "quantity-trumps-quality" approach, but fans tout the "crowd-pleaser" as a "big night out" for "not a lot of money."

Magnolia Cafe M *American* | 23 | 20 | 20 | $39

Ravenswood | 1224 W. Wilson Ave. (Magnolia Ave.) | 773-728-8785 | www.magnoliacafeuptown.com

"Sophisticated yet approachable", this New American "neighborhood gem" in Ravenswood serves "succulent" "gourmet" fare, "with regular changes to the [seasonal] menu" and "without the pretentious surroundings"; though some say it's "not unique enough to travel to", for locals it's "warm and inviting" and makes you "feel like you're dining at your best friend's house."

Maiz M⇗ *Mexican* | ∇ 23 | 18 | 21 | $23

Humboldt Park | 1041 N. California Ave. (2 blocks south of Division St.) | 773-276-3149

This latest incarnation of Carlos Reyna's super-casual cantina in Humboldt Park pleases with "tasty and unique *antojitos*" ("Mexican-style tapas"), "dynamite" margaritas and "sinful corn-on-the-cob covered with cheese"; its "low prices" are almost as authentic as the south-of-the-border eats, enjoyed amid "simple decor" marked by "warm colors" and a "great patio in the summer"; N.B. they don't accept reservations.

Mama Desta's Red Sea *Ethiopian* | ∇ 21 | 10 | 20 | $20

Lakeview | 3216 N. Clark St. (Belmont Ave.) | 773-935-7561

For almost 25 years, this no-reservations Lakeview standby has been dishing out "authentic Ethiopian dining" in the "traditional" "family style"; "go with a bunch of people and order different items to share", and don't be scared off by the low-scoring decor or "no silverware" custom: an "extremely friendly staff will show you how to eat with your hands."

Mambo Grill ⊠ *Nuevo Latino* | 20 | 15 | 18 | $30

River North | 412 N. Clark St. (bet. Hubbard & Kinzie Sts.) | 312-467-9797 | www.mambogrill.com

Amigos of this "low-key" River North Nuevo Latino praise the "tasty" cuisine, "great happy-hour specials" and "helpful" staff; disappointed dancers, however, say the "cramped" space is "not for someone claustrophobic" (though there's sidewalk seating in season), service can be "spacey" and the "menu reads better than the food tastes" – though with so many "inventive" cocktails on offer, some surmise "food is not the focus here."

Manny's *Deli* | 23 | 8 | 15 | $17

South Loop | 1141 S. Jefferson St. (Roosevelt Rd.) | 312-939-2855 ⊠
Southwest Side | Midway Int'l Airport | 5700 S. Cicero Ave. (55th St.) | 773-948-6300
www.mannysdeli.com

"The local color is laid on as thick as the corned beef" at this beloved South Loop breakfast-and-lunch "institution" (and its Southwest Side franchise), an "anachronistic" "steam-table cafeteria, with sand-wiches made to order", peopled "by old-timers, new wavers, tourists and politicians" enjoying a taste of "true Chicago" – so "just yell out what you want" to the "countermen, who are caricatures of them-selves"; N.B. they now serve dinner and alcohol, and take credit cards.

Marché French
22 | 25 | 22 | $48

Market District | 833 W. Randolph St. (Green St.) | 312-226-8399 | www.marche-chicago.com

This Market District anchor's "over-the-top" "French carnival" vibe with "pumping music" and "whimsical decor" is matched by "consis-tently creative" "riffs on bistro fare" delivered by "energetic" servers; even those who feel the "food never wows" admit that "it will always do", so it's "still a favorite after many years and much competition."

Margie's Candies American
22 | 15 | 18 | $11

Bucktown | 1960 N. Western Ave. (Armitage Ave.) | 773-384-1035 ◑
Ravenswood | 1813 W. Montrose Ave. (Ravenswood Ave.) | 773-348-0400

Though "you can eat lunch or dinner" here, "it's really about the ice cream" at this Bucktown American "classic" "with an old-fashioned parlor feel", "disabled table jukeboxes" and "staffers in bow ties and vests", where "sundaes as big as your head" topped "with home-made caramel and fudge sauce" are served in "giant seashell bowls" (and don't forget to take home some "hand-dipped chocolates"); P.S. sweet-toothers who gripe that "they haven't updated" the orig-inal in years may want to check out the newer Ravenswood location.

Marigold Ⓜ Indian
23 | 21 | 20 | $37

Uptown | 4832 N. Broadway (W. Lawrence Ave.) | 773-293-4653 | www.marigoldrestaurant.com

"Upscale" and "cutting-edge", this Uptowner has supporters "swear-ing off Devon Avenue" in favor of its "imaginative" Indian fusion with "unusual spicing" set against "understated modern decor" and a "trendy bar/lounge", all hidden behind a "deceptive storefront" with no "curb appeal"; purists, however, prefer the "cheaper" standard bearers where there's less "loud music and fussy presentation."

NEW Maya Del Sol Nuevo Latino
▽ 21 | 23 | 22 | $29

Oak Park | 144 S. Oak Park Ave. (bet. Pleasant St. & South Blvd.) | 708-358-9800 | www.mayadelsol.com

Oak Park's "upscale" "new hot spot" puts forth "innovative and yummy" Nuevo Latino dishes that "combine different styles and fla-vors" alongside "good cocktails", even if some feel they're "trying too hard" and "need to pick a specialty"; "live music" on Friday nights enlivens the "trendy" space staffed by "attentive" servers.

May Street Market Ⓩ American
23 | 19 | 21 | $50

West Loop | 1132 W. Grand Ave. (May St.) | 312-421-5547 | www.maystreetmarket.com

"Out of the way" in the West Loop, this "lucky find" offers "serious plates" of "creative" New American dishes showcasing "great fla-vors and fresh, local ingredients"; a few regulars report "inconsistent" food, though, and note that the "decibel rating" inside its modern space hovers near that of "an airport runway."

Maza *Mideastern*   23 | 16 | 20 | $30

Lincoln Park | 2748 N. Lincoln Ave. (Diversey Pkwy.) | 773-929-9600 | www.mazarestaurant.net

This "dreamy" Lincoln Park place for Middle Eastern meze ("a million little plates" of "excellent appetizers", including lots of veggie options) is "family-owned and -operated with Lebanese graciousness"; blessed with a "homey", "old-world feel" and an "eager-to-please staff", it's "just what you want in a neighborhood restaurant" – no wonder regulars "would eat here every night."

Z McCormick & Schmick's *Seafood*   21 | 20 | 21 | $43

Loop | 1 E. Wacker Dr. (bet. State St. & Wabash Ave.) | 312-923-7226

Gold Coast | 41 E. Chestnut St. (Rush St.) | 312-397-9500

NEW Skokie | Westfield Old Orchard | 4999 Old Orchard Ctr. (bet. Old Orchard Rd. & Skokie Blvd.) | 847-763-9811

NEW Schaumburg | 1140 E. Higgins Rd. (bet. Del Lago Dr. & National Pkwy.) | 847-517-1616

NEW Oak Brook | 3001 Butterfield Rd. (Meyers Dr.) | 630-571-3700 www.mccormickandschmicks.com

Its "endless menu" that "changes daily depending on what's freshly caught" reels folks into this "elevated seafood" chain where the quality is "high", the fish "refreshing" and the scene "clubby"; some protest the "kind-of-costly" tabs, but other's argue that if you have an "expense account" handy, the "unsurpassed variety" can't be beat.

Medici on 57th *American*   17 | 15 | 15 | $17

Hyde Park | 1327 E. 57th St. (bet. Kenwood & Kimbark Aves.) | 773-667-7394

A sentimental "favorite" of South-Siders, this "classic Hyde Park" "college hangout" and BYO comforts colleagues with "consistent" Traditional American fare, including "juicy burgers", "very good pizza" and "nice" "breads baked next door", all dished up in a "dark", "traditional grunge" "coffeehouse atmosphere" where it's "fun to read the writing on the walls"; P.S. "the patio garden is an oasis."

Meiji Z *Japanese*   25 | 23 | 23 | $47

West Loop | 623 W. Randolph St. (bet. Desplaines & Jefferson Sts.) | 312-887-9999 | www.meijirestaurant.com

"One of the most inventive sushi restaurants" around, this "new-wave" West Looper features "fabulous combinations of ingredients you would never imagine", enhanced by "fresh wasabi" that gives the rolls "extra kick"; it ends up being a "fair bit pricier" than usual, and some call the "intimate" setting somewhat "stark."

Melting Pot *Fondue*   19 | 18 | 20 | $45

River North | Millennium Center Towers | 609 N. Dearborn St. (bet. Ohio & Ontario Sts.) | 312-573-0011 ☻

Buffalo Grove | 1205 W. Dundee Rd. (Arlington Heights Rd.) | 847-342-6022

(continued)

(continued)

Melting Pot

Schaumburg | 255 W. Golf Rd. (bet. Higgins & Roselle Rds.) | 847-843-8970

Oakbrook Terrace | 17 W. 633 Roosevelt Rd. (Summit Rd.) | 630-495-5778
www.meltingpot.com

"Change-of-pace" mavens and "do-it-yourself" types are fond of this "novel" fondue franchise for its "interactive" approach, i.e. the chance to "cook your own" "tasty" dinner; the "long, slow meals" make it appropriate for "first dates" or "large crowds" who don't mind tariffs that can add up to "a lot of money."

NEW Mercat a la Planxa *Spanish*   - | - | - | M

South Loop | Blackstone Hotel | 638 S. Michigan Ave. (Balbo Ave.) | 312-765-0524 | www.mercatchicago.com

Chef Jose Garces (Philly's Amada and Tinto) serves classic Catalan tapas and *a la planxa* (grilled-to-order) seafood and steaks from an open kitchen in the South Loop's renovated Blackstone Hotel; the hip setting channels Barcelona with a winding central staircase, Gaudí-esque tile mosaics and views of Lake Michigan – a mood further fueled by seasonal sangrias and 40 wines by the bottle or glass.

Merle's Smokehouse *BBQ*   19 | 16 | 18 | $25

Evanston | 1727 Benson Ave. (Church St.) | 847-475-7766 | www.merlesbbq.com

Gluttons go for a "great meaty gnaw" at this "funky" North Suburban "palace of BBQ" that "delivers" "very good" "saliva-inducing" eats "with lots of options on the ribs preparation, sauces and sides", all served by a "friendly staff" in "relaxed", "barnlike" digs "that the college students love and adults enjoy" (there's also delivery or carryout); a rack of "unimpressed" raters, though, judges it "just average."

Merlo *Italian*   24 | 20 | 21 | $50

Gold Coast | 16 W. Maple St. (bet. Dearborn & State Sts.) | 312-335-8200

Lincoln Park | 2638 N. Lincoln Ave. (Wrightwood Ave.) | 773-529-0747
www.merlochicago.com

An "ever-changing menu" of "sophisticated" "totally authentic" Bolognese fare – "you can tell [the pasta] was just handmade" – with "authentic sauces" and "a quality wine list" are served in "charming, staid" settings to the tune of "opera music", making for "a special evening out" at this Northern Italian duo (in Lincoln Park and the Gold Coast); diners who "were expecting more", however, aver that it can be "expensive" and the "vibe is a little pretentious."

Mesón Sabika *Spanish*   24 | 23 | 21 | $36

Naperville | 1025 Aurora Ave. (east of West St.) | 630-983-3000 | www.mesonsabika.com

Tapas Valencia *Spanish*

Bloomingdale | 241 E. Lake St. (Lakeview Dr.) | 630-582-1500 | www.tapasvalencia.com

Experience a "garlic infusion" at this No. 1 rated tapas twosome purveying a "wonderful variety" of "real" Spanish small plates, including "plenty of vegetarian" bites, along with "wonderful Spanish wines"; in the ambiance department, it's hard for the Bloomingdale satellite to compete with the Naperville flagship's "charming" "historic manor" setting and "romantic" "outdoor patio" (plus, the original offers a "great Sunday brunch"); N.B. onetime sib Tapas Gitana is now separately owned.

☑ M. Henry Ⓜ American

26 | 21 | 21 | $17

Andersonville | 5707 N. Clark St. (Hollywood Ave.) | 773-561-1600 | www.mhenry.net

"Admit it, your mother never offered the caliber breakfast" that you get at this "funky" Andersonville BYO breakfast-brunch-and-luncher (no dinner, alas) meting out "veggie-centric" New American noshes rife with "novel pairings" of "often organic and/or local" ingredients; an "accommodating staff" and "quirky architectural decor" featuring "hanging windows" add to the appeal, as does its "bustling", "kid-friendly" vibe, so it's no wonder there's "always a line on the weekends" (though "they've expanded to accommodate the large crowds").

Mia Francesca Italian

25 | 19 | 21 | $35

Lakeview | 3311 N. Clark St. (School St.) | 773-281-3310 | www.miafrancesca.com

The mother of Francesca's "local chain" gang, this "crowded", "bohemian" Lakeview Italian has been "consistent for 15 years" with an "ever-changing menu" of "creative dishes with simple fresh ingredients", "upscale vibe", "affordable prices" and "funky staff" that's "quick" and "approachable"; "happy sardines" tolerate the "close-together" tables and "loud" acoustics, though peace-niks "try to eat in the garden, weather permitting."

☑ Michael ◑Ⓜ French

26 | 22 | 25 | $60

Winnetka | 64 Green Bay Rd. (Winnetka Ave.) | 847-441-3100 | www.restaurantmichael.com

Michael Lachowicz offers "adult dining with no attitude" at this "romantic" New French in Winnetka purveying "flavorful" fare that's "not the usual" (including a "to-die-for" foie gras appetizer), "decadent desserts" and a wine list "full of surprises"; fans call the expensive prices "reasonable" given the quality, and laud the "unstuffy but elegant" room (a trifle "too conservative" to some) and "professional", "friendly" service that's gotten a big ratings boost since the last Survey.

Mike Ditka's Steak

22 | 21 | 21 | $47

Gold Coast | Tremont Hotel | 100 E. Chestnut St. (Rush St.) | 312-587-8989

NEW Oakbrook Terrace | 2 Mid America Plaza, Ste. 100 (bet. 16th & 22nd Sts.) | 630-572-2200 ⚿Ⓜ
www.mikeditkaschicago.com

"Iron Mike's" "macho steak place" is a Gold Coast "must-stop for football fans" seeking "massive quantities" of "well-prepared meat" (including "worth-the-hype" pork chops and burgers), "high-class junk food" and "killer Bloody Marys"; the space is filled with "tourists", "Chicago Bears memorabilia" and "flat-screen TVs to monitor the game" (though thanks to the "smoking ban", no more cigar bar), but on the downside, a cadre of cost-conscious consumers "can't say the price of the food matches the quality"; N.B. the recent Oakbrook Terrace addition is unrated.

Milk & Honey *American*   22 | 16 | 15 | $16

Wicker Park | 1920 W. Division St. (bet. Damen & Wolcott Aves.) | 773-395-9434 | www.milkandhoneycafe.com

Expect New American food that's "particularly fresh" at this "cutie" of a Wicker Parker, where the morning meal is "better than breakfast in bed" (they mix "amazing" "granola you might dream about") and the "fantastic sandwiches" and "interesting salads" make for a "lovely lunch" – "whether you sit indoors or out"; "only counter orders are taken", and the "lines on weekends are out the door", but boosters who believe it's "worth it" ("if you can stand the cell phone and stroller" crowd) lament that "they're not open late enough."

Miller's Pub ◑ *Pub Food*   18 | 16 | 19 | $25

Loop | 134 S. Wabash Ave. (bet. Adams & Monroe Sts.) | 312-263-4988 | www.millerspub.com

A "time-tested" Loop "landmark", this "true Old Chicago" "holdout" is a "classic watering hole" "with celebrity pictures on the walls" and customers representing "a cross-section of humanity"; the "old-fashioned" American eats are "not haute cuisine", but they're "plain, good food" at a "bargain" price, and the "rough-around-the-edges but real" space is "bustling with activity at all hours" (the bar only closes between 4 and 10 AM); still, sterner surveyors deem it "dreary" and think "the menu, staff and decor all need an upgrade."

Minnies ◑ *American*   17 | 17 | 17 | $19

Lincoln Park | 1969 N. Halsted St. (Armitage Ave.) | 312-943-9900 | www.minnies.com

The "novelty" of this "darn cute" diminutive Lincoln Park "concept" cafe is that it proffers "small"-sized "samplings" of "tasty" Traditional American "tidbits" like "sandwiches and burgers" along with "airplane-sized liquor bottles" poured in a "'50s diner"-esque setting; pleased parents peg it a "perfect place for pre-adolescent and adolescent children", but jaded jurists call it a "one-note" "gimmick" offering "so-so" "mini food at a maxi price."

Mirabell 🅩 *German*   ▽ 21 | 16 | 24 | $30

Northwest Side | 3454 W. Addison St. (bet. Kimball & St. Louis Aves.) | 773-463-1962 | www.mirabellrestaurant.com

"Hearty", "stick-to-your-ribs" German vittles are the "star" at this "historic" Northwest Side "favorite" featuring "generous portions", a "great display of beer steins" and "friendly service" in traditional costume; "insist on sitting in the main dining room" to be immersed in the "authentic" atmosphere that, to some surveyors, is like "dining in a Hummel figurine."

	FOOD	DECOR	SERVICE	COST

Mirai Sushi ⊠ *Japanese* — 25 | 20 | 20 | $51

Wicker Park | 2020 W. Division St. (Damen Ave.) |
773-862-8500

"Amazing" "high-end" raw fish that "glides down your throat like
butter", whether in sashimi or "balanced" "well-presented" maki,
makes this Wicker Parker a "worth-it" "splurge" "for the hard-core
sushi fan"; the vibe is "low-key" if somewhat "sterile" "downstairs",
and "swank upstairs", where the "pretty people" quaff "carefully
crafted cocktails"; some suggest the service could be more "orga-
nized", and those who mention the "menu hasn't changed in years"
might want to "order their specials to try new things."

Miramar Bistro *French* — 20 | 19 | 19 | $39

Highwood | 301 Waukegan Ave. (Highwood Ave.) | 847-433-1078 |
www.miramarbistro.com

Fans of Gabriel Viti (Gabriel's) say "Highwood is hotter than ever"
thanks to this "hopping" French-ster "with a Cuban accent" and its
"very good" "take on bistro fare", "nice wine list (for a casual restaurant)", "well-made mojitos" and "great people-watching"; some say
they "expected more" and hint that "service can be a little overbear-
ing", but all agree the "outdoor seating is wonderful."

NEW Miss Asia ⊠Ⓜ *Pan-Asian* — - | - | - | I

Lakeview | 434 W. Diversey Pkwy. (bet. Pine Grove Ave. & Sheridan Rd.) |
773-248-3999

Culinary wanderlust drives this Lakeview Pan-Asian whose menu
travels extensively through Thailand and touches on the Pacific Rim
and elsewhere; the casual-chic neighborhood setting has a serene
feel enhanced by Buddhist artwork and Asian artifacts, and the mellow mood is matched by bargain prices and a BYO policy.

Mitchell's Fish Market *Seafood* — 21 | 19 | 19 | $38

Glenview | Glenview Town Ctr. | 2601 Navy Blvd. (Patriot Blvd.) |
847-729-3663 | www.mitchellsfishmarket.com

A "large menu" of "fresh fish with simple preparations" lures a
school of seafood lovers to this North Suburban chain outpost with
an "upscale nautical theme" that's "nice for business or social"
gatherings, even if doubters deem it "not terribly inspiring" with "inconsistent service and quality"; fin-fans who find it "pricey" prefer
to "go during luncheon hours" for the "same quality" at a "better
price than dinner."

Mity Nice Grill *American* — 17 | 15 | 19 | $29

Streeterville | Water Tower Pl. | 835 N. Michigan Ave., Mezzanine level
(bet. Chestnut & Pearson Sts.) | 312-335-4745 | www.leye.com

"Nicer than a diner but still affordable", this "oasis" "in the hubbub
of Water Tower Place" dishes out "dependable" Traditional
American "comfort food" and "tiny desserts" that "just hit the spot"
"for only one dollar"; the "welcoming staff" and "cozy" "supper-club
atmosphere" make it a "great place to relax" (if you can "find" it
"hidden away" "in back of [the] food court"), though a share of
shoppers takes its measure as "mighty average."

	FOOD	DECOR	SERVICE	COST

Mizu Yakitori & Sushi Lounge *Japanese* ▽ 27 | 21 | 22 | $34

Old Town | 315 W. North Ave. (N. Park Ave.) | 312-951-8880

"The yakitori make a great meal by themselves", but that would mean missing out on the "exceptional" "affordable" sushi at this Old Town "find" issuing some of "the best Japanese food around"; with "lovely" servers, a setting that's "closer to an upscale lounge than your standard" and "tasty martinis" and wines, it's no surprise surveyors "wish this spot would catch on."

⊿ mk *American* 26 | 24 | 24 | $68

Near North | 868 N. Franklin St. (bet. Chestnut & Locust Sts.) | 312-482-9179 | www.mkchicago.com

"mk stands for 'marvelous kitchen'" say fans of Michael Kornick's namesake "vibrant", "sexy" Near North New American that's becoming a "legend" for its "right-on" cuisine with an "innovative kick" – including the "consistently amazing tasting menu", "incredible desserts" and "truffle fries" that "can replace oysters as an aphrodisiac"; service is "attentive yet unobtrusive" (though some sense a whiff of "attitude"), and the "upscale loft environment" ("in an old paint factory") fosters "great people-watching"; P.S. "try for a table upstairs" where the noise is less "deafening" than below.

⊿ Mon Ami Gabi *French* 22 | 22 | 21 | $43

Lincoln Park | Belden-Stratford Hotel | 2300 N. Lincoln Park W. (Belden Ave.) | 773-348-8886

Oak Brook | Oakbrook Center Mall | 260 Oakbrook Ctr. (Rte. 83) | 630-472-1900

www.monamigabi.com

With outposts in Lincoln Park and Oak Brook, this "really solid" Lettuce Entertain You chain of "enjoyable" French bistros offers a taste of "Paris on the prairie" in the form of "classic preparations" that cost "not a lot of francs"; foes fault them for being "faux" and "not exceptional", but for most they're "steady" and "dependable" for a "date" or "dinner with a group of friends", though the "noise level makes that romantic tête-à-tête a shout-a-shout."

Montarra Ⓜ *American* ▽ 25 | 25 | 24 | $42

Algonquin | 1491 S. Randall Rd. (County Line Rd.) | 847-458-0505 | www.montarra.com

A "top-notch" array of "unusual" New American fare, including "to-die-for" steaks, wins accolades for this Northwest Suburban strip-mall surprise whose admirers also cite its "very good service"; as for the "comfortable" yet "elegant" "modern decor", the "curtains and Italian glass" add a "mystic" touch.

Moon Palace *Chinese* ▽ 24 | 13 | 19 | $19

Chinatown | 216 W. Cermak Rd. (Wentworth Ave.) | 312-225-4081

Shanghai-ed surveyors support this "longtime favorite" (since 1960) Chinatown "cornerstone" as a "great place for a family or business dinner" with offerings "for those non-adventurous types" as well as "more exotic dishes" too; the "decor is a bit shabby", but

	FOOD	DECOR	SERVICE	COST

at least it's "comfortable", "friendly" and "reasonably priced", and there's a "full bar."

☑ Morton's The Steakhouse *Steak* | 26 | 21 | 24 | $63 |

Loop | 65 E. Wacker Pl. (bet. Michigan & Wabash Aves.) | 312-201-0410
Gold Coast | Newberry Plaza | 1050 N. State St. (Maple St.) | 312-266-4820
Rosemont | 9525 Bryn Mawr Ave. (River Rd.) | 847-678-5155
Northbrook | 699 Skokie Blvd. (Dundee Rd.) | 847-205-5111
Schaumburg | 1470 McConnor Pkwy. (Meacham Rd.) | 847-413-8771
Westchester | 1 Westbrook Corporate Ctr. (22nd St.) | 708-562-7000
www.mortons.com

Some of the "best steak in town" is still served at the late Arnie Morton's Chicago "institution" (the Gold Coast "original" with "speakeasy atmosphere" spawned the national chain) where "dry-aged prime beef" meets an "extensive wine list" in a "men's club" milieu filled with "lots of suits" and "executive"-level service; some warn that "everything is à la carte, so the total creeps up on you", while others figure "you've seen one, you've seen them all"; P.S. "happy hour is a draw", and the Loop locale is an "excellent power-lunch option."

Moto ☒Ⓜ *Eclectic* | 25 | 22 | 26 | $150 |

Market District | 945 W. Fulton Mkt. (Sangamon St.) | 312-491-0058 | www.motorestaurant.com

It's like "having Willy Wonka cook you a 10-course meal" say admirers of Homaro Cantu's "hip", "hyper-modern" Market District "enclave" "for the adventurous" eater, combining "cutting-edge technology and molecular gastronomy" in spendy, Eclectic "small-course" tasting meals with "wild presentations" that include an "edible menu" and "a lot of liquid nitrogen"; the servers are "well-versed in the cuisine", and while its "shock value" "impresses" enthusiasts as "intriguing, interesting and inviting", others call it "more cool than genuinely delicious."

Mr. Beef ☒⊄ *Sandwiches* | 24 | 5 | 14 | $10 |

River North | 666 N. Orleans St. (bet. Erie & Huron Sts.) | 312-337-8500

"Digging in" to the "hot, delicious Italian beef" at this cash-only River North sandwich "dive" is "a Chicago tradition", as are the "surly guys behind the counter" and the "picnic tables" peopled by "cops, workers and execs"; as for "decor – who needs it?" ask insiders, considering you can just "close [your] eyes and feel the juice dripping down [your] arm"; P.S. rumor has it it's "Jay Leno's must-stop when in" town.

Mrs. Murphy & Sons Irish Bistro Ⓜ *Irish* | 18 | 23 | 20 | $35 |

North Center/St. Ben's | 3905 N. Lincoln Ave. (Byron St.) | 773-248-3905 | www.irishbistro.com

Set "in a converted funeral home" in North Center, this surprisingly "lovely" contemporary Irish eatery boasts a "beautiful" interior with bars handmade in Ireland and two fireplaces; lauders love the "great" menu featuring upscale "twists on pub fare", which is paired with tap pours of Gaelic and Belgian brews plus a big native whiskey selection, though voting vacillates on the service.

	FOOD	DECOR	SERVICE	COST

Mrs. Park's Tavern ● *American* — 16 | 16 | 17 | $31

Streeterville | Hilton Guest Suites | 198 E. Delaware Pl. (Michigan Ave.) |
312-280-8882

A "good Streeterville option" for "comforting" Traditional American eats (as well as offerings that are more "creative, but not bizarre"), this "hotel eatery [in the Hilton Guest Suites] is actually popular with locals as well as conventioneers" and a "pleasant" "spot to eat outside in the summer", though faultfinders feel the "fair food" "fails to wow."

Mt. Everest Restaurant *Indian* — 22 | 16 | 18 | $23

Evanston | 630 Church St. (bet. Chicago & Orrington Aves.) |
847-491-1069 | www.mteverestrestaurant.com

Goat is the signature dish at this "cheap", "offbeat" Evanston eatery offering a "nice variety" of Indian and "unusual Nepalese food" that can be "set to your heat level"; "fast, attentive service" works the "spacious, noisy" setting where Northwestern students and other bargain-hunters appreciate the "all-you-can-eat daily lunch buffet."

Mundial Cocina Mestiza *Mexican* — ▽ 24 | 11 | 17 | $29

University Village | 1640 W. 18th St. (bet. S. Marshfield Ave. &
S. Paulina St.) | 312-491-9908

Set in a casual Pilsen "storefront", this Mexican BYO turns out "intriguing", "almost gourmet" selections that are "tasty, tasty, tasty" and "different from the rest" of the area's offerings; despite quarters that are "not warm or inviting", optimists opine it's "too good to stay unknown."

My Pie Pizza *Pizza* — 20 | 11 | 17 | $17

Bucktown | 2010 N. Damen Ave. (Armitage Ave.) |
773-929-3380
Bucktown | 2417 N. Clark St. (Fullerton Pkwy.) | 773-394-6900
www.lilguysandwich.com

"Classic, crispy, gooey thin-crust" and "great deep-dish" "pizza is served in the pan so it stays hot at the table" at this pair of "old-school" Bucktown parlors where you can also indulge in "little sandwiches" and a "very good" salad bar; the "dark", "kitschy, comfy '70s decor" at the original "hasn't changed in [almost] 30 years" (though "the fireplace is a grand thing on a cold night"), while the North Clark offshoot is BYO with limited seating.

Myron & Phil's Steakhouse Ⓜ *Steak* — 22 | 15 | 21 | $40

Lincolnwood | 3900 W. Devon Ave. (Springfield Ave.) | 847-677-6663 |
www.myronandphils.com

"You never leave hungry" from this Lincolnwood "family-owned" "flashback", an "old-fashioned" steakhouse where "artery-unfriendly" entrees come with "complimentary" chopped liver, "relishes, salad and potato" ("oy, bubbie, such a place!"); a "caring", "veteran staff" serves a crowd sporting "lots of blue hair" amid "'70s decor" enlivened by Thursday–Sunday night piano music, monthly karaoke, patio seating and plasma TVs at the bar.

NEW Mythos M *Greek*

— | — | — | M

Lakeview | 2030-32 W. Montrose Ave. (Seeley Ave.) | 773-334-2000 | www.mythoschicago.com

"Two Greek sisters" are at the helm of this "little" Lakeview BYO that's more "upscale" than its Greektown competition and offers ambitious entrees and housemade pastries; the "exuberant" service can be "uneven" inside its double-storefront space, which is done up in dusty blue and peach with white tablecloths, candles, mosaics and stone floors, plus seasonal sidewalk seating.

Nacional 27 Z *Nuevo Latino*

23 | 24 | 21 | $47

River North | 325 W. Huron St. (Orleans St.) | 312-664-2727 | www.nacional27.net

"Cocktails, flavors, dancing . . . oh my!" coo compadres of this "sexy", "exciting" "River North treasure" that's "like a night at the Copa but with great food" in the form of "superbly seasoned and presented" provender that packs in a "variety of Latin influences" (try the "tasty small plates" and "steal of a lunch"); service that ranges from "efficient and professional" to "merely competent" is overshadowed by the "superb drinks" and "seductive" space, which "becomes a nightclub" after 11 PM on weekends; N.B. the Food score does not reflect the departure of chef Randy Zweiban.

Naha Z *American*

25 | 23 | 23 | $63

River North | 500 N. Clark St. (Illinois St.) | 312-321-6242 | www.naha-chicago.com

Carrie Nahabedian's "innovative fusion" of American cuisine with Mediterranean flair finds favor with "foodies" for its "clean" flavors and "locally sourced ingredients" (while on the "pricey" side, at least "you don't need a second mortgage"); generally "attentive service" and a "well-thought-out wine list" enhance this "detail-oriented" River North dining destination done in "cool, sleek lines and placid colors", and though a few report letdowns, they're in the minority; P.S. "power-lunch"-ers love the "fantastic burgers."

Nancy's Original Stuffed Pizza *Pizza*

22 | 10 | 16 | $17

Lakeview | 2930 N. Broadway St. (Wellington Ave.) | 773-883-1977 ●
Northwest Side | 3970 N. Elston Ave. (Irving Park Rd.) | 773-267-8182 ⌀
Niles | 8706 W. Golf Rd. (Milwaukee Ave.) | 847-824-8183
Elmhurst | 940 N. York St. (Grand Ave.) | 630-834-4374
www.nancyspizza.com

"Zesty sauce is slathered on top of gooey cheese and loads of toppings" to create the "delicious" stuffed pizza at this pie panoply, which also garners zealots for its "filling pasta entrees" and "good antipasto salad" – plus you can "feed your late-night cravings" at the Lakeview location; of course, since this is Chicago 'za we're talkin' about, not everyone agrees "you can't beat it."

NEW Natalino's ● *Italian*

— | — | — | M

West Town | 1523 W. Chicago Ave. (Armour St.) | 312-997-3700

This swanky-for–West Town Italian offers an *abbondanza* of moderately priced classic dishes with options aplenty for salad, pasta and

FOOD | DECOR | SERVICE | COST

chicken fans; the supper-clubby setting of toasty-warm colors and cozy booths provides a natural backdrop for sipping seasonal drink specials and wines from an Italian-influenced list; N.B. night owls can hoot till 2 AM Fridays and Saturdays.

New Three Happiness *Chinese* ▽ 20 | 13 | 17 | $20

Chinatown | 2130 S. Wentworth Ave. (Cermak Rd.) | 312-791-1228
"The carts move fast and the staff talks faster" at this "busy" Chinatown mainstay serving "great dim sum" daily, as well as traditional Cantonese cooking; it's a "good place for large groups and families", even if "the atmosphere is lacking and the service spotty"; N.B. no relation to the similarly named Three Happiness nearby.

Next Door Bistro Ⓜ⇗ *American/Italian* 22 | 14 | 20 | $34

Northbrook | 250 Skokie Blvd. (Lake Cook Rd.) | 847-272-1491
An "interesting mixture" of "very good" American (including "great roast chicken") and Italian favorites "for a remarkably low price" is the draw at this Suburban North "neighborhood" eatery that's "still good after all these years"; the sister of Francesco's Hole in the Wall, its co-owned next-door neighbor, it's always "crowded" with a "very loyal clientele" so expect to "wait" (some say it "helps to know the owner"); P.S. "bring cash."

🆕 Nia *Mediterranean* - | - | - | M

Market District | 803 W. Randolph St. (Halsted St.) | 312-226-3110
Mediterranean small plates invade the Market District at this mid-priced perch for sophisticated samplings from all over the region; the spotlight is on imported ingredients, charcuterie and cheeses – plus niceties like an olive-oil tasting and three sangrias (white, red, rose) – all served in a warmly lit, glass-faced modern storefront with mosaic-tile accents, banquette seating and a separate bar.

🄩 Niche Ⓢ Ⓜ *American* 28 | 26 | 28 | $58

Geneva | 14 S. Third St. (State St.) | 630-262-1000 | www.nichegeneva.com
"Amazingly fresh, seasonal and unique" New American cuisine "paired with awesome wines" "at all price ranges" has voters convinced that this "worthy" West Suburban "successor to 302 West" (chef-owner Jeremy Lycan, sommelier-owner Jody Richardson and most of the staff hail from that late pioneer) "rivals its big-city competition"; the service is "knowledgeable" and has a "genuine sense of caring", the dining room boasts a "beautiful urban feel" and though prices qualify as "expensive", you "don't have to break the bank."

Nick's Fishmarket Ⓢ *Seafood* 24 | 21 | 23 | $57

Loop | Bank One Plaza | 51 S. Clark St. (Monroe St.) | 312-621-0200
Rosemont | O'Hare Int'l Ctr. | 10275 W. Higgins Rd. (bet. Higgins & Mannheim Rds.) | 847-298-8200
Deerfield | 483 Lake Cook Rd. (bet. S. Pfingsten & Waukegan Rds.) | 847-412-4800
www.nicksfishmarketchicago.com
"Clubby" environs and "fresh fish" meet at this "old-boy-style" seafood trio where "discreet but constant service" sets the tone in the

"formal" confines; skeptics who find the bill of fare "boring" feel the "high prices" are "only worth it on an expense account", noting that the "best deal is in the bar during happy hour"; P.S. lamenters of the Loop locale's "cold atmosphere" will appreciate that they've lightened it up.

N9ne 🅱 *Seafood/Steak*   24 | 25 | 21 | $58

Loop | 440 W. Randolph St. (Canal St.) | 312-575-9900 | www.n9ne.com
This "splashy" "modern steakhouse" that's "not just a scene" surprises surveyors with its "unique" meat and seafood spread, "root beer floats" and "romantic s'mores" "that you cook yourself"; add in an "ultratrendy" Loop setting full of "beautiful people", and you get "cloud nine" for a "date or any celebration" – though some critics call the service "only satisfactory"; P.S. "if you're still raring to go, there's a terrific nightclub [The Ghost Bar] upstairs."

Niu Japanese   ▽ 21 | 22 | 19 | $39
Fusion Lounge ◑ *Asian Fusion*

Streeterville | 332 E. Illinois St. (bet. Columbus Dr. & McClurg Ct.) | 312-527-2888 | www.niusushi.com
"Sushi, Japanese classics" and other Asian fare with "innovative fusion spins" are the draw at this "classy", "decently priced" Streeterville spot serving up "zany" "specialty rolls" that represent a "unique combination of epicurean feast and huge portions"; go for a "low-key meal before or after a movie" or even "for a night out", since they have "yummy drinks", though no one raves about the service.

Ⓩ NoMI *French*   26 | 28 | 26 | $78

Gold Coast | Park Hyatt Chicago | 800 N. Michigan Ave. (Chicago Ave.) | 312-239-4030 | www.nomirestaurant.com
Top Decor honors go once again to this "swoon-worthy", "sophisticated" Gold Coast slice of "heaven", prized as much for its "majestic" Water Tower view as for its "refined", "elegant" New French cuisine, sushi station with its own chef's table and "standout" 1,500-bottle wine list; the "calm" setting with "well-spaced tables" is home to "superb service that's personal but not abrasive" – in short, it's a "great place to propose", if you can swallow the "epic bill"; P.S. the weekend brunch, "swank" bar menu and "rooftop" "dining in the summer" also rate raves.

Nookies *Diner*   19 | 10 | 18 | $15

Old Town | 1746 N. Wells St. (bet. Lincoln & North Aves.) | 312-337-2454
Nookies Too *Diner*
Lincoln Park | 2114 N. Halsted St. (bet. Dickens & Webster Aves.) | 773-327-1400
Nookies Tree ◑ ⇄ *Diner*
Lakeview | 3334 N. Halsted St. (Buckingham Pl.) | 773-248-9888
"Tried-and-true", this trio of Traditional Americans slings "simply great breakfasts" ("wonderful pancakes", "large omelets") "any time of the day", and "diner" lunches and dinners, all at a "good value"; despite "mixed service", they're a "favorite" "for families", and "you can always find the boys out" at the Boys Town "gaybor-

hood staple", "especially during the late night" (Too and Tree are open 24 hours on Friday and Saturday) – after which "the 'hangover helper' does not disappoint"; P.S. "get up early because the lines get long."

Noon-O-Kabab *Persian*
24 | 14 | 20 | $23

Northwest Side | 4661 N. Kedzie Ave. (Leland Ave.) | 773-279-8899 | www.noonokabab.com

This "mosaic-walled" Northwest Side "hole-in-the-wall" gives a "good introduction to Persian food" with "wonderful" "juicy kebabs", "amazing baklava", fesenjan and "primeval stews and pilafs", plus they serve beer and wine; the "big portions" are "so cheap" that some feasters "feel guilty", saying they "should pay more" for such a "splendid" "neighborhood spot."

⊠ North Pond Ⓜ *American*
25 | 26 | 24 | $62

Lincoln Park | 2610 N. Cannon Dr. (bet. Diversey & Fullerton Pkwys.) | 773-477-5845 | www.northpondrestaurant.com

There's a "1920s-Chicago" feel to its setting inside a "former ice rink warming house", but Bruce Sherman's "über-fresh", "exquisite 21st-century sustainable cuisine" ("including game" and "excellent Sunday brunch") is decidedly modern at this "special", "hard-to-find" Lincoln Park New American where the "Arts and Crafts decor" "oozes rustic luxury"; though nitpickers perceive it as "pretentious" and suggest "take the in-laws and make them pay" the "dear" price, most can't find fault with the "engaging service" and "astonishing" "ground-level view of the city and park."

Nosh *Eclectic*
▽ 24 | 17 | 20 | $19

Geneva | 211 James St. (3rd St.) | 630-845-1570

They "work for the customer" at this "local secret" in West Suburban Geneva with "excellent", "interesting twists" on Eclectic "breakfast/lunch" "food that you won't make at home" (e.g. "hot chocolate French toast stuffed with marshmallow fluff"), matched by a short wine list and fruity nonalcoholic drinks; the setting is "bright" with a retro diner-counter option, and its "new patio is a nice addition."

𝗡𝗘𝗪 NXXT Restaurant & Bar *American*
- | - | - | M

Humboldt Park | 2700 W. Chicago Ave. (Washtenaw Ave.) | 773-489-6998 | www.nxxtchicago.com

Upscale American comfort food is served with a large selection of beer (including a half-dozen micros on tap) and domestic wines plus a handful of culinary cocktails (lavender margarita, lemon-basil martini) at this ultramodern, bi-level Humboldt Park newcomer that's loft-y upstairs and loungey down; a corner location and big windows give passersby a 'fishbowl' view of the scene that unfolds around the prominent white-marble bar.

Oak Tree *American*
16 | 11 | 15 | $21

Gold Coast | Bloomingdale's Bldg. | 900 N. Michigan Ave., 6th fl. (bet. Delaware Pl. & Walton St.) | 312-751-1988

Gold Coasters hit this American "respite" "hidden" in 900 North Michigan for "breakfast or lunch", "meeting friends or family" or when they're "hungry but don't want to get too far away from the shopping"; its "dependable" eats rate "a little better than diner food" ("everything from matzo ball soup to a tasty shrimp salad") in "a little better than diner atmosphere" – just "don't expect a little better service"; P.S. "ask for the tables with a view."

☑ Oceanique ☒ *French/Seafood*   26 | 20 | 23 | $60

Evanston | 505 Main St. (bet. Chicago & Hinman Aves.) | 847-864-3435 | www.oceanique.com

Coming up on 20 years, this "romantic" New French once again totes up "tops for seafood" scores thanks to its "stellar preparation and ingredients" (its "meats are good too", and they still serve foie gras) and "outstanding" wines, "especially the reserve collection"; so "do not be deterred by the storefront" say devotees of this "safe harbor" in the Northern Suburbs, even if the service can occasionally be "erratic" and tabs "very expensive"; N.B. there's a weeknight prix fixe and seasonal sidewalk seating.

O'Famé *Pizza*   19 | 12 | 16 | $22

Lincoln Park | 4159 N. Western Ave. (Halsted St.) | 773-929-5111 | www.ofame.com

"Both the thick and thin pizza", as well as "their signature salad", are "great" at this "friendly" and "unpretentious" Lincoln Park parlor with "fair prices" and "efficient service"; "everything else is pretty average", but at least the staff knows how to handle "groups and kids", making it a "good-in-'hood choice" – and "delivery is a plus"; N.B. the Decor score does not reflect its post-Survey move to Western Avenue.

Old Jerusalem *Mideastern*   19 | 7 | 15 | $14

Old Town | 1411 N. Wells St. (bet. North Ave. & Schiller St.) | 312-944-0459 | www.oldjerusalemrestaurant.com

Some of "the best cheap food" in town is the "great Middle Eastern grub" – such as "yummy falafel" and "melt-in-your-mouth shawarma" – at this "laid-back" Old Town BYO that's been in business for three decades; the "simple" "small storefront" space is "friendly" and "family-run", but it's "not a date place, dude" (possibly why many consider it "great for delivery").

🆕 Old Town Brasserie   24 | 21 | 20 | $56
Market ☒ *French*

Old Town | 1209 N. Wells St. (Division St.) | 312-943-3000 | www.oldtownbrasserie.com

Veteran restaurateur Bob Djahanguiri teams up with chef Roland Liccioni (ex Le Francais, Les Nomades) at this "beautifully appointed" Old Town "new kid on the block" where the "gourmet" French cookery includes many of the toque's former signature dishes; a faction feels it's "not worth the high price" considering the "bistro feel" and sometimes "shaky" service, while others opine it's a "value" given the provender's "pedigree"; P.S. "you'll need a reservation" for "one of the few tables", though there's also a "large comfortable bar."

	FOOD	DECOR	SERVICE	COST

Olé Olé ● *Nuevo Latino* — 20 | 20 | 20 | $31

Andersonville | 5413 N. Clark St. (Balmoral Ave.) | 773-293-2222

"Trendy" Nuevo Latino nosh lures Andersonville eaters into this "dark, atmospheric" "split-level" space done up with "cool light fixtures and traditional Mexican music"; sippers split over "specialty drinks" like caipirinhas and margaritas ("yummy" vs. "weak"), and some suggest that while the "ceviche flights" are "excellent, the rest of the menu is so-so", as is the service.

NEW Omaggio *Italian* — ∇ 20 | 21 | 22 | $27

Evanston | 1639 Orrington Ave. (bet. Church & Davis Sts.) | 847-570-0500

A "beautiful", "casual" "addition to Downtown Evanston", this "friendly" Italian "grazing" destination, a sibling of La Petite Amelia, fares well with its "unique (but not too) menu selections"; the "comfortable space" boasts a brick oven and attached specialty store/deli, all of which has well-wishers crowing "keep up the good food and great prices."

One North ☒ *American* — 18 | 18 | 17 | $36

Loop | UBS Building | 1 N. Wacker Dr. (Madison St.) | 312-750-9700 | www.restaurants-america.com

"Cozy yet sophisticated decor", a "nice outdoor eating area" and a "convenient" locale in the Loop make this "bustling" New American a "great location for an after-work" "or pre-theater dinner" (plus there's a happenin' if very noisy lunch scene); to some, the "consistent" comestibles are "very good", but badgers deduct points for "unimaginative" fare, "spotty service" and "horrible acoustics."

one sixtyblue ☒ *French* — 25 | 23 | 24 | $65

Market District | 1400 W. Randolph St. (Ogden Ave.) | 312-850-0303 | www.onesixtyblue.com

"Charming" chef Martial Noguier's "imaginative" French preparations are "always spot-on", "using the freshest ingredients without being science-experiment weird", at this "hip, modern" "out-of-the-way" Market District alternative; a "swanky staff that is not too full of itself" can help find the "perfect wines to pair with each menu choice", and the "clean-lined", "industrial" interior comes as a "great surprise after seeing the outside of the building", which "used to be a pickle factory."

OPA Estiatorio *Greek* — 19 | 20 | 20 | $34

Vernon Hills | 950 Lakeview Pkwy. (Hawthorn Pkwy.) | 847-968-4300 | www.oparestaurant.com

"Very good Greek cuisine" "at a value", including plentiful seafood, with "wine prices" reminiscent of "what Greektown charged decades ago", lures Hellen-ophiles to this "pleasant" room in North Suburban Vernon Hills boasting "a nice patio overlooking" Bear Lake; P.S. it "can be noisy and crowded, especially on the weekends – lunch is much more sedate and comfortable."

	FOOD	DECOR	SERVICE	COST

Opera *Asian*　　　　　　　　　| 22 | 24 | 21 | $43 |

South Loop | 1301 S. Wabash Ave. (13th St.) | 312-461-0161 |
www.opera-chicago.com

"Upscale", "cross-cultural [Asian] flavors" from a menu as "varied"
as the "pierced" and "costumed" though "professional" staff ("it's
not every day that you're served by a waiter wearing pajamas")
tempt a "see-and-be-seen" crowd at this South Looper with prix fixe
options, a "lively vibe", "fabulous" decor and "huge bar"; a segment
of "disappointed" divas, however, describes the food as "overpriced
for what you get", and those who lament the "loud" acoustics recommend "reserving a vault table" for "privacy."

Orange *Eclectic*　　　　　　　| 22 | 17 | 18 | $19 |

Lakeview | 3231 N. Clark St. (Belmont Ave.) | 773-549-4400
Printer's Row | 75 W. Harrison St. (bet. Clark & Federal Sts.) |
312-447-1000

Orange on Roscoe *Eclectic*

NEW Roscoe Village | 2011 W. Roscoe St. (Damen Ave.) | 773-248-0999
www.orangebrunch.com

For "out-of-the-norm" Eclectic nourishment like "chai French
toast", "fruit sushi" and "surprisingly good orange coffee", consider these "innovative", "arty" breakfast/brunch/lunch brothers; their "funky" (if "too cute") settings are full of "friendly
service" that "struggles at times with the weekend crowds", and
tabs can inch up high "for breakfast", yet fans find them "worth
getting up early for"; N.B. the Lakeview and Printer's Row locations are BYO, while Roscoe Village has a liquor license and is open
for dinner Wednesday–Sunday.

Original Gino's East, The *Pizza*　| 21 | 15 | 17 | $21 |

River North | 633 N. Wells St. (Ontario St.) | 312-943-1124
Streeterville | 162 E. Superior St. (Michigan Ave.) | 312-266-3337
Lincoln Park | 2801 N. Lincoln Ave. (Diversey Pkwy.) | 773-327-3737
O'Hare Area | 8725 W. Higgins Rd. (bet. Cumberland & East River Rds.) |
773-444-2244
Rolling Meadows | 1321 W. Golf Rd. (Algonquin Rd.) |
847-364-6644
Orland Park | 15840 S. Harlem Ave. (159th St.) | 708-633-1300
Naperville | 1807 S. Washington St. (bet. Foxcroft & Redstart Rds.) |
630-548-9555
St. Charles | Tin Cup Pass Shopping Ctr. | 1590 E. Main St. (Tyler Rd.) |
630-513-1311
Wheaton | 315 W. Front St. (West St.) | 630-588-1010
www.ginoseast.com

Supporters "stand in line" to savor this "veritable institution's" "hot,
deep-dish Chicago-style pizza" with "that great cornmeal crust"
("and wonderful thin crust" too), swearing "even though owner-
ships keep changing, the pie still continues to be great"; though the
querulous quibble "quantity has overruled quality" and say some locations have seen better days (nostalgists note the newer spots
"lack the ambiance of the old really-original"), the "writing on the
walls" remains "quite entertaining" at the River North site.

	FOOD	DECOR	SERVICE	COST

Original Pancake House, The *American* 23 | 13 | 18 | $14

Streeterville | 22 E. Bellevue Pl. (bet. Michigan Ave. & Rush St.) | 312-642-7917

Lincoln Park | 2020 N. Lincoln Park W. (Clark St.) | 773-929-8130

Hyde Park | Village Ctr. | 1517 E. Hyde Park Blvd. (bet. 51st St. & Lake Park Blvd.) | 773-288-2323

Oak Forest | 5148 W. 159th St. (bet. Laramie & Le Claire Aves.) | 708-687-8282

Oak Park | 954 Lake St. (Forest St.) | 708-524-0955
www.originalpancakehouse.com

Walker Bros.
Original Pancake House *American*

Lincolnshire | 200 Marriott Dr. (Milwaukee Ave.) | 847-634-2220

Glenview | 1615 Waukegan Rd. (bet. Chestnut & Lake Aves.) | 847-724-0220

Highland Park | 620 Central Ave. (2nd St.) | 847-432-0660

Wilmette | 153 Green Bay Rd. (Isabella St.) | 847-251-6000

Arlington Heights | 825 W. Dundee Rd. (bet. Arlington Heights Rd. & Rte. 53) | 847-392-6600

Lake Zurich | Lake Zurich Theatre Development | 767 S. Rand Rd. (Jun Terr.) | 847-550-0006
www.walkerbrosoph.com

A "seemingly endless variety of pancakes" (especially the "don't-miss" apple and "unusual" Dutch Baby versions) makes fans flip for this "always-crowded" "real-deal" American chain that supplies "Sunday morning comfort" for many; service is "fast (if not so friendly)" and the price is right, but "better coffee would be an improvement"; N.B. not all locations are open for dinner.

Osteria di Tramonto *Italian* 21 | 23 | 19 | $46

Wheeling | Westin Chicago North Shore | 601 N. Milwaukee Ave. (N. Wolf Rd.) | 847-777-6570 | www.cenitare.com

Wheeling's Westin Chicago North Shore houses this "trendy", "high-profile package", "one of the most enjoyable in the area" courtesy of Rick Tramonto's (Tru) "sophisticated rustic Italian" fare matched by an "enormous" wine list in a "noisy, city-chic" setting – and, "of course, don't miss Gale Gand's desserts"; still, diners "disappointed" to see this "major league chef serving minor league" food ushered by "unreliable service" (staffers are "friendly if you can grab one") tally it "too little bang for the buck."

Osteria Via Stato *Italian* 22 | 20 | 21 | $45

River North | 620 N. State St. (Ontario St.) | 312-642-8450

Pizzeria Via Stato *Italian*

River North | 620 N. State St. (Ontario St.) | 312-337-6634
www.leye.com

A "boffo" "family-style" Italian dining experience is on the table at this Lettuce Entertain You "all-you-can-eat free-for-all" in River North, where "you pick the main dish" from a "few choices" and "the food just keeps coming"; the "stone-and-dark-wood decor provides a warm atmosphere", made even more "cozy" by "some communal seating", but respondents who feel "rushed" gripe that the "gimmick" is "too much circus" and say "service is a work-in-progress"; P.S. "try the new pizzeria" adjacent to the main restaurant.

☑ NEW Otom Ⓢ American 23 | 23 | 25 | $45

Market District | 951 W. Fulton Mkt. (bet. Morgan & Sangamon Sts.) | 312-491-5804 | www.otomrestaurant.com

Moto's "funky" "sister restaurant" in the Market District focuses on "affordable" New American "comfort cuisine" with "no pretensions", which most maintain is "terrific"; "genuinely friendly, knowledgeable servers" work a "modern, warm" setting with "exposed brick, soft lighting", "orange chairs" and "little details" like "nifty purse hooks."

Over Easy Café Ⓜ American ▽ 25 | 20 | 21 | $16

Ravenswood | 4943 N. Damen Ave. (bet. Ainslie & Argyle Sts.) | 773-506-2605

"Inspired" New American brunch and lunch "that actually lives up to its description" (like the "upside-down apple pancake baked with fresh apples in an iron skillet") explains why the line "can be long" at this "tiny" Ravenswood BYO with a "small waiting area"; the "owners are eager to please", just get there early, because they close daily at 3 PM.

Oysy Japanese 21 | 18 | 20 | $29

River North | 50 E. Grand Ave. (bet. Rush St. & Wabash Ave.) | 312-670-6750
South Loop | 888 S. Michigan Ave. (9th St.) | 312-922-1127
Northbrook | 315 Skokie Blvd. (Dundee Rd.) | 847-714-1188
www.oysysushi.com

Enthusiasts explain that "everything's fresh and tasty" at these "stylish and hip" South Loop, River North and Northbrook spots with "succulent sushi" and a "good selection" of cooked Japanese fare, including "nice small plates", served in a "minimal" "space-age environment"; lauders also love the "lunch specials", but some suggest that the "pleasant" servers are "not very knowledgeable."

Palm, The Steak 23 | 20 | 23 | $59

Loop | Swissôtel | 323 E. Wacker Dr. (bet. Lake Shore Dr. & Michigan Ave.) | 312-616-1000
Northbrook | Northbrook Court Shopping Ctr. | 2000 Northbrook Court (Lake Cook Rd.) | 847-239-7256
www.thepalm.com

"Old-school dining" is alive and well at this "distinguished" chain carnivorium, born in NYC in 1926 (now with Loop and Northbrook branches) and drawing "movers and shakers" ever since with its "enormous" steaks and lobsters served in "distinguished" settings adorned with celebrity "caricatures"; sure, the tabs are reminiscent of "mortgage payments" and service can careen from "top-notch" to "surly", but ultimately they're "consistently good."

Pane Caldo Italian 24 | 20 | 23 | $67

Gold Coast | 72 E. Walton St. (bet. Michigan Ave. & Rush St.) | 312-649-0055 | www.pane-caldo.com

"Top shelf" Northern Italian dining, an "exceptional wine list" and "knowledgeable service" distinguish this "quaint", "intimate" "res-

	FOOD	DECOR	SERVICE	COST

taurant off Michigan Avenue" in the Gold Coast; its "measured portions and astronomical pricing" are "not for the light of wallet", but that doesn't faze the "power money crowd" that finds it "fabulous" for a "work lunch" and dinners at the "window table" where you can "watch the world go by."

Pappadeaux Seafood Kitchen *Seafood*
| 21 | 18 | 19 | $34 |

Arlington Heights | 798 W. Algonquin Rd. (Golf Rd.) | 847-228-9551
Westmont | 921 Pasquinelli Dr. (Oakmont Ln.) | 630-455-9846
www.pappas.com

"Good commercial" Cajun-Creole seafood is the "star" at these "loud, bustling" suburban sibs that get boosters through their "New Orleans 'jones'" with a "value"-priced "happy hour" and "all-you-can-eat-lobster nights"; critics who "don't understand the crowds" label the food "mediocre", "overthought, oversauced" and "overpriced for the quality"; N.B. Arlington Heights does both buffet and à la carte Sunday brunch, and both sites have weekend entertainment.

NEW Paramount Room, The *American*
| - | - | - | M |

Near West | 415 N. Milwaukee Ave. (bet. Hubbard & Kinzie Sts.) | 312-829-6300 | www.paramountroom.com

Classic pub eats join gastropub gourmet (peekytoe crab salad, tempura-fried green beans) at this upscale Near West American tavern proffering a connoisseur's beer list and exotic bar-chef cocktails like a blackberry-sage gin fizz; thanks to high coved ceilings with rafters and open ductwork, its candlelit space has a vintage-warehouse feel; N.B. you'll find plasmas and a pool table in the cellar.

NEW Park 52 ⊠ Ⓜ *American*
| - | - | - | M |

Hyde Park | 5201 S. Harper Ave. (52nd St.) | 773-241-5200

The long-awaited Hyde Park grill from high-profile restaurateur Jerry Kleiner (Room 21, Red Light) combines his notoriously flamboyant decor - wildly colorful walls, polka-dot chairs, glitzy photography, palm trees and silk shantung light fixtures - with moderately priced American classics such as lettuce-wedge salad, steak and onion rings and cheesecake; there's also a big bar for socializing over a reasonably priced domestic wine list and specialty cocktails.

Parkers' Ocean Grill *Seafood*
| 24 | 23 | 23 | $45 |

Downers Grove | 1000 31st St. (Highland Ave.) | 630-960-5701 | www.selectrestaurants.com

Some of the "freshest seafood around" the Western Suburbs comes from this "comfortable", "corporate" catch with an "accommodating staff"; the "well-spaced tables" work for "business" or "romance", so while a-fish-ionados admit the "common man might find the prices a bit steep", most maintain the "atmosphere, service and food quality make up for it"; P.S. there's a "pianist in the bar" on weekends.

Park Grill *American*   19 | 20 | 18 | $36

Loop | Millennium Park | 11 N. Michigan Ave. (bet. Madison & Washington Sts.) | 312-521-7275 | www.parkgrillchicago.com
"Amazing Millennium Park" is home to this "awesomely located New American" whose "varied" menu "will please upscale tourists and locals alike" (the "great burgers" get the most raves), as will the "fun view of the [ice] skaters", "nice fireplace" in winter and "fabulous outdoor area in summer"; picky eaters postulate the "pretty good" "but expensive" "food isn't up to the challenge", though, making the "beautiful scenery" "the real star here", and advise that "service is uneven" since the "staff is stretched too thin."

Parrot Cage, The 🗷Ⓜ *American*   - | - | - | M

Far South Side | South Shore Cultural Ctr. | 7059 S South Shore Dr. (71st St.) | 773-602-5333
The seasonal New American "results are right on" at this "quaint little restaurant" with a "beautiful location" in the South Shore Cultural Center; it's part of the Far South Side's Washburne Culinary Institute "cooking program" and is staffed by "very professional" "students" in a space with "nice decor" and patio seating (and oddly, parrot nests nearby, hence the name); P.S. those in-the-know say don't miss the "wine at a fabulously low price."

Parthenon ❶ *Greek*   22 | 17 | 21 | $28

Greektown | 314 S. Halsted St. (bet. Jackson Blvd. & Van Buren St.) | 312-726-2407 | www.theparthenon.com
In the "epicenter" of Greektown, "the food is cheap, the atmosphere festive" and the "service more than accommodating" at this "old standby" (since 1968) serving "authentic" "family-style" Grecian goodies ("flaming cheese", "lamb this and lamb that", "great gyros" and "gooey baklava"); "roasted" animals "paraded around the dining room" "upon the shoulders of handsome young Greeks" distracts a bit from the "dated" decor that "needs a face-lift."

Pasta Palazzo ⊄ *Italian*   ▽ 22 | 15 | 20 | $16

Lincoln Park | 1966 N. Halsted St. (Armitage Ave.) | 773-248-1400 | www.pastapalazzo.com
This "small", "casual" "neighborhood" Italian in Lincoln Park is "quick and reliable" "when you don't feel like making" your own "jalapeño gnocchi", "grilled calamari" or "creative salads"; its "amazing value" makes it popular, so "prepare for the possibility of sharing your table" in the "cozy but comfortable" "mosaic-walled" space"; P.S. it's "cash only" unless you order carryout over the Internet.

Pegasus *Greek*   21 | 18 | 20 | $28

Greektown | 130 S. Halsted St. (bet. Adams & Monroe Sts.) | 312-226-4666
Pegasus on the Fly ❶ *Greek*
Southwest Side | Midway Int'l Airport | 5700 S. Cicero Ave. (55th St.) | 773-581-1522
www.pegasuschicago.com
"More upscale than some Greektown establishments", this "consistent" "favorite" "goes beyond the typical gyros or souvlaki" with

FOOD DECOR SERVICE COST

"never-ending choices" of "hubcap-sized" Hellenic plates presented with "warm service" in a "bright, decorated room" – or "in summer" you can "sit on the rooftop deck" "overlooking Downtown", either "for drinks" or to order from "a smaller menu"; P.S. the airport stand is "a great quick meal at Midway."

Penang ● *Malaysian* | 22 | 14 | 15 | $20 |

Chinatown | 2201 S. Wentworth Ave. (Cermak Rd.) | 312-326-6888
Expect "spicy", "no-nonsense Malaysian cuisine" that's "as close as it gets" to "its tropical island namesake" at this no-reserving Chinatown "chain" member that also offers Japanese dishes and sushi; if there's a long "wait", cool your heels over karaoke upstairs on weekends, or get the grub to go, as "these dishes freeze well for future enjoyment."

Penny's Noodle Shop *Asian* | 18 | 12 | 17 | $14 |

Lakeview | 3400 N. Sheffield Ave. (Roscoe St.) | 773-281-8222 | www.pennysnoodleshop.com Ⓜ
Lincoln Park | 950 W. Diversey Pkwy. (Sheffield Ave.) | 773-281-8448 | www.pennysnoodleshop.com
Wicker Park | 1542 N. Damen Ave. (North Ave.) | 773-394-0100 | www.pennysnoodleshop.com Ⓜ
NEW Northfield | 320 S. Happ Rd. (Mt. Pleasant St.) | 847-446-4747 | www.pennysnoodleshop.com Ⓢ
Oak Park | 1130 Chicago Ave. (Harlem Ave.) | 708-660-1300 | www.pennysnoodleshopoakpark.com

Oodles of slurpers support these "no-frills" noodleries as "nice to have in the neighborhood" for their "great selection" of "amazingly affordable" "quickie Asian" eats, which are "tasty" (if "not haute cuisine") and offered in "casual", "packed" digs with "quick service" (for many, the chain's also a "regular on the takeout-restaurant rotation"); skeptics, though, sigh "same old, same old", saying "everything's bland" at these "run-of-the-mill" eateries "for beginners"; N.B. Lakeview and Northfield are BYO, the others serve beer and wine.

NEW Pepitone's *American/Italian* | ▽ 20 | 22 | 18 | $27 |

Edgewater | 5437 N. Broadway St. (bet. Balmoral & Catalpa Aves.) | 773-293-3730 | www.pepitones.com
A blend of upscale sports bar and affordable eatery, this stylish Edgewater hybrid offers a lengthy Traditional American and Italian menu of salads, sandwiches, pastas and pizzas (plus a few pricier entrees); up front, a welcoming mahogany bar with a dozen-plus beer handles and a cozy little lounge (both with plasmas aplenty) give way to a rustic-chic, earth-toned dining room with warm lighting.

Pete Miller's Seafood & Prime Steak *Seafood/Steak* | 22 | 21 | 21 | $47 |

Evanston | 1557 Sherman Ave. (bet. Davis & Grove Sts.) | 847-328-0399 ●
Wheeling | 412 N. Milwaukee Ave. (Lake Cook Rd.) | 847-243-3700 | www.petemillers.com
Now staking a claim in two suburban sites, these "classic", "casual" "supper clubs" serve what supporters sum up as "excellent prime steaks", seafood and "garbage salad" in "bustling" but "intimate"

| | FOOD | DECOR | SERVICE | COST |

settings with "romantic booths", "cool jazz" most nights and "pool tables"; regulars rank them "reasonably priced", but quibblers call the "quality average for the cost" and complain of "uneven service."

Petterino's *American*   20 | 20 | 20 | $39

Loop | Goodman Theatre Bldg. | 150 N. Dearborn St. (Randolph St.) | 312-422-0150 | www.petterinos.com

Loop locals and Goodman Theatre-goers feel "welcome" at this "convenient", "consistent" Traditional American with "old-fashioned, fun" fare (some Italian) and "caricatures of celebs" in a "red-velvet" "'40s" "supper-club" setting; granted, it gets "hectic before a show", but they "really hustle to make sure you make the curtain"; however, tougher critics lower that curtain on this "cliché" "attempt at Rat Pack" "retro", saying "lackluster food" makes it "one of the least interesting of the Lettuce Entertain You restaurants."

☑ P.F. Chang's China Bistro *Chinese*   21 | 20 | 19 | $30

River North | 530 N. Wabash Ave. (Grand Ave.) | 312-828-9977
Northbrook | Northbrook Mall | 1819 Lake Cook Rd.
(Northbrook Court Dr.) | 847-509-8844
Schaumburg | Woodfield Mall | 5 Woodfield Mall (bet. Frontage & Golf Rds.) | 847-610-8000
Orland Park | Orland Park Crossing | 14135 S. La Grange Rd.
(Southwest Hwy.) | 708-675-3970
Lombard | 2361 Fountain Square Dr. (bet. Butterfield & Meyers Rds.) | 630-652-9977
www.pfchangs.com

Expect "major hustle-bustle" at this "noisy" Chinese chain where the "sanitized", "mass-produced" menus "aren't really authentic" yet do "appeal to most palates" (when in doubt, the "lettuce wraps rule"); no one minds the "spotty" service and "ersatz" Sino decor since they "have the formula down" – starting with "nothing-fancy" prices and an overall "fun" vibe.

Philander's Oak Park *American*   ▽ 21 | 21 | 22 | $38

Oak Park | Carleton Hotel | 1110 Pleasant St. (bet. Maple Ave. & Marion St.) | 708-848-4250 | www.carletonhotel.com

Named for village historian Philander Barclay (not for wayward spouses), Oak Park's "classy", "comfortable" American "neighborhood hangout" in the Carleton Hotel offers "good seafood and steaks" and "friendly service" with an "old-time feel"; there's "outdoor seating" and a "nightlife" vibe in the bar with "cool jazz" every night; P.S. bargain-hunters "go next door to Poor Phil's" for burgers.

Philly G's *Italian*   22 | 18 | 19 | $33

Vernon Hills | 1252 E. Hwy. 45 (Rte. 21) | 847-634-1811 | www.phillygs.com

Retaining its "proud family" heritage, this Northwest Suburban "casa de garlic" serves "good roadhouse-y Italian" (including "great veal") within the "beautiful, comfortable rooms" of a restored home; the "charming" patio and weekend entertainment help make it "a nice date restaurant", but some judges jibe "the service is hit-or-miss."

	FOOD	DECOR	SERVICE	COST

Phil Stefani's 437 Rush ⊠ *Italian/Steak*   21 | 20 | 23 | $49

River North | 437 N. Rush St. (Hubbard St.) | 312-222-0101 |
www.stefanirestaurants.com

"Well-prepared" "classic Italian steakhouse" cooking in "grand proportions" is the draw at this "clubby", "comfortable" River Norther "with old-time service" and a "lively", "large bar area" (it's also "great for a business lunch or dinner"); still, voters who deem it "reliable but never spectacular" – with prices that are "a bit high" – assign it "secondary" status on their personal lists.

Phoenix *Chinese*   21 | 13 | 15 | $22

Chinatown | 2131 S. Archer Ave., 2nd fl. (Wentworth Ave.) |
312-328-0848 | www.chinatownphoenix.com

Patrons of this Chinatown chow-palace are pleased by its "great variety, freshness and service", pronouncing it "one of the best places for daily dim sum" and deeming "dinner a gracious experience" as well, with a menu that focuses on Hong Kong–style Cantonese cuisine; an abundance of "families adds to the cheer" of its "relaxed, open" space, though at peak hours "its popularity can be a bit daunting" due to the resulting "long lines and crowded rooms."

Piazza Bella *Italian*   20 | 19 | 21 | $30

Roscoe Village | 2116 W. Roscoe St. (bet. Damen & Western Aves.) |
773-477-7330

"Romantic, candlelit and casual", this Roscoe Village "neighborhood Italian trattoria" is "well-frequented" for its "classic dishes", such as "cracker thin–crusted pizzas" and "nice pastas", plus "good steak and fish as well" ("the specials are usually impressive" too); a "welcoming staff" and "nice wine list" further enhance the "happy atmosphere"; P.S. "if you want to sit outside", be warned that the patio gets "very crowded in the summer."

Piece *Pizza*   23 | 15 | 16 | $20

Wicker Park | 1927 W. North Ave. (Damen Ave.) | 773-772-4422 |
www.piecechicago.com

If you believe "beer and pizza [are the] staples of life" and "you're not in the mood for traditional Chicago" pie, check out this "large, industrial" Wicker Parker; its "great New Haven-style" thin-crust 'za "with interesting combinations" of toppings, plus "excellent large salads" and "tasty" microbrews, appeal to a "young, hip" crowd, making it a favorite place to "watch a game" or cut loose on the "loud", "wacky karaoke nights" (Thursdays, and with a live band on Saturdays).

Pierrot Gourmet *French*   21 | 20 | 17 | $28

River North | Peninsula Hotel | 108 E. Superior St. (bet. Michigan Ave. & Rush St.) | 312-573-6749 | www.peninsula.com

"High-quality" if "rather pricey" French salads, soups and pastries, "wonderful European breakfast", "weekend brunch" and "lots of good nibbly things to share" win friends for this "open, airy" River North "gem" "attached to the Peninsula Hotel"; added enticements are a "pleasant" staff and "huge doors" that open onto a patio, and

	FOOD	DECOR	SERVICE	COST

if its "dinner selections aren't that diverse, the wine list makes up for it"; N.B. they close at 7 PM in winter, 9 PM in summer.

Pine Yard *Chinese*
| | 20 | 13 | 17 | $20 |

Evanston | 1033 Davis St. (Oak St.) | 847-475-4940 | www.pineyardrestaurant.com

An "old-school Chinese" "standard", this stalwart is "convenient for Evanstonians" in search of "tasty" if "greasy" Mandarin and Sichuan meals; service ranges from "lightning quick" to "strained when busy" to downright "oddball", but glitches are offset by the "excellent lunch deals"; N.B. they serve wine and beer only.

pingpong ◐ *Asian Fusion*
| | 22 | 20 | 15 | $24 |

Lakeview | 3322 N. Broadway St. (Aldine Ave.) | 773-281-7575 | www.pingpongrestaurant.com

Its "wide variety" of "playful Asian fusion" is presented "at a decent price" by "too-cool-for-school" servers at this "minimalist" spot that's "in the heart of Lakeview's Boys Town"; the "crowded", "club-like" scene comes "complete with boom boom and flash flash" ("OMG, turn down the music in the dining area"); N.B. no reservations, and though they serve beer and wine, you can also BYO.

NEW Pinstripes *American/Italian*
| | 18 | 20 | 18 | $27 |

Northbrook | 1150 Willow Rd. (bet. Patriot Blvd. & Waukegan Rd.) | 847-480-2323 | www.pinstripes.com

"Leather couches, high ceilings and bocce add to the atmosphere" at this "classy bowling alley" in Northbrook with "tasty, well-presented" Traditional American and Italian eats that "exceed expectations" considering the game-hall context (though others find the "prices a bit steep" for the same reason); it's "nice for a party", particularly on the patio, but "slow", "awkward service" "does not bowl" anyone over.

Pita Inn *Mideastern/Mediterranean*
| | 24 | 9 | 15 | $10 |

Glenview | 9854 N. Milwaukee Ave. (Golf Rd.) | 847-759-9990
Skokie | 3910 Dempster St. (Crawford St.) | 847-677-0211
Wheeling | 122 S. Elmhurst Rd. (Dundee Rd.) | 847-808-7733

"Fabulous" and "healthy" Middle-Eastern" and "Med favorites" accompanied by "fresh-out-of-the-oven pita" make for "high-quality" "fast food" at this North Suburban trio with "quick service"; the "unassuming" settings ("who needs decor when the food is so great?") are "packed every night of the week" with "every type of person" (it's "great for vegetarians") – after all, who wouldn't want to "eat like a king [on] a pauper's budget"?

Pizza Capri *Pizza*
| | 20 | 13 | 17 | $20 |

Lakeview | 962 W. Belmont Ave. (Sheffield Ave.) | 773-296-6000
Lincoln Park | 1733 N. Halsted St. (Willow St.) | 312-280-5700
Hyde Park | 1501 E. 53rd St. (Harper Ave.) | 773-324-7777
www.pizzacapri.com

"Unique pizza" "that is a little more grown-up" thanks to "interesting toppings" (some "love the BBQ chicken" variety, while others say "try the rosemary potato" version), as well as "solid pastas", "great sandwiches" and "terrific salads" have surveyors saying this "unpretentious", "efficiently run" Italian trio "is excellent for what it aims to be"; regulars who report that the decor "could use some sprucing up" opt for the always "on-time" delivery.

Pizza D.O.C. *Pizza* 22 | 14 | 17 | $25
Lincoln Square | 2251 W. Lawrence Ave. (Oakley Ave.) | 773-784-8777
"Wonderful", "refined" "Italian-style pizzas" with "crackerlike crust" from a "wood-burning oven", plus "fresh" pastas, "terrific" antipasto and a "nice wine list" woo lovers of this "casual" Lincoln Square spot; still, some swear the pie "sometimes comes out more soggy than crisp", and say the "lacking service" and "rustic" "interior could use some work" (though "the open kitchen cozies up the space").

Pizzeria Uno ☻ *Pizza* 21 | 13 | 15 | $22
River North | 29 E. Ohio St. (Wabash Ave.) | 312-321-1000
Pizzeria Due ☻ *Pizza*
River North | 619 N. Wabash Ave. (bet. Ohio & Ontario Sts.) |
312-943-2400
www.unos.com
"The wait is always long" and the "quarters tight" at these "atmospheric", "authentic" River North "landmarks" slicing up "heaven on a thick crust" and helping give "deep-dish pizza" its "Chicago-style reputation"; a faction of former fans lament the pair "still attracts the tourists but aren't what they used to be for locals."

P.J. Clarke's *American* 16 | 15 | 16 | $26
Streeterville | Embassy Suites Hotel | 302 E. Illinois St. (Columbus Dr.) |
312-670-7500
Gold Coast | 1204 N. State Pkwy. (Division St.) | 312-664-1650
NEW Lincoln Park | 1141 W. Armitage Ave. (Clifton Ave.) |
773-327-8000
www.pjclarkeschicago.com
"Lively" and "crowded", this triplet of "watering holes" serving "standard" Traditional American provender are "popular" "for a casual beer and burger", "watching a game", "good people-watching on weekdays for the after-work crowd" and as "meeting spots" for "over-35 singles"; rueful raters, however, report that the original on State, a "once-great neighborhood haunt", now "reminds [them] of a chain" with "ho-hum" eats – though both branches are unrelated to and "without the history of the NY original."

Poag Mahone's 19 | 17 | 18 | $18
Carvery & Ale House ☒ *Pub Food*
Loop | 175 W. Jackson Blvd. (bet. LaSalle & Wells Sts.) | 312-566-9100 |
www.poagmahone.com
A "comfortable" lunch and "happy-hour" "option in the Loop", this Traditional American tavern "whose name translated from Gaelic means 'kiss my arse'" serves "pretty good bar food" including "great burgers", hand-carved sandwiches and salads at "decent prices"; surveyors' only serious complaint is that this find in the financial district ("an area with too few choices") is "not open on weekends."

	FOOD	DECOR	SERVICE	COST

NEW Pomegranate *Med./Mideastern*   ▽ 19 | 13 | 17 | $12

Evanston | 1633 Orrington Ave. (bet. Church & Davis Sts.) | 847-475-6002
Middle Eastern–Mediterranean sandwiches, salads, hummus and shawarma are all featured at this Evanston BYO that "caters to the university crowd" with "bargain" prices; if the "student atmosphere" can be "too bright and informal", the "food makes up for it" boast boosters who outnumber the doubters who dis the "dull flavors."

Pompei Bakery *Italian*   20 | 15 | 17 | $14

Streeterville | 212 E. Ohio St. (bet. N. State St. & N. Wabash Ave.) | 312-482-9900 🛃 Ⓜ
Lakeview | 2955 N. Sheffield Ave. (Wellington Ave.) | 773-325-1900
Little Italy | 1531 W. Taylor St. (bet. Ashland Ave. & Laflin St.) | 312-421-5179
Schaumburg | 1261 E. Higgins Rd. (bet. Meacham Rd. & National Pkwy.) | 847-619-5001
Oakbrook Terrace | 17 W. 744 22nd St. (Summit Ave.) | 630-620-0600
River Forest | 7215 Lake St. (Harlem Ave.) | 708-488-9800
www.pompeibakery.com

First opened in Little Italy in 1909 (though at a different location from that nabe's current branch, today a rater "favorite"), this "cheap, dependable" chain of "solid" "cafeteria-style Italians" issues "very good pizzas" that qualify as "comfort by the slice", plus "unique sandwiches" and "great soups and salads"; it's "not quite fast food – but service is quick", making it an "easy" stop with kids.

Pops for Champagne ● *American*   16 | 21 | 19 | $42

River North | Tree Studios | 601 N. State St. (Ohio St.) | 312-266-7677 | www.popsforchampagne.com

An "excellent, thorough champagne list" overshadows the American "small-plates selection" at this prime "venue for people-watching" that gets packed with "customers dressed to kill" who convene around the "live" "jazz nightly downstairs" and "nice outdoor patio in summer", making it all-in-all "so cool it's hot"; some sippers see the "sleek" River North space as "one damn sexy place" for a "first date", but others tag it "overpriced" and marred by "attitude from the staff" that's as "hard to swallow" as the "underwhelming food."

Potbelly Sandwich Works *Sandwiches*   19 | 15 | 18 | $9

Loop | One Illinois Ctr. | 111 E. Wacker Dr. (Michigan Ave.) | 312-861-0013 🛃
Loop | 175 W. Jackson Blvd. (bet. Financial Pl. & Wells St.) | 312-588-1150 🛃
Loop | 190 N. State St. (Lake St.) | 312-683-1234
Loop | 303 W. Madison St. (Franklin St.) | 312-346-1234 🛃
Loop | 55 W. Monroe St. (Dearborn St.) | 312-577-0070 🛃
River North | 508 N. Clark St. (bet. Grand Ave. & Illinois St.) | 312-644-9131
River North | The Shops at North Bridge | 520 N. Michigan Ave., 4th fl. (Grand Ave.) | 312-644-1008
Lakeview | 3424 N. Southport Ave. (Roscoe St.) | 773-289-1807
Lincoln Park | 1422 W. Webster Ave. (Clybourn Ave.) | 773-755-1234

(continued)

(continued)

Potbelly Sandwich Works

Lincoln Park | 2264 N. Lincoln Ave. (bet. Belden & Webster Aves.) | 773-528-1405

www.potbelly.com

Additional locations throughout the Chicago area

"Where else can you get live music and lunch for under 10 bucks?" ask admirers of this "comfy", "consistent" "sandwich chain" (the Survey's Top Bang for the Buck) conveying "manageably sized" subs, "veggie wraps", the "best milkshakes around" and salads too, making it a "hipper, higher-quality answer" to "other over-commercialized shops"; "even with a long line, they zip you out of there", so about the only complaint is "lack of seating during peak times."

NEW Powerhouse
Restaurant & Bar *American*

∇ 23 | 22 | 23 | $69

Loop | 215 N. Clinton St. (Lake St.) | 312-928-0800 | www.powerhouserestaurant.com

This Loop "emporium" of "upscale" seasonal New American cuisine with "bold flavors" is situated in a "renovated old industrial building" that's "tastefully decorated with rich colors and fabrics"; service that's "professional without being pretentious" can tend to be "slow", and those who point out how "pricey" it is say "eat on the bar side", where the "small plates" allow for "sampling more dishes."

Prairie Grass Cafe *American*

21 | 18 | 19 | $39

Northbrook | 601 Skokie Blvd. (bet. Dundee & Lake Cook Rds.) | 847-205-4433 | www.prairiegrasscafe.com

"Chefs [Sarah] Stegner and [George] Bumbaris bring their Ritz-Carlton pedigree" to this North Suburban "neighborhood benchmark", where the "upscale" New American "comfort food" showcases "high-quality ingredients" ("don't miss the shepherd's pie") and is served in a "cavernous", "polished, prairie-style setting" that's a "nod to Chicago's history"; but the "disappointed" "expected more from such talented" toques and criticize the "noisy" atmosphere.

NEW Prosecco 🅢 *Italian*

∇ 25 | 25 | 25 | $59

River North | 710 N. Wells St. (bet. Huron & Superior Sts.) | 312-951-9500

It's "hard to choose with so many choices" at this "welcoming" River Norther proffering "interesting, authentic" Italian eats, vino (with a strength in bubbly) and specialty martinis; "concerned and attentive service" keeps diners happy in the "conversation-friendly", "bright yellow" environs that's inspired by Venice and features patio seating.

P.S. Bangkok Ⓜ *Thai*

21 | 15 | 18 | $21

Lakeview | 3345 N. Clark St. (bet. Aldine Ave. & Roscoe St.) | 773-871-7777 | www.psbangkok.com

P.S. Bangkok 2 *Thai*

Lincoln Park | 2521 N. Halsted St. (bet. Fullerton Pkwy. & Wrightwood Ave.) | 773-348-0072 | www.psbangkok2.com

Separately owned, these fraternal Siamese twins dish up "delicious", "consistently good" Thai "with great versions of classics as well as regional" treats, plus beer and wine at the Lakeview location (Lincoln Park is BYO); their "casual" settings, however, are marred by what some Thai-rants target as "inconsistent service", making them take-out and "delivery favorites."

Puck's at the MCA ☒ *American*   20 | 18 | 16 | $24

Streeterville | Museum of Contemporary Art | 220 E. Chicago Ave. (Mies van der Rohe Way) | 312-397-4034 | www.mcachicago.org

Wolfgang Puck's "chic" Streeterville lunch and brunch (but no dinner) spot is a "favorite" for "after browsing contemporary art at the MCA", winning points for making a New American burger, pizza and salad menu "somehow sophisticated" (even if the signature "Chinois chicken salad" is "less cutting-edge" than it once was); the "sunny, modern" scene features murals that change with the museum exhibits, a "floor-to-ceiling glass wall" and seasonal patio where feasters "sit amid the terraced sculpture garden and look out at Lake Michigan."

Pump Room, The *American*   20 | 24 | 23 | $65

Gold Coast | Ambassador East Hotel | 1301 N. State Pkwy. (Goethe St.) | 312-266-0360 | www.pumproom.com

"Experience the life of a celebrity" from the "golden age on the Gold Coast" at this "wonderful" "old-money" "Chicago haunt" that "can still strut its stuff" thanks to "classic clublike" decor, "historic" star photos on the walls, American "cuisine of the 21st century" and "friendly atmosphere at the bar"; diners are divided over the "so-so food" and service, but "nostalgia" nudges fence-sitters who feel that though it's "lost a step or two, it's still a nice evening out", since "there's nowhere like it"; N.B. jackets are suggested.

NEW Purgatory Pizza ☒☒ *Pizza*   - | - | - | M

Wrigleyville | 3415 N. Clark St. (bet. Newport Ave. & Roscoe St.) | 773-975-6677

At this Wrigleyville pizzeria, pies come in two versions – St. Louis cracker crust (with Pabst Blue Ribbon in the dough) or rustic hand-tossed; each has six cheeses and a choice of toppings including offbeat picks such as beef brisket and calamari; Italian comfort-food sandwiches and bar basics are also served amid heaven-meets-hell decor of painted flames on the walls and clouds on the ceiling.

Quartino ● *Italian*   21 | 18 | 20 | $32

River North | 626 N. State St. (Ontario St.) | 312-698-5000 | www.quartinochicago.com

"Quality" "salumi and related small plates" including antipasto, cheeses, salads and fondue from Italy are made for "sharing" at this "bustling" River North noshery that feels "like you're in an Italian subway" due to the often "deafening noise", wall tiles and "crammed" seating – which can be avoided by perching at the bar or the "outside tables"; still, few complain, since the staff is "convivial" and "their motto 'where wine is cheaper than water' rings true."

	FOOD	DECOR	SERVICE	COST

Quince ⓜ *American*

| 24 | 21 | 21 | $47 |

Evanston | Homestead Hotel | 1625 Hinman Ave. (Davis St.) | 847-570-8400 | www.quincerestaurant.net

With "fresh ingredients and an emphasis on presentation", this "inspired" New American "successor to Trio" is a "strong addition to the Evanston scene"; other perks include its "tranquil", "upscale" yet "comfortable" "surroundings", "deep and affordable wine list", "personal service" and a "pleasant front porch" that's perfect for "imbibing before dining" "in good weather."

Radhuni Indian Kitchen *Indian/Pakistani*

| ▽ 15 | 9 | 16 | $21 |

Lakeview | 3227 N. Clark St. (bet. Belmont Ave. & School St.) | 773-404-5670

Gracious hospitality warms the casually elegant, curry-hued dining room at this Indian and Pakistani eatery in Lakeview; patrons can BYO or just enjoy its lassi drinks and lime soda.

Raj Darbar *Indian*

| 20 | 12 | 14 | $24 |

Lincoln Park | 2660 N. Halsted St. (Wrightwood Ave.) | 773-348-1010

"Excellent lentil dishes", "authentic paneer" and other "quality Indian fare" make this subcontinental a "popular local choice in the heart of Lincoln Park", especially for those "not feeling up to the trek to Devon"; some assess the food as "not the greatest" of the genre, and others feel the "reasonable prices" are undercut by the "spotty" service and decor that "needs help", but at least the "good" fixed-price Sunday buffet is all you can eat.

RA Sushi *Japanese*

| 18 | 18 | 17 | $34 |

Gold Coast | 1139 N. State St. (Elm St.) | 312-274-0011
Glenview | 2601 Aviator Ln. (Patriot Blvd.) | 847-510-1100
Lombard | Shops on Butterfield, The | 310 Yorktown Ctr. (S. Highland Ave.) | 630-627-6800 Ⓢ ⓜ
www.rasushi.com

"Great choices of creative rolls" and "delicious noodle dishes" – plus a "good lunch menu as well" – find favor with fans of these "fun" Gold Coast Japanese chainsters with an "amazing happy hour on weekdays" and "excellent crowd on Friday and Saturday nights" (some say the "great people-watching", "decor and scene are really the reason to come"); "outside seating is nice in the summer", and at the Gold Coast location there's a late-night bar menu until 1 AM.

Red Light *Pan-Asian*

| 22 | 22 | 20 | $45 |

Market District | 820 W. Randolph St. (Green St.) | 312-733-8880 | www.redlight-chicago.com

"Upholding high food standards", chef "Jackie Shen works her magic" at this "intoxicating", "hopping" Market District fusion "fantasy" where "Pan-Asian meets the club scene"; "delighted" denizens who "never tire of dining" on her "high-quality" cuisine, accompanied by "refreshing mango martinis" and served in a "flashy, over-the-top" setting, admit it's "expensive" but insist it's "still a value in the see-and-be-seen category."

	FOOD	DECOR	SERVICE	COST

Red Lion Pub *British* | 15 | 17 | 18 | $20 |

Lincoln Park | 2446 N. Lincoln Ave. (Fullerton Pkwy.) | 773-348-2695

"More authentic than many", this "classic British pub" in Lincoln Park possesses an "intimate" "dive" atmosphere that matches its "good draughts", "cider on tap" and "traditional English fare at a reasonable price" (seems "every patron in the place is eating the fish 'n' chips"); there's also the promise of "fun, intelligent conversation with the bartender and patrons" and the "friendly" "servers who are always willing to tell of their experiences with the ghosts" that "supposedly" inhabit the premises.

NEW Reel Club *Seafood* | 20 | 21 | 18 | $47 |

Oak Brook | Oakbrook Ctr. | 272 Oakbrook Ctr. (Kingery Hwy.) | 630-368-9400 | www.leye.com

"Lettuce Entertain You has done it again" say supporters of this "fresh take on seafood" in the Western Suburbs with "imaginative dishes", "good choices" even for those not in the aquatic mood and "oversized, tasty drinks"; faultfinders, however, see "growing pains", noting that the "service hopefully will improve" and the ratings might rise "if only they would bring the prices down a bit."

Republic Pan-Asian Restaurant & Lounge *Asian* | 19 | 21 | 16 | $36 |

River North | 58 E. Ontario St. (Rush St.) | 312-440-1818 | www.republicrestaurant.us

This River North entry aims to create a "young, hip professional singles scene without being over-the-top", supplying a "unique combination" of sushi and other Asian eats in a "stylish" setting; dissenters are down on the "Chinatown fare at downtown prices" (the "innovative" apps outshine the "basic entrees") and the sometimes "lacking" service, but maybe it just "needs time for the menu and service to mature."

Z Retro Bistro Z *French* | 25 | 18 | 24 | $41 |

Mt. Prospect | Mount Prospect Commons | 1746 W. Golf Rd. (Busse Rd.) | 847-439-2424 | www.retrobistro.com

At this "diamond in the rough" offering a "little taste of France" in the Northwest Suburbs, the "creative menu" and "well-versed" staff eclipse a "rather plain" "interior" in an "ugly" "strip mall"; the prix fixe and "lunchtime specials are a great value", and the secret's out, so make reservations, since it can get "busy on weekends."

Reza's *Mediterranean/Mideastern* | 20 | 15 | 17 | $26 |

River North | 432 W. Ontario St. (Orleans St.) | 312-664-4500 ◗
Andersonville | 5255 N. Clark St. (Berwyn Ave.) | 773-561-1898 ◗
Oak Brook | 40 N. Tower Rd. (Butterfield Rd.) | 630-424-9900 | www.rezasrestaurant.com

Whether you perceive their provender "healthy" or "heavy", you can bet portions will be "ridiculously large" at this bevy of "busy", "dependable" Middle Eastern–Med eateries with "massive menus" plus brunch and "weekday lunch buffets"; faulters find the fare "forgettable" and service "uninspired", and no one's raving about the decor, but still a majority maintains these "standbys" are an "outstanding value" "if you're not out for anything fancy."

Rhapsody *American*
21 | 22 | 21 | $48

Loop | Symphony Ctr. | 65 E. Adams St. (bet. Michigan & Wabash Aves.) | 312-786-9911 | www.rhapsodychicago.com

The "seasonal offerings" of "innovative but restrained" New American cuisine are "music to the taste buds" at this Loop "lovely" in the Symphony Center with a "tranquil" dining room, "lively bar" and "gorgeous patio"; proponents pick it as "the perfect overture" to a concert or Art Institute visit (and recommend it for "power lunches" too), though dissidents detect dissonance in the form of "unpolished" service; N.B. performance-night "reservations are a necessity."

Ribs 'n' Bibs ● *BBQ*
20 | 6 | 14 | $15

Hyde Park | 5300 S. Dorchester Ave. (53rd St.) | 773-493-0400

You'll be "planning another pilgrimage" after your first visit to this Hyde Park "carry-out place" (with limited counter perches and outdoor seating in summer) where the "aroma of barbecue" makes for "great advertising" – "walk downwind and savor the smell"; "you get an entire bucket" of "real ribs vs. Northside counterparts" "slathered in great sauce", "each one as delicious as the next", but be aware that management "doesn't mess around with decor", and "don't come for the service, unless you call 'take-a-number' service."

☒ Riccardo Trattoria *Italian*
26 | 18 | 22 | $41

Lincoln Park | 2119 N. Clark St. (bet. Dickens & Webster Aves.) | 773-549-0038 | www.riccardotrattoria.com

"Mama mia", "close your eyes and you're eating at someone's home in Italy" aver *amici* of this "top-notch" Northern Italian set in an "unpretentious" Lincoln Park storefront where the "freshest" seasonal "ingredients" are served in "sensible portions" at "sane prices"; with an "open kitchen" and "tight seating", it's often "noisy", and service can be "simply wonderful" or less so, yet loyalists would "eat a Lincoln Park squirrel if Riccardo prepared it and served it over his wife's heavenly pasta"; P.S. "reservations are essential, especially on weekends."

Rinconcito Sudamericano *S American*
▽ 18 | 12 | 16 | $27

Bucktown | 1954 W. Armitage Ave. (Damen Ave.) | 773-489-3126

Rios d' Sudamerica Ⓜ *S American*

Bucktown | 2010 W. Armitage Ave. (Damen Ave.) | 773-276-0170 | www.riosdesudamerica.com

"Comfort food Peruvian-style" satisfies surveyors who savor this affordable Bucktown BYO; quaffing "a few pisco sours" helps distract from service that can be "hit-or-miss" and decor that seems "dated" at the original, especially compared to the "clubby" conditions (with liquor license) at the newer sibling up the street, which serves a "much more varied menu" of South American cuisine.

Ringo *Japanese* ∇ 23 | 11 | 20 | $24

Lincoln Park | 2507 N. Lincoln Ave. (bet. Fullerton Pkwy. & Wrightwood Ave.) | 773-248-5788 | www.rin-go.us
Raw-fish lovers cheer this Lincoln Park local "treasure" serving "tasty rolls", "terrific specials" and "good rice-bowl dishes"; voters vacillate on the "utilitarian" space's recent expansion ("comfortable" vs. "a little weird"), and the "food may lack some imagination, but this is a great entry-level sushi house" where you "can't beat the BYO policy, friendly service" and "bargain" prices.

Riques *Mexican* 20 | 10 | 17 | $18

Uptown | 5004 N. Sheridan Rd. (Argyle St.) | 773-728-6200
"Wonderful, fresh" and "authentic Mexican food" – "not just burritos and tacos" – served "at a great price" in an "out-of-the-way" Uptown location ("don't be put off by the neighborhood") has contributors crowing they "can't get enough of" this "friendly" (and "vegetarian-friendly") BYO; the "nothing-too-special" decor does little to deter regulars, though a few lament that a recent "management change" may "not be a change for the better."

Rise *Japanese* 22 | 20 | 18 | $38

Wrigleyville | 3401 N. Southport Ave. (Roscoe St.) | 773-525-3535 | www.risesushi.com
Expect "quality that's very good" at this "trendy" Wrigleyville "neighborhood sushi spot" venerated for its "generous pieces", "inventive rolls" and other "terrific" Japanese specialties like "black cod in miso and teriyakis"; traditionalists call the "pricey" concoctions "too creative" and suggest service isn't their strength.

NEW Risqué Café 🅂 🅜 *BBQ* - | - | - | M

Lakeview | 3419 N. Clark St. (bet. Roscoe St. & W. Newport Ave.) | 773-525-7711
The owner of Fixture and the late Meritage is smokin' meats (pulled pork, brisket and babybacks, duck wings and turkey legs) in bourbon-barrel chips and pouring 200-plus craft beers and 45-plus bourbons at his new Lakeview BBQ joint, where WWII-era cheesecake girls adorn the walls and campy B-movies play on the plasmas; N.B. a buffet is offered for lunch on Saturday and all day Sunday.

ristorante we *Italian* 17 | 18 | 13 | $47

Loop | W Hotel | 172 W. Adams St. (LaSalle St.) | 312-917-5608 | www.ristorantewe.com
Its food may be "good" and the ambiance "cool", but it "seems to be a requirement for the staff to be ditzy" and the "interior noisy" at the Loop W's Northern Italian steakhouse, where "thumping" DJ "music" fills the airwaves; eaters who find it "inconsistent in all categories" say it "could be a nice spot with better service" and a lowering of the "hotel prices"; N.B. they offer a pre-theater prix fixe menu.

	FOOD	DECOR	SERVICE	COST

Ritz-Carlton Café *American* `23` `23` `24` `$52`

Streeterville | Ritz-Carlton Hotel | 160 E. Pearson St., 12th fl. (Michigan Ave.) | 312-573-5160 | www.fourseasons.com

"Surprisingly creative", "delightful" New American meals served in an area "open" to the "ritzy" Ritz hotel lobby (adorned with a "gorgeous fountain") make this a "peaceful oasis amid the madness of Michigan Avenue's crowds"; though some discern a disconnect between the "casual" setting and "outrageous prices", even critics concede it's a "bargain" compared to the now-shuttered formal dining room.

Riva *Seafood* `18` `21` `19` `$48`

Streeterville | Navy Pier | 700 E. Grand Ave. (Lake Shore Dr.) | 312-644-7482

Naperville | 2020 Calamos Court (Westings Ave.) | 630-718-1010 ⊠

www.stefanirestaurants.com

"Knockout Lake Michigan and city views" are the backdrop for "fresh fish, simply cooked", steaks and Italian dishes at this "upscale" Streeterville spot where a "special for Shakespeare theatergoers" and "excellent wine list" are "appreciated" by some surveyors; others, however, out it as an "overpriced tourist trap" with "uninspired" eats and "marginal" service (it's "the best thing on Navy Pier, which isn't saying much"), and while the "Naperville location has a great floor layout with beautiful windows", "unfortunately the view is of I-88."

R.J. Grunts *American* `19` `17` `19` `$22`

Lincoln Park | 2056 N. Lincoln Park W. (Dickens Ave.) | 773-929-5363 | www.leye.com

"Sentimental" surveyors trust this "loud, crowded" Lincoln Park "classic" – "the first 'Lettuce' restaurant" – known for "hearty" American fare proffered by "cheeky" servers in a setting dominated by "groovy music" and "photos of staffers over the years"; it "feels very '70s", and perhaps it's "not up with the latest things people like to eat", but for every dismisser who dubs it "dated" there's a diehard declaring "try and close it and I'll chain myself to the doors in protest."

☑ RL *American* `23` `25` `22` `$50`

Gold Coast | 115 E. Chicago Ave. (Michigan Ave.) | 312-475-1100 | www.rlrestaurant.com

"There is always a buzz" at this "clubby" Gold Coast getaway oozing an "old-money" feel "right out of a Ralph Lauren ad" (he owns the spot) with "vintage paintings and a "cozy bar with fireplace"; the "classic American" fare (from fish 'n' chips to Dover sole, burgers to steaks) feeds a "variety of tastes and budgets", the bartenders "pour an excellent drink" and it's "perfect for people-watching", since the crowd encompasses the "crème de la crème", "power-lunchers", "tourists", "gossip columnists", "blue hairs, fake boobs and professional shoppers."

	FOOD	DECOR	SERVICE	COST

Robinson's No. 1 Ribs *BBQ*   22 | 6 | 13 | $18

Loop | Union Station | 225 S. Canal St. (bet. Adams St. & Jackson Blvd.) | 312-258-8477 ⊞
Lincoln Park | 655 W. Armitage Ave. (Orchard St.) | 312-337-1399 Ⓜ
Oak Park | 940 W. Madison St. (Clinton St.) | 708-383-8452
www.rib1.com

"Real barbecue, paper plates and all", is the draw at this "no-atmosphere" city and suburban BYO trio where "fine" ribs, sides, a "very good pulled pork sandwich" and "homemade peach cobbler" stand in for decor; the "so-so service" nudges a number of 'cue-cravers to consider "carryout"; N.B. the Lincoln Park location has a dog-friendly patio.

Rockit Bar & Grill ◑ *American*   19 | 17 | 17 | $28

River North | 22 W. Hubbard St. (bet. Dearborn & State Sts.) | 312-645-6000 | www.rockitbarandgrill.com

A "fun" "30-and-under" crowd of "frat" types and "eye candy in skimpy outfits" convenes at this "rockin'" River North Traditional American "sandwich-and-easy-meal place", a "much-needed happy-hour destination" and "pre-partying" staging area with "above-average bar food" and a Bloody Mary cart that's becoming "one of the great Chicago brunch traditions"; diners who "don't quite understand all the hubbub" are "disappointed by the food" and "overpriced drinks", and say the staff is sometimes "overwhelmed."

NEW Rock-N-Roll Sushi Ⓢ *Japanese*   - | - | - | M
(fka Sushi Ai)

Palatine | 710 W. Euclid Ave. (Parkside Dr.) | 847-221-5100

Bright renovations with '50s-era rock 'n' roll memorabilia and "loud music" have this Northwest Suburban raw-fish purveyor (formerly Sushi Ai) living up to its new name, matching the tunes to a "wide choice of maki and nigiri", including both "innovative combinations" and "typical favorites"; raters haven't reconciled whether tabs are "reasonable" or "a bit pricey", but fans swear this "small, out-of-the-way place" is "like finding a pearl in an oyster."

NEW Rockstar Dogs ◑⊞ *Hot Dogs*   - | - | - | I

West Town | 801 N. Ashland Ave. (Chicago Ave.) | 312-421-2364 | www.rockstar-dogs.com

Nightlife nabob Dion Antic (Iggy's, Harry's Velvet Room) lives up to his name with his latest – a West Town fast-fooder featuring tube steaks and a stripper pole in a space decked out with rock photos and autographed axes; the specialty hot dog–and–topping combos are named after rockers, with free franks furnished to pole-dancing patrons after 10 PM (it serves till 4 AM Thursday–Saturday); N.B. it's cash only, with an ATM on hand.

Roditys ◑ *Greek*   22 | 17 | 22 | $28

Greektown | 222 S. Halsted St. (bet. Adams St. & Jackson Blvd.) | 312-454-0800 | www.roditys.com

Long a Greektown "classic", this "authentic" Hellenic "fave" "holds its own" and "can always be counted on" for "consistently good", "quality" food at a "value" served in a "family-style atmosphere that will have you swilling ouzo and breaking plates (well, almost)"; N.B. they're open till midnight on weeknights, and 1 AM on weekends.

☑ **Room 21** *Steak* | 21 | 26 | 21 | $46 |

South Loop | 2110 S. Wabash Ave. (bet. Cermac Rd. & 21st St.) | 312-328-1198 | www.room21chicago.com

A "surreal blend of *The Untouchables* and postmodern glam" sets the stage for "very good" vittles at this New American steakhouse addition to the "upcoming" South Loop scene, complete with "Al Capone mystique" (it's in his former bootlegging factory, and his escape tunnels now lead to a "glass-paneled chef's table"); "specialty" libations, servers who "know the menu forward and backward" and an "over-the-top romantic patio" pull pros, while cons who consider the food "boring" may be happy to hear that they've recently "juggled chefs."

RoSal's Italian Kitchen ⊠ *Italian* | 22 | 18 | 21 | $32 |

Little Italy | 1154 W. Taylor St. (Racine Ave.) | 312-243-2357 | www.rosals.com

"Excellent", "hearty" Southern Italian and a "staff that makes you feel at home" lure loyalists to this "quaint" Little Italy "storefront space" with "a lot of charm" and "a real family-owned feeling"; P.S. the "Sicilian wine is a wonderful surprise."

Rose Angelis ⓜ *Italian* | 22 | 19 | 21 | $31 |

Lincoln Park | 1314 W. Wrightwood Ave. (bet. Racine & Southport Aves.) | 773-296-0081 | www.roseangelis.com

Enthusiasm runs high from eaters who enjoy the "hearty portions" of "dependably good" "homemade Italian" (including "veggie-friendly" selections)" and "incredible value" at this "sweet, romantic" Lincoln Park "institution" in a "cozy" townhouse "with tons of character"; it can be "tough to get into as they don't take reservations", and dubious diners "don't know why people tolerate the long waits" (especially "when you can get takeaway") for what they consider "heavy" fare.

☑ **Rosebud, The** *Italian* | 22 | 18 | 19 | $39 |

Little Italy | 1500 W. Taylor St. (Laflin St.) | 312-942-1117

☑ **Rosebud of Highland Park** *Italian*

Highland Park | 1850 Second St. (Central Ave.) | 847-926-4800

☑ **Rosebud of Naperville** *Italian*

Naperville | 48 W. Chicago Ave. (Washington St.) | 630-548-9800

☑ **Rosebud of Schaumburg** *Italian*

Schaumburg | 1370 Bank Dr. (Meacham Rd.) | 847-240-1414

☑ **Rosebud on Rush** *Italian*

Gold Coast | 720 N. Rush St. (Superior St.) | 312-266-6444

☑ **Rosebud Theater District** ⊠ *Italian*

Loop | 3 First National Plaza | 70 W. Madison St. (bet. Clark & Dearborn Sts.) | 312-332-9500
www.rosebudrestaurants.com

Combining the "charm of a local restaurant" with the "class of a big-city institution" this "noisy" "Taylor Street original" ("packing in tourists and locals like olives in a jar") and its offshoots offer "enormous portions" of "*delizioso*" "basic red-sauce" Italian in "classic", "Old Chicago" settings; holdouts who hint that they're all "a tad tired" cite "hit-or-miss service" that can be "pushy" and "abrupt", and call the "quantity-over-quality" cuisine "unspectacular for the price."

☑ Rosebud Prime *Steak* | 23 | 20 | 22 | $52 |
NEW Loop | 1 S. Dearborn St. (Madison St.) | 312-384-1900

☑ Rosebud Steakhouse *Steak*
Streeterville | 192 E. Walton St. (Mies van der Rohe Way) | 312-397-1000
www.rosebudrestaurants.com

Streeterville and Loop locals can "see and be seen" at these purveyors of "gargantuan steaks" and one of the "best burgers in the city", served in "great locations" that are like "laid-back" "private clubs" (albeit ones that can be "unbearably noisy"); the "staffers are real pros" who "take good care of you, especially if you are a regular."

Roy's *Hawaiian* | 24 | 22 | 24 | $51 |
River North | 720 N. State St. (Superior St.) | 312-787-7599 |
www.roysrestaurant.com

The "beautiful presentations" of "classy", "creative" Hawaiian cuisine include "high-quality fresh seafood" and "great desserts" at this River North link in a chain; "terrific" service and "awesome pineapple martinis" lure land-locked beach worshipers, though some insist the original, in Hawaii, is "better" – and the penny-wise peg it "on the pricier side, but perfect for a special occasion"; P.S. "there's a nice outdoor patio in good weather."

Ruby of Siam *Thai* | 20 | 13 | 18 | $19 |
Evanston | 1125 Emerson St. (Ridge Ave.) | 847-492-1008
Skokie | Skokie Fashion Sq. | 9420 Skokie Blvd. (Gross Point Rd.) |
847-675-7008
www.rubyofsiam.com

Insiders insist "if you live near" a branch of this Northern Suburban BYO duo, "you don't really have to bother finding any other place for Thai", since each offers a "huge menu" of "reliable selections" from a "kitchen willing to substitute", making them "frequent destinations for vegetarians" and "good places to take kids with an adventurous palate"; add in "fabulous value", and you can see why touters tolerate "average atmosphere" and "iffy service."

Rumba ☒Ⓜ *Nuevo Latino* | ▽ 21 | 25 | 17 | $42 |
River North | 351 W. Hubbard St. (bet. Kingsbury & Orleans Sts.) |
312-222-1226 | www.rumba351.com

This "pickup joint's" "diverse crowd" doesn't mind going "out of the way" in River North for "spicy" Nuevo Latino eats and drinks in a "trendy setting" that's set up for "salsa dancing"; "go on the weekends" when the lessons are free and the ambiance is "hot, hot, hot", just know that at peak hours the "noise level makes it less than ideal for dining" and can lead to "distracted" service.

Russell's Barbecue *BBQ*

20 | 11 | 13 | $13

Rolling Meadows | 2885 Algonquin Rd. (bet. Carriageway & Newport Drs.) | 847-259-5710
Elmwood Park | 1621 N. Thatcher Ave. (North Ave.) | 708-453-7065
www.russellsbarbecue.com

A "no-nonsense" West Suburban "institution", this "trusty old BBQ stop" that's "been there forever" (since 1930) is a "favorite" for "pork and beef sandwiches" and "fallin'-off-the-bone tender" ribs; even devotees who rave that the fare "is great" admit the "decor and service aren't", while some tepid tasters "think you had to grow up with this food" "to really appreciate" it; N.B. at a mere 27 years of age, the Rolling Meadows location is a relative newcomer.

Russian Tea Time *Russian*

22 | 21 | 22 | $38

Loop | 77 E. Adams St. (bet. Michigan & Wabash Aves.) | 312-360-0000 | www.russianteatime.com

Take "a real culinary trip" "right in the heart of" the Loop at this "cozy" "hideaway" presenting a "menu that reads like a Russian novel, with a story explaining the history of each" "trusty" dish; respondents also revere the "old-world service", "burgundy-and-brass" interior "filled" with "lovely flowers", "samovars and velvet", "nice afternoon tea" and "flights" of "great infused vodkas", calling it "the best choice if you are bound for the symphony or Art Institute."

NEW Rustik *American*

- | - | - | M

Logan Square | 2515 N. California Ave. (Altgeld St.) | 773-235-0002 | www.rustikrestaurant.com

Tweaked versions of "trendy" New American "comfort food" such as mac 'n' cheese, BLTs, stuffed meatloaf, tomato soup and grilled cheese, plus a Latin-leaning brunch, are "priced very affordably" at this "sophisticated but warm" Logan Square "neighborhood" niche; the "north-woods atmosphere" includes antler light fixtures, stonework, a glass atrium garden, semicircular bar and communal table; N.B. they don't take reservations.

NEW Rusty Armadillo Grill & Cantina 🅂🅜 *Mexican*

- | - | - | I

Northwest Side | 6154 N. Milwaukee Ave. (bet. Huntington & Hyacinth Sts.) | 773-792-8360

Casual, colorful Mex at bargain prices takes over a former Northwest Side hardware store where you'll now find both classic and playful dishes (think Southwestern egg rolls) plus frozen fruit-flavored margaritas; a year-round rooftop patio crowns the bi-level space outfitted with exposed brick, a painted-concrete floor and giant plasma TVs.

Ruth's Chris Steak House *Steak*

25 | 21 | 23 | $58

River North | 431 N. Dearborn St. (Hubbard St.) | 312-321-2725
Northbrook | Renaissance Hotel | 933 Skokie Blvd. (Dundee Rd.) | 847-498-6889
www.ruthschris.com

"Nothing beats a steak sizzling in butter" at this "special-occasion" New Orleans–based chain with Northbrook and River North outposts where the "melt-in-your-mouth" chops are "cooked to perfection" and presented on "hot plates"; sure, the "decor varies" – from "blah" to "old-fashioned in a good way" – but service is "attentive" and the "off-the-charts" pricing manageable "so long as your boss doesn't care how much you spend."

Sabatino's ◑ *Italian* `22` `16` `22` `$32`

Northwest Side | 4441 W. Irving Park Rd. (bet. Cicero & Pulaski Aves.) | 773-283-8331 | www.sabatinoschicago.com

This Northwest Side "classic" is "a time warp" of "old Chicago Italian" dining, doing an "excellent job with the standard menu" (plus "great specials") served in "plentiful portions" that "preclude even the contemplation of dessert"; the "warmly bustling" setting is "like stepping into an old-time movie", "with the baby grand piano [played live on weekends], dim lighting, and booths tucked into corners" – part of why it "draws crowds" ranging from "families with kids" to "older" folks.

Sabor do Brasil Ⓜ *Brazilian* ▽ `22` `19` `23` `$49`

Orland Park | 15750 S. Harlem Ave. (157th St.) | 708-444-2770 | www.sabor-do-brasil.com

A "paradise for meat lovers" and "big-volume eaters", this Southwest Suburban Brazilian all-you-can-eat churrascaria relies on "prompt" servers in "authentic gaucho garb" to deliver the "various cuts" of "mouthwatering" beef; there's a "good salad bar for veggie lovers too", though a few feasters fear it "does not compare with others like it."

Sage Grille *American* `22` `20` `20` `$51`

Highwood | 260 Green Bay Rd. (Highwood Ave.) | 847-433-7005 | www.sagegrille.com

The "menu is creative" with "fresh ingredients" and "choices for everyone including vegetarians" at this "upscale" New American in North Suburban Highwood; though some sages see it as "too expensive for what you get", another segment labels it "one of the cooler spots" in the area thanks to its "minimalistic" "California" decor, "well-orchestrated" service and "splendid wine list."

Sai Café *Japanese* `24` `17` `22` `$32`

Lincoln Park | 2010 N. Sheffield Ave. (Armitage Ave.) | 773-472-8080 | www.saicafe.com

"For the love of maki, just go" to this "wonderful neighborhood sushi bar" that's "been around Lincoln Park for [more than 20] years" urge enthusiasts of its "nice, large cuts" of "fresh fish" "and other Japanese preparations" "prepared by super chefs"; with its "homey", "relaxing" feel, it's "not as flashy" "as the trendy places", but most agree it's a "value" – so "plan ahead to get a table" or expect "lengthy waits on weekend nights."

Sakuma's Japanese Restaurant *Japanese* `–` `–` `–` `M`

Streamwood | 43 S. Sutton Rd. (Schaumburg Rd.) | 630-483-0289

In a Suburban Northwest strip-mall, this midpriced spot is on a roll with fanciers of fresh raw fish (from a vast list), creative maki and sashimi preps, and Japanese classics, plus three omakase (chef's choice) menus; the simple setting features a long sushi bar and white walls hung with traditional artifacts.

Saloon Steakhouse, The *Steak* | 22 | 19 | 23 | $53 |

Streeterville | Seneca Hotel | 200 E. Chestnut St. (bet. Lake Shore Dr. & Michigan Ave.) | 312-280-5454 | www.saloonsteakhouse.com

A Streeterville "locals'" "secret" that "does just what it should do", this "clubby" steakhouse serves "some of the finest beef", including "succulent Wagyu" (prized by patrons as "on the money") and "fine, fine martinis too" in "classy", "pleasant surroundings" (the "perfect place for a business lunch"); the "nice" "older" clientele values the "friendly", "professional staff" and also likes that this "meat and potatoes" "standby" is "less crowded and noisy than nearby competitors" – and "without the attitude."

Salpicón *Mexican* | 24 | 19 | 22 | $45 |

Old Town | 1252 N. Wells St. (bet. Goethe & Scott Sts.) | 312-988-7811 | www.salpicon.com

"Every dish seems new, inventive and delicious" at this "colorful" Old Town "gem" showcasing Priscila Satkoff's "haute", "authentic" "Mexican with elegant presentation and savory sauces", plus "tons of tequila options" and a "surprisingly" "great wine list"; surveyor service assessments seesaw from "fabulous" to "snooty", and budgeters believe it's "a bit pricey", but it's a "must for anyone who likes their Mex with a modern twist."

Salud Tequila Lounge ⬤ *Mexican* | - | - | - | M |

Wicker Park | 1471 N. Milwaukee Ave. (Honore St.) | 773-235-5577 | www.saludlounge.com

A selection of 75-plus 100% agave tequilas for sipping or mixing is served alongside a creative Mexican menu with everything from nachos and tacos to Latin-influenced sautéed snapper, grilled rib-eye and pork chops at this Wicker Parker; the loungey lair has an upscale, see-and-be-seen vibe with settee seating and colorful murals; N.B. DJs spin Wednesday–Saturday after 10 PM.

Salvatore's Ristorante Ⓜ *Italian* | ▽ 21 | 21 | 21 | $32 |

Lincoln Park | 525 W. Arlington Pl. (Clark St.) | 773-528-1200 | www.salvatores-chicago.com

In business for over 30 years, this "hidden" Lincoln Park Northern Italian "tucked away on a side street" "charms" chowhounds who favor "old-fashioned, quiet" dining (it's "not a place to see and be seen"); "underpriced" eats with "good sauces" are served in a "romantic" "ballroom"-like setting or on the "terrace overlooking a garden" (it's "popular for weddings and special events").

Sam & Harry's Steakhouse *Steak* 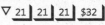 | ▽ 27 | 24 | 24 | $57 |

Schaumburg | Renaissance Schaumburg Hotel & Convention Ctr. | 1551 N. Thoreau Dr. (Meacham Rd.) | 847-303-4050 | www.samandharrys.com

"For a hotel restaurant, this is among the best" declare devotees of this "impressive" Northwest Suburban installation offering "great steak", "world-class crab cakes" and "fabulous" "modern decor" that some call "comfortable" (sofa booths piled with pillows) and others deem "cold" and "noisy"; the consensus is that the "quality is very good, but it's pricey."

San Gabriel Mexican Cafe Mexican   20 | 17 | 19 | $27

Bannockburn | Bannockburn Green Shopping Ctr. | 2535 Waukegan Rd. (Half Day Rd.) | 847-940-0200 | www.sangabcafe.com

"A nicely balanced menu" of "very good, fresh Mexican" fare "with some interesting specials", plus "great tableside guacamole" and a "good tequila selection (especially for the [Northern] Suburbs)" appeal to amigos of this "casual" "strip-mall" spot; some surveyors, though, can't get past certain "ups and downs" they perceive, most notably in relation to the "uneven service."

Sangria Restaurant &   ∇ 14 | 17 | 13 | $36
Tapas Bar ⊠Ⓜ Nuevo Latino

Lincoln Park | 901 W. Weed St. (Fremont St.) | 312-266-1200 | www.sangriachicago.com

As you'd guess, this "colorful", "happening" Nuevo Latino "hangout" in Lincoln Park has a "great sangria selection", but it also serves "fun" small plates; still, voters maintain "the point of going here is not the food" (most find the "average" offerings "uninteresting") or service (which many feel "is worse than a coffeehouse"), but rather "the cool atmosphere and beautiful people" – though a recent chef change may make a difference.

San Soo Gab San ❶ Korean   ∇ 21 | 8 | 14 | $23

Northwest Side | 5247 N. Western Ave. (Foster Ave.) | 773-334-1589

For an "interesting experience", investigate this "authentic" Northwest Sider's "excellent Korean barbecue" that comes with a "ton of side dishes"; due to "poor ventilation", expect to go home with smoke smells "embedded into your hair, clothing and entire being" – a discomfort that's offset by "extremely affordable" tabs and the fact that it's "open 24 hours" to "satisfy those late-night cravings."

Santorini ❶ Greek/Seafood   22 | 19 | 20 | $35

Greektown | 800 W. Adams St. (Halsted St.) | 312-829-8820 | www.santorinichicago.com

If you "need an evening in the Greek Islands", try this "more upscale" and "enlightened" "white-tablecloth" Hellenic "specializing in seafood" with "tableside filleting" (they "do the other specialties equally well"); veterans vow that the "very comfortable, almost elegant" environs are "quieter" and "not so touristy" as "most of its [Greektown] neighbors", and it's especially "warm and inviting by the fireplace" "on a cold night"; still, some say "service is hit-or-miss."

Sapore di Napoli Ⓜ Pizza   22 | 11 | 18 | $22

Lakeview | 1406 W. Belmont Ave. (N. Southport Ave.) | 773-935-1212 | www.saporedinapoli.net

This "gem" of an entrant into the "Neapolitan-style wood-fired pizza" "restaurant trend" is a "tiny" Lakeview BYO that's "crowded for a reason" – namely the "crisp, delicious" pies that "take little time to make", "wonderful gelato" and other Italian dishes for "eat-in or takeout"; few mind that there's "no ambiance", since the owners are so "lovely" and the service "very personal."

Sapori Trattoria *Italian*   22 | 19 | 21 | $31

Lincoln Park | 2701 N. Halsted St. (Schubert Ave.) | 773-832-9999 | www.saporitrattoria.net

It's "always packed" at this "charming" Lincoln Park "favorite", so "reserve for sure" for a "warm and friendly", "authentic" "trattoria experience" with "fresh Italian food" including "homemade pastas" (habitués are "hooked" on both the pumpkin and lobster ravioli) and "delicious specials" that are "so good, you always feel like you're getting a deal" (there's also an "extensive list of wines at reasonable prices"); P.S. garden seating helps alleviate the "crowded", sometimes "noisy" conditions inside.

Sayat Nova *Armenian*   20 | 15 | 19 | $31

Streeterville | 157 E. Ohio St. (bet. Michigan Ave. & St. Clair St.) | 312-644-9159 | www.sayatnovachicago.com

The "lively", "authentic Armenian fare" is a "great value" at this "cozy", "family-run" Streeterville "treasure tucked away just off Michigan Avenue", an "offbeat choice for something out of the ordinary", with "interesting" if "somewhat seedy decor"; most of the time it's a "quiet hideaway", but DJs (two Saturdays a month) heat up the scene.

Schwa ⧈Ⓜ *American*   - | - | - | E

Wicker Park | 1466 N. Ashland Ave. (LeMoyne St.) | 773-252-1466 | www.schwarestaurant.com

Acolytes of chef Michael Carlson "dream" about his "spectacular" "seasonal" New American cuisine, "artfully presented" in the "minimalist, unpretentious atmosphere" of the "smallest dining room and kitchen imaginable" in Wicker Park; bargain-hunters find it "a bit pricey", but supporters swear this BYO "little-restaurant-that-could" (its temporary closing last year is the reason for the lack of scores) is "a must"; P.S. "plan ahead", given the space limitations.

Scoozi! *Italian*   20 | 20 | 20 | $36

River North | 410 W. Huron St. (bet. Kingsbury & Orleans Sts.) | 312-943-5900 | www.leye.com

"Still fun" and "consistent", this River North "crowd-pleaser" "never gets tired" to surveyors supportive of its "solid execution" of "Americanized Italian" fare served at "fair prices" by a "happy" staff within a "huge", "noisy" and "rustic" warehouse setting; tarter tongues tell us this "typical Lettuce operation" "is a bit passé" and there's "nothing original" on its "generic" menu, but it's "good" "for the whole family"; P.S. there's a "hopping" "happy-hour scene."

ⓩ Seasons *American*   27 | 26 | 27 | $80

Gold Coast | Four Seasons Hotel | 120 E. Delaware Pl., 7th fl. (bet. Michigan Ave. & Rush St.) | 312-649-2349 | www.fourseasons.com

"Pure elegance" describes this "outstanding" Gold Coast hotel restaurant where Kevin Hickey's "inspired" seasonal New American prix fixe menus are matched by "sensitive service" and "expensive" tabs; the "spacious", "beautiful" and some say "slightly stuffy" setting features a "great view of the lake" and Michigan Avenue, drawing in supporters for a "special night out", "business or shopper's lunch" or "impressive Sunday brunch"; N.B. jackets suggested.

☑ Seasons Café ● *American*   `21` `24` `25` `$53`

Gold Coast | Four Seasons Hotel | 120 E. Delaware Pl., 7th fl.
(bet. Michigan Ave. & Rush St.) | 312 649 2349 | www.fourseasons.com
"Delightful service" and a "clubby", "upscale" atmosphere make this a "relaxing place" for Gold Coast grazing and shopping breaks, with a Traditional American menu that "works for appetites large and small" thanks to its "delightful" "luncheon buffets" ("reasonably priced for a top hotel") and prix fixe dinner option; the "decor hasn't changed in 20 years", but major renovations were in the works at press time.

☑ NEW Sepia *American*   `22` `25` `21` `$54`

Market District | 123 N. Jefferson St. (bet. Randolph & Washington Sts.) | 312-441-1920 | www.sepiachicago.com
The "theme of subtle-but-sensational echoes throughout" this "new star of the Market District", drawing an "attractive" "mix of people" to an "old Chicago print shop" for "delicious" "local/seasonal" New American food ("don't pass up the tiny flatbreads to start") and "original drinks"; some wish the service lived up to the "super-trendy room", and waverers warn "at its best it sparkles . . . but hit an off night and the food is in sepia tones as well as the decor."

☑ 1776 ☒ *American*   `26` `18` `24` `$40`

Crystal Lake | 397 W. Virginia St./Rte. 14 (bet. Dole & McHenry Aves.) | 815-356-1776 | www.1776restaurant.com
The "impressively diverse menu" is stocked with "excellent game dishes" at this Northwest Suburban New American where the service is "attentive and friendly" and the interior "cozy" if "drab"; it's a "treat to just read" the worldly 600-bottle wine list (ask owner Andy Andresky for advice, since he "knows it all"), and regulars recommend trying the Wednesday–Thursday night nine-course tapas menu.

Shallots Bistro *French/Mediterranean*   `-` `-` `-` `E`

Skokie | 4741 Main St. (Skokie Blvd.) | 847-677-3463 | www.shallotsbistro.com
Anointed the "best kosher restaurant in Chicago" by fans, this "superb" North Suburban French-Med bistro caters to diners who "observe the Jewish dietary laws" yet still crave "great desserts" and specialty martinis; you "can talk most of the time" in the "upscale" setting, just know that "they keep short hours" – service ends at 9 PM most nights, and they're closed on Fridays and summer Saturdays.

☑ Shanghai Terrace *Asian*   `25` `26` `26` `$66`

River North | Peninsula Hotel | 108 E. Superior St., 5th fl.
(bet. Michigan Ave. & Rush St.) | 312-573-6744 |
www.chicago.peninsula.com
Serving some of the "best-in-the-city" "pampered" Asian cuisine, this "exquisite" River North Peninsula Hotel canteen reminds raters

of "upmarket places in Hong Kong, Taipei or Shanghai"; its "attentive service" and "elegant, serene" setting (there's "nothing like overlooking Michigan Avenue from the beautifully appointed" "roof" terrace) are well-suited for an "important business meeting or the big date", given that it's "expensive and wonderful all in the same breath"; N.B. Sunday brunch, but not dinner, is served.

Z Shaw's Crab House *Seafood*   24 | 19 | 21 | $47

River North | 21 E. Hubbard St. (bet. State St. & Wabash Ave.) | 312-527-2722
Schaumburg | 1900 E. Higgins Rd. (Rte. 53) | 847-517-2722
www.shawscrabhouse.com

"You can almost hear the surf" at this "classy", "East Coast–style seafooder", a River North and Northwest Suburb "keeper" from the Lettuce Entertain You crew that reels 'em in with "worldwide-sourced" fish and shellfish including "oysters from both coasts" and a "selection of sushi"; the decor evokes "Miami Beach in the 1940s" with both a "formal" room and more "laid-back oyster bar", so while a few fear it costs too many "clams", the majority feels the prices are "justified by the quality."

NEW Shikago Ⓢ *Asian*   20 | 16 | 18 | $40

Loop | 190 S. LaSalle St. (Adams St.) | 312-781-7300 | www.shikagorestaurant.com

"Famed" chef Kevin Shikami oversees an "inventive" Asian menu that "merges the best of East and West" at this Loop locale with both counter and "restaurant-style service" for "takeaway" or "sit-down" in a setting within a "great historic building"; however, critics call the food "average", the service "spotty" and the room "cold and uninviting."

Shine & Morida *Chinese/Japanese*   18 | 16 | 16 | $30

Lincoln Park | 901 W. Armitage Ave. (Fremont St.) | 773-296-0101 | www.shinemorida.com

Admirers of this "upscale" Lincoln Parker aver it serves "surprisingly good" Mandarin Chinese food "as well as delicious, fresh sushi" and other Japanese "standards" in a "fun", "trendy atmosphere", with "lightning-fast delivery" too; however antis insist it "tries to be too many things" and question the "varying" quality of its food and service; P.S. the "patio seating is pet-friendly."

NEW Shochu Ⓢ Ⓜ *American/Japanese*   – | – | – | M

Lakeview | 3313 N. Clark St. (bet. Adeline Ave. & Buckingham Pl.) | 773-348-3313

From the owners of Deleece comes this American-style take on a Japanese izakaya featuring moderately priced Eclectic small plates (including sushi and yakitori) to pair with the namesake aromatic spirit (mixed in various cocktails); the contemporary Lakeview storefront room, complete with a fireplace, feels deceptively spacious thanks to its high ceilings and a combination of banquettes and ethereal white chairs – plus there is a seasonal landscaped patio.

	FOOD	DECOR	SERVICE	COST

Shor *American*
| - | - | - | E |

South Loop | Hyatt Regency McCormick Pl. | 2233 S. Martin Luther King Dr.
(Cermak Rd.) | 312-528-4140 | www.mccormickplace.hyatt.com

Tucked in the back of the South Loop's Hyatt Regency McCormick
Place, this Traditional American grill offers a limited, straightforward menu of pricey prime beef plus a few seafood and poultry
dishes, all served against a modern backdrop with raised banquettes and warm pendant lighting; breakfast and lunch are also offered to hungry conventioneers.

Shula's Steakhouse *Steak*
| 19 | 18 | 18 | $58 |

Streeterville | Sheraton Chicago Hotel & Towers | 301 E. North Water St.
(Columbus Dr.) | 312-670-0788
Itasca | Westin Chicago NW | 400 Park Blvd. (Thorndale Ave.) |
630-775-1499

"If you like the 1972 Dolphins, you'll like" these two members of a
national team of "upscale" "sports-themed steakhouses celebrating
Shula's splendid career"; the defense deems them "well done", with
"great service and food" ("huge" "aged steaks" and seafood too),
but the offense scores them "too expensive for the quality" (the
"black Angus offerings can't stand up to the prime cuts" elsewhere)
and thinks "the coach should have stuck with football."

Siam Café *Thai*
| ▽ 22 | 12 | 19 | $20 |

Uptown | 4712 N. Sheridan Rd. (bet. Lawrence & Leland Aves.) |
773-769-6602

A "neighborhood treasure" "since forever" (1969), this Uptown
Siamese "favorite" features "inexpensive" "savory" Thai "standbys"
alongside "unique dishes"; the "dated" decor "could be improved" –
perhaps that's why it's also known for its "carry-out business";
N.B. they also serve a bargain lunch buffet and are newly BYO.

☑ Signature Room *American*
| 19 | 25 | 20 | $60 |

Streeterville | John Hancock Ctr. | 875 N. Michigan Ave., 95th fl.
(bet. Chestnut St. & Delaware Pl.) | 312-787-9596 |
www.signatureroom.com

You "cannot beat the view" from this Streeterville New American
"on the 95th floor of the John Hancock Center" offering "dinner in
the clouds" with vistas so "breathtaking" that few mind the "tired"
interior and "mediocre" menu; smart shoppers suggest the "eco-
nomical weekday lunch buffet" or "delightful Sunday brunch", noting
it's "great to take out-of-towners, even if only for a drink"; P.S. the
"best" lookout over the city "can be found in the ladies room."

Silver Cloud Bar & Grill *American*
| 19 | 15 | 18 | $19 |

Bucktown | 1700 N. Damen Ave. (Wabansia Ave.) | 773-489-6212 |
www.silvercloudchicago.com

Bucktown's "quintessential neighborhood place" qualifies as a "low-
key hangout" and "hangover" cure with "homey", "artery-clogging"
Traditional American "comfort food" reminiscent of "elementary
school" – "go for the sloppy joes or the grilled cheese and tomato
soup" – and a "great drink selection"; it "looks like a trashy diner" with

	FOOD	DECOR	SERVICE	COST

"'70s sparkle furniture", plus there's "great outdoor seating" ("you can bring your dog", though Fido has to stay outside the fence).

Silver Seafood ● *Chinese/Seafood* | 20 | 6 | 13 | $24 |

Uptown | 4829 N. Broadway St. (Lawrence Ave.) | 773-784-0668
An "unpretentious" Uptown storefront houses this "raucous" "immersion experience into Asian family life and eating", with diners of "all ages" filing in for "inexpensive" Cantonese seafood (nods go to the "mixed" "basket" and "salt and pepper anything", but "avoid" the "gloppy" "gringo dishes"); service can be "slow, as English is a real problem", yet for the "adventurous" eater, it's a "good alternative to Chinatown"; N.B. beer and wine only.

Simply It ⓜ *Vietnamese* | 22 | 14 | 17 | $22 |

Lincoln Park | 2269 N. Lincoln Ave. (W. Belden Ave.) | 773-248-0884
Partialists praise the "Pasteur food" "without the pretense" (but with plenty of "complex flavors") at this "wonderful" Lincoln Park Vietnamese from a "former owner" of that defunct longtime favorite; if there's "no decor to speak of" and the "service needs just a bit of evening out", at least the owner himself is "the nicest" and it's BYO, which means "prices are quite reasonable."

NEW Sixteen *American* | - | - | - | E |

River North | Trump International Hotel & Tower | 401 N. Wabash Ave. (Kinzie St.) | 312-588-8030 | www.trumpchicagohotel.com
The 16th floor of River North's Trump International Hotel & Tower Chicago is home to this flashy New American, where globally influenced fare is offered à la carte (expensive) and in 'blind tastings' (very expensive); a showstopping Swarovski-crystal chandelier sets a posh tone, while soaring windows provide dramatic city views; N.B. there's 'high champagne' on Saturday afternoons and high-in-the-sky outdoor dining come summer.

Smith & Wollensky *Steak* | 22 | 20 | 21 | $58 |

River North | 318 N. State St. (Upper Wacker Dr.) | 312-670-9900 | www.smithandwollensky.com
This River North "businessman's" lunch and dinner "mecca" "doesn't feel like a chain" declare devotees of its "solid", "huge" steaks, "amazing seafood tray" and "enormous" sides, all priced "for the expense-account set"; the space is filled with "lots of testosterone" (and some say "'tude") and sports "one of the better late-night munchie menus" "downstairs at the grill"; even though some find it "frustratingly inconsistent", all agree there's "no place better in summer than on the terrace overlooking the river."

Smoke Daddy *BBQ* | 21 | 13 | 16 | $22 |

Wicker Park | 1804 W. Division St. (Woods St.) | 773-772-6656 | www.thesmokedaddy.com
Fans of "good, smoky flavor" "love the great ribs, sweet potato fries" and "yummy pulled pork" at this Wicker Park "local hangout" serving "just plain ol'" "bodacious" BBQ; supporters also like its "barlike" setting decorated with vintage Chicago photos and guitars on the

walls and say another "plus" is that there's "a live band every night with no cover"; still, some say the "service is slow."

Smoque BBQ Ⓜ *BBQ*

24 | 9 | 17 | $16

Northwest Side | 3800 N. Pulaski Rd. (Grace St.) | 773-545-7427 | www.smoquebbq.com

"Finally, respectable BBQ on the North[west] side" crow cronies who wait in the "long lines" at this "chaotic" "counter-service" BYO canteen for platefuls of "fine pulled pork", "brisket that rocks", "smoky" "St. Louis and babyback ribs" and "tasty sides"; there's "no fancy atmosphere", "sometimes they run out of food" and portions can be "small for the price", but don't blame the "courteous" staff, since they're "anxious to please."

socca *French/Italian*

24 | 20 | 23 | $35

Lakeview | 3301 N. Clark St. (Aldine Ave.) | 773-248-1155 | www.soccachicago.com

French-Italian bistro "basics" get "spiffed up with modern twists" at this Lakeview lair that pleases with "healthy-sized" portions at "affordable prices" ("no itty-bitty fancy plates here"), a "great wine list" and "friendly, informative staff"; depending on when you go, it could be "classy, quiet" and "comfortable" or a "cool scene" that's "crowded and loud", especially in the "trendy bar area"; N.B. there's patio dining in season.

sola *American*

25 | 22 | 22 | $44

Lakeview | 3868 N. Lincoln Ave. (Byron St.) | 773-327-3868 | www.sola-restaurant.com

Carol Wallack's "excellent" New American cuisine "draws from many inspirations", including Asia, Hawaii and "the bounty of the season", at this "lively" ("very noisy when busy") Lakeview "fine-dining" destination; additional assets include "attentive service", a "fair-priced wine list", "great" weekend "brunch options" and an "outdoor terrace in the summer"; N.B. they also offer curbside carryout.

Sol de Mexico *Mexican*

∇ 25 | 18 | 22 | $29

Northwest Side | 3018 N. Cicero Ave. (bet. Nelson St. & Wellington Ave.) | 773-282-4119

"Explosively original" "regional" Mexican meals with "BYO prices and no waiting for tables" have "foodies and Mexican families" alike anointing this Northwest Sider the city's most "serious mole outpost"; though "hard to get to", feasters who make the "worth-it" drive are rewarded with "warm service", "funky artwork" and "easy parking" – in fact, boosters beg "please don't publicize" this "hidden treasure."

NEW Sopa *American/Mediterranean*

- | - | - | M

Highwood | Fort Sheridan Plaza | 752 Sheridan Rd. (bet. Old Elm & Sheridan Rds.) | 847-433-3434 | www.soparestaurant.com

This North Suburban strip-mall spot (previously Erik's) from former staffers of Restaurant Michael offers midpriced, hearty New American–Mediterranean fare with a Cal-Ital wine list; rustic brick and warm wood are balanced by mod design elements (track lighting, sleek semi-open kitchen, metallic place mats) in the dining room.

	FOOD	DECOR	SERVICE	COST

South Gate Cafe *American*

20 | 19 | 20 | $33

Lake Forest | 655 Forest Ave. (Deerpath Rd.) | 847-234-8800 |
www.southgatecafe.com

Adherents of this "Lake Forest classic" appreciate its "inviting"
("particularly on the patio in summertime") setting in a turn-of-the-
last-century building and note the "new chef has done wonders"
with his "nice selection" of "flavorful" American "menu items"
paired with a "growing wine list"; however, gate-crashers gripe "the
quality of the food changes often" and wonder "will it ever break
free" of "mediocrity"?

South Water Kitchen *American*

17 | 17 | 18 | $33

Loop | Hotel Monaco | 225 N. Wabash Ave. (Lake St.) | 312-236-9300 |
www.southwaterkitchen.com

Traditional American "home cooking" "with modern twists" and a
"cute" "high-ceiling room" have some Loop denizens grading this
"great" "for a quick and hearty" lunch, a "drink after work" or a "pre-
theater" dinner; others cite "average" food – though it's "convenient
if you're staying at the hotel."

Spacca Napoli Pizzeria Ⓜ *Pizza*

24 | 17 | 18 | $24

Ravenswood | 1769 W. Sunnyside Ave. (bet. Hermitage &
Ravenswood Aves.) | 773-878-2420 | www.spaccanapolipizzeria.com

The coveted No. 1 pizza prize goes to this Ravenswood "thin-crust"
upstart whose "sincere" owner "traveled the whole of Italy to learn
his craft" – and "you can taste the love" in his "fabulous", "authentic
Neapolitan" pies whose "slightly charred", "bubbly" crusts are
topped with "high-quality ingredients"; the menu is all 'za, antipasto, *bierra* and wine, the "noisy" environs are "low-key" and "the
wait may be long" but it's "worth it."

NEW Spertus Cafe *American*

- | - | - | I

South Loop | Spertus Museum | 618 S. Michigan Ave. (Harrison St.) |
312-322-1700 | www.spertus.edu

The counter-service cafe at Spertus' fancy new South Loop building
is the only kosher option Downtown, and it offers inexpensive New
American fare (salads, sandwiches, sushi and sweets) from
Wolfgang Puck no less; its airy, white-and-metal space with a futur-
istic food-court feel and views of Grant Park is open from 8:30 AM
to early dinner (with a 3 PM closing on Fridays).

Ⓩ Spiaggia *Italian*

27 | 26 | 26 | $90

Gold Coast | One Magnificent Mile Bldg. | 980 N. Michigan Ave., 2nd fl.
(Oak St.) | 312-280-2750 | www.spiaggiarestaurant.com

Ranked the "best Italian in the city", this "haute" Gold Coast "institution" gets gold stars for Tony Mantuano's "exquisite composi-
tions", a "deep" and "wide" Cal-Ital wine list, "personalized,
knowledgeable service" (including a "fromagier who helps you select" from the cheese cart) and a jackets-required "tiered dining
room" that provides "gorgeous views of the lake"; yet still surveyors
are split on whether it's worth the "ginormous bucks", and some
who find it "too fussy" and "serious" prefer the adjacent cafe.

	FOOD	DECOR	SERVICE	COST

Spoon Thai *Thai*

20 | 10 | 15 | $16

Lincoln Square | 4608 N. Western Ave. (Wilson Ave.) | 773-769-1173 | www.spoonthai.com

"Not at all the usual Thai fare", this Lincoln Square BYO's "interesting", "authentic and aromatic" chow – including "edgy dishes" such as its "unique catfish curry with eggplant" – makes it a "cheap-eats" "favorite" that has devotees declaring the "owners should charge double (but we're glad they don't)"; if you aren't taken by the "no-frills" decor, remember that it's "great for pickup or delivery."

⚡ Spring Ⓜ *American/Seafood*

27 | 23 | 25 | $63

Wicker Park | 2039 W. North Ave. (Damen Ave.) | 773-395-7100 | www.springrestaurant.net

At this "oasis of calm in frenetic Wicker Park", Shawn McClain turns out "delicate", "fresh" New American seafood with Asian "flair" that devotees deem "exceptional both in taste and presentation"; adding to the allure, its "Zen-spa" setting features "original" tiles from its former incarnation as a bathhouse, the servers are "never intrusive but always there when you need them", and there's a "carefully chosen wine list" and "powerful, original cocktails"; as for the value, diners differ over whether it's "overpriced" or "reasonable" for the "excellent quality."

Stained Glass Wine Bar Bistro *American*

24 | 21 | 22 | $44

Evanston | 1735 Benson Ave. (bet. Church & Clark Sts.) | 847-864-8600 | www.thestainedglass.com

"Fun flights" and an "interesting modern American menu" served by a "knowledgeable", "unpretentious" staff make this "reliable" restaurant "tucked between Evanston storefronts" equally "great for a fancy dinner or just a bite after a movie"; "inventive wine pairings" from its "wide-ranging list" and its "warm" space are also enticing.

Stanley's Kitchen & Tap *American*

19 | 13 | 15 | $19

Lincoln Park | 1970 N. Lincoln Ave. (Armitage Ave.) | 312-642-0007 | www.stanleysrestaurant.com

Stanley's on Racine *American*

West Loop | 324 S. Racine Ave. (Van Buren St.) | 312-433-0007

"Good neighborhood joints" for "down-home" Traditional American eating, "drinking and hanging out", this "fun" "fake roadhouse" and "family restaurant hidden in a bar" in Lincoln Park and its newer West Loop locale sling "classic mac 'n' cheese" and "better meatloaf than mom's"; there's also a "maximum-cholesterol" weekend brunch that gets "very crowded" – especially "during football season."

Starfish Ⓢ *Japanese*

20 | 17 | 17 | $38

Market District | 804 W. Randolph St. (Halsted St.) | 312-997-2433 | www.starfishsushi.com

Sushi-lovers are split over this Market District raw-fish-monger, with some swearing by the "delicious nontraditional maki", "interesting appetizers", signature "Starfish martini" and "lovely outdoor patio" – and as for the "average" decor and service, they note it's "great for carryout" ("too bad they stopped doing delivery"); sliding food scores, however, support surveyors who see it as "past its prime", saying the once "serviceable" spot "has gone downhill."

Star of Siam *Thai*   20 | 14 | 18 | $19

River North | 11 E. Illinois St. (State St.) | 312-670-0100 |
www.starofsiamchicago.com

"Cheap and cheerful", this River North old-timer (opened in 1984) is "a humble choice" serving "reliably delicious" Thai with "no surprises" – "simply good stuff" that "they'll spice up if you request it hot"; in addition to "traditional tables and chairs", the "simple setting" offers "cubbyholes to sit in (a fun departure)", and "fast service" makes it a "great" place to "grab a quick lunch"; still, some surveyors score it as strictly "serviceable."

Stetson's Chop House *Steak*   23 | 18 | 19 | $52

Loop | Hyatt Regency | 151 E. Wacker Dr. (bet. Michigan & Stetson Aves.) | 312-239-4491 | www.hyatt.com

"Impressed" diners declare "don't dismiss" this "solid" meatery just "because it's in a tourist-filled [Loop] hotel", as it serves "huge portions" of prime beef in a "casual" setting with a "nice bar"; holdouts tally it a trifle "typical", though, and call it "a good steakhouse in a great steak town"; N.B. there's live jazz nightly except Sundays.

Stir Crazy *Asian*   21 | 17 | 17 | $23

Northbrook | Northbrook Court Shopping Ctr. | 1186 Northbrook Ct. (Lake Cook Rd.) | 847-562-4800

Schaumburg | Woodfield Mall | 5 Woodfield Mall (Frontage & Golf Rds.) | 847-330-1200

Oak Brook | Oakbrook Center Mall | 105 Oakbrook Ctr. (Rte. 83) | 630-575-0155

Warrenville | 28252 Diehl Rd. (Windfield Rd.) | 630-393-4700
www.stircrazy.com

Frequent fryers find "nothing more fun than choosing your own ingredients, heaping them as high as possible in a bowl", then "watching" as they're "cooked fresh in front of you" at this "convenient and friendly" clan of Asian stir-fry stations with "many menu options" (including "prepared dishes"); it's "quick" and "good for kids", though some raters rank the results "run-of-the-mill" and the settings sometimes "hectic" and "noisy enough to drive you stir crazy."

NEW Stretch Run ⊠Ⓜ *American*   - | - | - | I

River North | 544 N. LaSalle St. (Ohio St.) | 312-644-4477 |
www.stretchrunchicago.com

This upscale River North sports bar/restaurant is betting that diners will want a side of race wagering with their midpriced Traditional American fare (potato skins, burgers, planked salmon, sundaes); JumboTron and plasma screens are everywhere throughout the masculine, multilevel space, which includes an entire upstairs room of private cubicles with screens where bettors can eat, drink and play the ponies.

	FOOD	DECOR	SERVICE	COST

Sullivan's Steakhouse *Steak*

| | 22 | 21 | 21 | $54 |

River North | 415 N. Dearborn St. (Hubbard St.) | 312-527-3510
Naperville | 244 S. Main St. (bet. Chicago & Jackson Aves.) | 630-305-0230
www.sullivanssteakhouse.com

"They do a really nice job" "for either business or romance" at this "polished", "clubby" duo in River North and the Western Suburbs, where the certified Angus steaks are "excellent" and "the onion rings are as big as doughnuts"; some respondents regard it as "a notch below some of the other places" due to "disappointing service", but others observe "the jazz and the great bar set it apart" – plus it's "a bit less expensive"; P.S. "the pineapple martinis are addictive."

Superdawg Drive-In *Hot Dogs*

| | 22 | 18 | 18 | $10 |

Northwest Side | 6363 N. Milwaukee Ave. (Devon Ave.) | 773-763-0660 ●🚭
Southwest Side | Midway Int'l Airport | 5700 S. Cicero Ave. (55th St.) | 773-948-6300
www.superdawg.com

This "icon" of "Americana" on the Northwest Side is a "true drive-in" "of the 1950s era", delivering "dawgs to die for" in "amusing little boxes" plus "deeelicious" shakes and fries – all the ingredients of "perfect summer evenings" (and travelers can get a taste at the Midway Airport outpost); besides, you "gotta love the two flirting hot dogs on the roof", though smart alecks "don't understand why there isn't a little" cocktail weenie up there too, since the couple's "been standing there for years – perhaps they should lie down!"

Sura ● *Thai*

| | 21 | 23 | 19 | $24 |

Lakeview | 3124 N. Broadway (Briar Pl.) | 773-248-7872 | www.surachicago.com

The "hip" "stark white" and" "varnished wood" "space odyssey" ambiance at this Lakeview spot is a backdrop for "tasty, well-crafted Thai food" (they're "trying new things" with the genre) and a "great drink list"; portions are "tiny" "but appropriately priced", so "order a variety of dishes" – and don't be surprised to encounter "uneven service."

NEW Su-Ra Korean Restaurant Ⓜ *Korean*

| | ▽ 17 | 19 | 21 | $24 |

Wicker Park | 2257 W. North Ave. (bet. Bell & Oakley Aves.) | 773-276-9450

"Authentic Korean food" is the draw at this "beautiful" Wicker Park BYO with "lots of varieties" of "good" "bibimbop and appetizers" enhanced by a "warm and inviting interior" and "owner who truly cares about each diner's experience"; fresh-air fanatics whisper that the "back patio is a secret oasis in warm weather."

Sushi Naniwa *Japanese*

| | 23 | 13 | 19 | $33 |

River North | 607 N. Wells St. (bet. Ohio & Ontario Sts.) | 312-255-8555 | www.sushinaniwa.com

An "authentic sushi bar" "without all the fluff" of some newer competitors, this River North Japanese from owner Bob Bee (of Bob San fame) is known for "reliable", "very fresh fish" "at a reasonable price"; perhaps the "standard", "no-frills" decor is "not particularly memorable"; but the service is "attentive without being annoying" and there's "great outdoor seating in the summer" – plus it's also "good for takeout."

Z SushiSamba rio ● *Japanese/S American*   22 | 26 | 18 | $46

River North | 504 N. Wells St. (bet. Grand Ave. & Illinois St.) | 312-595-2300 | www.sushisamba.com

There's "lots to take in" at this "swanky" River North "scene" serving a "creative" "fusion" of "Brazilian-Peruvian-Japanese" cuisines to "giant crowds" of "eye candy and beautiful people" who coo over the cocktails; "service could be better" and some consider it "kind of expensive", but most insist it's "worth it" for the "gorgeous" decor, "high-octane atmosphere" and "covered rooftop deck"; P.S. "Wednesday nights with live samba music are an event."

Z sushi wabi *Japanese*   26 | 19 | 20 | $46

Market District | 842 W. Randolph St. (bet. Green & Peoria Sts.) | 312-563-1224 | www.sushiwabi.com

"Fabulous rolls" from "old-fashioned to funky" make friends for this top-ranked Market District Japanese also known for its "hipster" vibe and "dark", "sparse" setting; "service is good but can be lacking when things get hopping", and those not interested in a "loud", "crowded" scene complete with a DJ ("all the pre-clubbers and corporate folk come here, but they can't all fit") may "prefer takeout."

Sushi X *Japanese*   – | – | – | M

NEW **Lincoln Park** | 543 W. Diversey Pkwy. (bet. Clark St. & Broadway) | 773-248-1808

River West | 1136 W. Chicago Ave. (bet. May St. & Racine Ave.) | 312-491-9232

www.sushi-x.net

Lincoln Park gets a hip sushi haunt in the form of a larger spin-off of the River West original with minimal-chic quarters boasting a cool silver-and-blue color scheme, clubby music and Japanese animation for visual distraction; there's a lounge area as well but no sushi bar – and no liquor unless you BYO.

Swordfish *Japanese*   ∇ 26 | 23 | 22 | $42

Batavia | 207 N. Randall Rd. (McKee St.) | 630-406-6463 | www.swordfishsushi.com

"High-end, innovative sushi finally reaches the far West Suburbs", prompting novices to note "now I know why people like this stuff", at this "trendy" Japanese sister of Wildfish where "incredibly" "fresh fish" – and "much more" – is served in a "subtle, modern" setting that surveyors say will make you "feel like you're in a Downtown restaurant"; P.S. it also offers a "thoughtfully planned wine list."

NEW **TABLE fifty-two** Ⓜ *American*   24 | 25 | 24 | $56

Gold Coast | 52 W. Elm St. (bet. Clark & Dearborn Sts.) | 312-573-4000 | www.tablefifty-two.com

"Oprah's chef" Art Smith, the "king of down-home yet elegant" Southern-accented, seasonal American cookery (think "fried green tomato Napoleans", "succulent ancho-crusted pork chops" and "hummingbird cake"), has transformed the Gold Coast's former Albert's Patisserie into a "buttery-yellow" "tiny gem" with an "intimate country feel"; it's "hard to get into" and topped off with generally "friendly" service, though some encounter a bit of "attitude" that comes with the "hype."

NEW Takashi *American/French* ▽ 29 | 20 | 25 | $60

Bucktown | 1952 N. Damen Ave. (Armitage Ave.) | 773-772-6170 | www.takashichicago.com

Takashi Yagihashi (ex Ambria) brings "terrific, unusual" Japanese-inflected American and French flavors to this "sleek, smart, small new spot" in the former Scylla space, an "awesome addition to the Bucktown dining scene"; the "warm", "accommodating service" and "reasonably priced" "wine and sake lists" have enthusiasts gushing "there's not much else to say except 'go.'"

Z Tallgrass M *French* 29 | 25 | 29 | $77

Lockport | 1006 S. State St. (10th St.) | 815-838-5566 | www.tallgrassrestaurant.com

"Spectacular" rave satisfied surveyors who "can't help but feel that they are dining in a different, more refined era" at this top-rated Suburban Southwest "diamond" that's so "high-end" you'd "expect to find it only in a major metropolis"; a staff that "picks up on the little things" serves "impeccably, imaginatively prepared" New French fare that is rife with "rich sauces" in a "cozy", "vintage" setting; add in a "highly sophisticated wine list", and it's "worth the ride and the price."

NEW Tallulah ⊠ M *American* – | – | – | M

Lincoln Square | 4539 N. Lincoln Ave. (bet. Sunnyside & Wilson Aves.) | 773-942-7585 | www.tallulahchicago.com

Troy Graves (ex Meritage) brings Contemporary American bistro fare to Lincoln Square, tweaking classics with global flavors to yield midpriced offerings such as pork belly bulgoki and chai crème brûlée; the tiny space is minimally chic yet warm thanks to blond wood and a cream-and-coffee-bean color scheme; year-round outdoor dining and BYO Tuesdays are added enticements.

Tamarind *Pan-Asian* ▽ 21 | 18 | 18 | $25

South Loop | 614 S. Wabash Ave. (Harrison St.) | 312-379-0970 | www.tamarindsushi.com

The "expansive" Pan-Asian menu stretches "from China to Vietnam to Japan and everything in-between" with "many healthy" choices, "noodle dishes", sushi and "build-your-own stir fry" at this South Loop "secret" set in "spartan"-chic surroundings; though some scribes say it's "nothing-to-write-home-about", most concede it's a "welcome addition" to the area; N.B. they offer prix fixe and patio seating.

Tango *Argentinean* ▽ 22 | 18 | 21 | $39

Naperville | 5 W. Jackson Ave. (Washington St.) | 630-848-1818 | www.tangogrill.com

"Come hungry and be prepared to share" at this Naperville Argentinean small-plates-and-meats "favorite" that's "fun for tapas", red or white sangria "or a full casual meal" (with a "cold martini" from the 20-plus list at the "small bar"); the staff is "friendly", Sunday brunch a "pleasant surprise" and wags wonder if their 26-inch steak is really the "longest in the world."

Tango Sur *Argentinean/Steak*   25 | 18 | 19 | $31

Lakeview | 3763 N. Southport Ave. (Grace St.) | 773-477-5466

Carnivores "can't go wrong" with the "addictive, cheap steaks and authentic Argentinean food" at this "funky" Lakeview BYO where the "dark" space with "tight" seating is intimate enough for a date but festive enough for "dinner with friends"; "plan on waiting awhile for a table", especially on weekends when it can be a "painfully noisy" "madhouse" – though they do have a bar and "try to turn the table quickly."

Tank Sushi *Japanese*   22 | 19 | 18 | $34

Lincoln Square | 4514 N. Lincoln Ave. (Sunnyside Ave.) | 773-769-2600 | www.tanksushi.com

"Sleek" and "spiffy" for Lincoln Square, this "indulgent" Japanese "pleasure" combines "clever maki rolls" made from "fresh ingredients" – "if you're looking for traditional sushi, this isn't the place" – with "brilliant drinks, beautiful presentation and surroundings" that "can be very loud" ("ambient club music"); some feel it's "service-challenged", and wallet watchers say it's "slightly overpriced", so go between 1:30 and 6 PM on weekends for the "half-price deal."

Tapas Barcelona *Spanish*   21 | 19 | 18 | $27

Evanston | Northshore Hotel Retirement Home | 1615 Chicago Ave. (bet. Church & Davis Sts.) | 847-866-9900 | www.tapasbarcelona.com

"Eat communally to savor the most sensations" at this "festive" Spaniard serving North Suburbanites "very good" tapas, "great sangria" and the "best sherry selection" in the vicinity; pleased patrons praise it as "perfect in summer for dining in the pretty garden" "but also fun in the exciting but noisy dining room" done up in "lots of cool tiles and colors"; while some warn of "mediocre service" and say the food "never really surprises or wows", even they concede "the price is right."

Tapas Gitana *Spanish*   - | - | - | M

Northfield | Northfield Village Ctr. | 310 Happ Rd. (bet. Willow Rd. & Winnetka Ave.) | 847-784-9300

If you share well with others, try the traditional and creative tapas, hot and cold – and, of course, paella – at this quaint North Suburban Spanish small-plates specialist; the colorful setting is enhanced by tiles and murals, a bar and an outdoor dining area with more seating than the intimate interior.

Tarantino's *Italian*   22 | 22 | 21 | $37

Lincoln Park | 1112 W. Armitage Ave. (Seminary Ave.) | 773-871-2929 | www.tarantinos.com

John Tarantino's "upscale Lincoln Park" establishment is a "cozy place for a simple dinner or a romantic night out" over "quality

Italian" fare that's "consistently" "solid and fresh" – "without the high price tag"; some say "service can be on or off" and feel there are "probably better options out there", but more maintain it's "everything one could want in a neighborhood restaurant"; P.S. "have a martini at the bar", as there's a "great list" to choose from.

Tasting Room, The ● Ⓩ Eclectic   ▽ 15 | 18 | 19 | $36

Market District | 1415 W. Randolph St. (Ogden Ave.) | 312-942-1313 | www.tlcwine.com

"Tasty appetizers", "new entree options", "cheese plates" and desserts pair well with the "extensive selection" of pours "you can purchase next door", all brokered by "experienced stewards" in this "roomy" Market District Eclectic with "cozy" (some say "frat-house"-style) seating and "great views of Downtown"; aficionados who wonder "why it's never super-packed" are answered by "disappointed" diners who swear the "best thing here is the wine selection."

Tavern Ⓩ American   ▽ 25 | 23 | 24 | $49

Libertyville | 519 N. Milwaukee Ave. (bet. Cook Ave. & Lake St.) | 847-367-5755 | www.tavernlibertyville.com

"It may be a tavern, but the food continues to be first-class" at this New American "favorite" in Libertyville, where "excellent steaks", an "outstanding potato chip–caviar appetizer" and a "wonderful", "Yellow Pages"-esque wine list are managed by "concerned" staffers; the "whimsy"-filled interior features architectural artifacts, paper lanterns and retro touches – just know that a night here "can get pricey if you're not careful."

NEW Tavern at the Park Ⓩ American   17 | 19 | 18 | $36

Loop | 130 E. Randolph St. (Michigan Ave.) | 312-552-0070 | www.tavernatthepark.com

Millennium Park's "busy, slightly lower-scale version of the upscale Keefer's" "fills a hole in Loop offerings" with a "broad" American menu of "huge salads", chicken pot pie, short ribs and prime rib and a happy hour–friendly "oak paneled bar"; "disappointed" raters, however, report on "ordinary, overpriced food", "fairly confused" service and a "bland" setting where "you can't even see the park from most of the tables"; N.B. better vistas are on the horizon when they add rooftop dining.

Tavern on Rush ● Steak   20 | 20 | 19 | $47

Gold Coast | 1031 N. Rush St. (Bellevue Pl.) | 312-664-9600 | www.tavernonrush.com

"A Chicago staple" to supporters of its "solid [steakhouse] dining experience", "great people-watching" and "awesome outdoor" seating, this "crowded" Gold Coast "hot spot" is admittedly "high-priced, but you pay for the scenery", especially at the "meat market in the bar" ("breasts and booze, what a combo"); testy tavern-goers, however, say this "Silicone Valley of the Viagra Triangle" metes out "mediocre food" and "attitude" ("we don't want nobody that nobody sent").

Tempo ●⊅ *Diner* 20 | 11 | 18 | $17

Gold Coast | 6 E. Chestnut St. (State St.) | 312-943-4373

"Open 24 hours to better serve the late, late crowd", this "nice" Gold Coast "landmark" is a "classic diner" that's "great morning, noon and night" for "wonderful, enormous omelets" and other "tasty" "coffee-shop" fare; there's "pleasant sidewalk dining in season", but "expect to wait for breakfast/brunch on the weekends", when it's "a zoo" – though it can be "dead at dinner"; P.S. yep, it's still "cash only."

Tepatulco *Mexican* 23 | 13 | 17 | $36

Lincoln Park | 2558 N. Halsted St. (bet. W. Lill & Wrightwood Aves.) | 773-472-7419 | www.tepatulco.com

Las Fuentas' replacement in Lincoln Park issues "imaginative", "authentic" Mexican eats and "friendly" but "not especially helpful" service; they've "hardly remodeled the dining area", causing critics to carp the "decor doesn't match the food quality" – optimists, however, hold out hope for a renovation of the patio, "which has always been the reason to go."

Terragusto Italian Café Ⓜ *Italian* 24 | 15 | 21 | $37

Roscoe Village | 1851 W. Addison St. (bet. Ravenswood & Wolcott Aves.) | 773-248-2777 | www.terragustocafe.com

This "tiny jewel of a neighborhood restaurant" brings "BYO Italian with an organic twist" to Roscoe Village with its "small, well-crafted" menu that's "interesting enough for foodies and approachable enough for meat and potato types" (kudos for the "exceptionally fresh" "handmade pastas"); penne-pinchers perceive it as "pricey but worth the cost", and though the space "lacks any atmosphere", it remains "very popular" so "reservations are recommended."

Texas de Brazil Churrascaria *Brazilian* 25 | 22 | 22 | $55

Schaumburg | Woodfield Mall | 5 Woodfield Mall (Golf Rd.) | 847-413-1600 | www.texasdebrazil.com

"Meat eaters rejoice" at this Northwest Suburban "carnivore's dream" where "gauchos rotate through" the room serving a "great selection" of all-you-can-eat Brazilian steakhouse offerings alongside a "spectacular salad bar" with "everything from sushi to gourmet cheeses"; it's "fun for a noisy group", though some vets vow "one can only eat so much meat and it's very expensive", ergo "lunch is the time to go – much less crowded and cheaper."

Thai Classic *Thai* ▽ 23 | 19 | 21 | $23

Lakeview | 3332 N. Clark St. (Addison St.) | 773-404-2000 | www.thaiclassicrestaurant.com

Thai classics "done well" at "reasonable prices" and with "great delivery" and a casual vibe make this longtime-"favorite" Lakeview BYO a "solid neighborhood pick"; eaters also enthuse over their "excellent lunch specials" and the fact that they serve a fixed-price buffet all day Sunday.

	FOOD	DECOR	SERVICE	COST

Thai Pastry *Thai*

| 24 | 13 | 18 | $18 |

Uptown | 4925 N. Broadway St. (bet. Ainslie & Argyle Sts.) | 773-784-5399 | www.thaipastry.com

"High-quality", "creative" Siamese that goes "way beyond pad Thai" is a "bargain" at this "charming", "casual" Uptown "storefront" BYO where "attentive", "pleasant" servers deliver "dishes customized to your requested spice level"; it also doubles as a bakery, so "leave room for dessert"; P.S. "the lunch special is a huge value."

NEW Thai Urban Kitchen *Japanese/Pan-Asian*

| - | - | - | M |

Loop | Ogilvie Transportation Ctr. | 500 W. Madison St. (N. Canal St.) | 312-575-0266 | www.thaiurbankitchen.com

Unexpected amid the fast-fooders at Ogilvie train station, this stunning modern eatery from the Sura folks serves moderately priced Pan-Asian interpretations and sushi; its swanky room is all black and white and metal, with a waterfall table/rock garden, wood seating pavilions, frosted-glass globe lighting and windows, windows, windows.

NEW Thalia Spice *Pan-Asian*

| ∇ 25 | 18 | 19 | $27 |

River West | 833 W. Chicago Ave. (Green St.) | 312-226-6020 | www.thaliaspice.com

There's "something for everyone" at this "reasonably priced" funky-chic River Wester where "it's easy to make a meal of the small plates" featuring "unique" "Thai, Japanese (sushi) and Indian" "flavor combos"; the staff is "eager to please" and you "can even find free street parking", so it's no surprise raters rank it "highly recommended"; N.B. at press time this was still a BYO-in-waiting.

Think *American/Eclectic*

| 22 | 17 | 21 | $37 |

Bucktown | 2235 N. Western Ave. (Lyndale St.) | 773-394-0537 | www.think-cafe.com

Admirers "can't get enough" of the "offbeat combos of fresh ingredients" and "gargantuan desserts" at this "off-the-beaten-path" New American–Eclectic Bucktown BYO "in a converted house" where the "creative vibe" is "perfect" for "romance" or a "girls' night out"; "friendly owners" and sidewalk dining ice the cake, and though service vacillates between "excellent" and "lacking", diehards declare "don't think about it, just go."

Three Happiness ● *Chinese*

| 19 | 8 | 15 | $18 |

Chinatown | 209 W. Cermak Rd. (20th St.) | 312-842-1964

"A Chinatown classic" that's "been there forever" (since 1971), this "family-run casual Chinese kitchen" with Cantonese "home cooking" and "steam-cart dim sum" is "always packed" with folks who come for the "great food" (especially "late-night eats", as it's open 24 hours on the weekend, and only closed from 6–9 AM on weekdays), not the "lacking atmosphere" or "spotty service"; P.S. it's unrelated to the bigger, more visible New Three Happiness on the corner.

	FOOD	DECOR	SERVICE	COST

312 Chicago *American/Italian* — 19 | 18 | 19 | $41

Loop | Hotel Allegro | 136 N. LaSalle St. (Randolph St.) | 312-696-2420 | www.312chicago.com

Dialers declare this "convenient" "class act" in the Loop's Hotel Allegro a "good spot for breakfast", a "power lunch" or an "after-work or pre-theater bite" thanks to a "nice, varied menu" of "delicious" Italian-American cooking that's "better than typical hotel" fare, plus "great people-watching" – all "without breaking the bank"; still, some skeptical surveyors give it static, nagging about "noise", "pedestrian" provender and "rushed service" "before a show"; N.B. the Decor score does not reflect a post-Survey remodeling.

Tiffin *Indian* — 22 | 17 | 18 | $27

West Rogers Park | 2536 W. Devon Ave. (Maplewood Ave.) | 773-338-2143 | www.tiffinrestaurant.com

"Everything's great from soup to dessert" at this "upscale" "jewel among the cheap eateries on Devon Avenue" in West Rogers Park, where the Indian "menu is quite diverse" (with plenty of "vegetarian options"), the interior is "comfortable", the staff is "helpful" and the prices are "very reasonable" (the "weekday lunch buffet is a steal"); P.S. they offer a "good wine selection" – and beer too.

Timpano Chophouse *Italian/Steak* — 20 | 19 | 21 | $43

Naperville | 22 E. Chicago Ave. (Washington St.) | 630-753-0985 | www.timpanochophouse.net

"Tasty" dry-aged "steaks, delicious salads, a wonderful bar" and "live entertainment" bring a touch of "downtown" to the "lovely hamlet of Naperville" in the form of this Italian steakhouse chain outpost; it's considered a "date place" despite being "noisy" – and even those who are "not crazy about the food" say the "cool atmosphere" makes it a fun place to get a drink, especially outside in the summer."

Tin Fish *Seafood* — 21 | 17 | 20 | $37

Tinley Park | Cornerstone Ctr. | 18201 S. Harlem Ave. (183rd St.) | 708-532-0200 | www.tinfishrestaurant.com

A school of surveyors savors this suburban seafooder in Tinley Park for "extremely fresh" "edibles from the deep" "done your way", a "fantastic raw bar" and "well-thought-out, reasonably priced wine list"; the decor strikes some as "classy" and "clever", but a few fin-icky feeders feel both the "noisy" "chain" ambiance and "'you guys' service" are "more casual than expected, considering the food quality."

Tizi Melloul *Mediterranean/Mideastern* — 21 | 24 | 19 | $45

River North | 531 N. Wells St. (Grand Ave.) | 312-670-4338 | www.tizimelloul.com

For "something different", try the Middle Eastern–Med menu at this "Moroccan-influenced" River North "escape" offering "offbeat" dishes with "surprising flavors" and "accommodating" service; some call the eats "tamed for the not-so-adventurous", while critics carp the "tired" food takes a backseat to the "beautiful" "Casbah" setting, and the staff is "disinterested."

	FOOD	DECOR	SERVICE	COST

Toast *American*
22 | 14 | 17 | $18

Lincoln Park | 746 W. Webster Ave. (Halsted St.) | 773-935-5600
Bucktown | 2046 N. Damen Ave. (bet. Dickens & McLean Aves.) | 773-772-5600

"There's always a wait" for the "creative" "heart-attack brunch food" as well as the "quality salads and other healthier options" served for breakfast and lunch at these "small, lively and crowded" slices of Traditional American indulgence in Bucktown and Lincoln Park; "close quarters" may concern claustrophobes, and while some say the "real" "service cuts through the sales speak and gets to the freakin' point", others aren't won over by the "rude" 'tude.

Tomboy ☒ *American*
21 | 18 | 22 | $34

Andersonville | 5402 N. Clark St. (Balmoral Ave.) | 773-907-0636 | www.tomboyrestaurant.com

Supporters of this "original Andersonville trendsetter" say it's "still good after all these years", serving "hearty [New American] comfort food", including "Sunday brunch", in a "hip yet comfortable" "storefront"; tougher customers consider it a "great place for a hot date, when your companion can make up for the lackluster food"; P.S. formerly BYO, it has a "good wine list" now, and there's live jazz on Thursdays.

Topo Gigio Ristorante *Italian*
23 | 19 | 19 | $35

Old Town | 1516 N. Wells St. (North Ave.) | 312-266-9355 | www.topogigiochicago.com

"Regulars and families" "savor" the "affordable", "old-fashioned Italian cooking" at this "low-key", "homey" "Old Town classic" with "personal service" from a "down-to-earth staff"; the "outdoor garden" ("heated in winter") is "quite the scene for the over-30 crowd."

☒ Topolobampo ☒☒ *Mexican*
28 | 23 | 25 | $62

River North | 445 N. Clark St. (bet. Hubbard & Illinois Sts.) | 312-661-1434 | www.rickbayless.com

Surveyors swear you get the "best high-end Mexican food in Chicago" (or perhaps "anywhere"), "crafted from the freshest ingredients", at "creative" "celebrity chef" Rick Bayless' "must-go" River North "treasure", the "upscale sister to Frontera Grill" ("with prices to match"); its "cheerful" servers are "extremely knowledgeable", and the "fantastic wine pairings" and "awesome" margaritas are "standouts" as well; just know that the "intimate", art-filled "white tablecloth" setting is "always crowded", so "make your reservations early."

Townhouse Restaurant & Wine Bar ☒ *American*
▽ 16 | 18 | 16 | $30

Loop | DeLoitte Bldg. | 111 S. Wacker Dr. (Monroe St.) | 312-948-8240 | www.restaurants-america.com

"Considering the limited Loop happy-hour options", this New American is a "welcome addition" with "decent specialty drinks" and "average" appetizers; locals also drop in for "business lunches" and warn that the "crowds" can create an "incredible noise level", so conversationalists should try the quieter sidewalk seating in season.

	FOOD	DECOR	SERVICE	COST

☑ Tramonto's
Steak & Seafood *Seafood/Steak*

| 24 | 26 | 23 | $65 |

Wheeling | Westin Chicago North Shore | 601 N. Milwaukee Ave.
(E. Lake Cook Rd.) | 847-777-6575 | www.cenitare.com

"Vegas meets Wheeling" at Rick Tramonto's "stunning" namesake "steak and seafood restaurant" that's "beyond upscale for the suburbs" with "plush" elements like a "waterfall wall", "high-profile wine storage" (housing 10,000 bottles from their "deep list") and Gale Gand's "out-of-this-world tasty desserts, especially the peanut butter sundae"; P.S. tabs are "expensive", and the "layout made for people-watching" can get "noisy."

NEW Trattoria 225 *Italian*

| ▽ 19 | 19 | 19 | $25 |

Oak Park | 225 Harrison St. (Harvey Ave.) | 708-358-8555 | www.trattoria225.com

Seasonal Italian sustenance including "wood-fired pizza" and salads "using local produce" "delight" discoverers of this "warm yet family-friendly" West Suburbanite where the "staff is attentive without hovering"; in-season sidewalk seating makes up for an interior that's "noisy when crowded", and even eaters who experience it as "uneven" say "here's hoping it lives up to the possibilities."

Trattoria D.O.C. *Pizza*

| 19 | 15 | 18 | $29 |

Evanston | 706 Main St. (Custer Ave.) | 847-475-1111 | www.trattoria-doc.com

To a slice of surveyors, the "wood-burning oven yields crisp, tasty Neapolitan-style pizzas" at this "upscale"-"casual" Evanston Italian eatery that's "great with kids" and offers a "good" (and "improving") wine list; however, other noshers note it's "nothing special" and "not a great value", insisting if it "were only as good as its cousin [Pizza D.O.C.], it would be worthy of the appellation."

Trattoria Gianni Ⓜ *Italian*

| 21 | 17 | 21 | $35 |

Lincoln Park | 1711 N. Halsted St. (bet. North Ave. & Willow St.) | 312-266-1976 | www.trattoriagianni.com

"Generous portions" of "consistent" Italian come in a "cozy" "neighborhood atmosphere" that's "convenient for Steppenwolf Theatre-goers" (it's "across the street and patronized by the actors") at this Lincoln Park pioneer where the "owner is always present and it shows"; other enticements include a patio, two fireplaces and a "notable" "wine-by-the-glass list", though "service is just fair."

NEW Trattoria Isabella Ⓢ Ⓜ *Italian*

| - | - | - | M |

Market District | 217 N. Jefferson St. (bet. Fulton & Lake Sts.) | 312-207-1900

Though larger and more modern than a typical trattoria, this mid-priced Market District Southern Italian serves the sort of hearty fare – including housemade pastas and desserts – you'd expect for the genre; the warm, wood and earth-toned space boasts a large classic bar and floor-to-ceiling windows that afford lots of natural light during lunch and views of city lights at night.

	FOOD	DECOR	SERVICE	COST

Trattoria No. 10 ⓩ *Italian*

| | 23 | 20 | 22 | $42 |

Loop | 10 N. Dearborn St. (Madison St.) | 312-984-1718 |
www.trattoriaten.com

For nearly 20 years, the "food has been consistently excellent" (if "expensive") at this "sophisticated", "subterranean" Loop "hideout" where Italian "favorites" include "farfalle with duck confit" and "fresh butternut squash ravioli"; "prompt", "smart servers" who add a "personalized touch" make this a good bet for a "business lunch", "pre-concert or pre-theater dinner" in a "cavernous" but "charming" milieu; P.S. "the appetizer bar at happy hour is a great deal."

Trattoria Roma *Italian*

| | 21 | 17 | 21 | $34 |

Old Town | 1535 N. Wells St. (bet. North Ave. & Schiller St.) |
312-664-7907 | www.trattoriaroma.com

An Old Town "locals' favorite" for nearly 25 years, this "friendly" Italian hands out "handwritten menus" featuring "fresh and authentic pastas, meats, fish and pizza" ("no surprises, but sometimes that's a good thing") in a "homey" setting where the staff "treats you like family"; the "convenient locale" makes it a "good choice for a casual meal before going to Second City", and the "outdoor dining is wonderful all summer long."

Trattoria 31 Ⓜ *Italian*

| | - | - | - | M |

Southwest Side | 605 W. 31st St. (Wallace St.) | 312-326-3500 |
www.trattoria31.com

"Consistently solid" if "not mind-blowing" Italian cookery from a "truly warm and friendly chef" makes this one of South Side Bridgeport's "gems" – even if waverers label it "a bit pretentious for the area"; the "quaint", "inviting setting" is enlivened by photos of old Chicago.

Trattoria Trullo *Italian*

| | ▽ 21 | 19 | 20 | $32 |

Lincoln Square | 4767 N. Lincoln Ave. (Lawrence Ave.) |
773-506-0093

"Sweet people" run this "pleasing trattoria" where an "attentive staff" delivers "authentic" and "interesting" Italian eats ("the chef-owner hails from Puglia") at "reasonable prices"; the "move to Lincoln Square" means "they have a deli now", plus a "large bar" that helps ameliorate the "long wait if you don't have a reservation"; P.S. it's also "kid-friendly" with "kid-portion pastas."

Tre Kronor *Scandinavian*

| | 23 | 18 | 21 | $22 |

Northwest Side | 3258 W. Foster Ave. (Sawyer Ave.) |
773-267-9888

"A bit off the beaten track" on the Northwest Side, the city's "best" "Scandinavian restaurant" serves "Swedish and Norwegian home cooking" that includes "phenomenal" "handcut corned beef hash", "salmon omelets and pickled herring" "for breakfast, lunch or dinner"; a "sweet staff" and "charming troll paintings" enhance the "unpretentious" BYO milieu, which is "always deservedly crowded", "especially on weekends" and during the "sumptuous smorgasbord" at Christmas.

	FOOD	DECOR	SERVICE	COST

⊠ Tru ⊠ *French* — 27 | 26 | 27 | $125

Streeterville | 676 N. St. Clair St. (bet. Erie & Huron Sts.) | 312-202-0001 |
www.trurestaurant.com

"Still one of the best" despite Rick Tramonto and Gale Gand "not being
there full-time", Streeterville's "superb", "over-the-top" New French
has fans swooning over its "subtle but distinctive flavor combinations" and "sense of whimsy" ("chemistry or artistry? who cares!"),
plus "out-of-this-world wines", "incredible personal attention" from
"eerily clairvoyant" servers and a "hushed", "Zen-like" (if "austere")
"art-gallery" atmosphere; it all adds up to a "tru-ly" "memorable"
event that's "a must for foodies", at an "outrageous" ("dip into the
kids' college fund") but "worth-it" price; N.B. jackets required.

Tsuki *Japanese* — 24 | 23 | 20 | $38

Lincoln Park | 1441-45 W. Fullerton Ave. (Janssen Ave.) | 773-883-8722 |
www.tsuki.us

The "terrific menu delivers" "excellent", "fresh and interesting" raw
fin fare with a "nice selection of sakes" and "great cocktails" like the
"ginger martini" at this "upscale", "romantic and trendy"
Lincoln Park Japanese joint; the "cool interior" houses "varied venues" including a "sushi bar", bar and patio; N.B. DJs spin Thursday
through Saturday nights.

Tsunami *Japanese* — 23 | 19 | 21 | $41

Gold Coast | 1160 N. Dearborn St. (Division St.) | 312-642-9911 |
www.tsunamijapanese.com

The "food is much better than the unfortunate name" of this Gold
Coast Japanese wielding a "wide" selection of "above-average
sushi" (its "à la carte prices seem steep, but the dinners are reasonable" and portions "generous"); a "hip staff" delivers an "ok level of
service" in "busy" environs that some find "lush and sexy" – there's
a "sake bar" ("with fireplace") upstairs, and an outdoor patio – but
others deem "dated."

Tufano's Vernon Park Tap ⊠⊅ *Italian* — 20 | 13 | 21 | $25

University Village | 1073 W. Vernon Park Pl. (Carpenter St.) |
312-733-3393

It's the "closest thing to being in a *Godfather* set" say supporters of
this "old-school [since 1930], no-frills" University Village "time
warp" serving "tasty" "traditional" Southern Italian in "gut-busting"
portions; "lacking" decor doesn't dissuade those who dub it "good for
family night out" as long as you "bring cash" ("no credit cards").

Turquoise *Turkish* — 22 | 18 | 16 | $29

Roscoe Village | 2147 W. Roscoe St. (bet. Hamilton Ave. & Leavitt St.) |
773-549-3523 | www.turquoisedining.com

"More than just the bar it appears to be", this "nice" entry offers
restless Roscoe Villagers a Turkish tour via the "bright Mediterranean
flavors" of its "reasonably priced fare", including "flavorful meats
and seafood"; some suggest the "genial" "though unpolished" staff
provides "splintered service", but at least "there's a friendly atmosphere", and "the owners try hard to make you feel welcome."

	FOOD	DECOR	SERVICE	COST

Tuscany *Italian*

22 | 19 | 21 | $37

Wrigleyville | 3700 N. Clark St. (Waveland Ave.) | 773-404-7700
Little Italy | 1014 W. Taylor St. (Morgan St.) | 312-829-1990
Wheeling | 550 S. Milwaukee Ave. (Manchester Dr.) | 847-465-9498
Oak Brook | 1415 W. 22nd St. (Rte. 83) | 630-990-1993
www.stefanirestaurants.com

"Tuscan before Tuscan was cool", these "lively", "dependable Phil Stefani outlets" – the Little Italy *paterfamilias* and its three offspring – dish out "hearty" "traditional" Northern Italian fare plus "original dishes" ("two words: pear ravioli"); each manages to seem "elegant and homey at the same time", though "every location is a little different", and the original has a "cool throwback bar"; but the testy type it as "typical" and say "service can be slow."

Tweet ⌿ *Eclectic*

24 | 19 | 21 | $21

Uptown | 5020 N. Sheridan Rd. (Argyle St.) | 773-728-5576 |
www.tweet.biz

When you "want to feel cozy and welcome", join the "diverse clientele" dining on "overwhelming portions" of Eclectic "organic" breakfast/brunch/lunch at this cash-only Uptown coop where the favorites include "homestyle" French toast, breakfast burritos, crab cake sandwiches and "some surprises (bibimbop)"; "service is unusually friendly if not the most polished", and its decor is "granola-esque but with flair"; P.S. "go early to avoid the crowds."

Twin Anchors *BBQ*

22 | 16 | 19 | $29

Old Town | 1655 N. Sedgwick St. (bet. Eugenie St. & North Ave.) |
312-266-1616 | www.twinanchorsribs.com

"No bones about it", some of "the best" barbecue around includes the "legendary" ribs at this "wonderful dive", an Old Town "corner bar" "icon" that's "full of charm", "local color" and "lots of history" (Sinatra was a regular), as well as a "great selection of beer" and "snappy" servers; just be prepared for "impossible" waits, as they don't take reservations; P.S. "positively no dancing!"

Twist *Eclectic*

23 | 18 | 20 | $27

Lakeview | 3412 N. Sheffield Ave. (bet. Newport Ave. & Roscoe St.) |
773-388-2727 | www.twistinchicago.com

"The most inventive" Eclectic small plates, "good seasonal specials" and "traditional" Spanish tapas all fit in this "little" Lakeview lair with "a lot of character"; add in "awesome sangria" and "efficient servers" and it's a "fun place to start the night" and "a great group dining destination" – but it's "small and the tables are cramped" so "get there early to avoid a wait."

Twisted Spoke ● *Pub Food*

20 | 16 | 17 | $18

Near West | 501 N. Ogden Ave. (Grand Ave.) | 312-666-1500 |
www.twistedspoke.com

Roar up to this Near West "upscale dive" for some "big, big burgers and cold, cold beer" plus other "better-than-average" Traditional American "pub fare" and even some "respectable salads" served in a "pseudo-biker bar" setting with "metal tabletops, motorcycle parts everywhere" and "gruff service"; some say the "food's better with a hangover" – especially at the "great brunch" starring "killer Bloody Marys" – and the weekly "Smut and Eggs [event] at midnight on Saturdays" is "a must-see" for "porn" fanciers; N.B. the Decor score doesn't reflect a recent remodeling.

Udupi Palace *Indian*

19 | 8 | 16 | $19

West Rogers Park | 2543 W. Devon Ave. (bet. Maplewood Ave. & Rockwell St.) | 773-338-2152
Schaumburg | Market Sq. | 730 E. Schaumburg Rd. (Plum Grove Rd.) | 847-884-9510
www.udupipalace.com

"Huge servings of tasty", "solid and fresh regional Indian food" (including "wonderful dosas") satisfy supporters of this West Rogers Park BYO "vegetarian palace" with a Schaumburg spin-off; the staff is "not very informative but always polite and sincere", and "there's no mystery meat, so don't be afraid to dig in."

Uncle John's BBQ 🗷🍴 *BBQ*

‾ | ‾ | ‾ | I

Far South Side | 337 E. 69th St. (Calumet Ave.) | 773-892-1233

"Step up to the glass, place your order" and watch owner Mac Sevier "grab your ribs from the smoker or chop up your tips" at this "reasonably priced" cash-only Far South Side BBQ fast-fooder; though it's "probably not on the way to anywhere" and is "strictly takeout – so there's pretty much no atmosphere" – it serves some of the "meatiest, most carnally satisfying food in Chicagoland."

Uncommon Ground *Coffeehouse*

21 | 21 | 19 | $24

Lakeview | 3800 N. Clark St. (Grace St.) | 773-929-3680
NEW **Edgewater** | 1401 W. Devon Ave. (Glenwood Ave.) | 773-465-9801
www.uncommonground.com

"In the midst of the Wrigleyville madness", this "coffee shop/bar/restaurant" is a "favorite hangout" for a "diverse clientele", providing "room upon room" of "entertainment options", including "some of the best live acts", plus "fresh" Eclectic eats incorporating some "organic" ingredients (and "excellent brunches" all week long); loungers label the "laid-back atmosphere" "addictive", with some preferring the "front room with fireplace" and others heading for the "nice patio"; N.B. the green-minded Edgewater location in a former speakeasy space opened post-Survey.

NEW Union Pizzeria *Pizza*

‾ | ‾ | ‾ | M

Evanston | 1245 Chicago Ave. (bet. Dempster & Hamilton Sts.) | 847-475-2400

The Campagnola crew created this hip Evanston pizzeria serving rustic Tuscan pies, salads, pasta and Eclectic small plates along with 25 beers (bottled and tap, including Belgian and craft brews) and 50 wines under $50; a former Peugeot dealership, the open loft digs features full front windows, wood-beam-and-ductwork ceilings and cement floors; N.B. the space also houses a performance venue.

	FOOD	DECOR	SERVICE	COST

⚡ Va Pensiero *Italian*   26 | 24 | 25 | $50

Evanston | Margarita Inn | 1566 Oak Ave. (Davis St.) | 847-475-7779 |
www.va-p.com

The "best Italian food on the North Shore" is backed by an "amazing selection" of vinos and "attentive" servers "who work together to make your experience a memorable one"; the "tasteful", "charming" if "offbeat location" features a fireplace and "exquisite outdoor patio", and if some diners deem it "sort of expensive for Evanston", most maintain this "upscale" ristorante is "worth every lire."

Venus Greek-Cypriot Cuisine *Greek*   ▽ 21 | 17 | 21 | $30

Greektown | 820 W. Jackson Blvd. (bet. Green & Halsted Sts.) |
312-714-1001 | www.venuschicago.com

Admirers of this "lovely", "adventurous" "addition to Greektown" delight in its "delicious and unique twist" on Hellenic fare, as it serves not only that cuisine but also dishes with a wider "Mediterranean flair", including "some typically Cypriot" dishes; it's "an interesting variation in a neighborhood where each place [serves] the same food", and there's also live entertainment on Saturdays; P.S. "follow the waiter's suggestions" – but don't miss "the slow-cooked lamb."

Vermilion *Indian/Nuevo Latino*   21 | 20 | 20 | $50

River North | 10 W. Hubbard St. (bet. Dearborn & State Sts.) |
312-527-4060 | www.thevermilionrestaurant.com

"An interesting mix of foodies" finds "delicious" "new things to try" on the "intriguing menu" of "cutting-edge" "Indian-Latin fusion" cuisine at this "hip", "intimate" River Norther with "simple but sexy decor"; still, some traditionalists assert that the "unique concept" "doesn't quite work" (and comes with a "steep price tag" to boot), adding that the "stark" setting can be "noisy"; N.B. the Food rating may not reflect a post-Survey menu revamp.

Via Carducci *Italian*   22 | 19 | 19 | $31

Lincoln Park | 1419 W. Fullerton Ave. (Southport Ave.) | 773-665-1981

NEW Via Carducci La Sorella *Italian*

Wicker Park | 1928 W. Division St. (Winchester Ave.) | 773-252-2246 |
www.viacarducci-lasorella.com

This Lincoln Park original and its Wicker Park spin-off specialize in "well-done", "authentic", "reasonably priced" Southern Italian that ranges "from thin-crust pizza to pasta to entrees" "with many daily specials"; both locations have a "cozy neighborhood vibe" and live entertainment one night a week, however, foes are "bored" by the "predictable menu", "average" execution and "inconsistent" service.

Viand Bar & Kitchen *American*   22 | 18 | 19 | $41

Streeterville | 155 E. Ontario St. (Michigan Ave.) | 312-255-8505 |
www.viandchicago.com

Veteran chef Steve Chiappetti's "largely locally sourced and delicious" seasonal New American cookery includes "veggie-friendly" options and "great bar specials" served by "warm, attentive" servers at this "slick" Streeterville spot; set in a Marriot Courtyard, the "quirky" "lobby setting" has a "definite hotel-restaurant vibe", and a cadre complain the "comfort-food concept" "isn't all that innovative."

Viceroy of India *Indian* 18 | 11 | 16 | $23

West Rogers Park | 2520 W. Devon Ave. (bet. Campbell & Maplewood Aves.) | 773-743-4100
Lombard | 233 E. Roosevelt Rd. (Highland Ave.) | 630-627-4411
www.viceroyofindia.com

"All the basics are covered well" at this "popular" West Rogers Park and West Suburban pair that some reporters rate as a "safe bet" for "tasty" Indian food that's definitely "the real thing" – and "reasonably priced", to boot; maybe the "decor is lacking", but they are "vegetarian-friendly" and midday feasters say the "lunch buffet is spot-on."

Victory's Banner *Eclectic* 23 | 14 | 21 | $15

Roscoe Village | 2100 W. Roscoe St. (Hoyne Ave.) | 773-665-0227 | www.victorysbanner.com

"Fantastic" Eclectic vegan-vegetarian fare for "brunch and lunch" is presented by a "genuinely kind staff" and comes with a "dose of serenity", even on weekends when this Roscoe Village respite is "bustling" (expect "lines" and early-morning "strollers and toddlers"); as for the "overt" spiritual "imagery", advocates advise "you have to choose whether to be inspired, tolerant or weirded-out by the religious spaciness surrounding you."

Z Vie S *American* 28 | 21 | 25 | $65

Western Springs | 4471 Lawn Ave. (Burlington Ave.) | 708-246-2082 | www.vierestaurant.com

"Outstanding" "fine dining" hits home in Western Springs with chef Paul Virant's "artfully prepared" New American cuisine that "highlights local producers/growers" (with "sources prominently featured on the menu") in meals rife with "wonderful tastes and textures", delivered by "down-to-earth", "professional" servers; the "super-chic" atmosphere seems "stark" to some, and a few habitués flinch at the "high price tag", but most insist the tabs would be far larger "in the city", so it's "well worth the drive" – or the Metra ride, since "it's near the train station."

Viet Bistro & Lounge *Vietnamese* ▽ 19 | 23 | 18 | $37

Rogers Park | 1346 W. Devon Ave. (bet. Glenwood & Wayne Aves.) | 773-465-5720

"A nice surprise" in a "stylish setting", this Rogers Park "find" woos with a "more elegant, more expensive" take on Vietnamese classics, which strikes some as "wonderful and creative" and others as "no better than what you'd find in a cheaper, neighborhood place"; while the owners are "wonderful", the "good" service can seem "slow."

Village, The ◐ *Italian* 20 | 20 | 20 | $35

Loop | Italian Vill. | 71 W. Monroe St., 2nd fl. (bet. Clark & Dearborn Sts.) | 312-332-7005 | www.italianvillage-chicago.com

The "last of the [Loop] survivors" "from days gone by", this "sentimental favorite" of the Italian Village trio plates "plentiful servings" of "predictable satisfying fare" (including "the best chicken Vesuvio") in a "wonderful interior" where "couples can enjoy private booths" with "twinkling lights"; modernists who find it "tired", however, say service swings from "charming" and "efficient" to "rushed" and "indifferent", and foodies find the fare "fancy eatin' for kids and tourists."

Vinci Ⓜ Italian

21 | 19 | 22 | $39

Lincoln Park | 1732 N. Halsted St. (Willow St.) | 312-266-1199 | www.vincichicago.com

Satisfied surveyors say that the "quiet, dignified Italian dining" "never goes out of style" at this "upscale" Lincoln Park "favorite" where Paul LoDuca continues to oversee a "warm place with excellent food" (props for the "amazing polenta with mushrooms"), a "good wine list and equitable pricing" in a "convenient" location that's "wonderful" for theatergoers; P.S. it's also "great for Sunday brunch" and "monthly wine dinners" that represent "a fantastic deal."

NEW Violet American

- | - | - | I

Lakeview | 3819 N. Southport Ave. (Grace St.) | 773-327-0234 | www.violetchicago.com

Think funky grown-up diner to get a feel for this Lakeview New American serving morning/daytime eats like custom omelets, salads and sandwiches complemented by items from its coffee/bakery bar; the airy storefront space is decorated with animation hand-painted by the staff, and there's a plush lounge area with fireplace and WiFi as well as a back garden.

Vito & Nick's ⊘ Pizza

▽ 23 | 13 | 20 | $19

Far South Side | 8433 S. Pulaski Rd. (84th Pl.) | 773-735-2050 | www.vitoandnick.com

"Snappy" cracker-style crust", the "right spices" and "delicious Italian sausage" make this "old-school"-er's pies some of "da best pizza" on the Far South Side; its "decor has barely changed in 30 years" ("be sure to see the grotto") and the service is "sometimes slow", yet still it's "worth the trek" – heck, some devotees would even "drive to Minnesota" for the privilege of partaking in these "old recipes."

Vivere Ⓢ Italian

23 | 23 | 22 | $48

Loop | Italian Vill. | 71 W. Monroe St. (bet. Clark & Dearborn Sts.) | 312-332-4040 | www.vivere-chicago.com

An "awesome" wine list complements the "mildly innovative, high-end Italian cuisine" at this "upscale" ristorante in the "heart of the Loop"; the "showpiece dining room" with "whimsical" "fantasyland decor" is home to a "different menu and higher prices" than its Italian Village "sisters", plus it offers "high service standards" and an "intimate bar"; P.S. the location is "excellent for lunch or pre-opera or theater."

Vivo Italian

21 | 20 | 20 | $42

Market District | 838 W. Randolph St. (bet. Green & Peoria Sts.) | 312-733-3379 | www.vivo-chicago.com

"Still a solid player" despite all the "new places in the area", this Market District pioneer continues to please with "excellent Italian cuisine" – including "heavenly gnocchi and fettuccine" and "outstanding fish specials" – served "in a trendy loft setting" that's "crowded, yet cozy"; it's "too loud sometimes" and "service can be a bit uneven", but the experience is otherwise "enjoyable"; P.S. many "love eating in the elevator shaft", whose table seats six.

Volare *Italian*
24 | 16 | 22 | $40

Streeterville | 201 E. Grand Ave. (St. Clair St.) | 312-410-9900
Oakbrook Terrace | 1919 S. Meyers Rd. (22nd St.) | 630-495-0200 Ⓢ Ⓜ
www.volarerestaurant.com

A taste of "true *Italiano*" "hidden away off Michigan Avenue" in Streeterville, this "friendly", "bustling" "backstreet trattoria" with the "feel of an old-fashioned neighborhood Italian supper club" and a "wonderful" patio puts out "big portions" of "delicious" "classics", including some of "the best osso buco and risotto" around and "well-prepared fresh seafood selections" – thus a visit here is "very enjoyable", except for the "close tables" and "terrible waits"; as for the new Oakrook Terrace branch, surveyors call it "spectacular."

Volo Restaurant & Wine Bar Ⓢ *American*
20 | 21 | 21 | $38

Roscoe Village | 2008 W. Roscoe St. (Damen Ave.) | 773-348-4600 | www.volorestaurant.com

Expect a "cool mood" with "fun and creative wine flights to match the creative" and "delectable" New American small plates at this "hip wine bar" in Roscoe Village, where the "welcoming atmosphere" includes "conviviality", "great background music" and a "huge wine list"; it can be "packed", but outdoor patio seating "practically doubles the number of tables" and "can't be beat" on a "summer night."

Vong's Thai Kitchen *Thai*
22 | 20 | 20 | $38

River North | 6 W. Hubbard St. (State St.) | 312-644-8664 | www.vongsthaikitchen.com

"Interesting" Thai with an "upscale", "metro flair" finds favor at this River North Lettuce Entertain You partnership with famed chef Jean-Georges Vongerichten; a "value" given the "quality", "good service" and "serene" "Far East" decor; diners "disappointed" by the "more casual food and presentation" at "the most down-market Vong there is" would "just as soon go to a neighborhood" Siamese and "save money" (though the "$1 dessert menu [at lunch] is the best concept ever").

Wakamono ◐ *Japanese*
∇ 23 | 21 | 18 | $30

Lakeview | 3317 N. Broadway St. (W. Buckingham Pl.) | 773-296-6800 | www.wakamonosushi.com

Serving "incredibly fresh" sushi in the "heart of East Lakeview", this "small" Japanese BYO has quickly become a "neighborhood favorite"; service is "not necessarily friendly", "tables are very close" and it gets "noisy at times", so "alfresco dining" "is an added plus."

Wave *Mediterranean*
∇ 20 | 20 | 20 | $42

Streeterville | W Chicago Lakeshore | 644 N. Lake Shore Dr. (Ontario St.) | 312-255-4460 | www.waverestaurant.com

Voters "willing to experiment" dive into the "delicious", "interesting tastes" on the Mediterranean "small-plates" menus at this "contemporary" lunch and dinner spot in the Streeterville W; the vibe is especially "loud, young and fun" on weekends, when a DJ spins, and there's a Lake Shore Drive view, sidewalk dining and "global cooking class every month."

⚡ Weber Grill *BBQ* | 19 | 17 | 18 | $34 |

River North | Hilton Garden Inn | 539 N. State St. (Grand Ave.) | 312-467-9696
Schaumburg | 1010 N. Meacham Rd. (American Ln.) | 847-413-0800
Lombard | 2331 Fountain Square Dr. (Meyers Rd.) | 630-953-8880
www.webergrillrestaurant.com

"Authentic American BBQ" aficionados who "camp out" at these "tourist-friendly" city and suburban sizzlefests – where virtually "everything" is grilled on "huge Weber kettles" – believe they bring "basic meat and potatoes" "to the highest level", making them a "lower-cost alternative to the high-priced steakhouses"; still, "char"-red chewers who chastise them for "generic chain" grub, "weak service" and "noisy atmospheres" brag "my backyard is much better."

Webster Wine Bar ● *Eclectic* | 20 | 21 | 21 | $31 |

Lincoln Park | 1480 W. Webster Ave. (bet. Ashland Ave. & Clybourn St.) | 773-868-0608 | www.websterwinebar.com

An early adopter of the wine bar trend, this "comfortable" Lincoln Park "neighborhood joint" is appropriate for a "post-movie date", "girls' night out" or "nightcap" "with friends" who want to sample "tasty" Eclectic "tapas" and "great wine flights" from an "excellent list"; the "knowledgeable bartenders" know how to "handle crowds quickly without brushing off customer service", and the confines are "dark" and "cozy."

West Town Tavern ⑤ *American* | 25 | 21 | 23 | $42 |

West Town | 1329 W. Chicago Ave. (Throop St.) | 312-666-6175 | www.westtowntavern.com

Its "loyal local following" "feels welcome" at this "cool but not trendy" West Town "keeper" where "creative" New American "comfort food with class" is paired with an "ambitious, moderately priced wine list"; it can get loud when it's "full", but service is "professional" and "they work really hard to keep quality high" – so even though "it's gotten a little pricey", tavern-goers wager it's "worth it" and wonder "why is this so hard to replicate?"

White Fence Farm Ⓜ *American* | 22 | 17 | 21 | $22 |

Romeoville | 1376 Joliet Rd. (Bolingbrook Dr.) | 630-739-1720 | www.whitefencefarm.com

The meal begins with an "old-fashioned" "relish tray" at this "massive" "family-style" Northwest Suburban "fried chicken heaven" that also serves other Traditional American "supper-club favorites" along with "remarkable corn fritters" and "great cinnamon rolls" – in other words, the "best comfort food at the lowest prices"; its "farmhouse decor" is "like something out of *The Andy Griffith Show*", and the service is "old-school"; P.S. "kids will love the petting zoo, and grandpa will love the antique cars."

	FOOD	DECOR	SERVICE	COST

Wiener's Circle, The ●⊉ *Hot Dogs* | 20 | 5 | 13 | $8 |

Lincoln Park | 2622 N. Clark St. (Wrightwood Ave.) | 773-477-7444
"Gimme a charred red hot dammit!" demand respondents who relish the "funny, filthy-mouthed" "late-night" shtick (from customers and staff) as much as the "outstanding Chicago dogs" and "amazing cheeseburgers" at this "one-of-a-kind" Lincoln Park "sitcom-in-waiting"; still, be warned that "the love goes in the bun, not the decor", there's "almost nowhere to sit" and some say "never go here sober."

☑ Wildfire *Steak* | 24 | 22 | 21 | $42 |

River North | 159 W. Erie St. (bet. LaSalle Blvd. & Wells St.) | 312-787-9000
Lincolnshire | 235 Parkway Dr. (Milwaukee Ave.) | 847-279-7900
Glenview | 1300 Patriot Blvd. (Lake Ave.) | 847-657-6363
Schaumburg | 1250 E. Higgins Rd. (National Pkwy.) | 847-995-0100
Oak Brook | Oakbrook Center Mall | 232 Oakbrook Ctr. (Rte. 83) | 630-586-9000
www.wildfirerestaurant.com

"Lettuce Entertain You's" "flamingly successful" (the Chicago Survey's No. 1 Most Popular) city-and-suburban steakhouse chain remains the "place to go" for "wood-fire-grilled meats", "good" Traditional American "basics" ("cedar plank salmon" and "chopped salad"), "divine desserts" and a "whole page of martinis in the menu", all arrayed in an atmosphere evocative of "a '40s supper club"; "service level can vary", "reservations are a must" and some participants "don't get the attraction" considering the "noise", "ridiculous waits"; N.B. River North serves dinner only.

Wildfish *Japanese* | 24 | 23 | 21 | $40 |

Deerfield | Deerfield Commons Shopping Ctr. | 730 Waukegan Rd. (bet. Deerfield Rd. & Osterman Ave.) | 847-317-9453
Arlington Heights | Arlington Town Sq. | 60 S. Arlington Heights Rd. (Northwest Hwy.) | 847-870-8260
www.wildfishsushi.com

There's "nothing fishy" about the "creative, delicious sushi" (including "innovative maki") and other Japanese fare that's "plated with fun, edible designs" at this "intimate little" Deerfield and Arlington Heights suburban twosome with a "great lounge vibe, chill music" and "attentive staff"; supporters say they may be "city priced" but they're also "city quality."

Wishbone *Southern* | 21 | 17 | 18 | $21 |

Roscoe Village | 3300 N. Lincoln Ave. (School St.) | 773-549-2663
West Loop | 1001 W. Washington Blvd. (Morgan St.) | 312-850-2663
Berwyn | 6611 Roosevelt Rd. (bet. Clarence Ave. & East Ave.) | 708-749-1295
www.wishbonechicago.com

This "boisterous", "family-friendly" trio dishes up "delicious" Southern and "sometime-Cajun" cooking with a side of "whimsy" ("note the 'chickeney' decor touches"); a sizable demographic deems it "dependable" for a "great brunch", plus "hearty and filling" lunches and "dinners as well", all at "tolerable prices"; still, a faction feels it's "fair to middling", with "long waits" and "hit-or-miss service."

subscribe to ZAGAT.com

	FOOD	DECOR	SERVICE	COST

Woo Lae Oak *Korean* ▽ 23 | 24 | 19 | $37

Rolling Meadows | 3201 Algonquin Rd. (Newport Dr.) | 847-870-9910
"Tasty", "upscale Korean BBQ" comes as a "surprise" among the "aging strip malls and gas stations" of Northwest Suburban Rolling Meadows, especially given the "nondescript building" that houses this "mega" spot; the "affordable" fare is matched by "unique and beautiful decorations" – so even if "service needs improvement", it's always an "eating experience, especially if you grill your own dinner."

Yard House *American* 17 | 16 | 16 | $26

Glenview | The Glen | 1880 Tower Dr. (Patriot Blvd.) | 847-729-9273 | www.yardhouse.com
With "over 100 on tap", "from all over the world", there may be "too many beers to choose from" – and "what a great problem to have" swoon suds lovers smitten with this North Suburban chainster that also offers a "varied, value-conscious menu" of American eats "for anytime, with or without kids"; the bonanza of brews, however, falls flat with those who perceive the provender as "pedestrian"; P.S. if the "lively" environs seem "loud", adjourn to the "great outside seating."

Yolk *American* 22 | 17 | 19 | $17

South Loop | 1120 S. Michigan Ave. (11th St.) | 312-789-9655
"Massive portions" of "creative breakfast foods and traditional [American] standbys" like "fabulous pancakes and egg concoctions", wraps and sandwiches add up to daylight dining a "cut above the usual" at this "energizing South Loop" spot with a "cheery", "sunny" setting ("if you're not a morning person, you'll find the decor too bright"); hard-boiled habitués say "too bad it's been discovered", since it's "insanely crowded during peak brunch time" when "service can be slow."

Yoshi's Café Ⓜ *French/Japanese* 25 | 18 | 23 | $47

Lakeview | 3257 N. Halsted St. (Aldine Ave.) | 773-248-6160 | www.yoshiscafe.com
Yoshi Katsumura's "delightful" Lakeview destination "has proven the test of time" with its Japanese-meets–"modern French" preparations and "attentive service"; it has "the feel of a fine local restaurant with a very loyal clientele", even if budgeters believe the price may "exceed the value" and some wags "wish it didn't look like it was in a Holiday Inn" (though remodeling was on the horizon at press time).

Zapatista *Mexican* 18 | 18 | 17 | $30

South Loop | 1307 S. Wabash Ave. (13th St.) | 312-435-1307 | www.zapatistamexicangrill.com
"Reasonably priced, good" Mexican food like "tasty tacos", "guac made tableside" and "fajita presentations that remind you of a volcano" are available at this "boisterous, kid-friendly" cantina that's "reliable" for a South Loop lunch or "night out"; still, seesawing surveyors say the quality can be "erratic" and the service "sometimes good, sometimes negligent" – as for the "loud" decibels, their "top margaritas will bring you up to the appropriate noise level."

	FOOD	DECOR	SERVICE	COST

Ⓩ Zealous ⓈⓂ *American* | 24 | 25 | 22 | $67 |

River North | 419 W. Superior St. (Sedgewick St.) | 312-475-9112 | www.zealousrestaurant.com

Chef-owner-manager Michael Taus is "not afraid to take chances" with "incredible combinations" of the "highest quality ingredients" on his "pricey" prix fixe–only New American menu at this "beautiful" "foodie" "discovery" in an "obscure" River North location; fans favor the "fantastically paired wines" from the "exposed vaulted cellar", but others hint service can be uneven and the vibe "a bit pretentious."

NEW ZED 451 *Eclectic* | ▽ 22 | 21 | 22 | $59 |

River North | 739 N. Clark St. (Superior St.) | 888-493-3451 ⓈⓂ
Schaumburg | 801 E. Algonquin Rd. (Hammond Dr.) | 847-925-0061 | www.zed451.com
Downers Grove | 3008 Finley Rd. (Butterfield Rd.) | 630-512-0900 | www.zed451.com

It's "bye-bye Brazil" at these "cool" Eclectic steakhouses where big makeovers, minor menu revisions and a name change have reinvented the former Sal & Carvao "churrascaria" concept; "the gauchos are gone, thank goodness", but the all-you-can-eat menu still features an "array of tasty meats" with some "delicious chef-created additions" plus a "harvest table" "buffet" of "unique savory offerings"; if some call it "overpriced", it's still "great for a special occasion"; N.B. the new River North locale has a roof lounge with city views.

Zest *American/Eclectic* | ▽ 18 | 15 | 16 | $39 |

Streeterville | Hotel InterContinental | 505 N. Michigan Ave. (Illinois St.) | 312-321-8766 | www.icchicagohotel.com

While some guests go for the "interesting, tasty" Eclectic–New American bites at the Intercontinental's installation, now in a "smaller location on the second floor", a good number find it "less interesting than the previous space" and "a bit too severe for comfortable dining."

Zia's Trattoria *Italian* | 25 | 19 | 21 | $34 |

Edison Park | 6699 N. Northwest Hwy. (Oliphant Ave.) | 773-775-0808 | www.ziaschicago.com

A Food score boost bodes well for this "cozy", "lively" Edison Park "treasure" where "quality, flavor and consistency are the name of the game" on its "real Italian" "comfort-food" menu full of dishes "just like nana makes" (the "squash ravioli" is "as good as a dessert"); locals lament that its "off-the-beaten-path" space can get "noisy", though few complain about the "friendly" staff and "great-value" price tag.

Zocalo *Mexican* | 23 | 20 | 20 | $35 |

River North | 358 W. Ontario St. (N. Orleans St.) | 312-302-9977 | www.zocalochicago.com

"Hidden" in River North, this midscale Mexican is relied on for "reasonable but still trendy food" (try the "out-of-this-world guacamole sampler"); its "dark", "sophisticated but comfortable" "environment" with "high ceilings and wood pillars" is "great for a date (especially "near the bar" where it's "cozier"), and they also offer live music on weekends, sidewalk seating and "prix fixe on Sunday and Tuesday."

CHICAGO
INDEXES

LOCATION MAPS

Cuisines

Includes restaurant names, locations and Food ratings. ☒ indicates places with the highest ratings, popularity and importance.

AFGHAN

Kabul Hse.	**Skokie**	21

AFRICAN

Icosium Kafe	**Andersonville**	19

AMERICAN (NEW)

Adelle's	**Wheaton**	24
Aigre Doux	**River N**	24
☒ Alinea	**Lincoln Pk**	29
Amber Cafe	**Westmont**	24
Aria	**Loop**	23
Atwater's	**Geneva**	21
Avenue M	**River W**	21
☒ Avenues	**River N**	25
BackStage	**River N**	22
NEW Balanced Kitchen	**NW Side**	–
Bank Lane	**Lake Forest**	23
NEW Bank Rest.	**Wheaton**	15
Bijan's	**River N**	18
Bin 36/Wine	**multi.**	20
☒ Blackbird	**W Loop**	27
NEW Bluebird, The	**Bucktown**	19
Blue Water	**River N**	23
NEW Bluprint	**River N**	22
BOKA	**Lincoln Pk**	24
Bonsoiree	**Logan Sq**	–
Broadway Cellars	**Edgewater**	21
Cab's Wine Bar	**Glen Ellyn**	22
Café Absinthe	**Bucktown**	24
NEW Café 103	**Far S Side**	–
Café Selmarie	**Lincoln Sq**	22
Caliterra	**Streeterville**	22
Chalkboard	**Lakeview**	22
☒ Charlie Trotter's	**Lincoln Pk**	27
Chef's Station	**Evanston**	22
Cité	**Streeterville**	24
Courtright's	**Willow Spgs**	25
Crofton on Wells	**River N**	25
Cru Café	**Gold Coast**	17
Custom Hse.	**Printer's Row**	25
David Burke Prime	**River N**	24
David's Bistro	**Des Plaines**	23
NEW Distinctive Cork	**Naperville**	22
NEW Drawing Rm/Le Passage	**Gold Coast**	–
Emilio's Sunflower	**La Grange**	24
erwin cafe	**Lakeview**	22

Feast	**Bucktown**	21
Fiddlehead	**Lincoln Sq**	19
545 North	**Libertyville**	20
Gage	**Loop**	21
Gordon Biersch	**Bolingbrook**	20
Green Dolphin St.	**Lincoln Pk**	19
Harvest	**St. Charles**	24
HB Home Bistro	**Lakeview**	24
Ina's	**W Loop**	22
Jack's on Halsted	**Lakeview**	21
Jacky's Bistro	**Evanston**	24
Jane's	**Bucktown**	21
Jilly's Cafe	**Evanston**	24
Landmark	**Lincoln Pk**	21
NEW Libertine	**Lincoln Pk**	–
NEW Lockwood	**Loop**	–
Lovells	**Lake Forest**	22
Magnolia Cafe	**Ravenswood**	23
May St. Market	**W Loop**	23
☒ M. Henry	**Andersonville**	26
Milk & Honey	**Wicker Pk**	22
☒ mk	**Near North**	26
Montarra	**Algonquin**	25
Naha	**River N**	25
☒ Niche	**Geneva**	28
☒ North Pond	**Lincoln Pk**	25
NEW NXXT	**Humboldt Pk**	–
One North	**Loop**	18
☒ NEW Otom	**Mkt Dist**	23
Over Easy	**Ravenswood**	25
NEW Paramount Rm.	**Near W**	–
Park Grill	**Loop**	19
Parrot Cage	**Far S Side**	–
Philander's	**Oak Pk**	21
Pops/Champagne	**River N**	16
NEW Powerhouse	**Loop**	23
Prairie Grass	**Northbrook**	21
Puck's at MCA	**Streeterville**	20
Pump Rm.	**Gold Coast**	20
Quince	**Evanston**	24
Rhapsody	**Loop**	21
Ritz Café	**Streeterville**	23
☒ Room 21	**S Loop**	21
NEW Rustik	**Logan Sq**	–
Sage Grille	**Highwood**	22
Schwa	**Wicker Pk**	–
☒ Seasons	**Gold Coast**	27

subscribe to ZAGAT.com

Ⓩ NEW Sepia | **Mkt Dist**	22
Ⓩ 1776 | **Crystal Lake**	26
NEW Shochu | **Lakeview**	–
Ⓩ Signature Rm. | **Streeterville**	19
NEW Sixteen | **River N**	–
sola | **Lakeview**	25
NEW Sopa | **Highwood**	–
NEW Spertus Cafe | **S Loop**	–
Ⓩ Spring | **Wicker Pk**	27
Stained Glass | **Evanston**	24
NEW TABLE 52 | **Gold Coast**	24
NEW Takashi | **Bucktown**	29
NEW Tallulah | **Lincoln Sq**	–
Tavern | **Libertyville**	25
NEW Tavern at the Park | **Loop**	17
Think | **Bucktown**	22
Tomboy | **Andersonville**	21
Townhouse | **Loop**	16
Tweet | **Uptown**	24
Viand Bar | **Streeterville**	22
Ⓩ Vie | **W Springs**	28
NEW Violet | **Lakeview**	–
Volo | **Roscoe Vill**	20
West Town Tavern | **W Town**	25
Ⓩ Zealous | **River N**	24
Zest | **Streeterville**	18

AMERICAN (TRADITIONAL)

American Girl | **Gold Coast**	13
Ann Sather | **multi.**	20
Atwood Cafe | **Loop**	21
Bandera | **Streeterville**	22
Billy Goat | **multi.**	15
Birch River | **Arlington Hts**	–
Bongo Room | **multi.**	24
Boston Blackies | **multi.**	19
Breakfast Club | **W Loop**	20
Ⓩ Cheesecake Factory | **multi.**	19
Chicago Firehse. | **S Loop**	22
NEW Cinners Chili | **Lincoln Sq**	–
Clubhouse | **Oak Brook**	20
Cordis Bros. | **Lakeview**	20
Depot Diner | **Far W**	–
Dine | **W Loop**	15
Entourage | **Schaumburg**	22
NEW Fat Cat | **Uptown**	18
NEW Fifty/50, The | **Wicker Pk**	–
Finley's Grill | **Downers Grove**	22
Flo | **W Town**	22
Gale St. Inn | **multi.**	21
Glenn's Diner | **Ravenswood**	23

Goose Is. Brewing | **multi.**	16
Grace O'Malley's | **S Loop**	18
Green Door | **River N**	15
Grill on Alley | **Streeterville**	20
Hackney's | **multi.**	18
Hard Rock | **River N**	12
Hemmingway's | **Oak Pk**	20
Hot Chocolate | **Bucktown**	24
J. Alexander's | **multi.**	20
John's Place | **Lincoln Pk**	17
Kroll's | **S Loop**	14
Kuma's | **Logan Sq**	24
Lawry's | **River N**	24
Lou Mitchell's | **multi.**	21
LuxBar | **Gold Coast**	19
L. Woods Lodge | **Lincolnwood**	20
Margie's Candies | **multi.**	22
Medici on 57th | **Hyde Pk**	17
Mike Ditka's | **multi.**	22
Miller's Pub | **Loop**	18
Minnies | **Lincoln Pk**	17
Mity Nice Grill | **Streeterville**	17
Mrs. Park's | **Streeterville**	16
Next Door | **Northbrook**	22
Nookies | **multi.**	19
Oak Tree | **Gold Coast**	16
Orange | **multi.**	22
Original Pancake/Walker Bros. | **multi.**	23
NEW Park 52 | **Hyde Pk**	–
NEW Pepitone's | **Edgewater**	20
Petterino's | **Loop**	20
NEW Pinstripes | **Northbrook**	18
P.J. Clarke's | **multi.**	16
Poag Mahone's | **Loop**	19
R.J. Grunts | **Lincoln Pk**	19
Ⓩ RL | **Gold Coast**	23
Rockit B&G | **River N**	19
Ⓩ Seasons Café | **Gold Coast**	21
Shor | **S Loop**	–
Silver Cloud B&G | **Bucktown**	19
South Gate | **Lake Forest**	20
South Water | **Loop**	17
Stanley's | **multi.**	19
NEW Stretch Run | **River N**	–
NEW Tavern at the Park | **Loop**	17
Tavern on Rush | **Gold Coast**	20
312 Chicago | **Loop**	19
Toast | **multi.**	22
Twisted Spoke | **Near W**	20
Ⓩ Weber Grill | **multi.**	19

White Fence | **Romeoville**	22
Z Wildfire | **multi.**	24
Yard House | **Glenview**	17
Yolk | **S Loop**	22

ARGENTINEAN

El Nandu | **Logan Sq**	19
Rinconcito | **Bucktown**	18
Tango | **Naperville**	22
Tango Sur | **Lakeview**	25

ARMENIAN

Sayat Nova | **Streeterville**	20

ASIAN

Big Bowl | **multi.**	19
NEW Chant | **Hyde Pk**	16
China Grill | **Loop**	20
Flat Top Grill | **multi.**	19
Z Karma | **Mundelein**	23
Le Lan | **River N**	25
Opera | **S Loop**	22
Penny's Noodle | **Northfield**	18
Republic | **River N**	19
Z Shanghai Terr. | **River N**	25
NEW Shikago | **Loop**	20
NEW Shochu | **Lakeview**	-
Stir Crazy | **multi.**	21

ASIAN FUSION

Niu | **Streeterville**	21
pingpong | **Lakeview**	22
Sura | **Lakeview**	21
NEW Thalia Spice | **River W**	25

AUSTRIAN

Julius Meinl | **Lakeview**	22

BARBECUE

Carson's Ribs | **multi.**	22
Fat Willy's | **Logan Sq**	23
Hecky's | **multi.**	21
Honey 1 BBQ | **Bucktown**	19
Lem's BBQ | **Far S Side**	25
Merle's Smokehse. | **Evanston**	19
Ribs 'n' Bibs | **Hyde Pk**	20
NEW Risqué Café | **Lakeview**	-
Robinson's Ribs | **multi.**	22
Russell's BBQ | **multi.**	20
Smoke Daddy | **Wicker Pk**	21
Smoque BBQ | **NW Side**	24
Twin Anchors | **Old Town**	22
Uncle John's | **Far S Side**	-
Z Weber Grill | **multi.**	19

BELGIAN

Hopleaf | **Andersonville**	23

BRAZILIAN

NEW Al Primo Canto | **NW Side**	-
Brazzaz | **River N**	22
Z Fogo de Chão | **River N**	25
Rinconcito | **Bucktown**	18
Sabor do Brasil | **Orland Pk**	22
Texas de Brazil | **Schaumburg**	25

BRITISH

Red Lion Pub | **Lincoln Pk**	15

BURGERS

Billy Goat | **multi.**	15
Boston Blackies | **multi.**	19
Ed Debevic's | **multi.**	13
fRedhots | **Glenview**	18
Goose Is. Brewing | **multi.**	16
Hackney's | **multi.**	18
Hamburger Mary's | **Andersonville**	16
Hop Häus | **River N**	18
P.J. Clarke's | **multi.**	16
Poag Mahone's | **Loop**	19
Twisted Spoke | **Near W**	20
Wiener's Circle | **Lincoln Pk**	20

CAJUN

Davis St. Fish | **multi.**	20
Dixie Kitchen | **multi.**	20
Z Heaven on Seven | **multi.**	21
Pappadeaux | **multi.**	21
Wishbone | **multi.**	21

CHINESE

(* dim sum specialist)

Ben Pao | **River N**	21
Chens | **Wrigleyville**	20
Dee's | **Lincoln Pk**	19
Emperor's Choice | **Chinatown**	22
Evergreen | **Chinatown**	22
Fornetto Mei | **Gold Coast**	21
Hai Yen | **multi.**	20
Happy Chef* | **Chinatown**	22
Koi | **Evanston**	20
Z Lao | **multi.**	26
LuLu's* | **Evanston**	19
Moon Palace | **Chinatown**	24
New Three Happiness* | **Chinatown**	20
Z P.F. Chang's | **multi.**	21
Phoenix* | **Chinatown**	21
Pine Yard | **Evanston**	20

Shine & Morida | **Lincoln Pk**	18
Silver Seafood | **Uptown**	20
Three Happiness* | **Chinatown**	19

COFFEEHOUSES

Julius Meinl | **Lakeview**	22
Uncommon Ground | **multi.**	21

COFFEE SHOPS/DINERS

Chicago Diner | **Lakeview**	21
Depot Diner | **Far W**	–
Ed Debevic's | **multi.**	13
Eleven City | **S Loop**	19
Glenn's Diner | **Ravenswood**	23
Lou Mitchell's | **multi.**	21
Manny's | **multi.**	23
Milk & Honey | **Wicker Pk**	22
Nookies | **multi.**	19
Orange | **multi.**	22
Original Pancake/Walker Bros. | **multi.**	23
Tempo | **Gold Coast**	20

COLOMBIAN

La Fonda | **Andersonville**	24
Las Tablas | **multi.**	20

CONTINENTAL

Café la Cave | **Des Plaines**	20
Le P'tit Paris | **Streeterville**	24
☑ Lobby | **River N**	24

COSTA RICAN

Irazu | **Bucktown**	23

CREOLE

☑ Heaven on Seven | **multi.**	21
Pappadeaux | **multi.**	21

CUBAN

Cafe Bolero | **Bucktown**	20
Cafe 28 | **North Ctr/St. Ben's**	24
Habana Libre | **W Town**	21

DELIS

Bagel | **multi.**	19
Eleven City | **S Loop**	19
Manny's | **multi.**	23

ECLECTIC

Aria | **Loop**	23
NEW Bank Rest. | **Wheaton**	15
NEW Between Boutique | **Wicker Pk**	–
NEW Café 103 | **Far S Side**	–
NEW Cellar | **Wheaton**	–
Châtaigne | **Near North**	–
NEW C.J.'s | **Humboldt Pk**	–

Deleece | **Lakeview**	20
NEW Exposure Tapas | **S Loop**	18
Flatwater | **River N**	15
Flight | **Glenview**	19
foodlife | **Streeterville**	16
Grand Lux | **River N**	19
Hamburger Mary's | **Andersonville**	16
Heartland Cafe | **Rogers Pk**	17
Jane's | **Bucktown**	21
Kit Kat | **Wrigleyville**	15
Kitsch'n | **multi.**	16
NEW La Brochette | **Wicker Pk**	–
Lula | **Logan Sq**	26
NEW Macarena | **Naperville**	–
Moto | **Mkt Dist**	25
Nosh | **Geneva**	24
Orange | **multi.**	22
NEW Shochu | **Lakeview**	–
Tasting Room | **Mkt Dist**	15
Think | **Bucktown**	22
Tweet | **Uptown**	24
Twist | **Lakeview**	23
Uncommon Ground | **Lakeview**	21
Victory's Banner | **Roscoe Vill**	23
Webster Wine | **Lincoln Pk**	20
NEW ZED 451 | **multi.**	22
Zest | **Streeterville**	18

ETHIOPIAN

NEW African Harambee | **Rogers Pk**	18
Ethiopian Diamond | **Edgewater**	22
Mama Desta's | **Lakeview**	21

FILIPINO

Coobah | **Lakeview**	20

FONDUE

Geja's Cafe | **Lincoln Pk**	22
Melting Pot | **multi.**	19

FRENCH

Atwater's | **Geneva**	21
Bonsoiree | **Logan Sq**	–
Café/Architectes | **Gold Coast**	23
Cafe Matou | **Bucktown**	23
☑ Carlos' | **Highland Pk**	28
Châtaigne | **Near North**	–
Convito | **Wilmette**	16
copperblue | **Streeterville**	21
Dining Rm./Kendall | **Near W**	24
Dorado | **Lincoln Sq**	25
☑ Everest | **Loop**	27

Froggy's | **Highwood**	23
🅩 Gabriel's | **Highwood**	26
Jilly's Cafe | **Evanston**	24
L'anne | **Wheaton**	21
la petite folie | **Hyde Pk**	23
Le Lan | **River N**	25
Le P'tit Paris | **Streeterville**	24
🅩 Les Nomades | **Streeterville**	28
🅩 Le Titi/Paris | **Arlington Hts**	28
Le Vichyssois | **Lakemoor**	27
🅩 Michael | **Winnetka**	26
🅩 NoMI | **Gold Coast**	26
🅩 Oceanique | **Evanston**	26
NEW Old Town Mkt. | **Old Town**	24
one sixtyblue | **Mkt Dist**	25
NEW Takashi | **Bucktown**	29
🅩 Tallgrass | **Lockport**	29
🅩 Tru | **Streeterville**	27
Yoshi's Café | **Lakeview**	25

FRENCH (BISTRO)

🅩 Barrington Country | **Barrington**	26
Bin 36/Wine | **multi.**	20
Bistro Campagne | **Lincoln Sq**	24
Bistro Monet | **Glen Ellyn**	23
Bistro 110 | **Gold Coast**	20
Bistro 22 | **Lake Zurich**	22
Bistrot Margot | **Old Town**	21
Bistrot Zinc | **Gold Coast**	20
Café Bernard | **Lincoln Pk**	19
Cafe Central | **Highland Pk**	23
Café le Coq | **Oak Pk**	23
Cafe Pyrenees | **Libertyville**	23
Chez Joël | **Little Italy**	23
Côtes/Rhône | **Edgewater**	18
Cyrano's Bistrot | **River N**	21
D & J Bistro | **Lake Zurich**	25
Hemmingway's | **Oak Pk**	20
Jacky's Bistro | **Evanston**	24
KiKi's Bistro | **Near North**	23
La Crêperie | **Lakeview**	21
La Petite Amelia | **Evanston**	20
La Sardine | **W Loop**	23
La Tache | **Andersonville**	22
Le Bouchon | **Bucktown**	24
Marché | **Mkt Dist**	22
Miramar Bistro | **Highwood**	20
🅩 Mon Ami Gabi | **multi.**	22
Pierrot Gourmet | **River N**	21
🅩 Retro Bistro | **Mt. Prospect**	25
Shallots Bistro | **Skokie**	–
socca | **Lakeview**	24

FRENCH (BRASSERIE)

Brasserie Jo | **River N**	22
🅩 **NEW** Brasserie Ruhlmann | **River N**	21

GERMAN

Berghoff | **multi.**	19
Edelweiss | **Norridge**	22
Mirabell | **NW Side**	21

GREEK

Artopolis | **Greektown**	23
Athena | **Greektown**	19
Costa's | **multi.**	22
Greek Islands | **multi.**	22
NEW Mythos | **Lakeview**	–
OPA Estiatorio | **Vernon Hills**	19
Parthenon | **Greektown**	22
Pegasus | **multi.**	21
Roditys | **Greektown**	22
Santorini | **Greektown**	22
Venus | **Greektown**	21

HAWAII REGIONAL

Roy's | **River N**	24

HOT DOGS

Al's #1 Beef | **multi.**	21
fRedhots | **Glenview**	18
Gold Coast | **multi.**	21
🅩 Hot Doug's | **NW Side**	27
NEW Rockstar Dogs | **W Town**	–
Superdawg | **multi.**	22
Wiener's Circle | **Lincoln Pk**	20

INDIAN

Essence of India | **Lincoln Sq**	21
Gaylord Indian | **Schaumburg**	21
Hema's Kitchen | **multi.**	21
India Hse. | **multi.**	24
Indian Gdn. | **multi.**	22
Klay Oven | **River N**	21
Marigold | **Uptown**	23
Mt. Everest | **Evanston**	22
Radhuni | **Lakeview**	15
Raj Darbar | **Lincoln Pk**	20
Tiffin | **W Rogers Pk**	22
Udupi Palace | **multi.**	19
Vermilion | **River N**	21
Viceroy of India | **multi.**	18

IRISH

Chief O'Neill's | **NW Side**	17
Grace O'Malley's | **S Loop**	18

Irish Oak | **Wrigleyville**	19
Mrs. Murphy | **North Ctr/St. Ben's**	18

ITALIAN

(N=Northern; S=Southern)

Adesso | **Lakeview**	18
NEW Al Primo Canto | **NW Side**	-
NEW A Mano | **River N**	21
Angelina | S | **Lakeview**	21
Anna Maria | **Ravenswood**	23
Anteprima | **Andersonville**	23
Antico Posto | **Oak Brook**	22
Z a tavola | N | **Ukrainian Vill**	26
Aurelio's Pizza | **multi.**	21
Bacchanalia | N | **SW Side**	24
Ballo | **River N**	20
Basil Leaf | N | **Lincoln Pk**	21
Bella Bacino's | **multi.**	20
Bella Notte | S | **W Loop**	22
Bice | **Streeterville**	21
NEW Brio | **Lombard**	21
Bruna's | **SW Side**	23
Buona Terra | N | **Logan Sq**	23
Café Bionda | **multi.**	22
Café Spiaggia | **Gold Coast**	25
Caliterra | N | **Streeterville**	22
Campagnola | **Evanston**	23
Carlos & Carlos | N | **Arlington Hts**	23
Carlucci | N | **multi.**	21
Carmine's | **Gold Coast**	21
Club Lucky | S | **Bucktown**	19
Coco Pazzo | N | **River N**	25
Coco Pazzo Café | N | **Streeterville**	23
Convito | **Wilmette**	16
NEW Cucina Paradiso | **Oak Pk**	25
Dave's Italian | S | **Evanston**	17
Del Rio | N | **Highwood**	22
Dinotto | **Old Town**	21
Di Pescara | **Northbrook**	21
EJ's Place | N | **Skokie**	20
Enoteca Piattini | S | **Lincoln Pk**	18
Erba | N | **Lincoln Sq**	20
Erie Cafe | **River N**	22
Filippo's | **Lincoln Pk**	22
Fiorentino's | S | **Lakeview**	22
FoLLia | N | **Mkt Dist**	23
Fornetto Mei | N | **Gold Coast**	21
Z Francesca's | N | **multi.**	24
Francesco's | S | **Northbrook**	25
NEW Frankie's Scaloppine | **Gold Coast**	-
Frasca Pizzeria | **Lakeview**	19
Z Gabriel's | **Highwood**	26
NEW Gaetano's | **Forest Pk**	-
Gio | N | **Evanston**	20
Gioco | N | **S Loop**	24
Gruppo/Amici | **Rogers Pk**	21
Harry Caray's | **multi.**	20
Il Covo | **Bucktown**	20
NEW Il Fiasco | **Andersonville**	19
Il Mulino | **Gold Coast**	24
La Bocca/Verità | **Lincoln Sq**	20
La Cantina | N | **Loop**	21
La Cucina/Donatella | **Rogers Pk**	24
La Donna | **Andersonville**	19
La Gondola | **Lakeview**	23
NEW La Madia | **River N**	22
La Scarola | **River W**	23
La Vita | N | **Little Italy**	22
Leonardo's | N | **Andersonville**	21
Lucia | **Wicker Pk**	23
Luna Caprese | S | **Lincoln Pk**	26
NEW Macello | **Mkt Dist**	19
NEW mado | **Bucktown**	-
Z Maggiano's | **multi.**	21
Merlo | N | **multi.**	24
Mia Francesca | **Lakeview**	25
NEW Natalino's | **W Town**	-
Next Door | **Northbrook**	22
NEW Omaggio | **Evanston**	20
Osteria/Tramonto | **Wheeling**	21
Osteria/Pizzeria Via Stato | S | **River N**	22
Pane Caldo | N | **Gold Coast**	24
Pasta Palazzo | **Lincoln Pk**	22
NEW Pepitone's | **Edgewater**	20
Philly G's | **Vernon Hills**	22
Phil Stefani's | **River N**	21
Piazza Bella | **Roscoe Vill**	20
NEW Pinstripes | **Northbrook**	18
Pizza Capri | **multi.**	20
Pizza D.O.C. | **Lincoln Sq**	22
Pompei Bakery | **multi.**	20
NEW Prosecco | **River N**	25
NEW Purgatory Pizza | **Wrigleyville**	-
Quartino | **River N**	21
Z Riccardo Tratt. | N | **Lincoln Pk**	26
rist. we | N | **Loop**	17
RoSal's Kitchen | S | **Little Italy**	22
Rose Angelis | **Lincoln Pk**	22
Z Rosebud | **multi.**	22
Z Rosebud Prime/Steak | **multi.**	23

Sabatino's | **NW Side**	22
Salvatore's | N | **Lincoln Pk**	21
Sapore/Napoli | **Lakeview**	22
Sapori Tratt. | **Lincoln Pk**	22
Scoozi! | **River N**	20
socca | **Lakeview**	24
Spacca Napoli | **Ravenswood**	24
Z Spiaggia | **Gold Coast**	27
Tarantino's | **Lincoln Pk**	22
Terragusto Cafe | **Roscoe Vill**	24
312 Chicago | **Loop**	19
Timpano Chophse. | **Naperville**	20
Topo Gigio | **Old Town**	23
NEW Trattoria 225 | **Oak Pk**	19
Tratt. D.O.C. | **Evanston**	19
Tratt. Gianni | **Lincoln Pk**	21
NEW Trattoria Isabella | **Mkt Dist**	–
Tratt. No. 10 | **Loop**	23
Tratt. Roma | **Old Town**	21
Tratt. 31 | **SW Side**	–
Trattoria Trullo | S | **Lincoln Sq**	21
Tufano's Tap | S | **University Vill**	20
Tuscany | N | **multi.**	22
Z Va Pensiero | **Evanston**	26
Via Carducci | S | **multi.**	22
Village | **Loop**	20
Vinci | **Lincoln Pk**	21
Vito & Nick's | **Far S Side**	23
Vivere | **Loop**	23
Vivo | **Mkt Dist**	21
Volare | **multi.**	24
Zia's Trattoria | **Edison Pk**	25

JAPANESE

(* sushi specialist)

Agami* | **Uptown**	25
NEW Ai Sushi* | **River N**	21
Akai Hana* | **Wilmette**	21
Benihana | **multi.**	20
Blu Coral* | **Wicker Pk**	22
Bob San* | **Wicker Pk**	24
Butterfly* | **W Loop**	21
Chens* | **Wrigleyville**	20
Coast Sushi/South Coast* | **multi.**	25
Dee's* | **Lincoln Pk**	19
Hachi's Kitchen* | **Logan Sq**	24
Indie Cafe* | **Edgewater**	23
Itto Sushi* | **Lincoln Pk**	23
Z Japonais* | **River N**	24
Kamehachi* | **multi.**	22
Kansaku* | **Evanston**	22

Katsu* | **NW Side**	24
Kaze Sushi* | **Roscoe Vill**	23
Koi* | **Evanston**	20
Kuni's* | **Evanston**	21
Meiji* | **W Loop**	25
Mirai Sushi* | **Wicker Pk**	25
Mizu Yakitori* | **Old Town**	27
Niu | **Streeterville**	21
Oysy* | **multi.**	21
RA Sushi* | **multi.**	18
Ringo* | **Lincoln Pk**	23
Rise* | **Wrigleyville**	22
NEW Rock-N-Roll* | **Palatine**	–
Sai Café* | **Lincoln Pk**	24
Sakuma's* | **Streamwood**	–
Shine & Morida* | **Lincoln Pk**	18
Starfish* | **Mkt Dist**	20
Sushi Naniwa* | **River N**	23
Z SushiSamba* | **River N**	22
Z sushi wabi* | **Mkt Dist**	26
Sushi X* | **multi.**	–
Swordfish* | **Batavia**	26
Tamarind* | S **Loop**	21
Tank Sushi* | **Lincoln Sq**	22
NEW Thai Urban* | **Loop**	–
Tsuki* | **Lincoln Pk**	24
Tsunami* | **Gold Coast**	23
Wakamono* | **Lakeview**	23
Wildfish* | **multi.**	24
Yoshi's Café | **Lakeview**	25

JEWISH

Bagel | **multi.**	19
Manny's | **multi.**	23

KOREAN

(* barbecue specialist)

NEW BBOP Lounge | **Old Town**	–
Jin Ju | **Andersonville**	21
Koryo | **Lakeview**	19
San Soo Gab San* | **NW Side**	21
NEW Su-Ra | **Wicker Pk**	17
Woo Lae Oak* | **Rolling Meadows**	23

KOSHER

Shallots Bistro | **Skokie**	–
NEW Spertus Cafe | S **Loop**	–

LEBANESE

Kan Zaman | **River N**	20
Maza | **Lincoln Pk**	23

MALAYSIAN

Penang | **Chinatown**	22

MEDITERRANEAN

Andies | **multi.**	19
Artopolis | **Greektown**	23
☑ Avec | **Loop**	27
Café/Architectes | **Gold Coast**	23
copperblue | **Streeterville**	21
Cousin's | **Lakeview**	19
Isabella's | **Geneva**	25
NEW La Brochette | **Wicker Pk**	–
NEW mado | **Bucktown**	–
NEW Nia | **Mkt Dist**	–
Pita Inn | **multi.**	24
NEW Pomegranate | **Evanston**	19
Reza's | **multi.**	20
Shallots Bistro | **Skokie**	–
NEW Sopa | **Highwood**	–
Tizi Melloul | **River N**	21
Turquoise | **Roscoe Vill**	22
Venus | **Greektown**	21
Wave | **Streeterville**	20

MEXICAN

Adobo Grill | **multi.**	21
Cafe 28 | **North Ctr/St. Ben's**	24
de cero | **Mkt Dist**	22
Don Juan's | **Edison Pk**	21
Dorado | **Lincoln Sq**	25
El Presidente | **Lincoln Pk**	15
Fonda del Mar | **Logan Sq**	24
☑ Frontera Grill | **River N**	27
Hot Tamales | **Highland Pk**	21
Irazu | **Bucktown**	23
NEW Jack Rabbit | **Lincoln Sq**	–
La Casa/Isaac | **Highland Pk**	22
NEW La Cocina/Frida | **Andersonville**	–
Lalo's | **multi.**	17
Las Palmas | **multi.**	22
Lupita's | **Evanston**	19
Maiz | **Humboldt Pk**	23
Mundial | **University Vill**	24
Riques | **Uptown**	20
NEW Rusty Armadillo | **NW Side**	–
Salpicón | **Old Town**	24
Salud Tequila | **Wicker Pk**	–
San Gabriel | **Bannockburn**	20
Sol de Mex. | **NW Side**	25
Tepatulco | **Lincoln Pk**	23
☑ Topolobampo | **River N**	28
Zapatista | **S Loop**	18
Zocalo | **River N**	23

MIDDLE EASTERN

Aladdin's Eatery | **Lincoln Pk**	21
☑ Alhambra | **Mkt Dist**	13
Andies | **multi.**	19
Babylon | **Bucktown**	20
NEW La Brochette | **Wicker Pk**	–
Old Jerusalem | **Old Town**	19
Pita Inn | **multi.**	24
NEW Pomegranate | **Evanston**	19
Tizi Melloul | **River N**	21

MOROCCAN

NEW La Brochette | **Wicker Pk**	–

NEPALESE

Mt. Everest | **Evanston**	22

NOODLE SHOPS

Joy Yee's | **multi.**	22
Penny's Noodle | **multi.**	18

NUEVO LATINO

☑ Carnivale | **Loop**	22
Coobah | **Lakeview**	20
Cuatro | **S Loop**	22
DeLaCosta | **Streeterville**	22
Mambo Grill | **River N**	20
NEW Maya Del Sol | **Oak Pk**	21
Nacional 27 | **River N**	23
Olé Olé | **Andersonville**	20
Rumba | **River N**	21
Sangria | **Lincoln Pk**	14
Vermilion | **River N**	21

PAKISTANI

Radhuni | **Lakeview**	15

PAN-ASIAN

LuLu's | **Evanston**	19
NEW Miss Asia | **Lakeview**	–
Red Light | **Mkt Dist**	22
Tamarind | **S Loop**	21
NEW Thai Urban | **Loop**	–
NEW Thalia Spice | **River W**	25

PERSIAN

Noon-O-Kabab | **NW Side**	24
Reza's | **multi.**	20

PERUVIAN

Rinconcito | **Bucktown**	18

PIZZA

Art of Pizza | **Lakeview**	21
Aurelio's Pizza | **multi.**	21

Bella Bacino's	**multi.**	20
Bricks	**Lincoln Pk**	22
Chicago Pizza	**Lincoln Pk**	22
Coalfire Pizza	**W Loop**	22
Crust	**Wicker Pk**	21
Edwardo's Pizza	**multi.**	20
NEW Frankie's Scaloppine	**Gold Coast**	–
Frasca Pizzeria	**Lakeview**	19
Gio	**Evanston**	20
Z Giordano's	**multi.**	21
Gruppo/Amici	**Rogers Pk**	21
Gulliver's Pizza	**Rogers Pk**	–
La Gondola	**Lakeview**	23
NEW La Madia	**River N**	22
Z Lou Malnati's	**multi.**	24
My Pie Pizza	**Bucktown**	20
Nancy's Pizza	**multi.**	22
O'Famé	**Lincoln Pk**	19
Original Gino's	**multi.**	21
Piece	**Wicker Pk**	23
Pizza Capri	**multi.**	20
Pizza D.O.C.	**Lincoln Sq**	22
Pizzeria Uno/Due	**River N**	21
Osteria/Pizzeria Via Stato	**River N**	22
Pompei Bakery	**multi.**	20
NEW Purgatory Pizza	**Wrigleyville**	–
Sapore/Napoli	**Lakeview**	22
Spacca Napoli	**Ravenswood**	24
Tratt. D.O.C.	**Evanston**	19
NEW Union Pizzeria	**Evanston**	–
Vito & Nick's	**Far S Side**	23

PUB FOOD

Bar Louie	**multi.**	15
Billy Goat	**multi.**	15
Boston Blackies	**multi.**	19
Chief O'Neill's	**NW Side**	17
Duke of Perth	**Lakeview**	21
Goose Is. Brewing	**multi.**	16
Grace O'Malley's	**S Loop**	18
Green Door	**River N**	15
Irish Oak	**Wrigleyville**	19
L. Woods Lodge	**Lincolnwood**	20
Mrs. Murphy	**North Ctr/St. Ben's**	18
Poag Mahone's	**Loop**	19
Red Lion Pub	**Lincoln Pk**	15
Twin Anchors	**Old Town**	22

RUSSIAN

Russian Tea	**Loop**	22

SANDWICHES

Al's #1 Beef	**multi.**	21
Bagel	**multi.**	19
Bar Louie	**Mkt Dist**	15
Berghoff	**multi.**	19
Hannah's Bretzel	**Loop**	23
NEW Jerry's	**Wicker Pk**	20
Mr. Beef	**River N**	24
Potbelly	**multi.**	19

SCANDINAVIAN

Tre Kronor	**NW Side**	23

SCOTTISH

Duke of Perth	**Lakeview**	21

SEAFOOD

Bob Chinn's	**Wheeling**	22
Cape Cod Rm.	**Streeterville**	22
Z Catch 35	**multi.**	24
Chinn's Fishery	**Lisle**	22
Davis St. Fish	**multi.**	20
Devon Seafood	**River N**	21
Di Pescara	**Northbrook**	21
Don Roth's	**Wheeling**	23
Drake Bros.'	**Streeterville**	20
Emperor's Choice	**Chinatown**	22
Fonda del Mar	**Logan Sq**	24
Froggy's	**Highwood**	23
Fulton's	**River N**	19
Glenn's Diner	**Ravenswood**	23
Half Shell	**Lincoln Pk**	22
NEW Holy Mackerel!	**Lombard**	19
Hugo's	**multi.**	23
Z Joe's Seafood	**River N**	26
Keefer's	**River N**	24
La Cantina	**Loop**	21
Z Lobby	**River N**	24
Z McCormick/Schmick's	**multi.**	21
Mitchell's Fish Mkt.	**Glenview**	21
Nick's Fishmkt.	**multi.**	24
N9ne	**Loop**	24
Z Oceanique	**Evanston**	26
Pappadeaux	**multi.**	21
Parkers'	**Downers Grove**	24
Pete Miller	**multi.**	22
NEW Reel Club	**Oak Brook**	20
Riva	**multi.**	18
Sam & Harry's	**Schaumburg**	27
Santorini	**Greektown**	22
Z Shaw's Crab	**multi.**	24
Shula's Steak	**multi.**	19
Silver Seafood	**Uptown**	20

Z Spring | **Wicker Pk**	27	
Tin Fish | **Tinley Park**	21	
Z Tramonto's | **Wheeling**	24	

SMALL PLATES

(See also Spanish tapas specialist)

Z Avec | Med. | **Loop**	27
NEW Bluebird, The | Amer. | **Bucktown**	19
BOKA | Amer. | **Lincoln Pk**	24
NEW Cellar | Eclectic | **Wheaton**	-
NEW Chant | Asian | **Hyde Pk**	16
NEW Drawing Rm/Le Passage | Amer. | **Gold Coast**	-
Enoteca Piattini | Italian | **Lincoln Pk**	18
NEW Exposure Tapas | Eclectic | **S Loop**	18
Flight | Eclectic | **Glenview**	19
Green Zebra | Veg. | **W Town**	26
Maza | Lebanese | **Lincoln Pk**	23
NEW Nia | Med. | **Mkt Dist**	-
Pops/Champagne | Amer. | **River N**	16
Quartino | Italian | **River N**	21
Sangria | Nuevo Latino | **Lincoln Pk**	14
NEW Shochu | Amer./Japanese | **Lakeview**	-
Tango | Argent. | **Naperville**	22
Volo | Amer. | **Roscoe Vill**	20
Wave | Med. | **Streeterville**	20
Webster Wine | Eclectic | **Lincoln Pk**	20

SOUL FOOD

Army & Lou's | **Far S Side**	24

SOUTH AMERICAN

La Peña | **NW Side**	18
Z SushiSamba | **River N**	22

SOUTHERN

Army & Lou's | **Far S Side**	24
NEW Big Jones | **Andersonville**	-
NEW C.J.'s | **Humboldt Pk**	-
Dixie Kitchen | **multi.**	20
Fat Willy's | **Logan Sq**	23
Wishbone | **multi.**	21

SOUTHWESTERN

Bandera | **Streeterville**	22
Flo | **W Town**	22
NEW Jack Rabbit | **Lincoln Sq**	-

SPANISH

(* tapas specialist)

Arco/Cuchilleros* | **Lakeview**	18
Azucar* | **Logan Sq**	23
Cafe Ba-Ba-Reeba!* | **Lincoln Pk**	22
Café Iberico* | **River N**	22
Emilio's Tapas* | **multi.**	22
1492 Tapas* | **River N**	19
La Tasca* | **Arlington Hts**	23
NEW Macarena* | **Naperville**	-
NEW Mercat | **S Loop**	-
Mesón Sabika/Tapas Valencia* | **multi.**	24
Tapas Barcelona* | **Evanston**	21
Tapas Gitana* | **Northfield**	-
Twist* | **Lakeview**	23

STEAKHOUSES

Avenue M | **River W**	21
Benihana | **multi.**	20
Bogart's | **multi.**	20
Z NEW Brasserie Ruhlmann | **River N**	21
Brazzaz | **River N**	22
Z Capital Grille | **multi.**	25
Carmichael's | **W Loop**	21
Z Chicago Chop | **River N**	25
David Burke Prime | **River N**	24
Don Roth's | **Wheeling**	23
Drake Bros.' | **Streeterville**	20
EJ's Place | **Skokie**	20
El Nandu | **Logan Sq**	19
Entourage | **Schaumburg**	22
Erie Cafe | **River N**	22
Five O'Clock Steak | **Fox Riv. Grove**	23
Fleming's | **Lincolnshire**	22
Z Fogo de Chão | **River N**	25
Fulton's | **River N**	19
Gene & Georgetti | **River N**	24
Z Gibsons | **multi.**	25
Grill on Alley | **Streeterville**	20
Grillroom | **Loop**	18
Harry Caray's | **multi.**	20
Hugo's | **multi.**	23
Z Joe's Seafood | **River N**	26
Keefer's | **River N**	24
Kinzie Chophse. | **River N**	20
Las Tablas | **multi.**	20
Lawry's | **River N**	24
Mike Ditka's | **multi.**	22
Montarra | **Algonquin**	25
Z Morton's | **multi.**	26

Myron & Phil's | **Lincolnwood**	22
N9ne | **Loop**	24
Palm, The | **multi.**	23
Pete Miller | **multi.**	22
Phil Stefani's | **River N**	21
rist. we | **Loop**	17
☑ Room 21 | **S Loop**	21
☑ Rosebud Prime/Steak | **multi.**	23
Ruth's Chris | **multi.**	25
Sabor do Brasil | **Orland Pk**	22
Sage Grille | **Highwood**	22
Saloon Steak | **Streeterville**	22
Sam & Harry's | **Schaumburg**	27
Shor | **S Loop**	-
Shula's Steak | **multi.**	19
Smith/Wollensky | **River N**	22
Stetson's Chop Hse. | **Loop**	23
Sullivan's Steak | **multi.**	22
Tango | **Naperville**	22
Tango Sur | **Lakeview**	25
Tavern | **Libertyville**	25
Tavern on Rush | **Gold Coast**	20
Texas de Brazil | **Schaumburg**	25
Timpano Chophse. | **Naperville**	20
☑ Tramonto's | **Wheeling**	24
☑ Wildfire | **multi.**	24
NEW ZED 451 | **multi.**	22

SWEDISH

Ann Sather | **multi.**	20

THAI

☑ Arun's | **NW Side**	27
Butterfly | **W Loop**	21
Indie Cafe | **Edgewater**	23
NEW Miss Asia | **Lakeview**	-
P.S. Bangkok | **multi.**	21

Ruby of Siam | **multi.**	20
Siam Café | **Uptown**	22
Spoon Thai | **Lincoln Sq**	20
Star of Siam | **River N**	20
Sura | **Lakeview**	21
Thai Classic | **Lakeview**	23
Thai Pastry | **Uptown**	24
NEW Thai Urban | **Loop**	-
Vong's | **River N**	22

TURKISH

A La Turka | **Lakeview**	20
Cousin's | **Lakeview**	19
Turquoise | **Roscoe Vill**	22

VEGETARIAN

(* vegan)

Aladdin's Eatery | **Lincoln Pk**	21
Andies | **multi.**	19
NEW Balanced Kitchen* | **NW Side**	-
Blind Faith | **Evanston**	21
Chicago Diner | **Lakeview**	21
Ethiopian Diamond | **Edgewater**	22
Green Zebra | **W Town**	26
Heartland Cafe | **Rogers Pk**	17
Hema's Kitchen | **multi.**	21
Kabul Hse. | **Skokie**	21
Karyn's* | **multi.**	21
Tiffin | **W Rogers Pk**	22
Udupi Palace | **multi.**	19
Victory's Banner | **Roscoe Vill**	23

VIETNAMESE

Hai Yen | **multi.**	20
L'anne | **Wheaton**	21
Le Colonial | **Gold Coast**	23
Simply It | **Lincoln Pk**	22
Viet Bistro | **Rogers Pk**	19

subscribe to ZAGAT.com

Locations

Includes restaurant names, cuisines, Food ratings and, for locations that are mapped, top list and map coordinates. **Z** indicates places with the highest ratings, popularity and importance.

City North

ANDERSONVILLE/EDGEWATER

Andies	Med./Mideast	19
Ann Sather	Amer./Swedish	20
Anteprima	Italian	23
NEW Big Jones	Southern	-
Broadway Cellars	Amer.	21
Côtes/Rhône	French	18
Ethiopian Diamond	Ethiopian	22
Z Francesca's	Italian	24
Hamburger Mary's	Burgers	16
Hopleaf	Belgian	23
Icosium Kafe	African	19
NEW Il Fiasco	Italian	19
Indie Cafe	Japanese/Thai	23
Jin Ju	Korean	21
NEW La Cocina/Frida	Mex.	-
La Donna	Italian	19
La Fonda	Colombian	24
La Tache	French	22
Leonardo's	Italian	21
Z M. Henry	Amer.	26
Olé Olé	Nuevo Latino	20
NEW Pepitone's	Amer./Italian	20
Reza's	Med./Mideast.	20
Tomboy	Amer.	21
Uncommon Ground	Coffee	21

GOLD COAST

(See map on page 193)

TOP FOOD

Seasons	Amer.	**H3**	27
Spiaggia	Italian	**G4**	27
NoMI	French	**I3**	26
Morton's	Steak	**G2**	26
Gibsons	Steak	**G2**	25
Café Spiaggia	Italian	**G4**	25
Pane Caldo	Italian	**H3**	24
Il Mulino	Italian	**F1**	24
TABLE 52	Amer.	**F1**	24
Merlo	Italian	**G2**	24

LISTING

American Girl	Amer.	13
Big Bowl	Asian	19
Bistro 110	French	20
Bistrot Zinc	French	20
Café/Architectes	French/Med.	23
Café Spiaggia	Italian	25
Carmine's	Italian	21
Cru Café	Amer.	17
NEW Drawing Rm/Le Passage	Amer.	-
Edwardo's Pizza	Pizza	20
Fornetto Mei	Chinese/Italian	21
NEW Frankie's Scaloppine	Pizza	-
Z Gibsons	Steak	25
Hugo's	Seafood	23
Il Mulino	Italian	24
Le Colonial	Viet.	23
LuxBar	Amer.	19
Z McCormick/Schmick's	Seafood	21
Merlo	Italian	24
Mike Ditka's	Steak	22
Z Morton's	Steak	26
Z NoMI	French	26
Oak Tree	Amer.	16
Pane Caldo	Italian	24
P.J. Clarke's	Amer.	16
Pump Rm.	Amer.	20
RA Sushi	Japanese	18
Z RL	Amer.	23
Z Rosebud	Italian	22
Z Seasons	Amer.	27
Z Seasons Café	Amer.	21
Z Spiaggia	Italian	27
NEW TABLE 52	Amer.	24
Tavern on Rush	Steak	20
Tempo	Diner	20
Tsunami	Japanese	23

LAKEVIEW/WRIGLEYVILLE

Adesso	Italian	18
A La Turka	Turkish	20
Angelina	Italian	21
Ann Sather	Amer./Swedish	20
Arco/Cuchilleros	Spanish	18
Art of Pizza	Pizza	21
Bagel	Deli	19
Bar Louie	Pub	15
Chalkboard	Amer.	22
Chens	Chinese/Japanese	20

Chicago Diner	*Diner*	21
Coobah	*Filipino/Nuevo Latino*	20
Cordis Bros.	*Amer.*	20
Cousin's	*Med.*	19
Deleece	*Eclectic*	20
Duke of Perth	*Scottish*	21
erwin cafe	*Amer.*	22
Fiorentino's	*Italian*	22
Flat Top Grill	*Asian*	19
Frasca Pizzeria	*Pizza*	19
🆉 Giordano's	*Pizza*	21
Goose Is. Brewing	*Pub*	16
HB Home Bistro	*Amer.*	24
Irish Oak	*Pub*	19
Jack's on Halsted	*Amer.*	21
Julius Meinl	*Austrian*	22
Kit Kat	*Eclectic*	15
Koryo	*Korean*	19
La Crêperie	*French*	21
La Gondola	*Italian*	23
Las Tablas	*Colombian/Steak*	20
Mama Desta's	*Ethiopian*	21
Mia Francesca	*Italian*	25
🆃🅴🆆 Miss Asia	*Pan-Asian*	-
🆃🅴🆆 Mythos	*Greek*	-
Nancy's Pizza	*Pizza*	22
Nookies	*Diner*	19
Orange	*Eclectic*	22
Penny's Noodle	*Asian*	18
pingpong	*Asian Fusion*	22
Pizza Capri	*Pizza*	20
Pompei Bakery	*Italian*	20
Potbelly	*Sandwiches*	19
P.S. Bangkok	*Thai*	21
🆃🅴🆆 Purgatory Pizza	*Pizza*	-
Radhuni	*Indian/Pakistani*	15
Rise	*Japanese*	22
🆃🅴🆆 Risqué Café	*BBQ*	-
Sapore/Napoli	*Pizza*	22
🆃🅴🆆 Shochu	*Amer./Japanese*	-
socca	*French/Italian*	24
sola	*Amer.*	25
Sura	*Thai*	21
Tango Sur	*Argent./Steak*	25
Thai Classic	*Thai*	23
Tuscany	*Italian*	22
Twist	*Eclectic*	23
Uncommon Ground	*Coffee*	21
🆃🅴🆆 Violet	*Amer.*	-
Wakamono	*Japanese*	23
Yoshi's Café	*French/Japanese*	25

LINCOLN PARK

(See map on page 194)

TOP FOOD

Alinea	*Amer.*	**I7**	29
Charlie Trotter's	*Amer.*	**G6**	27
Riccardo Tratt.	*Italian*	**F10**	26
North Pond	*Amer.*	**B11**	25
Tsuki	*Japanese*	**D2**	24
Sai Café	*Japanese*	**G5**	24
Merlo	*Italian*	**B5**	24
BOKA	*Amer.*	**I7**	24
Lou Malnati's	*Pizza*	24
Itto Sushi	*Japanese*	**B6**	23
Maza	*Mideast.*	**A4**	23
Tepatulco	*Mex.*	**B6**	23
Original Pancake/Walker Bros.	*Amer.*	**G9**	23
Tarantino's	*Italian*	**G4**	22
Filippo's	*Italian*	**E2**	22

LISTING

Aladdin's Eatery	*Mideast.*	21
🆉 Alinea	*Amer.*	29
Basil Leaf	*Italian*	21
Bella Bacino's	*Italian*	20
BOKA	*Amer.*	24
Bricks	*Pizza*	22
Cafe Ba-Ba-Reeba!	*Spanish*	22
Café Bernard	*French*	19
🆉 Charlie Trotter's	*Amer.*	27
Chicago Pizza	*Pizza*	22
Dee's	*Asian*	19
Edwardo's Pizza	*Pizza*	20
El Presidente	*Mex.*	15
Emilio's Tapas	*Spanish*	22
Enoteca Piattini	*Italian*	18
Filippo's	*Italian*	22
Geja's Cafe	*Fondue*	22
Goose Is. Brewing	*Pub*	16
Green Dolphin St.	*Amer.*	19
Hai Yen	*Chinese/Viet.*	20
Half Shell	*Seafood*	22
Hema's Kitchen	*Indian*	21
Itto Sushi	*Japanese*	23
J. Alexander's	*Amer.*	20
John's Place	*Amer.*	17
Karyn's	*Veg.*	21
Lalo's	*Mex.*	17
Landmark	*Amer.*	21
🆃🅴🆆 Libertine	*Amer.*	-
🆉 Lou Malnati's	*Pizza*	24
Luna Caprese	*Italian*	26

Maza	*Mideast.*	23
Merlo	*Italian*	24
Minnies	*Amer.*	17
Z Mon Ami Gabi	*French*	22
Nookies	*Diner*	19
Z North Pond	*Amer.*	25
O'Famé	*Pizza*	19
Original Gino's	*Pizza*	21
Original Pancake/Walker Bros.	*Amer.*	23
Pasta Palazzo	*Italian*	22
Penny's Noodle	*Asian*	18
Pizza Capri	*Pizza*	20
P.J. Clarke's	*Amer.*	16
Potbelly	*Sandwiches*	19
P.S. Bangkok	*Thai*	21
Raj Darbar	*Indian*	20
Red Lion Pub	*British*	15
Z Riccardo Tratt.	*Italian*	26
Ringo	*Japanese*	23
R.J. Grunts	*Amer.*	19
Robinson's Ribs	*BBQ*	22
Rose Angelis	*Italian*	22
Sai Café	*Japanese*	24
Salvatore's	*Italian*	21
Sangria	*Nuevo Latino*	14
Sapori Tratt.	*Italian*	22
Shine & Morida	*Chinese/Japanese*	18
Simply It	*Viet.*	22
Stanley's	*Amer.*	19
Sushi X	*Japanese*	-
Tarantino's	*Italian*	22
Tepatulco	*Mex.*	23
Toast	*Amer.*	22
Tratt. Gianni	*Italian*	21
Tsuki	*Japanese*	24
Via Carducci	*Italian*	22
Vinci	*Italian*	21
Webster Wine	*Eclectic*	20
Wiener's Circle	*Hot Dogs*	20

LINCOLN SQUARE/ UPTOWN

Agami	*Japanese*	25
Bistro Campagne	*French*	24
Café Selmarie	*Amer.*	22
NEW Cinners Chili	*Amer.*	-
Dorado	*French/Mex.*	25
Erba	*Italian*	20
Essence of India	*Indian*	21
NEW Fat Cat	*Amer.*	18
Fiddlehead	*Amer.*	19

Hai Yen	*Chinese/Viet.*	20
NEW Jack Rabbit	*SW*	-
La Bocca/Verità	*Italian*	20
Marigold	*Indian*	23
Pizza D.O.C.	*Pizza*	22
Riques	*Mex.*	20
Siam Café	*Thai*	22
Silver Seafood	*Chinese/Seafood*	20
Spoon Thai	*Thai*	20
NEW Tallulah	*Amer.*	-
Tank Sushi	*Japanese*	22
Thai Pastry	*Thai*	24
Trattoria Trullo	*Italian*	21
Tweet	*Eclectic*	24

NEAR NORTH

Châtaigne	*Eclectic/French*	-
KiKi's Bistro	*French*	23
Z mk	*Amer.*	26

NORTH CENTER/ST. BEN'S

Cafe 28	*Cuban/Mex.*	24
Mrs. Murphy	*Irish*	18

OLD TOWN

Adobo Grill	*Mex.*	21
NEW BBOP Lounge	*Korean*	-
Bistrot Margot	*French*	21
Dinotto	*Italian*	21
Flat Top Grill	*Asian*	19
Kamehachi	*Japanese*	22
Mizu Yakitori	*Japanese*	27
Nookies	*Diner*	19
Old Jerusalem	*Mideast.*	19
NEW Old Town Mkt.	*French*	24
Salpicón	*Mex.*	24
Topo Gigio	*Italian*	23
Tratt. Roma	*Italian*	21
Twin Anchors	*BBQ*	22

ROGERS PARK/ WEST ROGERS PARK

NEW African Harambee	*African*	18
Gold Coast	*Hot Dogs*	21
Gruppo/Amici	*Pizza*	21
Gulliver's Pizza	*Pizza*	-
Heartland Cafe	*Eclectic/Veg.*	17
Hema's Kitchen	*Indian*	21
Indian Gdn.	*Indian*	22
La Cucina/Donatella	*Italian*	24
Tiffin	*Indian*	22
Udupi Palace	*Indian*	19
Viceroy of India	*Indian*	18
Viet Bistro	*Viet.*	19

Downtown

LOOP

Aria	*Amer./Eclectic*	23
Atwood Cafe	*Amer.*	21
Aurelio's Pizza	*Pizza*	21
Z Avec	*Med.*	27
Bella Bacino's	*Italian*	20
Berghoff	*German*	19
Billy Goat	*Amer.*	15
Boston Blackies	*Burgers*	19
Z Carnivale	*Nuevo Latino*	22
Z Catch 35	*Seafood*	24
China Grill	*Asian*	20
Z Everest	*French*	27
Gage	*Amer.*	21
Z Giordano's	*Pizza*	21
Gold Coast	*Hot Dogs*	21
Grillroom	*Steak*	18
Hannah's Bretzel	*Sandwiches*	23
Z Heaven on Seven	*Cajun/Creole*	21
La Cantina	*Italian/Seafood*	21
NEW Lockwood	*Amer.*	-
Lou Mitchell's	*Diner*	21
Z McCormick/Schmick's	*Seafood*	21
Miller's Pub	*Pub*	18
Z Morton's	*Steak*	26
Nick's Fishmkt.	*Seafood*	24
N9ne	*Seafood/Steak*	24
One North	*Amer.*	18
Palm, The	*Steak*	23
Park Grill	*Amer.*	19
Petterino's	*Amer.*	20
Poag Mahone's	*Pub*	19
Potbelly	*Sandwiches*	19
NEW Powerhouse	*Amer.*	23
Rhapsody	*Amer.*	21
rist. we	*Italian*	17
Robinson's Ribs	*BBQ*	22
Z Rosebud	*Italian*	22
Z Rosebud Prime/Steak	*Steak*	23
Russian Tea	*Russian*	22
NEW Shikago	*Asian*	20
South Water	*Amer.*	17
Stetson's Chop Hse.	*Steak*	23
NEW Tavern at the Park	*Amer.*	17
NEW Thai Urban	*Japanese/Pan-Asian*	-
312 Chicago	*Amer./Italian*	19
Townhouse	*Amer.*	16

Tratt. No. 10	*Italian*	23
Village	*Italian*	20
Vivere	*Italian*	23

RIVER NORTH

(See map on page 192)

TOP FOOD

Topolobampo	*Mex.*	**D6**	28
Frontera Grill	*Mex.*	**D6**	27
Joe's Seafood	*Seafood/Steak*	**C8**	26
Avenues	*Amer.*	**A8**	25
Le Lan	*Asian/French*	**A6**	25
Naha	*Amer.*	**C6**	25
Ruth's Chris	*Steak*	**D7**	25
Crofton on Wells	*Amer.*	**C5**	25
Chicago Chop	*Steak*	**B7**	25
Shanghai Terr.	*Asian*	**A8**	25
Coco Pazzo	*Italian*	**D5**	25
Fogo de Chão	*Brazilian/Steak*	**B6**	25
David Burke Prime	*Steak*	**C8**	24
Aigre Doux	*Amer.*	**D5**	24
Japonais	*Japanese*	**A2**	24

LISTING

Aigre Doux	*Amer.*	24
NEW Ai Sushi	*Japanese*	21
Al's #1 Beef	*Sandwiches*	21
NEW A Mano	*Italian*	21
Z Avenues	*Amer.*	25
BackStage	*Amer.*	22
Ballo	*Italian*	20
Bar Louie	*Pub*	15
Ben Pao	*Chinese*	21
Big Bowl	*Asian*	19
Bijan's	*Amer.*	18
Billy Goat	*Amer.*	15
Bin 36/Wine	*Amer./French*	20
Blue Water	*Amer.*	23
NEW Bluprint	*Amer.*	22
Brasserie Jo	*French*	22
Z NEW Brasserie Ruhlmann	*French*	21
Brazzaz	*Brazilian/Steak*	22
Café Iberico	*Spanish*	22
Carson's Ribs	*BBQ*	22
Z Chicago Chop	*Steak*	25
Coco Pazzo	*Italian*	25
Crofton on Wells	*Amer.*	25
Cyrano's Bistrot	*French*	21
David Burke Prime	*Steak*	24
Devon Seafood	*Seafood*	21
Ed Debevic's	*Diner*	13
Erie Cafe	*Italian/Steak*	22

Flatwater	*Eclectic*	15
🆉 Fogo de Chão	*Brazilian/Steak*	25
1492 Tapas	*Spanish*	19
🆉 Frontera Grill	*Mex.*	27
Fulton's	*Seafood/Steak*	19
Gene & Georgetti	*Steak*	24
🆉 Giordano's	*Pizza*	21
Grand Lux	*Eclectic*	19
Green Door	*Amer.*	15
Hard Rock	*Amer.*	12
Harry Caray's	*Itallan/Steak*	20
🆉 Heaven on Seven	*Cajun/Creole*	21
Hop Häus	*Burgers*	18
India Hse.	*Indian*	24
🆉 Japonais	*Japanese*	24
🆉 Joe's Seafood	*Seafood/Steak*	26
Kan Zaman	*Lebanese*	20
Karyn's	*Veg.*	21
Keefer's	*Amer.*	24
Kinzie Chophse.	*Steak*	20
Kitsch'n	*Eclectic*	16
Klay Oven	*Indian*	21
Lalo's	*Mex.*	17
🆕 La Madia	*Italian*	22
Lawry's	*Steak*	24
Le Lan	*Asian/French*	25
🆉 Lobby	*Continental/Seafood*	24
🆉 Lou Malnati's	*Pizza*	24
🆉 Maggiano's	*Italian*	21
Mambo Grill	*Nuevo Latino*	20
Melting Pot	*Fondue*	19
Mr. Beef	*Sandwiches*	24
Nacional 27	*Nuevo Latino*	23
Naha	*Amer.*	25
Original Gino's	*Pizza*	21
Osteria/Pizzeria Via Stato	*Italian*	22
Oysy	*Japanese*	21
🆉 P.F. Chang's	*Chinese*	21
Phil Stefani's	*Italian/Steak*	21
Pierrot Gourmet	*French*	21
Pizzeria Uno/Due	*Pizza*	21
Pops/Champagne	*Amer.*	16
Potbelly	*Sandwiches*	19
🆕 Prosecco	*Italian*	25
Quartino	*Italian*	21
Republic	*Asian*	19
Reza's	*Med./Mideast.*	20
Rockit B&G	*Amer.*	19
Roy's	*Hawaiian*	24
Rumba	*Nuevo Latino*	21

Ruth's Chris	*Steak*	25
Scoozi!	*Italian*	20
🆉 Shanghai Terr.	*Asian*	25
🆉 Shaw's Crab	*Seafood*	24
🆕 Sixteen	*Amer.*	-
Smith/Wollensky	*Steak*	22
Star of Siam	*Thai*	20
🆕 Stretch Run	*Amer.*	-
Sullivan's Steak	*Steak*	22
Sushi Naniwa	*Japanese*	23
🆉 SushiSamba	*Japanese/S Amer.*	22
Tizi Melloul	*Med./Mideast.*	21
🆉 Topolobampo	*Mex.*	28
Vermilion	*Indian/Nuevo Latino*	21
Vong's	*Thai*	22
🆉 Weber Grill	*BBQ*	19
🆉 Wildfire	*Steak*	24
🆉 Zealous	*Amer.*	24
🆕 ZED 451	*Eclectic*	22
Zocalo	*Mex.*	23

STREETERVILLE

Bandera	*Amer.*	22
Bice	*Italian*	22
Billy Goat	*Amer.*	15
Boston Blackies	*Burgers*	19
Caliterra	*Amer./Italian*	22
Cape Cod Rm.	*Seafood*	22
🆉 Capital Grille	*Steak*	25
🆉 Cheesecake Factory	*Amer.*	19
Cité	*Amer.*	24
Coco Pazzo Café	*Italian*	23
copperblue	*French/Med.*	21
DeLaCosta	*Nuevo Latino*	22
Drake Bros.'	*Seafood/Steak*	20
Emilio's Tapas	*Spanish*	22
foodlife	*Eclectic*	16
Grill on Alley	*Amer.*	20
Indian Gdn.	*Indian*	22
Kamehachi	*Japanese*	22
Le P'tit Paris	*Continental/French*	24
🆉 Les Nomades	*French*	28
Mity Nice Grill	*Amer.*	17
Mrs. Park's	*Amer.*	16
Niu	*Asian Fusion*	21
Original Gino's	*Pizza*	21
Original Pancake/Walker Bros.	*Amer.*	23
P.J. Clarke's	*Amer.*	16
Pompei Bakery	*Italian*	20
Puck's at MCA	*Amer.*	20
Ritz Café	*Amer.*	23

Riva	*Seafood*	18
🔲 Rosebud Prime/Steak	*Steak*	23
Saloon Steak	*Steak*	22
Sayat Nova	*Armenian*	20
Shula's Steak	*Steak*	19
🔲 Signature Rm.	*Amer.*	19
🔲 Tru	*French*	27
Viand Bar	*Amer.*	22
Volare	*Italian*	24
Wave	*Med.*	20
Zest	*Amer./Eclectic*	18

City Northwest

BUCKTOWN

(See map on page 196)

TOP FOOD

Coast Sushi/South Coast	*Japanese*	**D5**	25
Café Absinthe	*Amer.*	**H5**	24
Le Bouchon	*French*	**E5**	24
Hot Chocolate	*Amer.*	**F5**	24
Irazu	*Costa Rican*	**F2**	23

LISTING

Babylon	*Mideast.*	20
Bar Louie	*Pub*	15
NEW Bluebird, The	*Amer.*	19
Café Absinthe	*Amer.*	24
Cafe Bolero	*Cuban*	20
Cafe Matou	*French*	23
Club Lucky	*Italian*	19
Coast Sushi/South Coast	*Japanese*	25
Feast	*Amer.*	21
Honey 1 BBQ	*BBQ*	19
Hot Chocolate	*Amer.*	24
Il Covo	*Italian*	20
Irazu	*Costa Rican*	23
Jane's	*Amer./Eclectic*	21
Las Palmas	*Mex.*	22
Le Bouchon	*French*	24
NEW mado	*Italian*	-
Margie's Candies	*Amer.*	22
My Pie Pizza	*Pizza*	20
Rinconcito	*S Amer.*	18
Silver Cloud B&G	*Amer.*	19
NEW Takashi	*Amer./French*	29
Think	*Amer./Eclectic*	22
Toast	*Amer.*	22

EDISON PARK/
O'HARE AREA

Berghoff	*German*	19
Big Bowl	*Asian*	19

Billy Goat	*Amer.*	15
Café la Cave	*Continental*	20
Carlucci	*Italian*	21
🔲 Cheesecake Factory	*Amer.*	19
David's Bistro	*Amer./French*	23
Don Juan's	*Mex.*	21
Fleming's	*Steak*	22
🔲 Gibsons	*Steak*	25
🔲 Giordano's	*Pizza*	21
Gold Coast	*Hot Dogs*	21
Harry Caray's	*Italian/Steak*	20
Lalo's	*Mex.*	17
Lou Mitchell's	*Diner*	21
🔲 Morton's	*Steak*	26
Nick's Fishmkt.	*Seafood*	24
Original Gino's	*Pizza*	21
Original Pancake/Walker Bros.	*Amer.*	23
🔲 Wildfire	*Steak*	24
Zia's Trattoria	*Italian*	25

HUMBOLDT PARK

NEW C.J.'s	*Eclectic*	-
Maiz	*Mex.*	23
NEW NXXT	*Amer.*	-

LOGAN SQUARE

Azucar	*Spanish*	23
Bonsoiree	*Amer./French*	-
Buona Terra	*Italian*	23
El Nandu	*Argent.*	19
Fat Willy's	*BBQ/Southern*	23
Fonda del Mar	*Mex./Seafood*	24
Hachi's Kitchen	*Japanese*	24
Kuma's	*Amer.*	24
Lula	*Eclectic*	26
NEW Rustik	*Amer.*	-

NORTHWEST SIDE/
RAVENSWOOD

NEW Al Primo Canto	*Brazilian/Italian*	-
Andies	*Med./Mideast*	19
Anna Maria	*Italian*	23
🔲 Arun's	*Thai*	27
NEW Balanced Kitchen	*Amer.*	-
Chief O'Neill's	*Pub*	17
Gale St. Inn	*Amer.*	21
🔲 Giordano's	*Pizza*	21
Glenn's Diner	*Diner*	23
Gold Coast	*Hot Dogs*	21
🔲 Hot Doug's	*Hot Dogs*	27
Katsu	*Japanese*	24
La Peña	*S Amer.*	18

Las Tablas | *Colombian/Steak*	20
Magnolia Cafe | *Amer.*	23
Margie's Candies | *Amer.*	22
Mirabell | *German*	21
Nancy's Pizza | *Pizza*	22
Noon-O-Kabab | *Persian*	24
Over Easy | *Amer.*	25
NEW Rusty Armadillo | *Mex.*	-
Sabatino's | *Italian*	22
San Soo Gab San | *Korean*	21
Smoque BBQ | *BBQ*	24
Sol de Mex. | *Mex.*	25
Spacca Napoli | *Pizza*	24
Superdawg | *Hot Dogs*	22
Tre Kronor | *Scan.*	23

ROSCOE VILLAGE

Kaze Sushi | *Japanese*	23
Kitsch'n | *Eclectic*	16
Orange | *Eclectic*	22
Piazza Bella | *Italian*	20
Terragusto Cafe | *Italian*	24
Turquoise | *Turkish*	22
Victory's Banner | *Eclectic*	23
Volo | *Amer.*	20
Wishbone | *Southern*	21

WICKER PARK

(See map on page 196)

TOP FOOD

Spring | *Amer./Seafood* | **H4**	27
Mirai Sushi | *Japanese* | **K4**	25
Francesca's | *Italian* | **H5**	24
Bongo Room | *Amer.* | **I5**	24
Bob San | *Japanese* | **K6**	24

LISTING

Adobo Grill | *Mex.*	21
NEW Between Boutique | *Eclectic*	-
Bin 36/Wine | *Amer./French*	20
Blu Coral | *Japanese*	22
Bob San | *Japanese*	24
Bongo Room | *Amer.*	24
Café Bionda | *Italian*	22
Crust | *Pizza*	21
NEW Fifty/50, The | *Amer.*	-
Z Francesca's | *Italian*	24
NEW Jerry's | *Sandwiches*	20
NEW La Brochette | *Mideast./Moroccan*	-
Lucia | *Italian*	23
Milk & Honey | *Amer.*	22
Mirai Sushi | *Japanese*	25
Penny's Noodle | *Asian*	18

Piece | *Pizza*	23
Salud Tequila | *Mex.*	-
Schwa | *Amer.*	-
Smoke Daddy | *BBQ*	21
Z Spring | *Amer./Seafood*	27
NEW Su-Ra | *Korean*	17
Via Carducci | *Italian*	22

City South

CHINATOWN

Emperor's Choice | *Chinese*	22
Evergreen | *Chinese*	22
Happy Chef | *Chinese*	22
Joy Yee's | *Asian*	22
Z Lao | *Chinese*	26
Moon Palace | *Chinese*	24
New Three Happiness | *Chinese*	20
Penang | *Malaysian*	22
Phoenix | *Chinese*	21
Three Happiness | *Chinese*	19

FAR SOUTH SIDE

Army & Lou's | *Southern*	24
NEW Café 103 | *Amer./Eclectic*	-
Lalo's | *Mex.*	17
Lem's BBQ | *BBQ*	25
Parrot Cage | *Amer.*	-
Uncle John's | *BBQ*	-
Vito & Nick's | *Pizza*	23

HYDE PARK/KENWOOD

Bar Louie | *Pub*	15
NEW Chant | *Asian*	16
Dixie Kitchen | *Cajun/Southern*	20
Edwardo's Pizza | *Pizza*	20
la petite folie | *French*	23
Medici on 57th | *Amer.*	17
Original Pancake/Walker Bros. | *Amer.*	23
NEW Park 52 | *Amer.*	-
Pizza Capri | *Pizza*	20
Ribs 'n' Bibs | *BBQ*	20

PRINTER'S ROW

Bar Louie | *Pub*	15
Custom Hse. | *Amer.*	25
Hackney's | *Amer.*	18
Orange | *Eclectic*	22

SOUTH LOOP

Bongo Room | *Amer.*	24
Café Bionda | *Italian*	22
Chicago Firehse. | *Amer.*	22
Coast Sushi/South Coast | *Japanese*	25

Cuatro | *Nuevo Latino* — 22
Edwardo's Pizza | *Pizza* — 20
Eleven City | *Diner* — 19
NEW Exposure Tapas | *Eclectic* — 18
Gioco | *Italian* — 24
Grace O'Malley's | *Pub* — 18
Joy Yee's | *Asian* — 22
Kroll's | *Amer.* — 14
Manny's | *Deli* — 23
NEW Mercat | *Spanish* — -
Opera | *Asian* — 22
Oysy | *Japanese* — 21
Z Room 21 | *Steak* — 21
Shor | *Amer.* — -
NEW Spertus Cafe | *Amer.* — -
Tamarind | *Pan-Asian* — 21
Yolk | *Amer.* — 22
Zapatista | *Mex.* — 18

SOUTHWEST SIDE

Bacchanalia | *Italian* — 24
Bruna's | *Italian* — 23
Z Giordano's | *Pizza* — 21
Gold Coast | *Hot Dogs* — 21
Harry Caray's | *Italian/Steak* — 20
Lalo's | *Mex.* — 17
Z Lou Malnati's | *Pizza* — 24
Manny's | *Deli* — 23
Pegasus | *Greek* — 21
Superdawg | *Hot Dogs* — 22
Tratt. 31 | *Italian* — -

City West

FAR WEST

Depot Diner | *Diner* — -

GREEKTOWN

Artopolis | *Greek/Med.* — 23
Athena | *Greek* — 19
Costa's | *Greek* — 22
Z Giordano's | *Pizza* — 21
Greek Islands | *Greek* — 22
Parthenon | *Greek* — 22
Pegasus | *Greek* — 21
Roditys | *Greek* — 22
Santorini | *Greek/Seafood* — 22
Venus | *Greek* — 21

LITTLE ITALY/
UNIVERSITY VILLAGE

Al's #1 Beef | *Sandwiches* — 21
Bar Louie | *Pub* — 15
Chez Joël | *French* — 23

Z Francesca's | *Italian* — 24
La Vita | *Italian* — 22
Mundial | *Mex.* — 24
Pompei Bakery | *Italian* — 20
RoSal's Kitchen | *Italian* — 22
Z Rosebud | *Italian* — 22
Tufano's Tap | *Italian* — 20
Tuscany | *Italian* — 22

MARKET DISTRICT

Z Alhambra | *Mideast.* — 13
Bar Louie | *Pub* — 15
de cero | *Mex.* — 22
Flat Top Grill | *Asian* — 19
FoLLia | *Italian* — 23
NEW Macello | *Italian* — 19
Marché | *French* — 22
Moto | *Eclectic* — 25
NEW Nia | *Med.* — -
one sixtyblue | *French* — 25
Z NEW Otom | *Amer.* — 23
Red Light | *Pan-Asian* — 22
Z NEW Sepia | *Amer.* — 22
Starfish | *Japanese* — 20
Z sushi wabi | *Japanese* — 26
Tasting Room | *Eclectic* — 15
NEW Trattoria Isabella | *Italian* — -
Vivo | *Italian* — 21

NEAR WEST

Dining Rm./Kendall | *French* — 24
Hecky's | *BBQ* — 21
NEW Paramount Rm. | *Amer.* — -
Twisted Spoke | *Pub* — 20

RIVER WEST

Avenue M | *Amer.* — 21
La Scarola | *Italian* — 23
Sushi X | *Japanese* — -
NEW Thalia Spice | *Pan-Asian* — 25

UKRAINIAN VILLAGE

Z a tavola | *Italian* — 26

WEST LOOP

Bella Notte | *Italian* — 22
Billy Goat | *Amer.* — 15
Z Blackbird | *Amer.* — 27
Breakfast Club | *Amer.* — 20
Butterfly | *Japanese/Thai* — 21
Carmichael's | *Steak* — 21
Coalfire Pizza | *Pizza* — 22
Dine | *Amer.* — 15
Ina's | *Amer.* — 22

La Sardine	*French*	23
May St. Market	*Amer.*	23
Meiji	*Japanese*	25
Stanley's	*Amer.*	19
Wishbone	*Southern*	21

WEST TOWN

Flo	*Amer.*	22
Green Zebra	*Veg.*	26
Habana Libre	*Cuban*	21
NEW Natalino's	*Italian*	-
NEW Rockstar Dogs	*Hot Dogs*	-
West Town Tavern	*Amer.*	25

Suburbs

SUBURBAN NORTH

Akai Hana	*Japanese*	21
Al's #1 Beef	*Sandwiches*	21
Bagel	*Deli*	19
Bank Lane	*Amer.*	23
Bar Louie	*Pub*	15
Benihana	*Japanese/Steak*	20
Blind Faith	*Veg.*	21
Bob Chinn's	*Seafood*	22
Boston Blackies	*Burgers*	19
Cafe Central	*French*	23
Cafe Pyrenees	*French*	23
Campagnola	*Italian*	23
☑ Carlos'	*French*	28
Carson's Ribs	*BBQ*	22
☑ Cheesecake Factory	*Amer.*	19
Chef's Station	*Amer.*	22
Convito	*French/Italian*	16
Dave's Italian	*Italian*	17
Davis St. Fish	*Seafood*	20
Del Rio	*Italian*	22
Di Pescara	*Italian/Seafood*	21
Dixie Kitchen	*Cajun/Southern*	20
Don Roth's	*Seafood/Steak*	23
Edwardo's Pizza	*Pizza*	20
EJ's Place	*Italian/Steak*	20
545 North	*Amer.*	20
Flat Top Grill	*Asian*	19
Flight	*Eclectic*	19
☑ Francesca's	*Italian*	24
Francesco's	*Italian*	25
fRedhots	*Hot Dogs*	18
Froggy's	*French*	23
☑ Gabriel's	*French/Italian*	26
Gale St. Inn	*Amer.*	21
Gio	*Italian*	20
Gold Coast	*Hot Dogs*	21

Hackney's	*Amer.*	18
Hecky's	*BBQ*	21
Hot Tamales	*Mex.*	21
Jacky's Bistro	*Amer./French*	24
J. Alexander's	*Amer.*	20
Jilly's Cafe	*Amer./French*	24
Joy Yee's	*Asian*	22
Kabul Hse.	*Afghan*	21
Kamehachi	*Japanese*	22
Kansaku	*Japanese*	22
☑ Karma	*Asian*	23
Koi	*Asian*	20
Kuni's	*Japanese*	21
La Casa/Isaac	*Mex.*	22
Lalo's	*Mex.*	17
La Petite Amelia	*French*	20
☑ Lou Malnati's	*Pizza*	24
Lovells	*Amer.*	22
LuLu's	*Pan-Asian*	19
Lupita's	*Mex.*	19
L. Woods Lodge	*Amer.*	20
☑ Maggiano's	*Italian*	21
☑ McCormick/Schmick's	*Seafood*	21
Merle's Smokehse.	*BBQ*	19
☑ Michael	*French*	26
Miramar Bistro	*French*	20
Mitchell's Fish Mkt.	*Seafood*	21
☑ Morton's	*Steak*	26
Mt. Everest	*Indian*	22
Myron & Phil's	*Steak*	22
Next Door	*Amer./Italian*	22
Nick's Fishmkt.	*Seafood*	24
☑ Oceanique	*French/Seafood*	26
NEW Omaggio	*Italian*	20
OPA Estiatorio	*Greek*	19
Original Pancake/Walker Bros.	*Amer.*	23
Osteria/Tramonto	*Italian*	21
Oysy	*Japanese*	21
Palm, The	*Steak*	23
Penny's Noodle	*Asian*	18
Pete Miller	*Seafood/Steak*	22
☑ P.F. Chang's	*Chinese*	21
Philly G's	*Italian*	22
Pine Yard	*Chinese*	20
NEW Pinstripes	*Amer./Italian*	18
Pita Inn	*Mideast.*	24
NEW Pomegranate	*Med./Mideast.*	19
Prairie Grass	*Amer.*	21
Quince	*Amer.*	24

RA Sushi | *Japanese*	18
Z Rosebud | *Italian*	22
Ruby of Siam | *Thai*	20
Ruth's Chris | *Steak*	25
Sage Grille | *Amer.*	22
San Gabriel | *Mex.*	20
Shallots Bistro | *French/Med.*	-
NEW Sopa | *Amer./Med.*	-
South Gate | *Amer.*	20
Stained Glass | *Amer.*	24
Stir Crazy | *Asian*	21
Tapas Barcelona | *Spanish*	21
Tapas Gitana | *Spanish*	-
Tavern | *Amer.*	25
Z Tramonto's | *Seafood/Steak*	24
Tratt. D.O.C. | *Pizza*	19
Tuscany | *Italian*	22
NEW Union Pizzeria | *Pizza*	-
Z Va Pensiero | *Italian*	26
Z Wildfire | *Steak*	24
Wildfish | *Japanese*	24
Yard House | *Amer.*	17

SUBURBAN NW

Al's #1 Beef | *Sandwiches*	21
Aurelio's Pizza | *Pizza*	21
Z Barrington Country | *French*	26
Benihana | *Japanese/Steak*	20
Big Bowl | *Asian*	19
Birch River | *Amer.*	-
Bistro 22 | *French*	22
Boston Blackies | *Burgers*	19
Carlos & Carlos | *Italian*	23
Z Cheesecake Factory | *Amer.*	19
D & J Bistro | *French*	25
Davis St. Fish | *Seafood*	20
Edelweiss | *German*	22
Entourage | *Amer.*	22
Five O'Clock Steak | *Steak*	23
Z Francesca's | *Italian*	24
Gaylord Indian | *Indian*	21
Hackney's | *Amer.*	18
India Hse. | *Indian*	24
Indian Gdn. | *Indian*	22
Lalo's | *Mex.*	17
Las Palmas | *Mex.*	22
La Tasca | *Spanish*	23
Z Le Titi/Paris | *French*	28
Le Vichyssois | *French*	27
Z Lou Malnati's | *Pizza*	24
Z Maggano's | *Italian*	21

Z McCormick/Schmick's | *Seafood*	21
Melting Pot | *Fondue*	19
Montarra | *Amer.*	25
Z Morton's | *Steak*	26
Nancy's Pizza | *Pizza*	22
Original Gino's | *Pizza*	21
Original Pancake/Walker Bros. | *Amer.*	23
Pappadeaux | *Seafood*	21
Z P.F. Chang's | *Chinese*	21
Pompei Bakery | *Italian*	20
Z Retro Bistro | *French*	25
NEW Rock-N-Roll | *Japanese*	-
Z Rosebud | *Italian*	22
Russell's BBQ | *BBQ*	20
Sakuma's | *Japanese*	-
Sam & Harry's | *Steak*	27
Z 1776 | *Amer.*	26
Z Shaw's Crab | *Seafood*	24
Shula's Steak | *Steak*	19
Stir Crazy | *Asian*	21
Texas de Brazil | *Brazilian*	25
Udupi Palace | *Indian*	19
Z Weber Grill | *BBQ*	19
White Fence | *Amer.*	22
Z Wildfire | *Steak*	24
Wildfish | *Japanese*	24
Woo Lae Oak | *Korean*	23
NEW ZED 451 | *Eclectic*	22

SUBURBAN SOUTH

Al's #1 Beef | *Sandwiches*	21
Aurelio's Pizza | *Pizza*	21
Bogart's | *Steak*	20
Dixie Kitchen | *Cajun/Southern*	20
Original Pancake/Walker Bros. | *Amer.*	23

SUBURBAN SW

Al's #1 Beef | *Sandwiches*	21
Aurelio's Pizza | *Pizza*	21
Bar Louie | *Pub*	15
Bogart's | *Steak*	20
Courtright's | *Amer.*	25
Hackney's | *Amer.*	18
Original Gino's | *Pizza*	21
Z P.F. Chang's | *Chinese*	21
Sabor do Brasil | *Brazilian*	22
Z Tallgrass | *French*	29
Tin Fish | *Seafood*	21

subscribe to ZAGAT.com

SUBURBAN WEST

Adelle's	*Amer.*	24
Adobo Grill	*Mex.*	21
Amber Cafe	*Amer.*	24
Antico Posto	*Italian*	22
Atwater's	*Amer./French*	21
Aurelio's Pizza	*Pizza*	21
NEW Bank Rest.	*Amer.*	15
Bar Louie	*Pub*	15
Bella Bacino's	*Italian*	20
Benihana	*Japanese/Steak*	20
Bistro Monet	*French*	23
NEW Brio	*Italian*	21
Cab's Wine Bar	*Amer.*	22
Café le Coq	*French*	23
Z Capital Grille	*Steak*	25
Carlucci	*Italian*	21
Z Catch 35	*Seafood*	24
NEW Cellar	*Eclectic*	-
Z Cheesecake Factory	*Amer.*	19
Chinn's Fishery	*Seafood*	22
Clubhouse	*Amer.*	20
Costa's	*Greek*	22
NEW Cucina Paradiso	*Italian*	25
NEW Distinctive Cork	*Amer.*	22
Ed Debevic's	*Diner*	13
Edwardo's Pizza	*Pizza*	20
Emilio's Sunflower	*Amer.*	24
Emilio's Tapas	*Spanish*	22
Finley's Grill	*Amer.*	22
Flat Top Grill	*Asian*	19
Z Francesca's	*Italian*	24
NEW Gaetano's	*Italian*	-
Gordon Biersch	*Amer.*	20
Greek Islands	*Greek*	22
Harry Caray's	*Italian/Steak*	20
Harvest	*Amer.*	24
Z Heaven on Seven	*Cajun/Creole*	21
Hemmingway's	*Amer./French*	20
NEW Holy Mackerel!	*Seafood*	19
Hugo's	*Seafood*	23
India Hse.	*Indian*	24
Isabella's	*Med.*	25
J. Alexander's	*Amer.*	20
Joy Yee's	*Asian*	22
Lalo's	*Mex.*	17

L'anne	*Viet.*	21
Z Lao	*Chinese*	26
Z Lou Malnati's	*Pizza*	24
NEW Macarena	*Eclectic*	-
Z Maggiano's	*Italian*	21
NEW Maya Del Sol	*Nuevo Latino*	21
Z McCormick/Schmick's	*Seafood*	21
Melting Pot	*Fondue*	19
Mesón Sabika/Tapas Valencia	*Spanish*	24
Mike Ditka's	*Steak*	22
Z Mon Ami Gabi	*French*	22
Z Morton's	*Steak*	26
Nancy's Pizza	*Pizza*	22
Z Niche	*Amer.*	28
Nosh	*Eclectic*	24
Original Gino's	*Pizza*	21
Original Pancake/Walker Bros.	*Amer.*	23
Pappadeaux	*Seafood*	21
Parkers'	*Seafood*	24
Penny's Noodle	*Asian*	18
Z P.F. Chang's	*Chinese*	21
Philander's	*Amer.*	21
Pompei Bakery	*Italian*	20
RA Sushi	*Japanese*	18
NEW Reel Club	*Seafood*	20
Reza's	*Med./Mideast.*	20
Riva	*Seafood*	18
Robinson's Ribs	*BBQ*	22
Z Rosebud	*Italian*	22
Russell's BBQ	*BBQ*	20
Stir Crazy	*Asian*	21
Sullivan's Steak	*Steak*	22
Swordfish	*Japanese*	26
Tango	*Argent.*	22
Timpano Chophse.	*Italian/Steak*	20
NEW Trattoria 225	*Italian*	19
Tuscany	*Italian*	22
Viceroy of India	*Indian*	18
Z Vie	*Amer.*	28
Volare	*Italian*	24
Z Weber Grill	*BBQ*	19
Z Wildfire	*Steak*	24
Wishbone	*Southern*	21
NEW ZED 451	*Eclectic*	22

CHICAGO

LOCATIONS

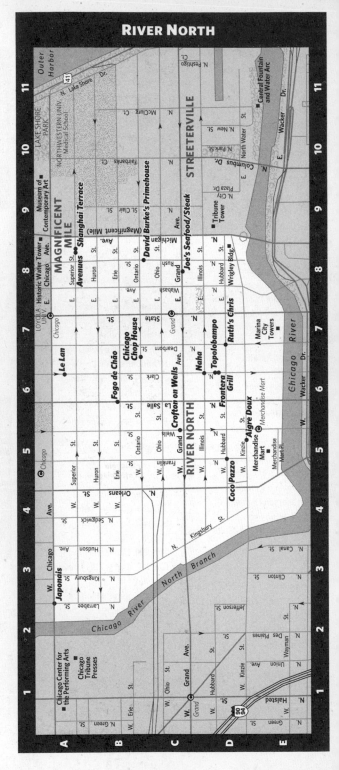

Outer Harbor

LAKE SHORE PARK

NORTHWESTERN UNIV. Medical School

■ Museum of Contemporary Art

MAGNIFICENT MILE

Avenues ■ Shanghai Terrace

Historic Water Tower ■

LOYOLA UNIV.

● Le Lan

● Fogo de Chão

● David Burke's Primehouse

STREETERVILLE

● Joe's Seafood/Steak

Chicago Chop House ●

Crofton on Wells ●

Naha ●

● Topolobampo

● Ruth's Chris

Frontera Grill ●

Aigre Doux ●

■ Tribune Tower

Wrigley Bldg. ■

Marina City Towers ■

Chicago River

W. Wacker Dr.

● Merchandise Mart

Merchandise Mart ●

RIVER NORTH

Coco Pazzo ●

Chicago River North Branch

● Japonais

■ Chicago Center for the Performing Arts

■ Chicago Tribune Presses

Kingsbury St.

Chicago River

90 94

N. Central Fountain and Water Arc ■

E. Wacker Dr.

Columbus Dr.

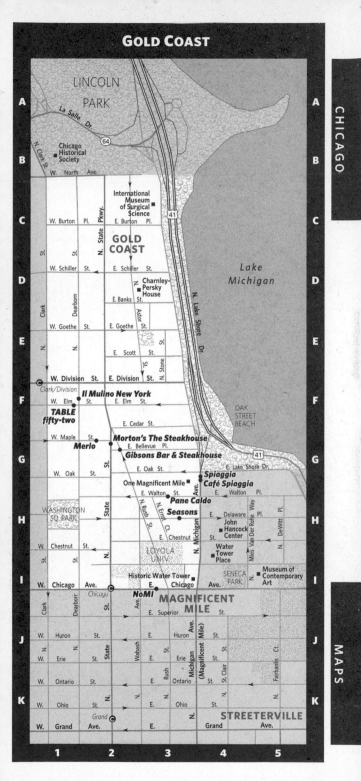

LINCOLN PARK

La Salle Dr.

N. Clark St.

Chicago Historical Society

W. North Ave.

International Museum of Surgical Science

W. Burton Pl.　E. Burton Pl.

N. State Pkwy.

GOLD COAST

W. Schiller St.

Clark St.

Dearborn St.

W. Goethe St.

E. Schiller St.

Charnley-Persky House

E. Banks St.

Astor St.

E. Goethe St.

E. Scott St.

N. Stone St.

N. Lake Shore Dr.

Lake Michigan

W. Division St.　E. Division St.

Clark/Division

Il Mulino New York

W. Elm St.　E. Elm St.

OAK STREET BEACH

TABLE fifty-two

E. Cedar St.

W. Maple St.

Morton's The Steakhouse

Merlo

E. Bellevue Pl.

Gibsons Bar & Steakhouse

W. Oak St.

E. Oak St.

One Magnificent Mile

Spiaggia

Café Spiaggia

E. Walton St.

N. Michigan Ave.

E. Walton Pl.

WASHINGTON SQ PARK

State St.

N. Rush St.

N. Ernst Ct.

Pane Caldo

Seasons

E. Delaware Pl.

John Hancock Center

Mies Van Der Rohe Way

DeWitt Pl.

W. Chestnut St.

St. N.

E. Chestnut St.

LOYOLA UNIV.

Water Tower Place

Historic Water Tower

SENECA PARK

Museum of Contemporary Art

W. Chicago Ave.　E. Chicago Ave.

Chicago

NoMI

MAGNIFICENT MILE

E. Superior St.

Clark St.

Dearborn St.

N. State St.

Ave. (Magnificent Mile)

W. Huron St.　Huron St.

W. Erie St.　Erie St.

Wabash St.

Rush St.

Michigan Ave. (Magnificent Mile)

St. Clair St.

W. Ontario St.　Ontario St.

W. Ohio St.　Ohio St.

STREETERVILLE

Fairbanks Ct.

W. Grand Ave.　Grand Ave.

Grand Ave.

MAPS

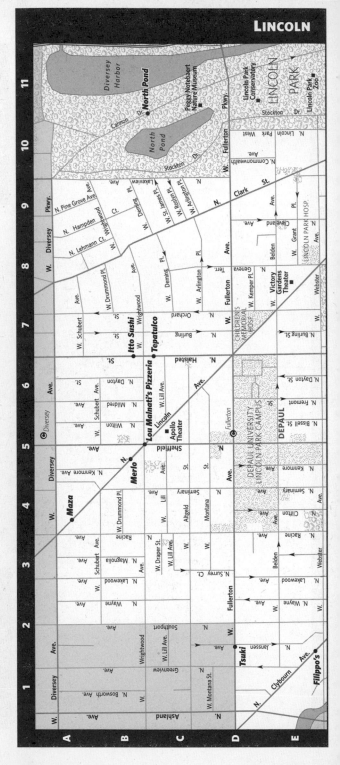

LINCOLN

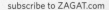

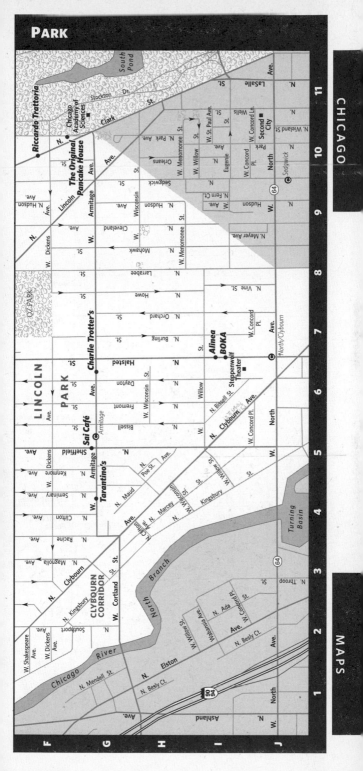

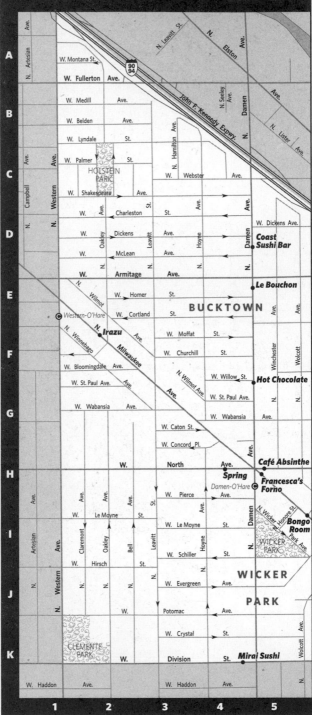

BUCKTOWN

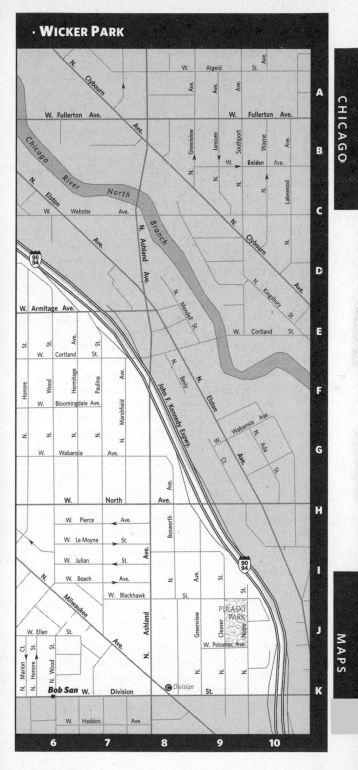

Special Features

Listings cover the best in each category and include names, locations and Food ratings. Multi-location restaurants' features may vary by branch.
Z indicates places with the highest ratings, popularity and importance.

BREAKFAST

(See also Hotel Dining)

Ann Sather | **multi.**	20
Army & Lou's | **Far S Side**	24
Bagel | **multi.**	19
Billy Goat | **multi.**	15
Bin 36/Wine | **River N**	20
Blind Faith | **Evanston**	21
Bongo Room | **Wicker Pk**	24
Breakfast Club | **W Loop**	20
Café Selmarie | **Lincoln Sq**	22
Chicago Diner | **Lakeview**	21
Dixie Kitchen | **Evanston**	20
Ed Debevic's | **River N**	13
Flo | **W Town**	22
foodlife | **Streeterville**	16
Harry Caray's | **SW Side**	20
Heartland Cafe | **Rogers Pk**	17
Z Heaven on Seven | **Loop**	21
Ina's | **W Loop**	22
Irazu | **Bucktown**	23
Kitsch'n | **multi.**	16
Lou Mitchell's | **multi.**	21
Lula | **Logan Sq**	26
Manny's | **multi.**	23
Z M. Henry | **Andersonville**	26
Milk & Honey | **Wicker Pk**	22
Nookies | **multi.**	19
Nosh | **Geneva**	24
Oak Tree | **Gold Coast**	16
Orange | **Lakeview**	22
Original Pancake/Walker Bros. | **multi.**	23
Over Easy | **Ravenswood**	25
Pegasus | **SW Side**	21
Phoenix | **Chinatown**	21
San Soo Gab San | **NW Side**	21
Tempo | **Gold Coast**	20
Three Happiness | **Chinatown**	19
Toast | **multi.**	22
Tre Kronor | **NW Side**	23
Uncommon Ground | **Lakeview**	21
Viand Bar | **Streeterville**	22
Victory's Banner | **Roscoe Vill**	23
Wishbone | **multi.**	21
Yolk | **S Loop**	22

BRUNCH

Adobo Grill | **multi.**	21
American Girl | **Gold Coast**	13
Andies | **Andersonville**	19
Angelina | **Lakeview**	21
Ann Sather | **Andersonville**	20
Atwater's | **Geneva**	21
Atwood Cafe | **Loop**	21
Bistro 110 | **Gold Coast**	20
Bistrot Margot | **Old Town**	21
Bistrot Zinc | **Gold Coast**	20
Bongo Room | **Wicker Pk**	24
Café/Architectes | **Gold Coast**	23
Café Selmarie | **Lincoln Sq**	22
Café Spiaggia | **Gold Coast**	25
Cafe 28 | **North Ctr/St. Ben's**	24
Z Cheesecake Factory | **multi.**	19
Chicago Diner | **Lakeview**	21
Clubhouse | **Oak Brook**	20
Coobah | **Lakeview**	20
erwin cafe | **Lakeview**	22
Flo | **W Town**	22
Z Frontera Grill | **River N**	27
Grand Lux | **River N**	19
Hackney's | **Palos Pk**	18
Z Heaven on Seven | **multi.**	21
Hemmingway's | **Oak Pk**	20
Jane's | **Bucktown**	21
Jilly's Cafe | **Evanston**	24
John's Place | **Lincoln Pk**	17
Kitsch'n | **multi.**	16
La Crêperie | **Lakeview**	21
La Donna | **Andersonville**	19
La Tache | **Andersonville**	22
Z Lobby | **River N**	24
Magnolia Cafe | **Ravenswood**	23
Mesón Sabika/Tapas Valencia | **Naperville**	24
Z M. Henry | **Andersonville**	26
Mike Ditka's | **Gold Coast**	22
Milk & Honey | **Wicker Pk**	22
Z North Pond | **Lincoln Pk**	25
Orange | **Lakeview**	22
Pizza Capri | **multi.**	20
P.J. Clarke's | **multi.**	16
Pump Rm. | **Gold Coast**	20

subscribe to ZAGAT.com

rist. we | **Loop**	17
Z RL | **Gold Coast**	23
Salpicón | **Old Town**	24
Z Seasons | **Gold Coast**	27
Z Signature Rm. | **Streeterville**	19
Silver Cloud B&G | **Bucktown**	19
Smith/Wollensky | **River N**	22
South Water | **Loop**	17
Stanley's | **Lincoln Pk**	19
Z SushiSamba | **River N**	22
Tavern on Rush | **Gold Coast**	20
312 Chicago | **Loop**	19
Toast | **Lincoln Pk**	22
Tre Kronor | **NW Side**	23
Tweet | **Uptown**	24
Twisted Spoke | **Near W**	20
Uncommon Ground | **Lakeview**	21
Vinci | **Lincoln Pk**	21
Wishbone | **multi.**	21
Yoshi's Café | **Lakeview**	25

BUFFET

(Check availability)

Andies | **Andersonville**	19
Aria | **Loop**	23
Aurelio's Pizza | **multi.**	21
Drake Bros.' | **Streeterville**	20
Edwardo's Pizza | **Oak Pk**	20
Essence of India | **Lincoln Sq**	21
Z Fogo de Chão | **River N**	25
Gale St. Inn | **Jefferson Pk**	21
Gaylord Indian | **Schaumburg**	21
Grace O'Malley's | **S Loop**	18
Hackney's | **Palos Pk**	18
Hemmingway's | **Oak Pk**	20
India Hse. | **multi.**	24
Indian Gdn. | **multi.**	22
Karyn's | **Lincoln Pk**	21
Klay Oven | **River N**	21
La Fonda | **Andersonville**	24
Las Tablas | **Lakeview**	20
Z Lobby | **River N**	24
LuxBar | **Gold Coast**	19
Mesón Sabika/Tapas Valencia | **Naperville**	24
Miramar Bistro | **Highwood**	20
Mt. Everest | **Evanston**	22
Z NoMI | **Gold Coast**	26
Pappadeaux | **Arlington Hts**	21
P.S. Bangkok | **Lakeview**	21
Puck's at MCA | **Streeterville**	20
Radhuni | **Lakeview**	15

Raj Darbar | **Lincoln Pk**	20
Reza's | **multi.**	20
Robinson's Ribs | **Oak Pk**	22
Ruby of Siam | **multi.**	20
Z Seasons | **Gold Coast**	27
Shor | **S Loop**	–
Siam Café | **Uptown**	22
Z Signature Rm. | **Streeterville**	19
NEW Sixteen | **River N**	–
Stanley's | **multi.**	19
Tango | **Naperville**	22
Thai Classic | **Lakeview**	23
Tiffin | **W Rogers Pk**	22
Udupi Palace | **Schaumburg**	19
Viceroy of India | **multi.**	18
Z Weber Grill | **River N**	19

BUSINESS DINING

Aigre Doux | **River N**	24
NEW Ai Sushi | **River N**	21
Z Alinea | **Lincoln Pk**	29
NEW A Mano | **River N**	21
Aria | **Loop**	23
Atwood Cafe | **Loop**	21
Z Avenues | **River N**	25
NEW Bank Rest. | **Wheaton**	15
Ben Pao | **River N**	21
Bice | **Streeterville**	22
Bistro Monet | **Glen Ellyn**	23
Bistro 22 | **Lake Zurich**	22
Z Blackbird | **W Loop**	27
Blue Water | **River N**	23
NEW Bluprint | **River N**	22
Brasserie Jo | **River N**	22
Z NEW Brasserie Ruhlmann | **River N**	21
Brazzaz | **River N**	22
NEW Brio | **Lombard**	21
Café/Architectes | **Gold Coast**	23
Caliterra | **Streeterville**	22
Z Capital Grille | **Streeterville**	25
Carlucci | **multi.**	21
Carmichael's | **W Loop**	21
Z Catch 35 | **Loop**	24
Z Charlie Trotter's | **Lincoln Pk**	27
Z Chicago Chop | **River N**	25
Coco Pazzo | **River N**	25
Crofton on Wells | **River N**	25
Custom Hse. | **Printer's Row**	25
David Burke Prime | **River N**	24
David's Bistro | **Des Plaines**	23

Devon Seafood	**River N**	21
Dine	**W Loop**	15
Drake Bros.'	**Streeterville**	20
Erie Cafe	**River N**	22
🆉 Everest	**Loop**	27
🆕 Fifty/50, The	**Wicker Pk**	–
Finley's Grill	**Downers Grove**	22
Flatwater	**River N**	15
Fleming's	**Lincolnshire**	22
🆉 Fogo de Chão	**River N**	25
Fulton's	**River N**	19
Gage	**Loop**	21
Gene & Georgetti	**River N**	24
🆉 Gibsons	**multi.**	25
Grill on Alley	**Streeterville**	20
Grillroom	**Loop**	18
Harry Caray's	**multi.**	20
🆕 Holy Mackerel!	**Lombard**	19
Il Mulino	**Gold Coast**	24
🆉 Japonais	**River N**	24
🆉 Joe's Seafood	**River N**	26
🆉 Karma	**Mundelein**	23
Keefer's	**River N**	24
Kinzie Chophse.	**River N**	20
Lawry's	**River N**	24
Le Colonial	**Gold Coast**	23
🆉 Les Nomades	**Streeterville**	28
🆉 Le Titi/Paris	**Arlington Hts**	28
🆕 Lockwood	**Loop**	–
LuxBar	**Gold Coast**	19
🆕 Macello	**Mkt Dist**	19
🆉 McCormick/Schmick's	**Gold Coast**	21
🆉 Michael	**Winnetka**	26
Mike Ditka's	**Gold Coast**	22
🆉 mk	**Near North**	26
🆉 Morton's	**multi.**	26
Mrs. Park's	**Streeterville**	16
Naha	**River N**	25
Nick's Fishmkt.	**multi.**	24
N9ne	**Loop**	24
Niu	**Streeterville**	21
🆉 NoMI	**Gold Coast**	26
One North	**Loop**	18
one sixtyblue	**Mkt Dist**	25
Osteria/Tramonto	**Wheeling**	21
Palm, The	**Loop**	23
🆕 Park 52	**Hyde Pk**	–
Park Grill	**Loop**	19
Petterino's	**Loop**	20
Phil Stefani's	**River N**	21

🆕 Powerhouse	**Loop**	23
Quince	**Evanston**	24
🆕 Reel Club	**Oak Brook**	20
Rhapsody	**Loop**	21
rist. we	**Loop**	17
Ritz Café	**Streeterville**	23
🆉 RL	**Gold Coast**	23
Roy's	**River N**	24
Ruth's Chris	**multi.**	25
Saloon Steak	**Streeterville**	22
Sam & Harry's	**Schaumburg**	27
🆉 Seasons	**Gold Coast**	27
🆉🆕 Sepia	**Mkt Dist**	22
🆉 Shaw's Crab	**multi.**	24
🆕 Shikago	**Loop**	20
Shor	**S Loop**	–
🆕 Sixteen	**River N**	–
Smith/Wollensky	**River N**	22
South Water	**Loop**	17
🆉 Spiaggia	**Gold Coast**	27
🆕 Stretch Run	**River N**	–
Sullivan's Steak	**multi.**	22
🆕 Tavern at the Park	**Loop**	17
312 Chicago	**Loop**	19
Timpano Chophse.	**Naperville**	20
🆉 Topolobampo	**River N**	28
Townhouse	**Loop**	16
🆉 Tramonto's	**Wheeling**	24
Tuscany	**multi.**	22
Vivere	**Loop**	22
Vivo	**Mkt Dist**	23
Vong's	**River N**	21
🆉 Weber Grill	**River N**	22
🆕 ZED 451	**multi.**	19

BYO

Adesso	**Lakeview**	18
Ann Sather	**multi.**	20
Babylon	**Bucktown**	20
Butterfly	**W Loop**	21
🆕 Café 103	**Far S Side**	–
Châtaigne	**Near North**	–
🆕 C.J.'s	**Humboldt Pk**	–
Coalfire Pizza	**W Loop**	22
Coast Sushi/South Coast	**multi.**	25
Côtes/Rhône	**Edgewater**	18
Dorado	**Lincoln Sq**	25
Edwardo's Pizza	**multi.**	20
El Presidente	**Lincoln Pk**	15
🆉 Giordano's	**Edison Pk**	21

Habana Libre | **W Town**	21
HB Home Bistro | **Lakeview**	24
Hecky's | **multi.**	21
Hema's Kitchen | **multi.**	21
Honey 1 BBQ | **Bucktown**	19
Icosium Kafe | **Andersonville**	19
Indie Cafe | **Edgewater**	23
Irazu | **Bucktown**	23
Joy Yee's | **multi.**	22
Kabul Hse. | **Skokie**	21
Karyn's | **Lincoln Pk**	21
NEW La Brochette | **Wicker Pk**	-
La Cucina/Donatella | **Rogers Pk**	24
Z Lao | **Chinatown**	26
Las Tablas | **multi.**	20
Lucia | **Wicker Pk**	23
Medici on 57th | **Hyde Pk**	17
Melting Pot | **multi.**	19
Z M. Henry | **Andersonville**	26
Mundial | **University Vill**	24
My Pie Pizza | **Bucktown**	20
NEW Mythos | **Lakeview**	-
Nookies | **multi.**	19
Old Jerusalem | **Old Town**	19
Orange | **multi.**	22
Original Gino's | **Lincoln Pk**	21
Over Easy | **Ravenswood**	25
Penny's Noodle | **multi.**	18
Pizza Capri | **Lincoln Pk**	20
NEW Pomegranate | **Evanston**	19
P.S. Bangkok | **Lincoln Pk**	21
Radhuni | **Lakeview**	15
Rinconcito | **Bucktown**	18
Riques | **Uptown**	20
Robinson's Ribs | **multi.**	22
Ruby of Siam | **Skokie**	20
Sapore/Napoli | **Lakeview**	22
Schwa | **Wicker Pk**	-
Siam Café | **Uptown**	22
Simply It | **Lincoln Pk**	22
Smoque BBQ | **NW Side**	24
Sol de Mex. | **NW Side**	25
Spoon Thai | **Lincoln Sq**	20
NEW Su-Ra | **Wicker Pk**	17
Sushi X | **River W**	-
Tango Sur | **Lakeview**	25
Terragusto Cafe | **Roscoe Vill**	24
Thai Classic | **Lakeview**	23
Thai Pastry | **Uptown**	24
Think | **Bucktown**	22
Tre Kronor | **NW Side**	23

Udupi Palace | **multi.**	19
Wakamono | **Lakeview**	23

CELEBRITY CHEFS

(Listed under their primary restaurants)

Z Alinea | *Grant Achatz* | **Lincoln Pk**	29
Z Arun's | *Arun Sampanthavivat* | **NW Side**	27
Z Avec | *Koren Grieveson* | **Loop**	27
Bistro Campagne | *M. Altenberg* | **Lincoln Sq**	24
Bistro 110 | *Dominique Tougne* | **Gold Coast**	20
Z Blackbird | *Paul Kahan* | **W Loop**	27
Cafe Matou | *Charlie Socher* | **Bucktown**	23
Z Charlie Trotter's | *Charlie Trotter* | **Lincoln Pk**	27
Crofton on Wells | *Suzy Crofton* | **River N**	25
DeLaCosta | *Douglas Rodriguez* | **Streeterville**	22
erwin cafe | *Erwin Drechsler* | **Lakeview**	22
Z Everest | *Jean Joho* | **Loop**	27
Z Frontera Grill | *Rick Bayless* | **River N**	27
Hot Chocolate | *Mindy Segal* | **Bucktown**	24
Keefer's | *John Hogan* | **River N**	24
Le Bouchon | *J-C Poilevey* | **Bucktown**	24
Z Le Titi/Paris | *M. Maddox* | **Arlington Hts**	28
Le Vichyssois | *Bernard Cretier* | **Lakemoor**	27
NEW Mercat | *Jose Garces* | **S Loop**	-
Z Michael | *Michael Lachowitz* | **Winnetka**	26
Z mk | *Michael Kornick* | **Near North**	26
Moto | *Homaro Cantu* | **Mkt Dist**	25
Naha | *Carrie Nahabedian* | **River N**	25
Z North Pond | *Bruce Sherman* | **Lincoln Pk**	25
NEW Old Town Mkt. | *Roland Liccioni* | **Old Town**	24
one sixtyblue | *Martial Noguier* | **Mkt Dist**	25
Opera | *Paul Wildermuth* | **S Loop**	22
Osteria/Tramonto | *Gale Gand & Rick Tramonto* | **Wheeling**	21

Prairie Grass	*George Bumbaris & Sarah Stegner*	**Northbrook**	21
Red Light	*Jackie Shen*	**Mkt Dist**	22
Salpicón	*Priscila Satkoff*	**Old Town**	24
Schwa	*Michael Carlson*	**Wicker Pk**	-
NEW Shikago	*Kevin Shikami*	**Loop**	20
Z Spiaggia	*Tony Mantuano*	**Gold Coast**	27
Z Spring	*Shawn McClain*	**Wicker Pk**	27
NEW TABLE 52	*Art Smith*	**Gold Coast**	24
NEW Takashi	*Takashi Yagihashi*	**Bucktown**	29
Z Tallgrass	*Robert Burcenski*	**Lockport**	29
Z Topolobampo	*Rick Bayless*	**River N**	28
Z Tramonto's	*Rick Tramonto*	**Wheeling**	24
West Town Tavern	*Susan Goss*	**W Town**	25
Yoshi's Café	*Yoshi Katsumura*	**Lakeview**	25
Z Zealous	*Michael Taus*	**River N**	24

CHILD-FRIENDLY

(Alternatives to the usual fast-food places; * children's menu available)

American Girl	**Gold Coast**	13
Ann Sather*	**multi.**	20
Antico Posto*	**Oak Brook**	22
Artopolis	**Greektown**	23
Bandera*	**Streeterville**	22
Benihana*	**multi.**	20
Berghoff	**O'Hare Area**	19
Big Bowl*	**multi.**	19
Bob Chinn's*	**Wheeling**	22
Breakfast Club	**W Loop**	20
Café Selmarie*	**Lincoln Sq**	22
Carson's Ribs*	**River N**	22
Z Cheesecake Factory*	**multi.**	19
Chicago Pizza	**Lincoln Pk**	22
Dave's Italian	**Evanston**	17
Davis St. Fish*	**Evanston**	20
Depot Diner	**Far W**	-
Ed Debevic's*	**River N**	13
Edwardo's Pizza*	**multi.**	20
Flat Top Grill*	**multi.**	19
foodlife*	**Streeterville**	16
Gold Coast	**Loop**	21

Gulliver's Pizza*	**Rogers Pk**	-
Hackney's*	**multi.**	18
Hard Rock*	**River N**	12
Harry Caray's*	**multi.**	20
Z Heaven on Seven*	**multi.**	21
Z Hot Doug's	**NW Side**	27
Ina's	**W Loop**	22
John's Place*	**Lincoln Pk**	17
Joy Yee's	**multi.**	22
Kansaku	**Evanston**	22
Kitsch'n*	**Roscoe Vill**	16
Lawry's*	**River N**	24
Z Lou Malnati's*	**multi.**	24
Lou Mitchell's*	**multi.**	21
LuLu's	**Evanston**	19
Z Maggiano's*	**multi.**	21
Manny's*	**SW Side**	23
Margie's Candies*	**Bucktown**	22
Mity Nice Grill*	**Streeterville**	17
Oak Tree	**Gold Coast**	16
OPA Estiatorio*	**Vernon Hills**	19
Orange*	**multi.**	22
Original Gino's*	**multi.**	21
Original Pancake/Walker Bros.*	**multi.**	23
Pegasus	**SW Side**	21
Z P.F. Chang's	**River N**	21
Pizza Capri*	**multi.**	20
Pizza D.O.C.	**Lincoln Sq**	22
Pizzeria Uno/Due*	**River N**	21
Potbelly	**multi.**	19
R.J. Grunts*	**Lincoln Pk**	19
Robinson's Ribs*	**multi.**	22
Russell's BBQ*	**Elmwood Pk**	20
Sapore/Napoli	**Lakeview**	22
Sapori Tratt.	**Lincoln Pk**	22
Scoozi!*	**River N**	20
Smoque BBQ*	**NW Side**	24
Stanley's*	**Lincoln Pk**	19
Stir Crazy*	**multi.**	21
Tempo	**Gold Coast**	20
Toast*	**multi.**	22
Tratt. D.O.C.	**Evanston**	19
Tufano's Tap	**University Vill**	20
Twin Anchors*	**Old Town**	22
Uncommon Ground*	**Lakeview**	21
White Fence*	**Romeoville**	22
Wishbone*	**multi.**	21

DANCING

| **Z** Alhambra | **Mkt Dist** | 13 |
| Ballo | **River N** | 20 |

Cordis Bros. | **Lakeview**	20
Gale St. Inn | **Mundelein**	21
La Peña | **NW Side**	18
Nacional 27 | **River N**	23
Nick's Fishmkt. | **Rosemont**	24
NEW Old Town Mkt. | **Old Town**	24
Pump Rm. | **Gold Coast**	20
Rumba | **River N**	21
Sayat Nova | **Streeterville**	20

DELIVERY/TAKEOUT

(D=delivery, T=takeout)

Adobo Grill | T | **multi.**	21
Akai Hana | D, T | **Wilmette**	21
Aladdin's Eatery | D, T | **Lincoln Pk**	21
A La Turka | T | **Lakeview**	20
Andies | D, T | **Andersonville**	19
Athena | T | **Greektown**	19
Bella Notte | D, T | **W Loop**	22
Benihana | T | **multi.**	20
Berghoff | T | **multi.**	19
Bijan's | T | **River N**	18
Bob Chinn's | T | **Wheeling**	22
Cafe Ba-Ba-Reeba! | T | **Lincoln Pk**	22
Café Spiaggia | T | **Gold Coast**	25
Coco Pazzo Café | T | **Streeterville**	23
Crofton on Wells | T | **River N**	25
D & J Bistro | T | **Lake Zurich**	25
Davis St. Fish | T | **Evanston**	20
Don Juan's | T | **Edison Pk**	21
Emilio's Tapas | T | **multi.**	22
erwin cafe | T | **Lakeview**	22
Filippo's | T | **Lincoln Pk**	22
foodlife | D, T | **Streeterville**	16
Z Francesca's | D, T | **multi.**	24
Gale St. Inn | D, T | **multi.**	21
Gene & Georgetti | T | **River N**	24
Z Gibsons | T | **multi.**	25
Gioco | T | **S Loop**	24
Z Heaven on Seven | D, T | **multi.**	21
Hema's Kitchen | D, T | **Lincoln Pk**	21
Z Japonais | T | **River N**	24
Z Joe's Seafood | T | **River N**	26
Keefer's | T | **River N**	24
La Sardine | T | **W Loop**	23
La Scarola | T | **River W**	23
La Tasca | T | **Arlington Hts**	23
Le Colonial | D, T | **Gold Coast**	23
Lula | T | **Logan Sq**	26
L. Woods Lodge | T | **Lincolnwood**	20
Z Maggiano's | T | **multi.**	21

Mesón Sabika/Tapas Valencia | T | **Naperville**	24
Mia Francesca | T | **Lakeview**	25
Mirai Sushi | T | **Wicker Pk**	25
Z Mon Ami Gabi | T | **multi.**	22
Old Jerusalem | D, T | **Old Town**	19
Opera | T | **S Loop**	22
Orange | T | **Lakeview**	22
Parthenon | T | **Greektown**	22
Penang | D, T | **Chinatown**	22
Pierrot Gourmet | T | **River N**	21
Poag Mahone's | T | **Loop**	19
Potbelly | D, T | **multi.**	19
Red Light | T | **Mkt Dist**	22
R.J. Grunts | T | **Lincoln Pk**	19
RoSal's Kitchen | T | **Little Italy**	22
Z Rosebud | D, T | **multi.**	22
Saloon Steak | D, T | **Streeterville**	22
San Soo Gab San | D, T | **NW Side**	21
Scoozi! | T | **River N**	20
Z Shaw's Crab | D, T | **multi.**	24
Smith/Wollensky | T | **River N**	22
Sullivan's Steak | T | **River N**	22
Sushi Naniwa | D, T | **River N**	23
Z sushi wabi | D, T | **Mkt Dist**	26
Swordfish | T | **Batavia**	26
Tapas Gitana | T | **Northfield**	–
Tarantino's | T | **Lincoln Pk**	22
Tizi Melloul | T | **River N**	21
Tratt. Roma | T | **Old Town**	21
Twin Anchors | T | **Old Town**	22
Village | D, T | **Loop**	20
Volare | D, T | **Streeterville**	24
Yoshi's Café | T | **Lakeview**	25

DINING ALONE

(Other than hotels and places with counter service)

Ann Sather | **multi.**	20
Bar Louie | **multi.**	15
Bin 36/Wine | **River N**	20
Blind Faith | **Evanston**	21
Blue Water | **River N**	23
Breakfast Club | **W Loop**	20
Chicago Diner | **Lakeview**	21
Eleven City | **S Loop**	19
Flat Top Grill | **multi.**	19
foodlife | **Streeterville**	16
Gold Coast | **Loop**	21
Heartland Cafe | **Rogers Pk**	17
Z Hot Doug's | **NW Side**	27
Indie Cafe | **Edgewater**	23

Kaze Sushi | **Roscoe Vill** 23

Kinzie Chophse. | **River N** 20

Koi | **Evanston** 20

Kroll's | **S Loop** 14

Lula | **Logan Sq** 26

Maiz | **Humboldt Pk** 23

Manny's | **S Loop** 23

Meiji | **W Loop** 25

Mrs. Murphy | **North Ctr/St. Ben's** 18

Nookies | **multi.** 19

Oak Tree | **Gold Coast** 16

Penny's Noodle | **multi.** 18

Puck's at MCA | **Streeterville** 20

Reza's | **multi.** 20

Toast | **multi.** 22

Tsuki | **Lincoln Pk** 24

Tweet | **Uptown** 24

Viand Bar | **Streeterville** 22

Wiener's Circle | **Lincoln Pk** 20

ENTERTAINMENT

(Call for days and times of performances)

A La Turka | belly dancing | **Lakeview** 20

Cafe Bolero | jazz/Latin | **Bucktown** 20

🆉 Catch 35 | piano | **Loop** 24

🆉 Chicago Chop | piano | **River N** 25

Chief O'Neill's | Irish | **NW Side** 17

Costa's | piano | **Oakbrook Terr** 22

Cyrano's Bistrot | cabaret | **River N** 21

Edelweiss | German | **Norridge** 22

El Nandu | guitar | **Logan Sq** 19

Emilio's Tapas | flamenco | **Lincoln Pk** 22

Geja's Cafe | flamenco/guitar | **Lincoln Pk** 22

Green Dolphin St. | jazz | **Lincoln Pk** 19

Hackney's | piano | **Wheeling** 18

Irish Oak | Irish/rock | **Wrigleyville** 19

Kit Kat | varies | **Wrigleyville** 15

Lalo's | DJ/mariachi | **multi.** 17

🆉 Lobby | jazz | **River N** 24

Mesón Sabika/Tapas Valencia | flamenco | **Naperville** 24

Myron & Phil's | piano | **Lincolnwood** 22

Nacional 27 | DJ/jazz | **River N** 23

Nick's Fishmkt. | jazz | **Rosemont** 24

Parkers' | jazz/piano | **Downers Grove** 24

Philander's | jazz | **Oak Pk** 21

Philly G's | piano | **Vernon Hills** 22

Pump Rm. | jazz | **Gold Coast** 20

Rumba | jazz | **River N** 21

Sabatino's | piano | **NW Side** 22

Sayat Nova | DJ | **Streeterville** 20

🆉 Shaw's Crab | blues/jazz | **multi.** 24

🆉 Signature Rm. | jazz | **Streeterville** 19

Smoke Daddy | blues/jazz | **Wicker Pk** 21

Sullivan's Steak | jazz | **multi.** 22

🆉 sushi wabi | DJ | **Mkt Dist** 26

Tapas Gitana | guitar | **Northfield** -

Tizi Melloul | belly dancing | **River N** 21

Uncommon Ground | varies | **Lakeview** 21

FIREPLACES

Adelle's | **Wheaton** 24

NEW Ai Sushi | **River N** 21

Andies | **Andersonville** 19

Ann Sather | **Lakeview** 20

Athena | **Greektown** 19

Atwater's | **Geneva** 21

NEW Bank Rest. | **Wheaton** 15

Bella Bacino's | **Loop** 20

Birch River | **Arlington Hts** -

Bistrot Margot | **Old Town** 21

NEW Bluebird, The | **Bucktown** 19

Boston Blackies | **Arlington Hts** 19

NEW Brio | **Lombard** 21

Café la Cave | **Des Plaines** 20

Carlucci | **Downers Grove** 21

Chens | **Wrigleyville** 20

Clubhouse | **Oak Brook** 20

Costa's | **multi.** 22

Courtright's | **Willow Spgs** 25

Cru Café | **Gold Coast** 17

David's Bistro | **Des Plaines** 23

Dee's | **Lincoln Pk** 19

Don Roth's | **Wheeling** 23

Edelweiss | **Norridge** 22

EJ's Place | **Skokie** 20

Enoteca Piattini | **Lincoln Pk** 18

Entourage | **Schaumburg** 22

Erie Cafe | **River N** 22

Finley's Grill | **Downers Grove** 22

Five O'Clock Steak | **Fox Riv. Grove** 23

1492 Tapas | **River N** 19

🆉 Francesca's | **multi.** 24

Froggy's | **Highwood** 23

Gale St. Inn | **Mundelein**	21
Gene & Georgetti | **River N**	24
Z Gibsons | **multi.**	25
Greek Islands | **multi.**	22
Green Door | **River N**	15
Hackney's | **Lake Zurich**	18
Half Shell | **Lincoln Pk**	22
Hecky's | **Evanston**	21
Il Covo | **Bucktown**	20
Il Mulino | **Gold Coast**	24
Z Japonals | **Rlver N**	24
NEW Jerry's | **Wicker Pk**	20
John's Place | **Lincoln Pk**	17
Keefer's | **River N**	24
Koi | **Evanston**	20
NEW La Madia | **River N**	22
Z Les Nomades | **Streeterville**	28
Le Vichyssois | **Lakemoor**	27
Lovells | **Lake Forest**	22
Z McCormick/Schmick's | **Gold Coast**	21
Melting Pot | **Schaumburg**	19
Milk & Honey | **Wicker Pk**	22
Mrs. Murphy | **North Ctr/St. Ben's**	18
My Pie Pizza | **Bucktown**	20
Z North Pond | **Lincoln Pk**	25
NEW Old Town Mkt. | **Old Town**	24
Original Pancake/Walker Bros. | **Lake Zurich**	23
Z NEW Otom | **Mkt Dist**	23
Oysy | **S Loop**	21
Parkers' | **Downers Grove**	24
Park Grill | **Loop**	19
Penny's Noodle | **multi.**	18
NEW Pepitone's | **Edgewater**	20
P.J. Clarke's | **Lincoln Pk**	16
Prairie Grass | **Northbrook**	21
Pump Rm. | **Gold Coast**	20
Quartino | **River N**	21
Quince | **Evanston**	24
Red Lion Pub | **Lincoln Pk**	15
Reza's | **River N**	20
Ribs 'n' Bibs | **Hyde Pk**	20
Z RL | **Gold Coast**	23
Robinson's Ribs | **Lincoln Pk**	22
Russell's BBQ | **Rolling Meadows**	20
Ruth's Chris | **Northbrook**	25
Sabor do Brasil | **Orland Pk**	22
Sage Grille | **Highwood**	22
Sai Café | **Lincoln Pk**	24
Santorini | **Greektown**	22

sola | **Lakeview**	25
Stanley's | **W Loop**	19
Swordfish | **Batavia**	26
Z Tallgrass | **Lockport**	29
NEW Tavern at the Park | **Loop**	17
Tratt. Gianni | **Lincoln Pk**	21
Tsuki | **Lincoln Pk**	24
Tsunami | **Gold Coast**	23
Udupi Palace | **W Rogers Pk**	19
Uncommon Ground | **multi.**	21
Z Va Pensiero | **Evanston**	26
Z Vie | **W Springs**	28
NEW Violet | **Lakeview**	–
Z Weber Grill | **multi.**	19
Webster Wine | **Lincoln Pk**	20

GAME IN SEASON

Adelle's | **Wheaton**	24
Adesso | **Lakeview**	18
Aigre Doux | **River N**	24
Z Alinea | **Lincoln Pk**	29
Aria | **Loop**	23
Atwater's | **Geneva**	21
Z Avenues | **River N**	25
Azucar | **Logan Sq**	23
Bank Lane | **Lake Forest**	23
Z Barrington Country | **Barrington**	26
Bice | **Streeterville**	22
Bistro Campagne | **Lincoln Sq**	24
Bistro 110 | **Gold Coast**	20
Bistrot Margot | **Old Town**	21
Bistrot Zinc | **Gold Coast**	20
NEW Bluebird, The | **Bucktown**	19
BOKA | **Lincoln Pk**	24
Brasserie Jo | **River N**	22
Buona Terra | **Logan Sq**	23
Cab's Wine Bar | **Glen Ellyn**	22
Café Absinthe | **Bucktown**	24
Café Bernard | **Lincoln Pk**	19
Café/Architectes | **Gold Coast**	23
Café la Cave | **Des Plaines**	20
Café le Coq | **Oak Pk**	23
Cafe Matou | **Bucktown**	23
Cafe Pyrenees | **Libertyville**	23
Campagnola | **Evanston**	23
Z Carlos' | **Highland Pk**	28
Carlucci | **Rosemont**	21
Chalkboard | **Lakeview**	22
Z Charlie Trotter's | **Lincoln Pk**	27
Châtaigne | **Near North**	–
Chicago Firehse. | **S Loop**	22

Cité | **Streeterville**	24	Mrs. Murphy | **North Ctr/St. Ben's**	18
Coco Pazzo | **River N**	25	Naha | **River N**	25
copperblue | **Streeterville**	21	**NEW** Nia | **Mkt Dist**	-
Côtes/Rhône | **Edgewater**	18	**Z** Niche | **Geneva**	28
Courtright's | **Willow Spgs**	25	Nick's Fishmkt. | **Deerfield**	24
Crofton on Wells | **River N**	25	**Z** North Pond | **Lincoln Pk**	25
Custom Hse. | **Printer's Row**	25	**Z** Oceanique | **Evanston**	26
Cyrano's Bistrot | **River N**	21	**NEW** Old Town Mkt. | **Old Town**	24
D & J Bistro | **Lake Zurich**	25	
David's Bistro | **Des Plaines**	23	**NEW** Omaggio | **Evanston**	20
de cero | **Mkt Dist**	22	One North | **Loop**	18
Emilio's Sunflower | **La Grange**	24	one sixtyblue | **Mkt Dist**	25
erwin cafe | **Lakeview**	22	Opera | **S Loop**	22
fRedhots | **Glenview**	18	**Z NEW** Otom | **Mkt Dist**	23
Froggy's | **Highwood**	23	**NEW** Paramount Rm. | **Near W**	-
Z Frontera Grill | **River N**	27	Park Grill | **Loop**	19
Z Gabriel's | **Highwood**	26	Philander's | **Oak Pk**	21
NEW Gaetano's | **Forest Pk**	-	**NEW** Prosecco | **River N**	25
Gage | **Loop**	21	P.S. Bangkok | **Lincoln Pk**	21
Gioco | **S Loop**	24	Pump Rm. | **Gold Coast**	20
Green Dolphin St. | **Lincoln Pk**	19	Quince | **Evanston**	24
Harvest | **St. Charles**	24	**Z** Retro Bistro | **Mt. Prospect**	25
HB Home Bistro | **Lakeview**	24	Riva | **Naperville**	18
Heartland Cafe | **Rogers Pk**	17	**Z** Room 21 | **S Loop**	21
Hemmingway's | **Oak Pk**	20	Rose Angelis | **Lincoln Pk**	22
Hop Häus | **River N**	18	Russian Tea | **Loop**	22
Z Hot Doug's | **NW Side**	27	Salpicón | **Old Town**	24
Isabella's | **Geneva**	25	Sapori Tratt. | **Lincoln Pk**	22
Jack's on Halsted | **Lakeview**	21	Schwa | **Wicker Pk**	-
Jilly's Cafe | **Evanston**	24	**Z** Seasons | **Gold Coast**	27
Z Karma | **Mundelein**	23	**Z** 1776 | **Crystal Lake**	26
Kaze Sushi | **Roscoe Vill**	23	**NEW** Shikago | **Loop**	20
Keefer's | **River N**	24	**NEW** Sixteen | **River N**	-
KiKi's Bistro | **Near North**	23	socca | **Lakeview**	24
La Petite Amelia | **Evanston**	20	**NEW** Sopa | **Highwood**	-
la petite folie | **Hyde Pk**	23	Stained Glass | **Evanston**	24
La Sardine | **W Loop**	23	Sura | **Lakeview**	21
La Scarola | **River W**	23	**Z** Tallgrass | **Lockport**	29
La Tache | **Andersonville**	22	Tarantino's | **Lincoln Pk**	22
La Tasca | **Arlington Hts**	23	Think | **Bucktown**	22
Le Bouchon | **Bucktown**	24	**Z** Va Pensiero | **Evanston**	26
Z Les Nomades | **Streeterville**	28	**Z** Vie | **W Springs**	28
Z Le Titi/Paris | **Arlington Hts**	28	Viet Bistro | **Rogers Pk**	19
Le Vichyssois | **Lakemoor**	27	Vivere | **Loop**	23
NEW Lockwood | **Loop**	-	Volo | **Roscoe Vill**	20
Lovells | **Lake Forest**	22	
May St. Market | **W Loop**	23	
NEW Mercat | **S Loop**	-	
Merlo | **Gold Coast**	24	
Z Michael | **Winnetka**	26	
Z mk | **Near North**	26	

HISTORIC PLACES

(Year opened; * building)

1800 | Chief O'Neill's* | **NW Side**	17
1847 | Mesón Sabika/ Tapas Valencia* | **Naperville**	24
1858 | Don Roth's* | **Wheeling**	23

1865 | Crofton on Wells* | **River N** 25	
1872 | Green Door* | **River N** 15	
1880 | West Town Tavern* | **W Town** 25	
1881 | Twin Anchors* | **Old Town** 22	
1885 | Red Lion Pub* | **Lincoln Pk** 15	
1890 | Pasta Palazzo* | **Lincoln Pk** 22	
1890 | Pizzeria Uno/Due* | **River N** 21	
1890 | Sapori Tratt.* | **Lincoln Pk** 22	
1890 | Webster Wine* | **Lincoln Pk** 20	
1893 | Tavern* | **Libertyville** 25	
1897 | Tallgrass* | **Lockport** 29	
1900 | Vivo* | **Mkt Dist** 21	
1901 | Bank Lane* | **Lake Forest** 23	
1901 | South Gate* | **Lake Forest** 20	
1905 | Carnivale* | **Loop** 22	
1905 | Chicago Firehse.* | **S Loop** 22	
1909 | Pompei Bakery | **Little Italy** 20	
1911 | Poag Mahone's* | **Loop** 19	
1912 | Eleven City* | **S Loop** 19	
1920 | Chef's Station* | **Evanston** 22	
1920 | Drake Bros.' | **Streeterville** 20	
1921 | Margie's Candies | **Bucktown** 22	
1923 | Lou Mitchell's | **Loop** 21	
1927 | Francesca's* | **Edgewater** 24	
1927 | Village* | **Loop** 20	
1927 | Vivere* | **Loop** 23	
1928 | Philander's* | **Oak Pk** 21	
1930 | Del Rio* | **Highwood** 22	
1930 | Russell's BBQ | **Elmwood Pk** 20	
1930 | Tufano's Tap* | **University Vill** 20	
1933 | Bruna's | **SW Side** 23	
1933 | Cape Cod Rm. | **Streeterville** 22	
1934 | Billy Goat | **multi.** 15	
1935 | Miller's Pub | **Loop** 18	
1937 | Café le Coq* | **Oak Pk** 23	
1938 | Al's #1 Beef | **Little Italy** 21	
1938 | Pump Rm. | **Gold Coast** 20	
1939 | Hackney's | **multi.** 18	
1941 | Gene & Georgetti | **River N** 24	
1942 | Manny's | **S Loop** 23	
1945 | Army & Lou's | **Far S Side** 24	
1948 | Superdawg | **NW Side** 22	
1954 | White Fence | **Romeoville** 22	
1955 | La Cantina | **Loop** 21	
1955 | Pizzeria Uno/Due | **River N** 21	

HOTEL DINING

Ambassador East Hotel
Pump Rm. \| **Gold Coast** 20

Belden-Stratford Hotel
🅩 Mon Ami Gabi \| **Lincoln Pk** 22

Blackstone Hotel
NEW Mercat \| **S Loop** – |

Carleton Hotel
Philander's \| **Oak Pk** 21

Crowne Plaza Chicago Metro
Dine \| **W Loop** 15

Crowne Plaza Hotel
🅩 Karma \| **Mundelein** 23

Doubletree Hotel
🅩 Gibsons \| **Rosemont** 25

Doubletree Hotel Arlington Hts
Birch River \| **Arlington Hts** – |

Drake Hotel
Cape Cod Rm. \| **Streeterville** 22
Drake Bros.' \| **Streeterville** 20

Embassy Suites Hotel
P.J. Clarke's \| **Streeterville** 16

Fairmont Chicago Hotel
Aria \| **Loop** 23

Four Seasons Hotel
🅩 Seasons \| **Gold Coast** 27
🅩 Seasons Café \| **Gold Coast** 21

Hard Rock Hotel
China Grill \| **Loop** 20

Herrington Inn
Atwater's \| **Geneva** 21

Hilton Garden Inn
🅩 Weber Grill \| **River N** 19

Hilton Guest Suites
Mrs. Park's \| **Streeterville** 16

Holiday Inn
Aurelio's Pizza \| **Loop** 21

Homestead Hotel
Quince \| **Evanston** 24

Hotel Allegro
312 Chicago \| **Loop** 19

Hotel Blake
Custom Hse. \| **Printer's Row** 25

Hotel Burnham
Atwood Cafe \| **Loop** 21

Hotel Monaco
South Water \| **Loop** 17

Hyatt Regency
Stetson's Chop Hse. \| **Loop** 23

Hyatt Regency McCormick Pl.
Shor \| **S Loop** – |

InterContinental, Hotel	
Zest | **Streeterville**	18
James Chicago Hotel	
David Burke Prime | **River N**	24
Margarita Inn	
☑ Va Pensiero | **Evanston**	26
Northshore Hotel	
Tapas Barcelona | **Evanston**	21
O'Hare International Ctr.	
Harry Caray's | **Rosemont**	20
Palmer House Hilton	
NEW Lockwood | **Loop**	–
Park Hyatt Chicago	
☑ NoMI | **Gold Coast**	26
Peninsula Hotel	
☑ Avenues | **River N**	25
☑ Lobby | **River N**	24
Pierrot Gourmet | **River N**	21
☑ Shanghai Terr. | **River N**	25
Pheasant Run Resort	
Harvest | **St. Charles**	24
Red Roof Inn	
Coco Pazzo Café | **Streeterville**	23
Renaissance Hotel	
Ruth's Chris | **Northbrook**	25
Renaissance Schaumburg Hotel	
Sam & Harry's | **Schaumburg**	27
Ritz-Carlton Hotel	
Ritz Café | **Streeterville**	23
Seneca Hotel	
Saloon Steak | **Streeterville**	22
Sheraton Chicago Hotel	
Shula's Steak | **Streeterville**	19
Sofitel Chicago Water Tower	
Café/Architectes | **Gold Coast**	23
Swissôtel	
Palm, The | **Loop**	23
Tremont Hotel	
Mike Ditka's | **Gold Coast**	22
Trump International Hotel	
NEW Sixteen | **River N**	–
W Chicago Lakeshore	
Wave | **Streeterville**	20
Westin Chicago North Shore	
Osteria/Tramonto | **Wheeling**	21
☑ Tramonto's | **Wheeling**	24
Westin Chicago NW	
Shula's Steak | **Itasca**	19
Westin Hotel	
Grill on Alley | **Streeterville**	20

Whitehall Hotel	
Fornetto Mei | **Gold Coast**	21
W Hotel	
rist. we | **Loop**	17
Write Inn	
Hemmingway's | **Oak Pk**	20
Wyndham Chicago	
Caliterra | **Streeterville**	22

JACKET REQUIRED

☑ Carlos' | **Highland Pk**	28
☑ Charlie Trotter's | **Lincoln Pk**	27
☑ Les Nomades | **Streeterville**	28
☑ Spiaggia | **Gold Coast**	27
☑ Tru | **Streeterville**	27

LATE DINING

(Weekday closing hour)

Agami | 12 AM | **Uptown**	25
Al's #1 Beef | varies | **River N**	21
Artopolis | 12 AM | **Greektown**	23
Athena | 12 AM | **Greektown**	19
☑ Avec | 12 AM | **Loop**	27
Avenue M | 2 AM | **River W**	21
Bar Louie | varies | **multi.**	15
NEW Between Boutique | 2:30 AM | **Wicker Pk**	–
Bijan's | 3:30 AM | **River N**	18
Billy Goat | varies | **River N**	15
NEW Bluebird, The | 1 AM | **Bucktown**	19
Boston Blackies | 12 AM | **Arlington Hts**	19
Carmichael's | 12 AM | **W Loop**	21
Carmine's | 12 AM | **Gold Coast**	21
Coast Sushi/South Coast | 12 AM | **Bucktown**	25
Coobah | 1 AM | **Lakeview**	20
Cru Café | 2 AM | **Gold Coast**	17
El Presidente | 24 hrs. | **Lincoln Pk**	15
Emperor's Choice | 12 AM | **Chinatown**	22
Evergreen | 12 AM | **Chinatown**	22
Finley's Grill | 1:30 AM | **Downers Grove**	22
Gene & Georgetti | 12 AM | **River N**	24
☑ Gibsons | varies | **multi.**	25
☑ Giordano's | varies | **SW Side**	21
Gold Coast | varies | **multi.**	21
Greek Islands | varies | **Greektown**	22
Happy Chef | 2 AM | **Chinatown**	22
Hard Rock | 12 AM | **River N**	12

subscribe to ZAGAT.com

Hop Häus	3:30 AM	**River N**	18
Hugo's	varies	**multi.**	23
Itto Sushi	12 AM	**Lincoln Pk**	23
Kamehachi	varies	**Old Town**	22
Kit Kat	12 AM	**Wrigleyville**	15
Kuma's	1 AM	**Logan Sq**	24
☑ Lao	varies	**Chinatown**	26
☑ Lobby	12 AM	**River N**	24
Lou Mitchell's	varies	**O'Hare Area**	21
LuxBar	1:30 AM	**Gold Coast**	19
Margie's Candies	varies	**Bucktown**	22
Melting Pot	varies	**River N**	19
Miller's Pub	2 AM	**Loop**	18
Minnies	2 AM	**Lincoln Pk**	17
Mrs. Park's	2 AM	**Streeterville**	16
Nancy's Pizza	varies	**Lakeview**	22
NEW Natalino's	2 AM	**W Town**	–
Niu	12 AM	**Streeterville**	21
Olé Olé	12 AM	**Andersonville**	20
Parthenon	12 AM	**Greektown**	22
Pegasus	varies	**SW Side**	21
Penang	1 AM	**Chinatown**	22
Pete Miller	varies	**Evanston**	22
Pizzeria Uno/Due	varies	**River N**	21
Pops/Champagne	1 AM	**River N**	16
Quartino	1 AM	**River N**	21
Reza's	varies	**multi.**	20
Ribs 'n' Bibs	12 AM	**Hyde Pk**	20
Rockit B&G	1:30 AM	**River N**	19
NEW Rockstar Dogs	3 AM	**W Town**	–
Roditys	12 AM	**Greektown**	22
Salud Tequila	2 AM	**Wicker Pk**	–
San Soo Gab San	24 hrs.	**NW Side**	21
Santorini	12 AM	**Greektown**	22
NEW Shochu	2 AM	**Lakeview**	–
Silver Seafood	1 AM	**Uptown**	20
Superdawg	varies	**NW Side**	22
☑ SushiSamba	1 AM	**River N**	22
Tasting Room	12 AM	**Mkt Dist**	15
Tavern on Rush	12 AM	**Gold Coast**	20
Tempo	24 hrs.	**Gold Coast**	20
Three Happiness	6 AM	**Chinatown**	19
Twisted Spoke	1 AM	**Near W**	20
Webster Wine	12:30 AM	**Lincoln Pk**	20
Wiener's Circle	4 AM	**Lincoln Pk**	20

MEET FOR A DRINK

(Most top hotels and the following standouts)

☑ Alhambra	**Mkt Dist**	13
NEW A Mano	**River N**	21
Avenue M	**River W**	21
Ballo	**River N**	20
Bandera	**Streeterville**	22
NEW Bank Rest.	**Wheaton**	15
Bar Louie	**multi.**	15
Bijan's	**River N**	18
Billy Goat	**multi.**	15
Bin 36/Wine	**multi.**	20
Bistro 110	**Gold Coast**	20
Blue Water	**River N**	23
NEW Bluprint	**River N**	22
BOKA	**Lincoln Pk**	24
Brasserie Jo	**River N**	22
NEW Brio	**Lombard**	21
Broadway Cellars	**Edgewater**	21
Cab's Wine Bar	**Glen Ellyn**	22
Café/Architectes	**Gold Coast**	23
☑ Carnivale	**Loop**	22
☑ Catch 35	**Loop**	24
NEW Chant	**Hyde Pk**	16
Chief O'Neill's	**NW Side**	17
China Grill	**Loop**	20
Coobah	**Lakeview**	20
Cordis Bros.	**Lakeview**	20
Cru Café	**Gold Coast**	17
Cuatro	**S Loop**	22
DeLaCosta	**Streeterville**	22
Dine	**W Loop**	15
Di Pescara	**Northbrook**	21
NEW Distinctive Cork	**Naperville**	22
NEW Drawing Rm/Le Passage	**Gold Coast**	–
Enoteca Piattini	**Lincoln Pk**	18
Entourage	**Schaumburg**	22
NEW Fifty/50, The	**Wicker Pk**	–
Finley's Grill	**Downers Grove**	22
Flatwater	**River N**	15
Fleming's	**Lincolnshire**	22
Flight	**Glenview**	19
☑ Frontera Grill	**River N**	27
Fulton's	**River N**	19
Gage	**Loop**	21
☑ Gibsons	**multi.**	25
Goose Is. Brewing	**multi.**	16
Gordon Biersch	**Bolingbrook**	20
Green Door	**River N**	15
Harry Caray's	**multi.**	20

NEW Holy Mackerel! | **Lombard**	19
Z Japonais | **River N**	24
Z Joe's Seafood | **River N**	26
Keefer's | **River N**	24
Landmark | **Lincoln Pk**	21
NEW Libertine | **Lincoln Pk**	-
LuxBar | **Gold Coast**	19
Mambo Grill | **River N**	20
Marché | **Mkt Dist**	22
Z McCormick/Schmick's | **Gold Coast**	21
Mike Ditka's | **Gold Coast**	22
Miramar Bistro | **Highwood**	20
Z mk | **Near North**	26
Nacional 27 | **River N**	23
N9ne | **Loop**	24
Niu | **Streeterville**	21
Z NoMI | **Gold Coast**	26
NEW NXXT | **Humboldt Pk**	-
One North | **Loop**	18
one sixtyblue | **Mkt Dist**	25
Osteria/Pizzeria Via Stato | **River N**	22
NEW Paramount Rm. | **Near W**	-
NEW Park 52 | **Hyde Pk**	-
NEW Pinstripes | **Northbrook**	18
P.J. Clarke's | **Gold Coast**	16
Pops/Champagne | **River N**	16
NEW Powerhouse | **Loop**	23
Prairie Grass | **Northbrook**	21
NEW Prosecco | **River N**	25
Quartino | **River N**	21
Red Light | **Mkt Dist**	22
Republic | **River N**	19
Rhapsody | **Loop**	21
Z RL | **Gold Coast**	23
Rockit B&G | **River N**	19
Z Room 21 | **S Loop**	21
Z Rosebud Prime/Steak | **Streeterville**	23
Rumba | **River N**	21
Scoozi! | **River N**	20
Z NEW Sepia | **Mkt Dist**	22
Z Shaw's Crab | **multi.**	24
NEW Shikago | **Loop**	20
NEW Shochu | **Lakeview**	-
Z Signature Rm. | **Streeterville**	19
NEW Sixteen | **River N**	-
Smith/Wollensky | **River N**	22
South Water | **Loop**	17
Stained Glass | **Evanston**	24
NEW Stretch Run | **River N**	-

Sullivan's Steak | **River N**	22
Sura | **Lakeview**	21
Z SushiSamba | **River N**	22
Tasting Room | **Mkt Dist**	15
NEW Tavern at the Park | **Loop**	17
Tavern on Rush | **Gold Coast**	20
Tepatulco | **Lincoln Pk**	23
312 Chicago | **Loop**	19
Timpano Chophse. | **Naperville**	20
Tizi Melloul | **River N**	21
Z Tramonto's | **Wheeling**	24
Tratt. No. 10 | **Loop**	23
Twisted Spoke | **Near W**	20
Viet Bistro | **Rogers Pk**	19
Volo | **Roscoe Vill**	20
Wave | **Streeterville**	20
Webster Wine | **Lincoln Pk**	20
Zapatista | **S Loop**	18
Zocalo | **River N**	23

MICROBREWERIES

Goose Is. Brewing | **multi.**	16
Gordon Biersch | **Bolingbrook**	20
Piece | **Wicker Pk**	23

NOTEWORTHY NEWCOMERS

African Harambee | **Rogers Pk**	18
Ai Sushi | **River N**	21
Al Primo Canto | **NW Side**	-
A Mano | **River N**	21
BackStage | **River N**	22
Balanced Kitchen | **NW Side**	-
Bank Rest. | **Wheaton**	15
BBOP Lounge | **Old Town**	-
Between Boutique | **Wicker Pk**	-
Big Jones | **Andersonville**	-
Bluebird, The | **Bucktown**	19
Bluprint | **River N**	22
Z Brasserie Ruhlmann | **River N**	21
Brio | **Lombard**	21
Café 103 | **Far S Side**	-
Cellar | **Wheaton**	-
Chant | **Hyde Pk**	16
Cinners Chili | **Lincoln Sq**	-
C.J.'s | **Humboldt Pk**	-
Cucina Paradiso | **Oak Pk**	25
Distinctive Cork | **Naperville**	22
Drawing Rm/Le Passage | **Gold Coast**	-
Exposure Tapas | **S Loop**	18
Fat Cat | **Uptown**	18

Fifty/50, The	Wicker Pk	-
Frankie's Scaloppine	Gold Coast	-
Gaetano's	Forest Pk	-
Holy Mackerel!	Lombard	19
Il Fiasco	Andersonville	19
Jack Rabbit	Lincoln Sq	-
Jerry's	Wicker Pk	20
La Brochette	Wicker Pk	-
La Cocina/Frida	Andersonville	-
La Madia	River N	22
Liberline	Lincoln Pk	-
Lockwood	Loop	-
Macarena	Naperville	-
Macello	Mkt Dist	19
mado	Bucktown	-
Maya Del Sol	Oak Pk	21
Mercat	S Loop	-
Mythos	Lakeview	-
Natalino's	W Town	-
Nia	Mkt Dist	-
Niu	Streeterville	21
NXXT	Humboldt Pk	-
Old Town Mkt.	Old Town	24
Omaggio	Evanston	20
Z Otom	Mkt Dist	23
Paramount Rm.	Near W	-
Park 52	Hyde Pk	-
Pepitone's	Edgewater	20
Pinstripes	Northbrook	18
Pomegranate	Evanston	19
Powerhouse	Loop	23
Prosecco	River N	25
Reel Club	Oak Brook	20
Risqué Café	Lakeview	-
Rock-N-Roll	Palatine	-
Rockstar Dogs	W Town	-
Rustik	Logan Sq	-
Rusty Armadillo	NW Side	-
Z Sepia	Mkt Dist	22
Shikago	Loop	20
Shochu	Lakeview	-
Sixteen	River N	-
Sopa	Highwood	-
Spertus Cafe	S Loop	-
Stretch Run	River N	-
Su-Ra	Wicker Pk	17
TABLE 52	Gold Coast	24
Takashi	Bucktown	29
Tallulah	Lincoln Sq	-
Tavern at the Park	Loop	17
Thai Urban	Loop	-
Thalia Spice	River W	25
Trattoria 225	Oak Pk	19
Trattoria Isabella	Mkt Dist	-
Union Pizzeria	Evanston	-
Violet	Lakeview	-
ZED 451	multi.	22

OUTDOOR DINING

(G=garden; P=patio; S=sidewalk; T=terrace; W=waterside)

Arco/Cuchilleros	P	Lakeview	18
Z a tavola	G	Ukrainian Vill	26
Athena	G	Greektown	19
Atwater's	P	Geneva	21
Avenue M	P	River W	21
Bank Lane	T	Lake Forest	23
Bice	S	Streeterville	22
Bijan's	S	River N	18
Bistro Campagne	G	Lincoln Sq	24
Bistro 110	S	Gold Coast	20
Bistrot Margot	S	Old Town	21
Z Blackbird	S	W Loop	27
BOKA	P	Lincoln Pk	24
Brasserie Jo	S	River N	22
Cafe Ba-Ba-Reeba!	P	Lincoln Pk	22
Café/Architectes	T	Gold Coast	23
Café Selmarie	S	Lincoln Sq	22
Campagnola	P	Evanston	23
Carmichael's	G	W Loop	21
Carmine's	P	Gold Coast	21
Z Carnivale	P	Loop	22
Chez Joël	P	Little Italy	23
Chicago Firehse.	P	S Loop	22
Coco Pazzo Café	P	Streeterville	23
Cru Café	S	Gold Coast	17
Cyrano's Bistrot	S	River N	21
Edwardo's Pizza	P	S Loop	20
Erie Cafe	T, W	River N	22
Feast	G	Bucktown	21
Five O'Clock Steak	P, W	Fox Riv. Grove	23
Flatwater	P, W	River N	15
Flight	P	Glenview	19
Z Frontera Grill	P	River N	27
Fulton's	P, W	River N	19
Z Gabriel's	T	Highwood	26
Greek Islands	P, S	multi.	22
Green Dolphin St.	P, W	Lincoln Pk	19
Il Mulino	P	Gold Coast	24
Isabella's	P	Geneva	25
Z Japonais	P	River N	24

John's Place | S | **Lincoln Pk**	17
Kamehachi | P, S | **multi.**	22
Le Colonial | S, T | **Gold Coast**	23
Z Maggiano's | P | **multi.**	21
Mesón Sabika/Tapas Valencia | G | **Naperville**	24
Mia Francesca | P | **Lakeview**	25
Z Mon Ami Gabi | G | **Lincoln Pk**	22
Z NoMI | G | **Gold Coast**	26
OPA Estiatorio | P | **Vernon Hills**	19
Park Grill | P | **Loop**	19
Pegasus | T | **Greektown**	21
Z P.F. Chang's | P | **Northbrook**	21
Phil Stefani's | S | **River N**	21
NEW Pinstripes | P | **Northbrook**	18
Pops/Champagne | P | **River N**	16
Potbelly | P | **multi.**	19
Puck's at MCA | P, W | **Streeterville**	20
Riva | P, W | **Streeterville**	18
Z RL | P | **Gold Coast**	23
Z Room 21 | G | **S Loop**	21
Z Rosebud | P, S, W | **multi.**	22
Salvatore's | G | **Lincoln Pk**	21
Z Shanghai Terr. | T | **River N**	25
Smith/Wollensky | G, P, T, W | **River N**	22
South Gate | P, S | **Lake Forest**	20
Z SushiSamba | S | **River N**	22
Tapas Barcelona | G, P | **Evanston**	21
Tapas Gitana | P | **Northfield**	–
Tavern on Rush | P, S | **Gold Coast**	20
Topo Gigio | G, S | **Old Town**	23
Tuscany | G, P | **multi.**	22
Twisted Spoke | P | **Near W**	20
Z Va Pensiero | T | **Evanston**	26

PEOPLE-WATCHING

Adobo Grill | **Old Town**	21
Z Alhambra | **Mkt Dist**	13
NEW A Mano | **River N**	21
American Girl | **Gold Coast**	13
Z Avec | **Loop**	27
Avenue M | **River W**	21
Bice | **Streeterville**	22
Bin 36/Wine | **River N**	20
Bistro 110 | **Gold Coast**	20
Z Blackbird | **W Loop**	27
BOKA | **Lincoln Pk**	24
Bongo Room | **Wicker Pk**	24
Brasserie Jo | **River N**	22

NEW Brasserie Ruhlmann | **River N**	21
Carmine's | **Gold Coast**	21
Z Carnivale | **Loop**	22
Z Chicago Chop | **River N**	25
Coobah | **Lakeview**	20
Cru Café | **Gold Coast**	17
Cuatro | **S Loop**	22
DeLaCosta | **Streeterville**	22
NEW Drawing Rm/Le Passage | **Gold Coast**	–
Entourage | **Schaumburg**	22
NEW Fifty/50, The | **Wicker Pk**	–
Z Gibsons | **Gold Coast**	25
Green Zebra | **W Town**	26
Hamburger Mary's | **Andersonville**	16
Harry Caray's | **River N**	20
Il Mulino | **Gold Coast**	24
Z Japonais | **River N**	24
Keefer's | **River N**	24
Landmark | **Lincoln Pk**	21
Le Colonial | **Gold Coast**	23
LuxBar | **Gold Coast**	19
Manny's | **S Loop**	23
Marché | **Mkt Dist**	22
NEW Mercat | **S Loop**	–
Mirai Sushi | **Wicker Pk**	25
Miramar Bistro | **Highwood**	20
Z mk | **Near North**	26
Naha | **River N**	25
N9ne | **Loop**	24
Niu | **Streeterville**	21
Z NoMI | **Gold Coast**	26
NEW NXXT | **Humboldt Pk**	–
Opera | **S Loop**	22
Osteria/Pizzeria Via Stato | **River N**	22
NEW Park 52 | **Hyde Pk**	–
Pops/Champagne | **River N**	16
NEW Powerhouse | **Loop**	23
NEW Prosecco | **River N**	25
Quartino | **River N**	21
Republic | **River N**	19
Z Room 21 | **S Loop**	21
Z Rosebud | **multi.**	22
Z Rosebud Prime/Steak | **Streeterville**	23
Scoozi! | **River N**	20
NEW Shikago | **Loop**	20
NEW Shochu | **Lakeview**	–
NEW Sixteen | **River N**	–

Z Spring | **Wicker Pk** — 27
NEW Stretch Run | **River N** — –
Sura | **Lakeview** — 21
Z SushiSamba | **River N** — 22
Tavern on Rush | **Gold Coast** — 20
Z Tramonto's | **Wheeling** — 24
Wave | **Streeterville** — 20
Zapatista | **S Loop** — 18

POWER SCENES

Z Alinea | **Lincoln Pk** — 29
Z Avenues | **River N** — 25
Bice | **Streeterville** — 22
Z NEW Brasserie Ruhlmann | **River N** — 21
Z Capital Grille | **Streeterville** — 25
Z Catch 35 | **Loop** — 24
Z Charlie Trotter's | **Lincoln Pk** — 27
Z Chicago Chop | **River N** — 25
Coco Pazzo | **River N** — 25
Custom Hse. | **Printer's Row** — 25
David Burke Prime | **River N** — 24
Entourage | **Schaumburg** — 22
Z Everest | **Loop** — 27
Fulton's | **River N** — 19
Gene & Georgetti | **River N** — 24
Z Gibsons | **multi.** — 25
Hugo's | **Gold Coast** — 23
Il Mulino | **Gold Coast** — 24
Keefer's | **River N** — 24
Z Les Nomades | **Streeterville** — 28
NEW Lockwood | **Loop** — –
Z mk | **Near North** — 26
Z Morton's | **multi.** — 26
Naha | **River N** — 25
Z NoMI | **Gold Coast** — 26
NEW Powerhouse | **Loop** — 23
Z RL | **Gold Coast** — 23
Ruth's Chris | **multi.** — 25
Z Seasons | **Gold Coast** — 27
NEW Shikago | **Loop** — 20
NEW Sixteen | **River N** — –
Smith/Wollensky | **River N** — 22
Z Spiaggia | **Gold Coast** — 27
Z Spring | **Wicker Pk** — 27
Z Tramonto's | **Wheeling** — 24
Z Tru | **Streeterville** — 27

PRIVATE ROOMS

(Restaurants charge less at off times; call for capacity)
Z Alinea | **Lincoln Pk** — 29
Athena | **Greektown** — 19

Ben Pao | **River N** — 21
Caliterra | **Streeterville** — 22
Z Carnivale | **Loop** — 22
Z Catch 35 | **multi.** — 24
Z Charlie Trotter's | **Lincoln Pk** — 27
Z Chicago Chop | **River N** — 25
Club Lucky | **Bucktown** — 19
Costa's | **multi.** — 22
Edwardo's Pizza | **multi.** — 20
Z Everest | **Loop** — 27
Z Francesca's | **multi.** — 24
Z Frontera Grill | **River N** — 27
Z Gabriel's | **Highwood** — 26
Gene & Georgetti | **River N** — 24
Z Gibsons | **multi.** — 25
Gioco | **S Loop** — 24
Goose Is. Brewing | **multi.** — 16
Greek Islands | **multi.** — 22
Z Joe's Seafood | **River N** — 26
Kamehachi | **multi.** — 22
Keefer's | **River N** — 24
NEW Lockwood | **Loop** — –
L. Woods Lodge | **Lincolnwood** — 20
NEW Mercat | **S Loop** — –
Mesón Sabika/Tapas Valencia | **Naperville** — 24
Z mk | **Near North** — 26
Naha | **River N** — 25
N9ne | **Loop** — 24
Z NoMI | **Gold Coast** — 26
Z North Pond | **Lincoln Pk** — 25
one sixtyblue | **Mkt Dist** — 25
Park Grill | **Loop** — 19
Pete Miller | **multi.** — 22
Red Light | **Mkt Dist** — 22
Z RL | **Gold Coast** — 23
Z Rosebud | **multi.** — 22
Russian Tea | **Loop** — 22
Ruth's Chris | **multi.** — 25
Scoozi! | **River N** — 20
Z NEW Sepia | **Mkt Dist** — 22
Z Shanghai Terr. | **River N** — 25
Z Shaw's Crab | **multi.** — 24
Z Spiaggia | **Gold Coast** — 27
Z SushiSamba | **River N** — 22
Z Tallgrass | **Lockport** — 29
312 Chicago | **Loop** — 19
Tizi Melloul | **River N** — 21
Z Topolobampo | **River N** — 28
Tratt. Roma | **Old Town** — 21
Z Va Pensiero | **Evanston** — 26

CHICAGO

SPECIAL FEATURES

Vivo | **Mkt Dist** 21
Z Wildfire | **multi.** 24

PRIX FIXE MENUS

(Call for prices and times)

Z Arun's | **NW Side** 27
Z Avenues | **River N** 25
Bank Lane | **Lake Forest** 23
Bin 36/Wine | **River N** 20
Bistro 110 | **Gold Coast** 20
Z Carlos' | **Highland Pk** 28
Z Charlie Trotter's | **Lincoln Pk** 27
Courtright's | **Willow Spgs** 25
Cyrano's Bistrot | **River N** 21
D & J Bistro | **Lake Zurich** 25
Z Everest | **Loop** 27
Froggy's | **Highwood** 23
Z Gabriel's | **Highwood** 26
La Sardine | **W Loop** 23
Z Les Nomades | **Streeterville** 28
Z mk | **Near North** 26
Moto | **Mkt Dist** 25
Z North Pond | **Lincoln Pk** 25
Z Oceanique | **Evanston** 26
Pump Rm. | **Gold Coast** 20
Red Light | **Mkt Dist** 22
Z Retro Bistro | **Mt. Prospect** 25
Roy's | **River N** 24
Salpicón | **Old Town** 24
Z Seasons | **Gold Coast** 27
Z Spiaggia | **Gold Coast** 27
Z Spring | **Wicker Pk** 27
Z Tallgrass | **Lockport** 29
Z Tru | **Streeterville** 27

QUICK BITES

Aladdin's Eatery | **Lincoln Pk** 21
Art of Pizza | **Lakeview** 21
Artopolis | **Greektown** 23
Azucar | **Logan Sq** 23
Babylon | **Bucktown** 20
Bagel | **multi.** 19
Bar Louie | **multi.** 15
Berghoff | **O'Hare Area** 19
Big Bowl | **multi.** 19
NEW Big Jones | **Andersonville** –
Bijan's | **River N** 18
Billy Goat | **multi.** 15
Bin 36/Wine | **multi.** 20
Café Selmarie | **Lincoln Sq** 22
NEW Cellar | **Wheaton** –
Chicago Pizza | **Lincoln Pk** 22

NEW Cinners Chili | **Lincoln Sq** –
Convito | **Wilmette** 16
Cru Café | **Gold Coast** 17
NEW Distinctive Cork | **Naperville** 22
NEW Drawing Rm/Le Passage | –
 Gold Coast
Eleven City | **S Loop** 19
El Presidente | **Lincoln Pk** 15
Flat Top Grill | **multi.** 19
foodlife | **Streeterville** 16
NEW Frankie's Scaloppine | –
 Gold Coast
fRedhots | **Glenview** 18
Gold Coast | **multi.** 21
Hannah's Bretzel | **Loop** 23
Honey 1 BBQ | **Bucktown** 19
Hot Chocolate | **Bucktown** 24
Z Hot Doug's | **NW Side** 27
NEW Jerry's | **Wicker Pk** 20
Lem's BBQ | **Far S Side** 25
NEW Macarena | **Naperville** –
Maiz | **Humboldt Pk** 23
Manny's | **multi.** 23
NEW Mercat | **S Loop** –
Minnies | **Lincoln Pk** 17
Mundial | **University Vill** 24
NEW Nia | **Mkt Dist** –
Noon-O-Kabab | **NW Side** 24
Oak Tree | **Gold Coast** 16
Old Jerusalem | **Old Town** 19
Pegasus | **SW Side** 21
Penny's Noodle | **multi.** 18
Pierrot Gourmet | **River N** 21
NEW Pomegranate | **Evanston** 19
Pompei Bakery | **multi.** 20
Potbelly | **multi.** 19
Puck's at MCA | **Streeterville** 20
Quartino | **River N** 21
NEW Rockstar Dogs | **W Town** –
Russell's BBQ | **Elmwood Pk** 20
NEW Shochu | **Lakeview** –
NEW Spertus Cafe | **S Loop** –
Stained Glass | **Evanston** 24
Stir Crazy | **multi.** 21
Superdawg | **NW Side** 22
Tasting Room | **Mkt Dist** 15
Tempo | **Gold Coast** 20
Trattoria Trullo | **Lincoln Sq** 21
Uncle John's | **Far S Side** –
Uncommon Ground | **Lakeview** 21
Viand Bar | **Streeterville** 22

subscribe to ZAGAT.com

Webster Wine	**Lincoln Pk**	20	RL	**Gold Coast**	23
Wiener's Circle	**Lincoln Pk**	20	Russian Tea	**Loop**	22

QUIET CONVERSATION

Akai Hana	**Wilmette**	21	Salvatore's	**Lincoln Pk**	21
Aria	**Loop**	23	Z Seasons	**Gold Coast**	27
Z Arun's	**NW Side**	27	Z Seasons Café	**Gold Coast**	21
Z a tavola	**Ukrainian Vill**	26	Z 1776	**Crystal Lake**	26
Bank Lane	**Lake Forest**	23	Z Shanghai Terr.	**River N**	25
Z Barrington Country	**Barrington**	26	Shor	**S Loop**	–
Bistro Monet	**Glen Ellyn**	23	Siam Café	**Uptown**	22
Café Bernard	**Lincoln Pk**	19	Z Signature Rm.	**Streeterville**	19
Café/Architectes	**Gold Coast**	23	South Gate	**Lake Forest**	20
Café la Cave	**Des Plaines**	20	South Water	**Loop**	17
Cafe Matou	**Bucktown**	23	NEW TABLE 52	**Gold Coast**	24
NEW Café 103	**Far S Side**	–	Z Tallgrass	**Lockport**	29
Cafe Pyrenees	**Libertyville**	23	Tasting Room	**Mkt Dist**	15
Café Selmarie	**Lincoln Sq**	22	Tavern	**Libertyville**	25
Café Spiaggia	**Gold Coast**	25	Tratt. No. 10	**Loop**	23
Caliterra	**Streeterville**	22	Tre Kronor	**NW Side**	23
Cape Cod Rm.	**Streeterville**	22	Z Tru	**Streeterville**	27
Z Carlos'	**Highland Pk**	28	Z Va Pensiero	**Evanston**	26
Z Charlie Trotter's	**Lincoln Pk**	27	Village	**Loop**	20
Cité	**Streeterville**	24	Vinci	**Lincoln Pk**	21
copperblue	**Streeterville**	21	Vivere	**Loop**	23
D & J Bistro	**Lake Zurich**	25	Vong's	**River N**	22
Don Roth's	**Wheeling**	23	Z Zealous	**River N**	24

erwin cafe	**Lakeview**	22
Z Everest	**Loop**	27

RAW BARS

NEW Gaetano's	**Forest Pk**	–	Blue Water	**River N**	23
Gale St. Inn	**Mundelein**	21	Bob Chinn's	**Wheeling**	22
Gaylord Indian	**Schaumburg**	21	Z NEW Brasserie Ruhlmann	**River N**	21
Geja's Cafe	**Lincoln Pk**	22	Cape Cod Rm.	**Streeterville**	22
Itto Sushi	**Lincoln Pk**	23	Davis St. Fish	**multi.**	20
Jilly's Cafe	**Evanston**	24	Fulton's	**River N**	19
Klay Oven	**River N**	21	Half Shell	**Lincoln Pk**	22
La Crêperie	**Lakeview**	21	Mitchell's Fish Mkt.	**Glenview**	21
La Gondola	**Lakeview**	23	Niu	**Streeterville**	21
Lawry's	**River N**	24	Pappadeaux	**Arlington Hts**	21
Le P'tit Paris	**Streeterville**	24	Pops/Champagne	**River N**	16
Z Les Nomades	**Streeterville**	28	Riva	**Streeterville**	18
Z Le Titi/Paris	**Arlington Hts**	28	Z Shaw's Crab	**multi.**	24
Le Vichyssois	**Lakemoor**	27	Tin Fish	**Tinley Park**	21

Lovells	**Lake Forest**	22
Z North Pond	**Lincoln Pk**	25

ROMANTIC PLACES

Z Oceanique	**Evanston**	26	NEW Ai Sushi	**River N**	21
One North	**Loop**	18	Z Alhambra	**Mkt Dist**	13
Pierrot Gourmet	**River N**	21	Avenue M	**River W**	21
Pump Rm.	**Gold Coast**	20	Z Avenues	**River N**	25
Quince	**Evanston**	24	Azucar	**Logan Sq**	23
Rhapsody	**Loop**	21	Z Barrington Country	**Barrington**	26
Ritz Café	**Streeterville**	23	NEW Between Boutique	**Wicker Pk**	–
			Bistro Campagne	**Lincoln Sq**	24

Bistro Monet | **Glen Ellyn**	23
Bistro 22 | **Lake Zurich**	22
Bistrot Margot | **Old Town**	21
Bistrot Zinc | **Gold Coast**	20
BOKA | **Lincoln Pk**	24
NEW Brasserie Ruhlmann | **River N**	21
Café Absinthe | **Bucktown**	24
Café Bernard | **Lincoln Pk**	19
Café la Cave | **Des Plaines**	20
Cafe Pyrenees | **Libertyville**	23
Cape Cod Rm. | **Streeterville**	22
Z Carlos' | **Highland Pk**	28
NEW Chant | **Hyde Pk**	16
Z Charlie Trotter's | **Lincoln Pk**	27
Chez Joël | **Little Italy**	23
Cité | **Streeterville**	24
Coco Pazzo | **River N**	25
copperblue | **Streeterville**	21
Côtes/Rhône | **Edgewater**	18
Courtright's | **Willow Spgs**	25
Crofton on Wells | **River N**	25
Cru Café | **Gold Coast**	17
Cuatro | **S Loop**	22
Cyrano's Bistrot | **River N**	21
D & J Bistro | **Lake Zurich**	25
DeLaCosta | **Streeterville**	22
NEW Drawing Rm/Le Passage | **Gold Coast**	–
Enoteca Piattini | **Lincoln Pk**	18
erwin cafe | **Lakeview**	22
Z Everest | **Loop**	27
Fiddlehead | **Lincoln Sq**	19
Fiorentino's | **Lakeview**	22
1492 Tapas | **River N**	19
Froggy's | **Highwood**	23
NEW Gaetano's | **Forest Pk**	–
Geja's Cafe | **Lincoln Pk**	22
Gioco | **S Loop**	24
Green Dolphin St. | **Lincoln Pk**	19
Il Covo | **Bucktown**	20
Il Mulino | **Gold Coast**	24
Jacky's Bistro | **Evanston**	24
Z Japonais | **River N**	24
Jilly's Cafe | **Evanston**	24
Kansaku | **Evanston**	22
KiKi's Bistro | **Near North**	23
La Crêperie | **Lakeview**	21
Landmark | **Lincoln Pk**	21
La Sardine | **W Loop**	23
La Tache | **Andersonville**	22
Le Bouchon | **Bucktown**	24
Le Colonial | **Gold Coast**	23
Le P'tit Paris | **Streeterville**	24
Z Les Nomades | **Streeterville**	28
Z Le Titi/Paris | **Arlington Hts**	28
Le Vichyssois | **Lakemoor**	27
Luna Caprese | **Lincoln Pk**	26
NEW Macarena | **Naperville**	–
Marigold | **Uptown**	23
May St. Market | **W Loop**	23
Z mk | **Near North**	26
Z Mon Ami Gabi | **multi.**	22
NEW Mythos | **Lakeview**	–
Nacional 27 | **River N**	23
Naha | **River N**	25
NEW Natalino's | **W Town**	–
Z Niche | **Geneva**	28
Z NoMI | **Gold Coast**	26
Z Oceanique | **Evanston**	26
Pane Caldo | **Gold Coast**	24
NEW Paramount Rm. | **Near W**	–
Pops/Champagne | **River N**	16
NEW Powerhouse | **Loop**	23
NEW Prosecco | **River N**	25
Pump Rm. | **Gold Coast**	20
Quince | **Evanston**	24
Rhapsody | **Loop**	21
Z Riccardo Tratt. | **Lincoln Pk**	26
Z RL | **Gold Coast**	23
RoSal's Kitchen | **Little Italy**	22
Z Seasons | **Gold Coast**	27
Z NEW Sepia | **Mkt Dist**	22
Z 1776 | **Crystal Lake**	26
Z Shanghai Terr. | **River N**	25
Z Signature Rm. | **Streeterville**	19
sola | **Lakeview**	25
South Gate | **Lake Forest**	20
Z Spring | **Wicker Pk**	27
Stained Glass | **Evanston**	24
NEW TABLE 52 | **Gold Coast**	24
Z Tallgrass | **Lockport**	29
NEW Tallulah | **Lincoln Sq**	–
Tango Sur | **Lakeview**	25
Tasting Room | **Mkt Dist**	15
Tavern | **Libertyville**	25
Tizi Melloul | **River N**	21
Topo Gigio | **Old Town**	23
NEW Trattoria 225 | **Oak Pk**	19
Trattoria Trullo | **Lincoln Sq**	21
Z Tru | **Streeterville**	27
Z Va Pensiero | **Evanston**	26

Vermilion | **River N**	21
Vinci | **Lincoln Pk**	21
Vivo | **Mkt Dist**	21
Vong's | **River N**	22
Wave | **Streeterville**	20
Webster Wine | **Lincoln Pk**	20
Wildfish | **Arlington Hts**	24
Zocalo | **River N**	23

SENIOR APPEAL

Andies | **Ravenswood**	19
Ann Sather | **multi.**	20
Army & Lou's | **Far S Side**	24
Bacchanalia | **SW Side**	24
Bagel | **multi.**	19
Berghoff | **Loop**	19
Bogart's | **multi.**	20
Bruna's | **SW Side**	23
NEW Café 103 | **Far S Side**	–
Cape Cod Rm. | **Streeterville**	22
Carson's Ribs | **River N**	22
Cordis Bros. | **Lakeview**	20
Dave's Italian | **Evanston**	17
Davis St. Fish | **Evanston**	20
Del Rio | **Highwood**	22
Don Roth's | **Wheeling**	23
Edelweiss | **Norridge**	22
Francesco's | **Northbrook**	25
Gale St. Inn | **multi.**	21
Hackney's | **multi.**	18
La Cantina | **Loop**	21
La Gondola | **Lakeview**	23
Lawry's | **River N**	24
Le P'tit Paris | **Streeterville**	24
Le Vichyssois | **Lakemoor**	27
Lou Mitchell's | **Loop**	21
Margie's Candies | **Bucktown**	22
Miller's Pub | **Loop**	18
Mirabell | **NW Side**	21
Myron & Phil's | **Lincolnwood**	22
Next Door | **Northbrook**	22
Nick's Fishmkt. | **multi.**	24
Oak Tree | **Gold Coast**	16
Original Pancake/Walker Bros. | **multi.**	23
Pump Rm. | **Gold Coast**	20
Ritz Café | **Streeterville**	23
Z Rosebud | **Loop**	22
Russell's BBQ | **Elmwood Pk**	20
Russian Tea | **Loop**	22
Sabatino's | **NW Side**	22
South Gate | **Lake Forest**	20

Tre Kronor | **NW Side**	23
Tufano's Tap | **University Vill**	20
Village | **Loop**	20
White Fence | **Romeoville**	22

SINGLES SCENES

Adobo Grill | **Old Town**	21
Bar Louie | **multi.**	15
BOKA | **Lincoln Pk**	24
Café Iberico | **River N**	22
Z Carnivale | **Loop**	22
Clubhouse | **Oak Brook**	20
DeLaCosta | **Streeterville**	22
NEW Drawing Rm/Le Passage | **Gold Coast**	–
Z Gibsons | **multi.**	25
Landmark | **Lincoln Pk**	21
LuxBar | **Gold Coast**	19
Mike Ditka's | **Gold Coast**	22
N9ne | **Loop**	24
P.J. Clarke's | **Gold Coast**	16
Red Light | **Mkt Dist**	22
Rockit B&G | **River N**	19
Scoozi! | **River N**	20
Stanley's | **Lincoln Pk**	19
Sullivan's Steak | **multi.**	22
Z SushiSamba | **River N**	22
Tavern on Rush | **Gold Coast**	20
Wave | **Streeterville**	20

SLEEPERS

(Good to excellent food, but little known)

Army & Lou's | **Far S Side**	24
Azucar | **Logan Sq**	23
Bacchanalia | **SW Side**	24
BackStage | **River N**	22
Bistro Monet | **Glen Ellyn**	23
Bruna's | **SW Side**	23
Carlos & Carlos | **Arlington Hts**	23
Cité | **Streeterville**	24
NEW Cucina Paradiso | **Oak Pk**	25
David's Bistro | **Des Plaines**	23
Dining Rm./Kendall | **Near W**	24
NEW Distinctive Cork | **Naperville**	22
Edelweiss | **Norridge**	22
Fiorentino's | **Lakeview**	22
Harvest | **St. Charles**	24
Indie Cafe | **Edgewater**	23
Kansaku | **Evanston**	22
La Cucina/Donatella | **Rogers Pk**	24
La Fonda | **Andersonville**	24
La Vita | **Little Italy**	22

Lem's BBQ | **Far S Side**	25
Le P'tit Paris | **Streeterville**	24
Le Vichyssois | **Lakemoor**	27
Lucia | **Wicker Pk**	23
Luna Caprese | **Lincoln Pk**	26
Maiz | **Humboldt Pk**	23
Mizu Yakitori | **Old Town**	27
Montarra | **Algonquin**	25
Moon Palace | **Chinatown**	24
Mundial | **University Vill**	24
Nosh | **Geneva**	24
Over Easy | **Ravenswood**	25
Pasta Palazzo | **Lincoln Pk**	22
NEW Powerhouse | **Loop**	23
NEW Prosecco | **River N**	25
Ringo | **Lincoln Pk**	23
Sabor do Brasil | **Orland Pk**	22
Sam & Harry's | **Schaumburg**	27
Siam Café | **Uptown**	22
Sol de Mex. | **NW Side**	25
Swordfish | **Batavia**	26
NEW Takashi | **Bucktown**	29
Tango | **Naperville**	22
Tavern | **Libertyville**	25
Thai Classic | **Lakeview**	23
NEW Thalia Spice | **River W**	25
Vito & Nick's | **Far S Side**	23
Wakamono | **Lakeview**	23
Woo Lae Oak | **Rolling Meadows**	23
NEW ZED 451 | **multi.**	22

TEEN APPEAL

Ann Sather | **multi.**	20
Arco/Cuchilleros | **Lakeview**	18
Aurelio's Pizza | **multi.**	21
Bandera | **Streeterville**	22
Bella Bacino's | **multi.**	20
Big Bowl | **multi.**	19
Z Cheesecake Factory | **multi.**	19
Chicago Pizza | **Lincoln Pk**	22
Edwardo's Pizza | **multi.**	20
EJ's Place | **Skokie**	20
Flat Top Grill | **multi.**	19
Z Giordano's | **multi.**	21
Gold Coast | **multi.**	21
Grand Lux | **River N**	19
Hackney's | **multi.**	18
Hard Rock | **River N**	12
Harry Caray's | **River N**	20
Z Heaven on Seven | **multi.**	21
Z Hot Doug's | **NW Side**	27
Hot Tamales | **Highland Pk**	21

Ina's | **W Loop**	22
Joy Yee's | **multi.**	22
Kroll's | **S Loop**	14
Z Lou Malnati's | **multi.**	24
Lou Mitchell's | **Loop**	21
LuLu's | **Evanston**	19
L. Woods Lodge | **Lincolnwood**	20
Margie's Candies | **Bucktown**	22
Mity Nice Grill | **Streeterville**	17
My Pie Pizza | **Bucktown**	20
Nancy's Pizza | **multi.**	22
Nookies | **multi.**	19
Original Gino's | **multi.**	21
Original Pancake/Walker Bros. | **multi.**	23
Penny's Noodle | **multi.**	18
Pizzeria Uno/Due | **River N**	21
Pompei Bakery | **multi.**	20
Potbelly | **multi.**	19
R.J. Grunts | **Lincoln Pk**	19
Robinson's Ribs | **multi.**	22
Russell's BBQ | **Elmwood Pk**	20
Stanley's | **Lincoln Pk**	19
Stir Crazy | **Northbrook**	21
Superdawg | **NW Side**	22
Tempo | **Gold Coast**	20
Toast | **multi.**	22
Wiener's Circle | **Lincoln Pk**	20
Wishbone | **multi.**	21

TRENDY

Adobo Grill | **Old Town**	21
Agami | **Uptown**	25
Aigre Doux | **River N**	24
Z Alhambra | **Mkt Dist**	13
Z Alinea | **Lincoln Pk**	29
NEW A Mano | **River N**	21
Z Avec | **Loop**	27
Avenue M | **River W**	21
Bin 36/Wine | **multi.**	20
Bistro Campagne | **Lincoln Sq**	24
Z Blackbird | **W Loop**	27
NEW Bluebird, The | **Bucktown**	19
NEW Bluprint | **River N**	22
BOKA | **Lincoln Pk**	24
Bongo Room | **Wicker Pk**	24
Bonsoiree | **Logan Sq**	–
Café Iberico | **River N**	22
Z Carnivale | **Loop**	22
NEW Cellar | **Wheaton**	–
Chalkboard | **Lakeview**	22
NEW Chant | **Hyde Pk**	16

China Grill	**Loop**	20
Coobah	**Lakeview**	20
Crust	**Wicker Pk**	21
Cuatro	**S Loop**	22
Custom Hse.	**Printer's Row**	25
David Burke Prime	**River N**	24
de cero	**Mkt Dist**	22
DeLaCosta	**Streeterville**	22
NEW Distinctive Cork	**Naperville**	22
NEW Drawing Rm/Le Passage	**Gold Coast**	-
545 North	**Libertyville**	20
Flatwater	**River N**	15
FoLLia	**Mkt Dist**	23
Z Frontera Grill	**River N**	27
Z Gibsons	**Gold Coast**	25
Gioco	**S Loop**	24
Green Zebra	**W Town**	26
Hamburger Mary's	**Andersonville**	16
Hot Chocolate	**Bucktown**	24
Z Hot Doug's	**NW Side**	27
Z Japonais	**River N**	24
NEW La Madia	**River N**	22
Landmark	**Lincoln Pk**	21
NEW Libertine	**Lincoln Pk**	-
LuxBar	**Gold Coast**	19
NEW Macarena	**Naperville**	-
NEW Macello	**Mkt Dist**	19
NEW mado	**Bucktown**	-
Marché	**Mkt Dist**	22
Marigold	**Uptown**	23
May St. Market	**W Loop**	23
NEW Mercat	**S Loop**	-
Mia Francesca	**Lakeview**	25
Mirai Sushi	**Wicker Pk**	25
Miramar Bistro	**Highwood**	20
Z mk	**Near North**	26
Naha	**River N**	25
NEW Nia	**Mkt Dist**	-
Z Niche	**Geneva**	28
N9ne	**Loop**	24
Niu	**Streeterville**	21
Z NoMI	**Gold Coast**	26
NEW NXXT	**Humboldt Pk**	-
Olé Olé	**Andersonville**	20
one sixtyblue	**Mkt Dist**	25
Opera	**S Loop**	22
Osteria/Pizzeria Via Stato	**River N**	22
Z NEW Otom	**Mkt Dist**	23
NEW Paramount Rm.	**Near W**	-

NEW Park 52	**Hyde Pk**	-
Pops/Champagne	**River N**	16
Prairie Grass	**Northbrook**	21
NEW Prosecco	**River N**	25
Quartino	**River N**	21
Red Light	**Mkt Dist**	22
Republic	**River N**	19
Z Room 21	**S Loop**	21
NEW Rustik	**Logan Sq**	-
Schwa	**Wicker Pk**	-
Z NEW Sepia	**Mkt Dist**	22
NEW Shikago	**Loop**	20
NEW Shochu	**Lakeview**	-
sola	**Lakeview**	25
Spacca Napoli	**Ravenswood**	24
Z Spring	**Wicker Pk**	27
Sura	**Lakeview**	21
NEW Su-Ra	**Wicker Pk**	17
Z SushiSamba	**River N**	22
Z sushi wabi	**Mkt Dist**	26
Sushi X	**Lincoln Pk**	-
Tamarind	**S Loop**	21
NEW Thalia Spice	**River W**	25
Z Tramonto's	**Wheeling**	24
Tratt. D.O.C.	**Evanston**	19
NEW Union Pizzeria	**Evanston**	-
Vermilion	**River N**	21
Viet Bistro	**Rogers Pk**	19
Volo	**Roscoe Vill**	20
Wakamono	**Lakeview**	23
Zapatista	**S Loop**	18

VIEWS

Atwater's	**Geneva**	21
Z Avenues	**River N**	25
Cité	**Streeterville**	24
Courtright's	**Willow Spgs**	25
DeLaCosta	**Streeterville**	22
Drake Bros.'	**Streeterville**	20
Z Everest	**Loop**	27
Five O'Clock Steak	**Fox Riv. Grove**	23
Flatwater	**River N**	15
Fulton's	**River N**	19
Gage	**Loop**	21
Green Dolphin St.	**Lincoln Pk**	19
Z Lobby	**River N**	24
NEW Mercat	**S Loop**	-
Nick's Fishmkt.	**Loop**	24
Z NoMI	**Gold Coast**	26
Z North Pond	**Lincoln Pk**	25
OPA Estiatorio	**Vernon Hills**	19

SPECIAL FEATURES

vote at ZAGAT.com

219

Park Grill	**Loop**	19
Puck's at MCA	**Streeterville**	20
Ritz Café	**Streeterville**	23
Riva	**Streeterville**	18
☑ Rosebud	**Naperville**	22
☑ Seasons	**Gold Coast**	27
☑ Shanghai Terr.	**River N**	25
☑ Signature Rm.	**Streeterville**	19
NEW Sixteen	**River N**	-
Smith/Wollensky	**River N**	22
South Gate	**Lake Forest**	20
☑ Spiaggia	**Gold Coast**	27
Tasting Room	**Mkt Dist**	15
Tavern on Rush	**Gold Coast**	20
NEW ZED 451	**multi.**	22

VISITORS ON EXPENSE ACCOUNT

☑ Alinea	**Lincoln Pk**	29
☑ Arun's	**NW Side**	27
☑ Avenues	**River N**	25
Bice	**Streeterville**	22
☑ Blackbird	**W Loop**	27
Bob Chinn's	**Wheeling**	22
Brazzaz	**River N**	22
Caliterra	**Streeterville**	22
Cape Cod Rm.	**Streeterville**	22
☑ Capital Grille	**Streeterville**	25
☑ Carlos'	**Highland Pk**	28
☑ Catch 35	**Loop**	24
☑ Charlie Trotter's	**Lincoln Pk**	27
☑ Chicago Chop	**River N**	25
Coco Pazzo	**River N**	25
Courtright's	**Willow Spgs**	25
Crofton on Wells	**River N**	25
Custom Hse.	**Printer's Row**	25
David Burke Prime	**River N**	24
Entourage	**Schaumburg**	22
☑ Everest	**Loop**	27
Gene & Georgetti	**River N**	24
☑ Gibsons	**multi.**	25
Il Mulino	**Gold Coast**	24
☑ Joe's Seafood	**River N**	26
Keefer's	**River N**	24
Lawry's	**River N**	24
Le Colonial	**Gold Coast**	23
☑ Les Nomades	**Streeterville**	28
☑ Le Titi/Paris	**Arlington Hts**	28
☑ Lobby	**River N**	24
NEW Lockwood	**Loop**	-
☑ mk	**Near North**	26
☑ Morton's	**multi.**	26

Naha	**River N**	25
N9ne	**Loop**	24
☑ NoMI	**Gold Coast**	26
☑ North Pond	**Lincoln Pk**	25
☑ Oceanique	**Evanston**	26
one sixtyblue	**Mkt Dist**	25
Palm, The	**Loop**	23
Pump Rm.	**Gold Coast**	20
NEW Risqué Café	**Lakeview**	-
Ritz Café	**Streeterville**	23
☑ RL	**Gold Coast**	23
☑ Rosebud Prime/Steak	**Streeterville**	23
Roy's	**River N**	24
Ruth's Chris	**multi.**	25
Saloon Steak	**Streeterville**	22
☑ Seasons	**Gold Coast**	27
☑ Shanghai Terr.	**River N**	25
☑ Shaw's Crab	**multi.**	24
☑ Signature Rm.	**Streeterville**	19
NEW Sixteen	**River N**	-
Smith/Wollensky	**River N**	22
☑ Spiaggia	**Gold Coast**	27
☑ Spring	**Wicker Pk**	27
NEW Takashi	**Bucktown**	29
☑ Tallgrass	**Lockport**	29
☑ Topolobampo	**River N**	28
☑ Tramonto's	**Wheeling**	24
☑ Tru	**Streeterville**	27
Vivere	**Loop**	23
Wave	**Streeterville**	20
☑ Zealous	**River N**	24

WINE BARS

☑ Avec	**Loop**	27
Bin 36/Wine	**Wicker Pk**	20
Broadway Cellars	**Edgewater**	21
Cab's Wine Bar	**Glen Ellyn**	22
Café Bernard	**Lincoln Pk**	19
Cru Café	**Gold Coast**	17
Cyrano's Bistrot	**River N**	21
Dine	**W Loop**	15
Enoteca Piattini	**Lincoln Pk**	18
Fleming's	**Lincolnshire**	22
Flight	**Glenview**	19
Frasca Pizzeria	**Lakeview**	19
Pops/Champagne	**River N**	16
Quartino	**River N**	21
South Water	**Loop**	17
Stained Glass	**Evanston**	24
Tasting Room	**Mkt Dist**	15
Townhouse	**Loop**	16

subscribe to ZAGAT.com

Volo | **Roscoe Vill**	20
Webster Wine | **Lincoln Pk**	20

WINNING WINE LISTS

Aigre Doux | **River N**	24
Z Alinea | **Lincoln Pk**	29
NEW A Mano | **River N**	21
Z Arun's | **NW Side**	27
Z Avec | **Loop**	27
Z Avenues | **River N**	25
Bin 36/Wine | **multi.**	20
Bistrot Margot | **Old Town**	21
Z Blackbird | **W Loop**	27
NEW Bluebird, The | **Bucktown**	19
Blue Water | **River N**	23
BOKA | **Lincoln Pk**	24
Z NEW Brasserie Ruhlmann | **River N**	21
Cab's Wine Bar | **Glen Ellyn**	22
Campagnola | **Evanston**	23
Z Capital Grille | **Streeterville**	25
Z Carlos' | **Highland Pk**	28
Chalkboard | **Lakeview**	22
Z Charlie Trotter's | **Lincoln Pk**	27
Courtright's | **Willow Spgs**	25
Cru Café | **Gold Coast**	17
Custom Hse. | **Printer's Row**	25
Cyrano's Bistrot | **River N**	21
DeLaCosta | **Streeterville**	22
Del Rio | **Highwood**	22
NEW Distinctive Cork | **Naperville**	22
Z Everest | **Loop**	27
Fiddlehead | **Lincoln Sq**	19
Fleming's | **Lincolnshire**	22
Flight | **Glenview**	19
Z Fogo de Chão | **River N**	25
Fornetto Mei | **Gold Coast**	21
Z Gabriel's | **Highwood**	26
Geja's Cafe | **Lincoln Pk**	22
Green Zebra | **W Town**	26
Isabella's | **Geneva**	25
Z Japonais | **River N**	24
NEW La Madia | **River N**	22
La Sardine | **W Loop**	23
La Tache | **Andersonville**	22
Le P'tit Paris | **Streeterville**	24
Z Les Nomades | **Streeterville**	28
Z Le Titi/Paris | **Arlington Hts**	28
NEW Lockwood | **Loop**	-
May St. Market | **W Loop**	23
Z Michael | **Winnetka**	26
Miramar Bistro | **Highwood**	20
Z mk | **Near North**	26
Moto | **Mkt Dist**	25
Naha | **River N**	25
Z Niche | **Geneva**	28
Z NoMI | **Gold Coast**	26
Z North Pond | **Lincoln Pk**	25
Z Oceanique | **Evanston**	26
NEW Omaggio | **Evanston**	20
one sixtyblue | **Mkt Dist**	25
Osteria/Tramonto | **Wheeling**	21
Pane Caldo | **Gold Coast**	24
Pops/Champagne | **River N**	16
NEW Powerhouse | **Loop**	23
NEW Prosecco | **River N**	25
Quince | **Evanston**	24
Rhapsody | **Loop**	21
Ritz Café | **Streeterville**	23
Salpicón | **Old Town**	24
Sam & Harry's | **Schaumburg**	27
Z Seasons | **Gold Coast**	27
Z NEW Sepia | **Mkt Dist**	22
Z 1776 | **Crystal Lake**	26
NEW Shikago | **Loop**	20
Z Signature Rm. | **Streeterville**	19
NEW Sixteen | **River N**	-
Smith/Wollensky | **River N**	22
Z Spiaggia | **Gold Coast**	27
Z Spring | **Wicker Pk**	27
Stained Glass | **Evanston**	24
NEW Takashi | **Bucktown**	29
Z Tallgrass | **Lockport**	29
Tasting Room | **Mkt Dist**	15
Z Topolobampo | **River N**	28
Z Tramonto's | **Wheeling**	24
Tratt. No. 10 | **Loop**	23
Z Tru | **Streeterville**	27
NEW Union Pizzeria | **Evanston**	-
Z Va Pensiero | **Evanston**	26
Vivere | **Loop**	23
Volo | **Roscoe Vill**	20
Webster Wine | **Lincoln Pk**	20
West Town Tavern | **W Town**	25
Z Zealous | **River N**	24

WORTH A TRIP

Arlington Heights	
Z Le Titi/Paris	28
Evanston	
Campagnola	23
Jacky's Bistro	24
Z Va Pensiero	26

MILWAUKEE

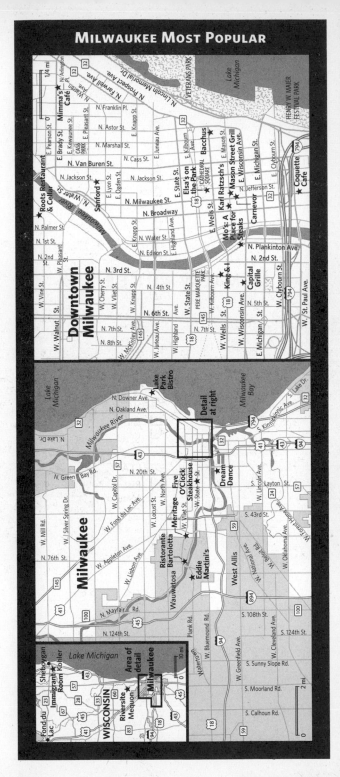

Top Food Ratings

MOST POPULAR

1. Sanford | *American*
2. Bacchus | *American*
3. Lake Park Bistro | *French*
4. Karl Ratzsch's | *German*
5. Eddie Martini's | *Steak*
6. Coquette Cafe | *French*
7. Mason St. Grill | *American*
8. Elsa's on the Park | *American*
9. Immigrant Room | *American*
10. Mo's | *Steak*
11. Roots | *Californian*
12. Carnevor | *Steak*
13. Dream Dance* | *American*
14. Meritage | *Eclectic*
15. Rist. Bartolotta | *Italian*
16. Riversite, The | *American*
17. Capital Grille | *Steak*
18. Mimma's Café | *Italian*
19. Five O'Clock Steak | *Steak*
20. King & I* | *Thai*

TOP FOOD

29 Sanford | *American*
28 Rist. Bartolotta | *Italian*
   Riversite, The | *American*
   Dream Dance | *American*
   Mangia* | *Italian*

26 Bacchus | *American*
   Lake Park Bistro | *French*
   Roots | *Californian*
   Osteria del Mondo | *Italian*
25 Capital Grille | *Steak*

BY CUISINE

AMERICAN (NEW)
29 Sanford
28 Dream Dance
26 Bacchus

AMERICAN (TRAD.)
28 Riversite, The
25 Mason St. Grill
23 Original Pancake

ASIAN (MISC.)
25 King & I
   Singha Thai
24 Nanakusa

ECLECTIC
24 Meritage
21 Knick
20 Eagan's

FRENCH
26 Lake Park Bistro
24 Coquette Cafe
21 Elliot's Bistro

ITALIAN
28 Rist. Bartolotta
   Mangia
26 Osteria del Mondo

JAPANESE
24 Nanakusa
21 Sake Tumi
20 Benihana

STEAKHOUSES
25 Capital Grille
   Eddie Martini's
24 Carnevor

BY LOCATION

DOWNTOWN
28 Dream Dance
26 Bacchus
   Osteria del Mondo

EAST SIDE
29 Sanford
26 Lake Park Bistro
24 Mimma's Café

* Indicates a tie with restaurant above

NORTH SHORE

23 River Lane Inn
19 North Shore Bistro
18 Hama

OUTLYING AREAS

28 Rist. Bartolotta
Riversite, The
Mangia

THIRD WARD

24 Nanakusa
Coquette Cafe

WEST SIDE

25 Eddie Martini's
24 Meritage
20 Edwardo's Pizza

TOP DECOR

26 Sanford
Bacchus
Kil@wat
Lake Park Bistro
25 Roots

24 Dream Dance
Coast
Capital Grille
23 Karl Ratzsch's
Nanakusa

TOP SERVICE

28 Sanford
27 Dream Dance
Riversite, The
Rist. Bartolotta
26 Eddie Martini's

Mangia
25 Bacchus
Lake Park Bistro
24 Capital Grille
Mimma's Café

BEST BUYS

In order of Bang for the Buck rating.

1. Potbelly Sandwich
2. Original Pancake
3. King & I
4. Elsa's on Park
5. Edwardo's Pizza

6. Cubanitas
7. Crawdaddy's
8. Rock Bottom
9. Three Brothers
10. Cheesecake Factory

MILWAUKEE
RESTAURANT
DIRECTORY

☑ Bacchus *American*

26 | 26 | 25 | $62

Downtown | Cudahy Tower | 925 E. Wells St. (Prospect Ave.) |
414-765-1166 | www.bacchusmke.com

This "elegant" "NY-style" Downtown New American (younger
sister to Lake Park Bistro and Ristorante Bartolotta) is the "ultimate" for "business" or a "special dress-up date" thanks to its
"indulgent", "exquisitely prepared" meals by "culinary master"
Adam Siegel; the "contemporary" decor (square lamp shades,
big mirrors) is "inviting" enough to "make you want to hang out
all night", especially with such "great lake [Michigan] views"
from the glassed-in conservatory.

Bayou *Cajun/Creole*

▽ 18 | 22 | 17 | $31

East Side | 2060 N. Humboldt Blvd. (Commerce Ave.) | 414-431-1511 |
www.bayoumilwaukee.com

For the feel of "New Orleans in the cold Midwest", hit up this East
Side Cajun-Creole canteen, a "fun place" with "beautiful views" of
the Milwaukee River (and a patio too); the Big Easy menu of jamba-
laya, blackened red fish and banana bread pudding hits its stride at
the "most amazing" brunch, although mates in Mardi Gras mode
mark the provisions "far from authentic."

Benihana *Japanese/Steak*

20 | 18 | 22 | $35

Downtown | 850 N. Plankinton Ave. (2nd St.) | 414-270-0890 |
www.benihana.com

See review in Chicago Directory.

Bosley on Brady ☒ *Seafood/Steak*

▽ 25 | 25 | 26 | $39

East Side | 815 E. Brady St. (Cass St.) | 414-727-7975 |
www.bosleyonbrady.com

"A place Jimmy Buffett could well envision", this "Key West"-esque
seafooder and steakhouse is a "wonderful" East Side "gathering"
spot where the "owners and staff make you feel as if you're dining in
their home"; the combo of "always-terrific" food (the "best
chocolate-dipped Key lime pie in the world!"), "colorful" decor and
possibly the "best bar manager in town" translates into a
"devoted regular clientele."

Capital Grille, The *Steak*

25 | 24 | 24 | $61

Downtown | 310 W. Wisconsin Ave. (N. 4th St.) | 414-223-0600 |
www.thecapitalgrille.com

See review in Chicago Directory.

Carnevor ☒ *Steak*

24 | 22 | 23 | $65

Downtown | 724 N. Milwaukee St. (Mason St.) | 414-223-2200 |
www.carnevor.com

"Boardroom execs and athletes" alike hie to this "very urbane"
Downtown steakhouse – a "breath of fresh air in a fine dining-
challenged town" – and tout its "well-designed" menu of "great
steaks" and other "pricey" carnivore fare; between the "huge portions" of "hip, fun food" and its "nightclub atmosphere", most don't
seem to mind if the "dark" environs can be "cramped."

	FOOD	DECOR	SERVICE	COST

Cempazuchi Ⓜ Mexican
21 18 20 $29

East Side | 1205 E. Brady St. (Franklin Pl.) | 414-291-5233 |
www.cempazuchi.com

Lovers of "the freshest", "top-notch" margaritas (try the variety of
the day) are in paradise at this "wonderful", "*muy auténtico*" East
Side Mexican where "family recipes" render "not-typical" dishes
"bursting with complex flavors" – "including several regional
moles", the "best fish tacos in town" and a shrimp sandwich that's
"so good [some] would consider it as a deathbed meal"; P.S. the
"festive" decor is nearly "as good as the food."

Cheesecake Factory American
19 19 18 $27

Glendale | Bayshore Mall | 5799 N. Bayshore Dr. (Port Washington Rd.) |
414-906-8550

Wauwatosa | 2350 N. Mayfair Rd. (North Ave.) | 414-257-2300
www.thecheesecakefactory.com
See review in Chicago Directory.

Coast American
18 24 19 $42

Downtown | O'Donnell Park Complex | 931 E. Wisconsin Ave. (Astor St.) |
414-727-5555 | www.coastrestaurant.com

An "amazing" view of Santiago Calatrava's addition to the
Milwaukee Art Museum, plus a "killer patio" anchor this "ideally located" Downtown New American that's run by the catering Zilli
family; while kudos go to the popovers, "competent seafood" and
prix fixe Sunday brunch, some mutineers cite "mediocre" food that
"hasn't lived up" to the "room with a view."

Coquette Cafe Ⓢ French
24 22 24 $37

Third Ward | 316 N. Milwaukee St. (St. Paul Ave.) | 414-291-2655 |
www.coquettecafe.com

This "consistent", "authentic" French bistro, the Third Ward "little
sister" of Sanford, "could be in Paris", "packing 'em in" for both "traditional items" and "unusual international specials"; with a "sophisticated" ambiance and "fun bar", it's "great for a date or business
lunch"; N.B. adjacent bakery Harlequin is Coquette's kin.

Crawdaddy's Ⓢ Ⓜ Cajun/Creole
22 16 21 $27

Southwest Side | 6414 W. Greenfield Ave. (National Ave.) | 414-778-2228 |
www.crawdaddysrestaurant.com

"Gotta get me some crawtails!" cry 'daddy devotees won over by
this "small", "crowded" Southwest Side Cajun-Creole's "menu as
big as the phone book", chock-full of "inexpensive" "seafood as
fresh as you can get it in the Midwest"; though some wizards of
roux maintain the fare is a "pale version of real Louisiana cooking", fans who can't get enough say "come early and have a drink
at the bar."

Cubanitas Ⓢ Cuban
21 16 19 $24

Downtown | 728 N. Milwaukee St. (bet. Mason St. & Wisconsin Ave.) |
414-225-1760 | www.cubanitas.us

"You could easily miss" this "casual" Downtown Cuban "if you
weren't looking for it" say surveyors who've sussed out its "awe-

some" eats and "top-notch" mojitos, making it a "real treat" for a "quick pre-theater bite" – though "packed" crowds call for getting there early; service ranges from "good" to "ok", and though the decor is "extremely basic", the sidewalk tables facing fashionable Milwaukee Street are a sweet respite in summer.

☑ Dream Dance ☒Ⓜ *American* — 28 | 24 | 27 | $62

Downtown | Potawatomi Bingo Casino | 1721 W. Canal St. (16th St.) | 414-847-7883 | www.paysbig.com

The "food is absolutely first-rate" (among the "best meals in the city") and so is the service at this Downtown "oasis" nestled inside the Potawatomi Bingo Casino, whose Red Deer Ranch supplies the venison for Jason Gorman's New American menu; foxtrotters fawn over the "sleek, hardwood interior" ("thanks for that champagne trolley!"), but admit they "would go more often" if they didn't have to pass through a "smoky" gambling arena to realize their "fondest culinary dreams."

Eagan's *Eclectic* — 20 | 19 | 21 | $37

Downtown | 1030 N. Water St. (State St.) | 414-271-6900 | www.eagansonwater.com

A "winner all the way", this "cosmopolitan" "standby" features "interesting items" (such as the "fantastic" lobster BLT) on its seafood-focused Eclectic menu and occupies a "wonderfully convenient" Downtown location that's close to concert and theater venues, meaning it's "easy to drop by for a [pre- or post-show] snack"; it's also a "great people-watching place", but unimpressed diners still size it up as "good – but nothing special."

Eddie Martini's *Steak* — 25 | 22 | 26 | $55

West Side | 8612 W. Watertown Plank Rd. (86th St.) | 414-771-6680 | www.eddiemartinis.com

Ravenous Rat Packers "step back" in time at this "quintessential '40s steakhouse", a "dependable" West Side "classic" where it's "a treat to come and eat" the "Midwest food" (filet mignon, NY strip and "also excellent seafood"); an "attentive staff" and "elegant decor" help make it "well worth the effort" to get a reservation, plus the "excellent" martinis "will make your nose numb."

Edwardo's Natural Pizza *Pizza* — 20 | 11 | 15 | $18

West Side | 10845 W. Bluemound Rd. (Hwy. 100) | 414-771-7770 | www.edwardos.com

See review in Chicago Directory.

Elliot's Bistro Ⓜ *French* — 21 | 16 | 21 | $35

East Side | 2321 N. Murray Ave. (North Ave.) | 414-273-1488 | www.elliotsbistro.com

"For the French bistro experience in Milwaukee", this "delightful" East Side "favorite" is "a definite must-do" "complete with an authentic [Gallic] chef", Pierre Briere, whose "traditional" cooking – from cassoulet to boeuf bourguignon – "rivals that of many Paris bistros"; "great for a dinner date or meeting old friends", it's also a "perfect spot for weekend brunch."

	FOOD	DECOR	SERVICE	COST

Elm Grove Inn, The 🗷 *American/Eclectic* — | — | — | M

Elm Grove | 13275 Watertown Plank Rd. (Elm Grove Rd.) |
262-782-7090 | www.elmgroveinn.com

Offering a "good selection of [New] American favorites", this "quiet
and inviting" Elm Grove Eclectic is "great for a special evening out"
in a "historic location" – its building dates to 1855 and has a "cozy,
romantic" atmosphere; some young folk find it all "rather staid", but
that's a boon for seniors ("my grandmother loved it"), who enjoy
taking advantage of the early-bird menu – half-off the second entree
from 4–5:30 PM.

Elsa's on the Park ◗ *American* 22 | 23 | 19 | $25

Downtown | 833 N. Jefferson St. (Wells St.) | 414-765-0615 |
www.elsas.com

"Beautiful people" flock to this "funky" 29-year-old Downtown
American for "fancy", "man-sized" burgers and prodigious pork
sandwiches; the "stylish" decor features rotating art by owner Karl
Kopp, of Kopp's Custard fame, and a "diverse", "always-crowded"
vibe makes it a prime "place to see or be seen over cocktails."

Envoy *American* — | — | — | M

Downtown | Ambassador Hotel | 2308 W. Wisconsin Ave. (bet. N. 23rd &
24th Sts.) | 414-345-5015 | www.envoymilwaukee.com

A "cool-looking" 120-room hotel restored to its 1927 art deco begin-
nings houses this Downtown New American whose "knockout" setting
makes it a "winner off the beaten path" (located west of Marquette
University); "good" specialties like filet of beef with porcini crust and
Thai curried rack of lamb please patrons, and seating is also available
in the adjacent lounge/bar, where there's live jazz on weekends.

Five O'Clock Steakhouse 🗷Ⓜ *Steak* 23 | 18 | 21 | $50

Central City | 2416 W. State St. (24th St.) | 414-342-3553 |
www.fiveoclocksteakhouse.com

"You can't beat" the "B-I-G steaks" that are "worth every penny" at
this "throwback to the great steakhouses of the '50s" (it was originally called "Coerper's 5 O'Clock Club"); at the "kitschy", "no-glitz"
Downtown Milwaukee mother ship, diners place their orders at the
bar before being seated, a "process" that adds to the "charm and experience"; as for the newer Fox River Grove outpost, serious stom-
achs are satisfied by the "tasty", "ample portions."

🆕 Fleming's Prime 22 | 22 | 22 | $57
Steakhouse & Wine Bar *Steak*

Brookfield | Brookfield Square Mall | 15665 W. Bluemound Rd.
(Moorland Rd.) | 262-782-9463 | www.flemingssteakhouse.com
See review in Chicago Directory.

Gilbert's *American* — | — | — | M

Lake Geneva | 327 Wrigley Dr. (Center St.) | 262-248-6680 |
www.gilbertsrestaurant.com

Fine foodies fancy this New American for its largely organic
menu that's rounded out by ripe releases fresh from its garden;

the gastronomy ranges from short ribs to grilled Hawaiian red snapper, all served in an 1885 Lake Geneva Queen Anne that's been restored in the style of an island plantation manor (albeit one with 13 fireplaces); N.B. there's a six-course tasting menu, and jackets are suggested.

Golden Mast Inn ☒ *American/German* ▽ 21 | 22 | 21 | $31

Okauchee | W349 N5293 Lacy's Ln. (Lake Dr.) | 262-567-7047 | www.weissgerbers.com/goldenmast

A waterfront setting with a "wonderful view" distinguishes this "beautiful" (if "kitschy") Traditional American that's outfitted like a castle overlooking Okauchee Lake; "sit by the fireplace in winter" while supping on the the Weissgerber family's "heavy", "consistently good" German productions (Wiener schnitzel, sauerbraten, beef Rouladen), or in warmer weather, amble out to the alfresco bar, open on weekend nights.

Hama ☒ *Asian Fusion/Japanese* 18 | 13 | 16 | $36

North Shore | 333 W. Brown Deer Rd. (Port Washington Rd.) | 414-352-5051

Sushi supporters are split on this North Shore hybrid of "Japanese–West Coast–style" Asian fusion "with a hint of Mexico": fans fawn over the "family favorite" for its "not-to-be-missed" specialties (and "original" desserts), while detractors say this 11-year-old is "not what it used to be", including the decor: "could use some plastic surgery."

Heaven City ☒☒ *American* - | - | - | M

Mukwonago | S91 W27850 National Ave./Hwy. ES (Edgewood Ave.) | 262-363-5191 | www.heavencity.com

A "restored old hotel with quite a history" (it was reputedly a hangout for mobster Al Capone) houses this Mukwonago New American, which originally opened in 1989 (under new ownership since 2005); with seating scattered in multiple wood-drenched rooms, it's "still one of the prettiest places to eat", though gatherers at the gates are divided on whether its nourishment satisfies or has "slipped."

NEW Hinterland Erie Street - | - | - | E
Gastropub ☒ *American*

Third Ward | 222 E. Erie St., Ste. 100 (Water St.) | 414-727-9300 | www.hinterlandbeer.com

The Third Ward's "new 'in' place" is this freshman New American offering "exquisite" if "pricey" fare from an "outstanding", ever-changing menu that spotlights fish (from big-eye tuna to Alaskan halibut) and game; its quiet, modern-meets-Montana-chic dining room contrasts with the bustle of the backside lounge, which features its own little lineup of noshables like elk meatloaf and Kobe sliders.

Il Mito Enoteca ☒ *Italian* - | - | - | M

Wauwatosa | 6913 W. North Ave. (N. 69th St.) | 414-443-1414 | www.ilmito.com

This "cozy", "moderately priced" Wauwatosa Italian "find" "always impresses with wonderful flavors" from chef-owner Michael Feker's "thoughtful", "rustic" pizza-to-osso buco menu; the "relaxing" (if sometimes "noisy") "wine-cellar" setting boasts wood and exposed beams, and there's an adjacent cooking school as well.

Immigrant Room & Winery, The 🅂🅼 *American*

24 | 21 | 23 | $65

Kohler | American Club | 419 Highland Dr. (School St.) | 920-457-8888 | www.destinationkohler.com

"New York is no match" for this "fabulous find" in Kohler's "chic" American Club with approriately American "inventive" eats, an "extensive wine list" and possibly the "best domestic cheese selection anywhere"; yes, the tabs can be "terribly expensive", but admirers insist it's a "real treat" and "worth every penny"; N.B. jackets are required in the dining room, but not at the attached wine bar.

Jackson Grill 🅂🅼 *Steak*

∇ 26 | 15 | 26 | $48

South Side | 3736 W. Mitchell St. (38th St.) | 414-384-7384

An "unimpressive exterior" "belies the wonders inside" this "tiny" South Side Traditional American meting out "big, big portions" of "unbelievable steaks" (rib-eye, flat iron) and "outstanding" ribs and seafood; the "unpretentious" interior evokes "'50s supper-club" chic with a "friendly" "neighborhood" vibe, prompting locals to label it the city's "best-kept secret."

Jake's Fine Dining 🅂 *Steak*

∇ 25 | 20 | 25 | $36

Brookfield | 21445 Gumina Rd. (Capital Dr.) | 262-781-7995 | www.jakes-restaurant.com

"Old school" meets "new school" at this 48-year-old Brookfield meatery with a "classic steak and comfort-food menu" (the tenderloin with onion rings is "a real treat") and also "innovative" "selections for more modern tastes"; "warm and cozy", its "relaxed" space is blessed with a "big hearth fireplace" and "attentive" service.

🆉 Karl Ratzsch's 🅂 *German*

24 | 23 | 22 | $40

Downtown | 320 E. Mason St. (bet. B'way & Milwaukee St.) | 414-276-2720 | www.karlratzsch.com

This Downtown Teutonic "landmark" (since 1904) is "a little bit of German heaven", wooing with "big portions" of "hearty", "authentic" Wiener schnitzel and sauerbraten that make it a "must-do Milwaukee experience"; the less enthused call its "festive" "Black Forest" decor "dated" and the tabs "pricey", yet insiders insist it remains an "old standard that holds its own."

🆉 Kil@wat Restaurant *American*

21 | 26 | 20 | $47

Downtown | Intercontinental Milwaukee Hotel | 139 E. Kilbourn Ave. (N. Water St.) | 414-291-4793 | www.kilawatcuisine.com

The "hip" "retro '70s flashback decor" of the Intercontinental Milwaukee Hotel's New American (part of a 2006 makeover) "has sexy written all over it", so no wonder it's the Downtown "place to eat before Milwaukee theater"; the high-voltage interior is home to a "fun", "inventive" and "expensive" menu, but some say it's "trying a bit too hard" and gets shorted out by "disorganized" service.

	FOOD	DECOR	SERVICE	COST

King & I, The *Thai*
| | 25 | 18 | 18 | $22 |

Downtown | 830 N. Old World Third St. (bet. Kilbourn Ave. & Wells St.) | 414-276-4181 | www.kingandirestaurant.com

When it comes to Bangkok bites, you "cannot go wrong" at this casual Downtown Thai where the riches range from a "heavenly" weekday lunch buffet to a "phenomenal satay presentation" and "great" curries; it's "fun for groups, especially if you go easy on the spices" and don't mind service that can be a bit "slow."

Knick, The ● *Eclectic*
| | 21 | 19 | 20 | $31 |

Downtown | Knickerbocker Hotel | 1030 E. Juneau Ave. (Astor St.) | 414-272-0011 | www.theknickrestaurant.com

"There's something for everyone" (from some of the "best appetizers" around to "great burgers" and "entrees that are good as well") on the "huge menu" at this "consistent" Downtown Eclectic that's "the place to be if you want to be seen"; it's "wonderful for Sunday brunch or a hearty lunch", and a "happy-hour favorite" too, with a "lively atmosphere" that attracts a "young and hip crowd" – no wonder the "terrace is a people-watcher's dream."

⊠ Lake Park Bistro *French*
| | 26 | 26 | 25 | $54 |

East Side | Lake Park Pavilion | 3133 E. Newberry Blvd. (N. Lake Dr.) | 414-962-6300 | www.lakeparkbistro.com

The Lake Michigan "view doesn't get any better" – or the setting more "romantic" – than at this "lovely" East Side French bistro located in the pavilion in Frederick Law Olmsted–designed Lake Park; its "outstanding" cuisine represents the "closest thing to being in France in Milwaukee", its wine list is a "revelation" with "reasonable" prices and the service is "impeccable" – just know that with the "wow!" factor comes crowds, so the "decibel level" of the dining room is "always up there."

Maggiano's Little Italy *Italian*
| | 21 | 19 | 20 | $32 |

Wauwatosa | Mayfair Mall | 2500 N. Mayfair Rd. (North Ave.) | 414-978-1000 | www.maggianos.com
See review in Chicago Directory.

Mangia *Italian*
| | 28 | 23 | 26 | $40 |

Kenosha | 5717 Sheridan Rd. (bet. 57th & 58th Sts.) | 262-652-4285
Kenosha's "best-kept secret" may be this affordable Italian that's "worth the drive from northern Illinois or Chicago" thanks to its "extraordinary" dishes ("to-die-for" white pizza, carpaccio and "wonderful, hearty" spaghetti with meat sauce) whose "aromas" "hit you immediately" upon entering; its "softly lit" interior "feels like a warm cave", and there's a "surprisingly beautiful" outdoor patio in summer.

Mason Street Grill *American*
| | 25 | 22 | 24 | $56 |

Downtown | Pfister Hotel | 425 E. Mason St. (bet. N. Jefferson & N. Milwaukee Sts.) | 414-298-3131 | www.masonstreetgrill.com
"There's something for everyone" – from "excellent" dry-aged steaks to sandwiches – at the "venerable" Pfister Hotel's "solid" Traditional American eatery that's "easy on the stomach and hard

on the wallet"; inquisitive gourmands go for the bar seating facing its open kitchen, where "you can strike up a friendly conversation with the staff", while leisurely sorts hang in the "enjoyable" lounge, where there's live music nightly.

NEW Maxie's Southern Comfort *Creole*

| – | – | – | I |

West Side | 6732 W. Fairview Ave. (68th St.) | 414-292-3969 | www.maxies.com

A "broad range" of "fantastic" Creole concoctions are the focus of this "relaxing", casual West Side Southerner, the sibling of a popular spot in Ithaca, NY; the "nicely revamped", two-level former grocery store digs, designed to look like a Southern brothel, "make one think of heading to the bayou."

NEW Meritage Ⓜ *Eclectic*

| 24 | 17 | 20 | $42 |

West Side | 5921 W. Vliet St. (60th St.) | 414-479-0620 | www.meritage.us

"There's a reason why it's packed" proclaim pleased patrons of this "charming" Eclectic, a "welcome addition" to the West Side thanks to chef-owner Jan Kelly (of the now-defunct Barossa) and her "unique", "homey" menu that's swayed by the seasons; with a "warm" atmosphere and midrange prices, most voters "can't wait to go back."

Milwaukee Chophouse Ⓩ *Steak*

| 22 | 22 | 21 | $55 |

Downtown | Hilton Milwaukee City Ctr. | 633 N. Fifth St. (bet. Michigan St. & Wisconsin Ave.) | 414-226-2467 | www.milwaukeechophouse.com

"Bring your grandparents, grandchildren" and "everyone" in-between to this "top-notch" steakhouse in Downtown's Hilton Milwaukee City Center, where the "excellent" steak-and-seafood fare is "cooked to perfection and served piping hot" by an "accommodating staff" in a "supper club-ish atmosphere"; some complain that it's "inconsistent" and "a bit pricey for what you get", but most maintain it's "well worth" the expense and an "overall good place to go for a nice night out."

Mimma's Café *Italian*

| 24 | 21 | 24 | $37 |

East Side | 1307 E. Brady St. (Arlington Pl.) | 414-271-7337 | www.mimmas.com

This "lovely" longtime "staple" of the East Side's "diverse" Brady Street serves "wonderful" "old-fashioned" Italian cuisine amid decor that some call "beautiful" and others rate "hopelessly dated"; its service is enhanced by the presence of "eccentric" chef-owner Mimma Megna, who "adds to the good time"

Mo's: A Place for Steaks Ⓩ *Steak*

| 21 | 19 | 21 | $59 |

Downtown | 720 N. Plankinton Ave. (Wisconsin Ave.) | 414-272-0720 | www.mosrestaurants.com

"Meat, meat and more meat" is the mantra at this "big-city" Downtown steakhouse that's also known for "classy" decor, "stiff cocktails" and "great people-watching", especially in the "large" "see-and-be-seen" bar; however, service can range from "fantastic" to "surly", and surveyors are split on whether the "high prices" are "worth it" or "for expense accounts only."

	FOOD	DECOR	SERVICE	COST

Mr. B's: At Bartolotta Steakhouse *Steak*
| 24 | 18 | 22 | $55 |

Brookfield | 17700 W. Capitol Dr. (Calhoun Rd.) | 262-790-7005 |
www.mrbssteakhouse.com

"Impressed" carnivores give the "expensive" beef an "A+" at this
"charming" steakhouse sibling in the Bartolotta Restaurant Group;
located in Brookfield's Stonewood Village shopping enclave, its mul-
tiroom interior evokes a rustic Italian bistro, complete with check-
ered tablecloths and conditions so "cramped", surveyors suggest "if
they packed any more tables in here, it would explode."

Nanakusa Ⓜ *Japanese*
| 24 | 23 | 22 | $40 |

Third Ward | 408 E. Chicago St. (Milwaukee St.) | 414-223-3200

"Traditional Japanese" "meets urban chic" at this "beautiful,
minimalist" Third Ward source for "top-quality sushi" fashioned
from "delicious" "fresh" fish, as well as "lovely cooked dishes",
all accompanied by "extensive wine and saki offerings"; lauders
"love" the semi-"private" 16-seat tatami room that contributes
to the "Zen atmosphere", but some note that the experience can
be "very expensive."

North Shore Bistro *American*
| 19 | 18 | 18 | $38 |

North Shore | River Point Vill. | 8649 N. Port Washington Rd.
(Brown Deer Rd.) | 414-351-6100 | www.northshorebistro.com

This North Shore "standby" coddles with "consistent" New
American fare that's "good" (if "not spectacular by gourmet standards") and features some "unusual combinations" (lobster
Reuben, Zinfandel-braised short ribs); folks who think the open,
upscale-casual dining room "feels too large" suggest snatching a
seat in the "urban patio jungle."

North Star American Bistro *American*
| 22 | 18 | 23 | $35 |

Brookfield | 19115 W. Capitol Dr. (Brookfield Rd.) | 262-754-1515
Shorewood | 4515 N. Oakland Ave. (Kensington Blvd.) |
414-964-4663
www.northstarbistro.com

"Good food at good prices" describes these Brookfield and Shorewood
twins, "romantic" bistros offering an "interesting" array of "well-
prepared" Traditional American fare in a "pleasant", "sparse" setting; the Brookfield branch is "great" before a show at the Sharon
Lynne Wilson Center, and also features live bands every Wednesday.

Original Pancake House, The *American*
| 23 | 13 | 18 | $14 |

East Side | 2621 N. Downer Ave. (E. Belleview Pl.) | 414-431-5055
Brookfield | 16460 W. Bluemound Rd. (Dechant Rd.) |
262-797-0800
www.originalpancakehouse.com
See review in Chicago Directory.

Osteria del Mondo Ⓢ *Italian*
| 26 | 22 | 23 | $51 |

Downtown | 1028 E. Juneau Ave. (Astor St.) | 414-291-3770 |
www.osteria.com

"Remaining solidly [near] the top of the ladder in Milwaukee", this
Downtown Italian delivers "outstanding meals" courtesy of chef/

co-owner Marc Bianchini, who "never ceases to amaze" with "elegant fare" that's "inventive" "without being strange"; combined with "wonderful service" and a "comfortable setting" (including "a great patio"), it amounts to a "fine-dining" experience that's "not to be missed"; N.B. a separate cigar lounge and valet parking are available.

Palms Bistro & Bar 🗷Ⓜ *American* ∇ 19 | 19 | 14 | $30

Third Ward | 221 N. Broadway (bet. Buffalo & Chicago Sts.) | 414 298 3000 | www.palmsbistrobar.com
Prime for "pre-theater" and post-shopping, this "extremely casual" canteen in the historic Third Ward offers a "nice variety" of "reasonably priced" New American vittles that range from Cobb salad to seared sea bass; its service doesn't win raves, and while some laud the "funky" setting, less-tropical sorts say the decor "gets tiresome."

P.F. Chang's China Bistro *Chinese* 21 | 20 | 19 | $30

Wauwatosa | Mayfair Mall | 2500 N. Mayfair Rd. (North Ave.) | 414-607-1029 | www.pfchangs.com
See review in Chicago Directory.

Polonez Ⓜ *Polish* – | – | – | I

South Side | 4016 S. Packard Ave. (Tesch St.) | 414-482-0080 | www.foodspot.com/polonez
"Rustic pleasures" abound at this South Sider from George and Aleksandra Burzynski that holds onto its standing as Milwaukee's "most authentic Polish restaurant", in part thanks to the traditional Friday night fish fry (lake perch, of course) that appeals to the pierogi-and-potato-pancake set; dessert wines and beer imported from the old country keep things lively in the two muraled dining rooms.

Potbelly Sandwich Works *Sandwiches* 19 | 15 | 18 | $9

Downtown | 135 W. Wisconsin Ave. (Plankinton Ave.) | 414-226-0014
Brookfield | 17800 W. Bluemound Rd. (bet. Brookfield & Calhoun Rds.) | 262-796-9845
www.potbelly.com
See review in Chicago Directory.

⧉ Ristorante Bartolotta *Italian* 28 | 23 | 27 | $41

Wauwatosa | 7616 W. State St. (Harwood Ave.) | 414-771-7910 | www.bartolottaristorante.com
Dining at this "lovely" Wauwatosa "original" – the oldest sibling in the Joe Bartolotta food family and the city's top-rated Italian – is "like eating in a quaint trattoria in Italy", complete with "superb" specialties like pappardelle that "makes the world melt away"; the "loud and lively" space inside a "cozy" 100-year-old stone building is "always packed", and the "thoughtful wine list" is poured by a "knowledgeable staff."

River Lane Inn 🗷 *Seafood* 23 | 19 | 24 | $42

North Shore | 4313 W. River Ln. (Brown Deer Rd.) | 414-354-1995
"Consistently good" "fresh" seafood makes this "casual" midpriced "favorite" (sibling to Mequon's Riversite) "well worth the drive to the North Shore", where it's perched in a "comfortable" turn-of-the-

century building; its "attentive" service rises above the tide, though a few critics float the idea that the experience "hasn't been the same" since they changed chefs.

ⓩ Riversite, The ⓔ *American*   28 | 23 | 27 | $56

Mequon | 11120 N. Cedarburg Rd. (Mequon Rd.) | 262-242-6050

"Beautifully situated along the Milwaukee River", "off the beaten path" in Mequon, this sister of the River Lane Inn excels with "excellent", "always-on-the-mark" Traditional American "fine dining" (game, rack of lamb, steaks and seafood) courtesy of longtime chef Tom Peschong; owner Jim Marks is "always there" overseeing the "warm, welcoming" service, and there's an "excellent" wine list.

Rock Bottom Brewery *American*   16 | 17 | 17 | $23

Downtown | 740 N. Plankinton Ave. (bet. Wells St. & Wisconsin Ave.) | 414-276-3030 | www.rockbottom.com

For some, "the beers are the reason to stop by" this "crowded, noisy", "comfortable" Downtown Traditional American, but in addition to the "great microbrews" ("amusing flights" and "seasonal" choices) there's "a nice variety" of "comfort food"; still, critics wonder "why go for chain conformity in a town with great watering holes?", contending the "run-of-the-mill" "pub fare" and service are "unremarkable."

Roots Restaurant & Cellar *Californian*   26 | 25 | 20 | $43

Brewers Hill | 1818 N. Hubbard St. (Vine St.) | 414-374-8480 | www.rootsmilwaukee.com

This "high-class, high-flavor" Brewers Hill beacon literally "brings the farm to the city" – co-owner Joe Schmidt cultivates an organic farm north of Milwaukee – with an "incredible", "ever-changing" Californian menu featuring "fresh", "locally produced" ingredients; the city views are especially "stunning" when it's "warm enough to sit outside" on the terrace, and despite tsk-tsks of "too much 'tude" from the staff, the food "leaves you wanting to return for more"; N.B. the lower-level Cellar offers a more casual menu.

Saffron Indian Bistro Ⓜ *Indian*   – | – | – | I

Brookfield | 17395D-1 W. Blue Mound Rd. (bet. Brookfield & Calhoun Rds.) | 262-784-1332

Located inside a nondescript strip mall, this small, casual Brookfield Indian draws diners with specialties like masala dosai, chicken tikka masala, tandoori lobster tail and saffron mango cheesecake; it also draws heavy eaters with its daily prix fixe lunch buffet.

Sake Tumi *Asian*   21 | 18 | 19 | $34

Downtown | 714 N. Milwaukee St. (bet. Mason St. & Wisconsin Ave.) | 414-224-7253 | www.sake-milwaukee.com

"Unique, tasty" sushi, Japanese specialties and Korean barbecue fuse on the "fun sharing menu" (don't be deterred by the "lame name") at this Downtowner set in a "narrow" storefront on modish Milwaukee Street; still, sometimes "slow" service and a "lack of ambiance" may help explain why a few critics feel it's "lost its mojo"; N.B. smoking permitted in the second-floor Buddha Lounge.

	FOOD	DECOR	SERVICE	COST

Sala da Pranzo *Italian*

▽ 23 | 17 | 22 | $28

East Side | 2613 E. Hampshire Ave. (Downer Ave.) | 414-964-2611 | www.sala-dapranzo.com

"As others come and go", this affordable family-run "little treasure" "tucked away" in the East Side's UW-Milwaukee area continues to woo "college students" and a "neighborhood" crowd with "abundant" plates of "good"-to-"marvelous" Italian fare; the staff and owners are "charming", and the "cozy", "comfortable" confines "get crowded fast", so "be sure to make reservations."

☑ Sanford ☒ *American*

29 | 26 | 28 | $76

East Side | 1547 N. Jackson St. (Pleasant St.) | 414-276-9608 | www.sanfordrestaurant.com

"Rapturous" "aromas emanate" from the kitchen of this "haute" East Side New American (big bro to Coquette Cafe) whose "amazing", "meticulous" cuisine causes epicures to exclaim "wow wow wow!" and vote it Most Popular and No. 1 for Food in the Milwaukee Survey (it's also tops for Decor and Service); an "impeccable and unhurried" staff adds to the "world-class" experience that's "splendid from start to finish", and its "intimate" space "makes you feel as though you're in [co-owner and chef] Sandy D'Amato's own home"; as for the "expensive" tabs, pleased palates would "pay twice as much – gladly."

Savoy Room, The *Italian*

- | - | - | M

East Side | Shorecrest Hotel | 1962 N. Prospect Ave. (Lafayette St.) | 414-270-9933

This "elegant" Italian steakhouse lodged in the lush lobby of the art deco Shorecrest Hotel serves staples "with a contemporary touch" in quarters that are "like an old supper club"; despite the passing of manager Sally Papia in 2005, it still fosters a fanbase; N.B. there's summer seating on the terrace facing busy Prospect Avenue.

Sebastian's ☒ *American*

- | - | - | M

Caledonia | 6025 Douglas Ave. (5 Mile Rd.) | 262-681-5465 | www.sebastiansfinefood.com

"Way off the beaten track, but worth the trip", this "very refined" New American "is the place to go" in Caledonia "for something different and reliably good" (to wit: chef/co-owner Scott Sebastian's potato-crusted grouper with champagne beurre blanc); it offers a "friendly" country vibe, and the "prices tend to be something of a bargain."

Singha Thai *Thai*

▽ 25 | 15 | 17 | $21

West Side | 2237 S. 108th St. (Lincoln Ave.) | 414-541-1234

Singha Thai II ☒ *Thai*

Downtown | 780 N. Jefferson St. (bet. Mason & Wells Sts.) | 414-226-0288

The kitchens of this Siamese twinset turn out an "incredible array" of "really good" spicy staples that may be the "best Thai in Milwaukee"; neither location earns accolades for service or decor – the West Side branch has a strip-mall ambiance, while the Downtowner steps it up slightly with an outdoor patio facing fashionable Jefferson Street.

	FOOD	DECOR	SERVICE	COST

Social, The *American* ▽ 18 | 15 | 16 | $30

Fifth Ward | 170 S. First St. (Pittsburgh Ave.) | 414-270-0438 |
www.the-social.com

Set in an old Fifth Ward foundry, this "quirky" New American proffers "interesting preparations" like "sinful" signature "goat cheese
macaroni" and sophisticated s'mores; still, the unconvinced feel the
staff needs "training" and the eats can be "hit-or-miss."

Tess 🅼 *Eclectic* ▽ 23 | 18 | 23 | $44

East Side | 2499 N. Bartlett Ave. (Bradford Ave.) | 414-964-8377

Savoring the "can't-miss" Eclectic menu of "excellent food" "from
both land and sea" "while sipping a cocktail" at this "quiet, romantic
bistro" adds up to the "perfect neighborhood night" for many East
Siders; some say the decor of its "small, intimate" dining room is
merely "so-so", but the "fabulous patio" "has the feel of a New
Orleans courtyard" – too bad it's only open "in summer."

Third Ward Caffe 🆂🅼 *Italian* ▽ 25 | 19 | 24 | $42

Third Ward | 225 E. St. Paul Ave. (bet. B'way & Water St.) | 414-224-0895

This "unpretentious" Third Ward "not-so-secret jewel" sates with
"well-prepared" Northern Italian that's "always great"; "spot-on"
service oversees the "cramped" confines in a landmark location that
underwent a face-lift in 2007, resulting in a more modern bar area.

Three Brothers 🅼🚫 *Serbian* 23 | 16 | 22 | $29

South Side | 2414 S. St. Clair St. (Russell Ave.) | 414-481-7530

"Bring an appetite" to this "delightful old-world tavern" in a former
Schlitz brewery, a 55-year-old South Side "institution" (still run by the
Radicevic family) that's "like hanging out at your grandma's kitchen
table" – if, that is, your nana made "lovingly presented" burek, goulash
and other "traditional" Serbian dishes; there's certainly "no pretense"
to the "rustic and homespun" (some say "nonexistent") decor, but
most find it "fun and kitschy"– just "don't expect it to be fast."

Yanni's 🆂 *Steak* 21 | 22 | 20 | $47

Downtown | 540 E. Mason St. (bet. Jackson & Jefferson Sts.) |
414-847-9264

Named for owner Danny Goumenos' Greek father, this "beautiful",
clubby 1940s-style steakhouse draws diners Downtown for "good"
Parmesan-crusted filet mignon, baked apple pie and a three-course
prix fixe lunch; while the "relaxed" atmosphere hits a high note, the
service strikes some as "too attentive" and "hovering" unnecessarily.

Zarletti 🆂 *Italian* 22 | 19 | 19 | $41

Downtown | 741 N. Milwaukee St. (Mason St.) | 414-225-0000 |
www.zarletti.net

"You feel like a regular on your second visit" to this "homey", "bustling"
Italian that entices with "well-prepared", "authentic" eats from a
somewhat "limited menu", layed out by an "attentive" staff; it "can get
a bit loud", and the problematic parking on mobbed Milwaukee Street
"might deter people" who don't know there's a valet (a "huge plus").

MILWAUKEE
INDEXES

Cuisines

Includes restaurant names, locations and Food ratings. ☒ indicates places with the highest ratings, popularity and importance.

AMERICAN (NEW)

☒ Bacchus | **Downtown**	26
Coast | **Downtown**	18
☒ Dream Dance | **Downtown**	28
Elm Grove Inn | **Elm Grove**	-
Envoy | **Downtown**	-
Gilbert's | **Lake Geneva**	-
Heaven City | **Mukwonago**	-
NEW Hinterland | **Third Ward**	-
Immigrant Rm. | **Kohler**	24
☒ Kil@wat | **Downtown**	21
North Shore | **N Shore**	19
Palms Bistro | **Third Ward**	19
☒ Sanford | **E Side**	29
Sebastian's | **Caledonia**	-
Social | **Fifth Ward**	18

AMERICAN (TRADITIONAL)

Cheesecake Factory | **multi.**	19
Elsa's on Park | **Downtown**	22
Golden Mast | **Okauchee**	21
Jackson Grill | **S Side**	26
Mason St. Grill | **Downtown**	25
North Star | **multi.**	22
Original Pancake/Walker Bros. | **multi.**	23
☒ Riversite, The | **Mequon**	28
Rock Bottom | **Downtown**	16

ASIAN FUSION

Hama | **N Shore**	18

BURGERS

Elsa's on Park | **Downtown**	22

CAJUN

Bayou | **E Side**	18
Crawdaddy's | **SW Side**	22
NEW Maxie's | **W Side**	-

CALIFORNIAN

Roots | **Brewers Hill**	26

CHINESE

P.F. Chang's | **Wauwatosa**	21

COFFEE SHOPS/DINERS

Original Pancake/Walker Bros. | **E Side**	23

CREOLE

Bayou | **E Side**	18
Crawdaddy's | **SW Side**	22
NEW Maxie's | **W Side**	-

CUBAN

Cubanitas | **Downtown**	21

DESSERT

Cheesecake Factory | **multi.**	19

ECLECTIC

Eagan's | **Downtown**	20
Elm Grove Inn | **Elm Grove**	-
Knick | **Downtown**	21
NEW Meritage | **W Side**	24
Tess | **E Side**	23

FRENCH

Coquette Cafe | **Third Ward**	24
☒ Lake Park | **E Side**	26

FRENCH (BISTRO)

Elliot's Bistro | **E Side**	21

GASTROPUB

NEW Hinterland | **Amer.** | **Third Ward**	-

GERMAN

Golden Mast | **Okauchee**	21
☒ Karl Ratzsch's | **Downtown**	24

INDIAN

Saffron Indian | **Brookfield**	-

ITALIAN

(N=Northern; S=Southern)

Il Mito Enoteca | **Wauwatosa**	-
Maggiano's | **Wauwatosa**	21

Mangia | **Kenosha** 28

Mimma's Café | **E Side** 24

Osteria/Mondo | N | **Downtown** 26

☑ Rist. Bartolotta | **Wauwatosa** 28

Sala da Pranzo | **E Side** 23

Savoy Rm. | S | **E Side** –

Third Ward Caffe | N | **Third Ward** 25

Zarletti | N | **Downtown** 22

JAPANESE
(* sushi specialist)

Benihana | **Downtown** 20

Hama | **N Shore** 18

Nanakusa* | **Third Ward** 24

Sake Tumi* | **Downtown** 21

KOREAN
(* barbecue specialist)

Sake Tumi* | **Downtown** 21

MEXICAN

Cempazuchi | **E Side** 21

PIZZA

Edwardo's Pizza | **W Side** 20

POLISH

Polonez | **S Side** –

SANDWICHES

Potbelly | **multi.** 19

SEAFOOD

Bosley on Brady | **E Side** 25

Eagan's | **Downtown** 20

Jackson Grill | **S Side** 26

River Ln. Inn | **N Shore** 23

SERBIAN

Three Brothers | **S Side** 23

SOUTHERN

NEW Maxie's | **W Side** –

STEAKHOUSES

Benihana | **Downtown** 20

Bosley on Brady | **E Side** 25

Capital Grille | **Downtown** 25

Carnevor | **Downtown** 24

Eddie Martini's | **W Side** 25

Five O'Clock | **Central City** 23

NEW Fleming's | **Brookfield** 22

Jackson Grill | **S Side** 26

Jake's | **Brookfield** 25

Milwaukee Chophse. | **Downtown** 22

Mo's: Steak | **Downtown** 21

Mr. B's | **Brookfield** 24

Savoy Rm. | **E Side** –

Yanni's | **Downtown** 21

THAI

King & I | **Downtown** 25

Singha Thai | **multi.** 25

Locations

Includes restaurant names, cuisines and Food ratings. ☑ indicates places with the highest ratings, popularity and importance.

Milwaukee

BREWERS HILL
Roots | *Calif.* — 26

CENTRAL CITY
Five O'Clock | *Steak* — 23

DOWNTOWN
☑ Bacchus | *Amer.* — 26
Benihana | *Japanese/Steak* — 20
Capital Grille | *Steak* — 25
Carnevor | *Steak* — 24
Coast | *Amer.* — 18
Cubanitas | *Cuban* — 21
☑ Dream Dance | *Amer.* — 28
Eagan's | *Eclectic* — 20
Elsa's on Park | *Amer.* — 22
Envoy | *Amer.* — -
☑ Karl Ratzsch's | *German* — 24
☑ Kil@wat | *Amer.* — 21
King & I | *Thai* — 25
Knick | *Eclectic* — 21
Mason St. Grill | *Amer.* — 25
Milwaukee Chophse. | *Steak* — 22
Mo's: Steak | *Steak* — 21
Osteria/Mondo | *Italian* — 26
Potbelly | *Sandwiches* — 19
Rock Bottom | *Amer.* — 16
Sake Tumi | *Asian* — 21
Singha Thai | *Thai* — 25
Yanni's | *Steak* — 21
Zarletti | *Italian* — 22

EAST SIDE
Bayou | *Cajun/Creole* — 18
Bosley on Brady | *Seafood/Steak* — 25
Cempazuchi | *Mex.* — 21
Elliot's Bistro | *French* — 21
☑ Lake Park | *French* — 26
Mimma's Café | *Italian* — 24
Original Pancake/Walker Bros. | *Amer.* — 23

FIFTH WARD
Social | *Amer.* — 18

Sala da Pranzo | *Italian* — 23
☑ Sanford | *Amer.* — 29
Savoy Rm. | *Italian* — -
Tess | *Eclectic* — 23

NORTH SHORE
Hama | *Asian Fusion/Japanese* — 18
North Shore | *Amer.* — 19
River Ln. Inn | *Seafood* — 23

SOUTH SIDE
Jackson Grill | *Steak* — 26
Polonez | *Polish* — -
Three Brothers | *Serbian* — 23

SOUTHWEST SIDE
Crawdaddy's | *Cajun/Creole* — 22

THIRD WARD
Coquette Cafe | *French* — 24
NEW Hinterland | *Amer.* — -
Nanakusa | *Japanese* — 24
Palms Bistro | *Amer.* — 19
Third Ward Caffe | *Italian* — 25

WEST SIDE
Eddie Martini's | *Steak* — 25
Edwardo's Pizza | *Pizza* — 20
NEW Maxie's | *Creole* — -
NEW Meritage | *Eclectic* — 24
Singha Thai | *Thai* — 25

Outlying Areas

BROOKFIELD
NEW Fleming's | *Steak* — 22
Jake's | *Steak* — 25
Mr. B's | *Steak* — 24
North Star | *Amer.* — 22
Original Pancake/Walker Bros. | *Amer.* — 23
Potbelly | *Sandwiches* — 19
Saffron Indian | *Indian* — -

CALEDONIA

Sebastian's | *Amer.*   -

ELM GROVE

Elm Grove Inn | *Amer./Eclectic*   -

GLENDALE

Cheesecake Factory | *Amer.*   19

KENOSHA

Mangia | *Italian*   28

KOHLER

Immigrant Rm. | *Amer.*   24

LAKE GENEVA

Gilbert's | *Amer.*   -

MEQUON

🛛 Riversite, The | *Amer.*   28

MUKWONAGO

Heaven City | *Amer.*   -

OKAUCHEE

Golden Mast | *Amer./German*   21

SHOREWOOD

North Star | *Amer.*   22

WAUWATOSA

Cheesecake Factory | *Amer.*   19
Il Mito Enoteca | *Italian*   -
Maggiano's | *Italian*   21
P.F. Chang's | *Chinese*   21
🛛 Rist. Bartolotta | *Italian*   28

Special Features

Listings cover the best in each category and include names, locations and Food ratings. Multi-location restaurants' features may vary by branch.
Z indicates places with the highest ratings, popularity and importance.

BRUNCH

Eagan's | **Downtown**	20
Elliot's Bistro | **E Side**	21
Golden Mast | **Okauchee**	21
Knick | **Downtown**	21
Polonez | **S Side**	–
Tess | **E Side**	23

BUFFET

(Check availability)

Eagan's | **Downtown**	20
King & I | **Downtown**	25
Polonez | **S Side**	–
Saffron Indian | **Brookfield**	–

BUSINESS DINING

Z Bacchus | **Downtown**	26
Carnevor | **Downtown**	24
Coast | **Downtown**	18
Coquette Cafe | **Third Ward**	24
Eagan's | **Downtown**	20
Eddie Martini's | **W Side**	25
Elm Grove Inn | **Elm Grove**	–
Envoy | **Downtown**	–
Jake's | **Brookfield**	25
Z Karl Ratzsch's | **Downtown**	24
Z Kil@wat | **Downtown**	21
Knick | **Downtown**	21
Z Lake Park | **E Side**	26
Mason St. Grill | **Downtown**	25
Milwaukee Chophse. | **Downtown**	22
Mo's: Steak | **Downtown**	21
Mr. B's | **Brookfield**	24
North Shore | **N Shore**	19
North Star | **Brookfield**	22
Z Rist. Bartolotta | **Wauwatosa**	28
River Ln. Inn | **N Shore**	23
Z Riversite, The | **Mequon**	28
Roots | **Brewers Hill**	26
Saffron Indian | **Brookfield**	–
Yanni's | **Downtown**	21

CELEBRITY CHEFS

(Listed under their primary restaurants)

Il Mito Enoteca | *Michael Feker* | **Wauwatosa**	–
Jackson Grill | *Jimmy Jackson* | **S Side**	26
Mason St. Grill | *Mark Weber* | **Downtown**	25
NEW Maxie's | *Joe Muench* | **W Side**	–
Mimma's Café | *Mimma Megna* | **E Side**	24
Osteria/Mondo | *Marc Bianchini* | **Downtown**	26
Z Riversite, The | *Tom Peschong* | **Mequon**	28
Z Sanford | *Sandy D'Amato* | **E Side**	29

CHILD-FRIENDLY

(Alternatives to the usual fast-food places; * children's menu available)

Benihana* | **Downtown**	20
Cempazuchi | **E Side**	21
Coast* | **Downtown**	18
Edwardo's Pizza* | **W Side**	20
Gilbert's* | **Lake Geneva**	–
Golden Mast* | **Okauchee**	21
Hama | **N Shore**	18
Z Karl Ratzsch's* | **Downtown**	24
Knick | **Downtown**	21
Maggiano's* | **Wauwatosa**	21
Mangia* | **Kenosha**	28
Palms Bistro | **Third Ward**	19
P.F. Chang's | **Wauwatosa**	21
Rock Bottom* | **Downtown**	16
Tess | **E Side**	23
Third Ward Caffe* | **Third Ward**	25

CIGARS WELCOME

Elm Grove Inn | **Elm Grove**	–
Heaven City | **Mukwonago**	–
Osteria/Mondo | **Downtown**	26
Yanni's | **Downtown**	21

DELIVERY/TAKEOUT

(D=delivery, T=takeout)

Benihana | T | **Downtown**	20
Cempazuchi | T | **E Side**	21
Crawdaddy's | T | **SW Side**	22
Elsa's on Park | T | **Downtown**	22
Hama | T | **N Shore**	18
Knick | T | **Downtown**	21
Maggiano's | T | **Wauwatosa**	21
Mimma's Café | T | **E Side**	24
Nanakusa | T | **Third Ward**	24
North Shore | T | **N Shore**	19
Palms Bistro | T | **Third Ward**	19
Polonez | T | **S Side**	-
Potbelly | D, T | **multi.**	19
River Ln. Inn | T | **N Shore**	23
Rock Bottom | T | **Downtown**	16
Roots | T | **Brewers Hill**	26
Singha Thai | T | **W Side**	25
Third Ward Caffe | T | **Third Ward**	25

DINING ALONE

(Other than hotels and places with counter service)

Benihana | **Downtown**	20
Cempazuchi | **E Side**	21
Coquette Cafe | **Third Ward**	24
Cubanitas | **Downtown**	21
Hama | **N Shore**	18
☑ Lake Park | **E Side**	26
Nanakusa | **Third Ward**	24
North Shore | **N Shore**	19
Potbelly | **Downtown**	19
Rock Bottom | **Downtown**	16
Singha Thai | **W Side**	25

ENTERTAINMENT

(Call for days and times of performances)

Coast | jazz/R&B | **Downtown**	18
Immigrant Rm. | piano | **Kohler**	24
☑ Karl Ratzsch's | piano | **Downtown**	24
North Shore | jazz | **N Shore**	19

FIREPLACES

Coast | **Downtown**	18
Elm Grove Inn | **Elm Grove**	-
Gilbert's | **Lake Geneva**	-
Golden Mast | **Okauchee**	21
Heaven City | **Mukwonago**	-
Jake's | **Brookfield**	25
Palms Bistro | **Third Ward**	19
Sebastian's | **Caledonia**	-

GAME IN SEASON

Coast | **Downtown**	18
Coquette Cafe | **Third Ward**	24
☑ Dream Dance | **Downtown**	28
Elliot's Bistro | **E Side**	21
Elm Grove Inn | **Elm Grove**	-
Gilbert's | **Lake Geneva**	-
Golden Mast | **Okauchee**	21
Heaven City | **Mukwonago**	-
NEW Hinterland | **Third Ward**	-
Immigrant Rm. | **Kohler**	24
Jake's | **Brookfield**	25

HISTORIC PLACES

(Year opened; * building)

1855 | Elm Grove Inn* | **Elm Grove**	-
1875 | Gilbert's* | **Lake Geneva**	-
1875 | Third Ward Caffe* | **Third Ward**	25
1890 | Elsa's on Park* | **Downtown**	22
1890 | Three Brothers* | **S Side**	23
1893 | Mason St. Grill* | **Downtown**	25
1900 | Rist. Bartolotta* | **Wauwatosa**	28
1900 | River Ln. Inn* | **N Shore**	23
1904 | Karl Ratzsch's | **Downtown**	24
1918 | Immigrant Rm.* | **Kohler**	24
1927 | Envoy* | **Downtown**	-
1948 | Five O'Clock | **Central City**	23

HOTEL DINING

Ambassador Hotel	
Envoy | **Downtown**	-
Hilton Milwaukee City Ctr.	
Milwaukee Chophse. | **Downtown**	22
Intercontinental Milwaukee	
☑ Kil@wat | **Downtown**	21
Knickerbocker Hotel	
Knick | **Downtown**	21

Pfister Hotel
   Mason St. Grill | **Downtown** _25_

Shorecrest Hotel
   Savoy Rm. | **E Side** _-_

JACKET REQUIRED

Immigrant Rm. | **Kohler** _24_

LATE DINING

(Weekday closing hour)
Elsa's on Park | 1 AM | **Downtown** _22_
Knick | 12 AM | **Downtown** _21_

MEET FOR A DRINK

(Most top hotels and the following standouts)
🆉 Bacchus | **Downtown** _26_
Bayou | **E Side** _18_
Bosley on Brady | **E Side** _25_
Carnevor | **Downtown** _24_
Cempazuchi | **E Side** _21_
Coast | **Downtown** _18_
Coquette Cafe | **Third Ward** _24_
Crawdaddy's | **SW Side** _22_
Cubanitas | **Downtown** _21_
Eagan's | **Downtown** _20_
Eddie Martini's | **W Side** _25_
Elsa's on Park | **Downtown** _22_
Envoy | **Downtown** _-_
Il Mito Enoteca | **Wauwatosa** _-_
Jackson Grill | **S Side** _26_
Knick | **Downtown** _21_
🆉 Lake Park | **E Side** _26_
Mason St. Grill | **Downtown** _25_
NEW Maxie's | **W Side** _-_
Mo's: Steak | **Downtown** _21_
Nanakusa | **Third Ward** _24_
North Shore | **N Shore** _19_
North Star | **multi.** _22_
Osteria/Mondo | **Downtown** _26_
Palms Bistro | **Third Ward** _19_
Rock Bottom | **Downtown** _16_
Sake Tumi | **Downtown** _21_
Savoy Rm. | **E Side** _-_
Social | **Fifth Ward** _18_
Tess | **E Side** _23_
Yanni's | **Downtown** _21_
Zarletti | **Downtown** _22_

MICROBREWERIES

Rock Bottom | **Downtown** _16_

NOTEWORTHY NEWCOMERS

Fleming's | **Brookfield** _22_
Hinterland | **Third Ward** _-_
Maxie's | **W Side** _-_
Meritage | **W Side** _24_
Original Pancake/Walker Bros. | **Brookfield** _23_

OUTDOOR DINING

(P=patio; S=sidewalk; T=terrace; W=waterside)
Coast | P | **Downtown** _18_
Eagan's | S | **Downtown** _20_
Edwardo's Pizza | P | **W Side** _20_
Golden Mast | P, W | **Okauchee** _21_
Knick | P | **Downtown** _21_
Maggiano's | P | **Wauwatosa** _21_
Mangia | P | **Kenosha** _28_
North Shore | P | **N Shore** _19_
Osteria/Mondo | P | **Downtown** _26_
Palms Bistro | S | **Third Ward** _19_
P.F. Chang's | P | **Wauwatosa** _21_
Potbelly | P, S | **multi.** _19_
🆉 Rist. Bartolotta | S | **Wauwatosa** _28_
River Ln. Inn | P | **N Shore** _23_
🆉 Riversite, The | P, W | **Mequon** _28_
Rock Bottom | P, W | **Downtown** _16_
Roots | P, T | **Brewers Hill** _26_
Savoy Rm. | S | **E Side** _-_
Tess | P | **E Side** _23_
Third Ward Caffe | S | **Third Ward** _25_

PEOPLE-WATCHING

🆉 Bacchus | **Downtown** _26_
Carnevor | **Downtown** _24_
Coast | **Downtown** _18_
Coquette Cafe | **Third Ward** _24_
Cubanitas | **Downtown** _21_
Eagan's | **Downtown** _20_
Eddie Martini's | **W Side** _25_
Elsa's on Park | **Downtown** _22_
Envoy | **Downtown** _-_
🆉 Kil@wat | **Downtown** _21_
Knick | **Downtown** _21_

Maggiano's | **Wauwatosa**	21
Mason St. Grill | **Downtown**	25
NEW Maxie's | **W Side**	–
Mimma's Café | **E Side**	24
Mo's: Steak | **Downtown**	21
Nanakusa | **Third Ward**	24
North Shore | **N Shore**	19
Palms Bistro | **Third Ward**	19
P.F. Chang's | **Wauwatosa**	21
Z Rist. Bartolotta | **Wauwatosa**	28
River Ln. Inn | **N Shore**	23
Rock Bottom | **Downtown**	16
Sake Tumi | **Downtown**	21
Z Sanford | **E Side**	29
Savoy Rm. | **E Side**	–
Three Brothers | **S Side**	23
Yanni's | **Downtown**	21

POWER SCENES

Z Bacchus | **Downtown**	26
Carnevor | **Downtown**	24
Eddie Martini's | **W Side**	25
Envoy | **Downtown**	–
Z Lake Park | **E Side**	26
Mason St. Grill | **Downtown**	25
Mo's: Steak | **Downtown**	21
Mr. B's | **Brookfield**	24
North Star | **Brookfield**	22
Savoy Rm. | **E Side**	–
Yanni's | **Downtown**	21

PRIVATE ROOMS

(Restaurants charge less at off times; call for capacity)

Coast | **Downtown**	18
Coquette Cafe | **Third Ward**	24
Eddie Martini's | **W Side**	25
Edwardo's Pizza | **W Side**	20
Elm Grove Inn | **Elm Grove**	–
Gilbert's | **Lake Geneva**	–
Golden Mast | **Okauchee**	21
Hama | **N Shore**	18
Heaven City | **Mukwonago**	–
Immigrant Rm. | **Kohler**	24
Maggiano's | **Wauwatosa**	21
Mangia | **Kenosha**	28
Mimma's Café | **E Side**	24
Mr. B's | **Brookfield**	24

Nanakusa | **Third Ward**	24
Osteria/Mondo | **Downtown**	26
Polonez | **S Side**	–
River Ln. Inn | **N Shore**	23
Z Riversite, The | **Mequon**	28
Rock Bottom | **Downtown**	16
Sebastian's | **Caledonia**	–

PRIX FIXE MENUS

(Call for prices and times)

Gilbert's | **Lake Geneva**	–
Immigrant Rm. | **Kohler**	24

QUICK BITES

Cubanitas | **Downtown**	21
Edwardo's Pizza | **W Side**	20
Elsa's on Park | **Downtown**	22
Hama | **N Shore**	18
Knick | **Downtown**	21
NEW Maxie's | **W Side**	–

QUIET CONVERSATION

Bosley on Brady | **E Side**	25
Z Dream Dance | **Downtown**	28
Eddie Martini's | **W Side**	25
Elliot's Bistro | **E Side**	21
Elm Grove Inn | **Elm Grove**	–
Envoy | **Downtown**	–
Golden Mast | **Okauchee**	21
Jake's | **Brookfield**	25
Z Karl Ratzsch's | **Downtown**	24
Z Kil@wat | **Downtown**	21
Milwaukee Chophse. | **Downtown**	22
North Star | **Brookfield**	22
Osteria/Mondo | **Downtown**	26
Polonez | **S Side**	–
Z Riversite, The | **Mequon**	28
Z Sanford | **E Side**	29
Third Ward Caffe | **Third Ward**	25

RAW BARS

Benihana | **Downtown**	20
Eagan's | **Downtown**	20
NEW Maxie's | **W Side**	–

ROMANTIC PLACES

Golden Mast | **Okauchee**	21
Heaven City | **Mukwonago**	–

MILWAUKEE

SPECIAL FEATURES

Il Mito Enoteca | **Wauwatosa** -|
Immigrant Rm. | **Kohler** 24|
☑ Lake Park | **E Side** 26|
Mimma's Café | **E Side** 24|
Osteria/Mondo | **Downtown** 26|
☑ Riversite, The | **Mequon** 28|
Third Ward Caffe | **Third Ward** 25|
Three Brothers | **S Side** 23|
Zarletti | **Downtown** 22|

SENIOR APPEAL

Elm Grove Inn | **Elm Grove** -|
Envoy | **Downtown** -|
Golden Mast | **Okauchee** 21|
Immigrant Rm. | **Kohler** 24|
Jake's | **Brookfield** 25|
☑ Karl Ratzsch's | **Downtown** 24|
North Star | **multi.** 22|
Polonez | **S Side** -|
☑ Riversite, The | **Mequon** 28|
Three Brothers | **S Side** 23|

SINGLES SCENES

Bayou | **E Side** 18|
Carnevor | **Downtown** 24|
Crawdaddy's | **SW Side** 22|
Cubanitas | **Downtown** 21|
Eagan's | **Downtown** 20|
Elsa's on Park | **Downtown** 22|
Knick | **Downtown** 21|
Mo's: Steak | **Downtown** 21|
Nanakusa | **Third Ward** 24|
Palms Bistro | **Third Ward** 19|
Rock Bottom | **Downtown** 16|
Sake Tumi | **Downtown** 21|
Social | **Fifth Ward** 18|

SLEEPERS

(Good to excellent food, but little known)
Bosley on Brady | **E Side** 25|
Jackson Grill | **S Side** 26|
Jake's | **Brookfield** 25|
Osteria/Mondo | **Downtown** 26|
Sala da Pranzo | **E Side** 23|
Singha Thai | **multi.** 25|
Tess | **E Side** 23|
Third Ward Caffe | **Third Ward** 25|

TEEN APPEAL

Edwardo's Pizza | **W Side** 20|
Maggiano's | **Wauwatosa** 21|
P.F. Chang's | **Wauwatosa** 21|
Potbelly | **Downtown** 19|
Rock Bottom | **Downtown** 16|

TRENDY

☑ Bacchus | **Downtown** 26|
Bayou | **E Side** 18|
Carnevor | **Downtown** 24|
Cempazuchi | **E Side** 21|
Coast | **Downtown** 18|
Cubanitas | **Downtown** 21|
Eddie Martini's | **W Side** 25|
Elsa's on Park | **Downtown** 22|
☑ Kil@wat | **Downtown** 21|
Knick | **Downtown** 21|
☑ Lake Park | **E Side** 26|
Maggiano's | **Wauwatosa** 21|
Mo's: Steak | **Downtown** 21|
Palms Bistro | **Third Ward** 19|
P.F. Chang's | **Wauwatosa** 21|
☑ Rist. Bartolotta | **Wauwatosa** 28|
Sake Tumi | **Downtown** 21|
☑ Sanford | **E Side** 29|
Social | **Fifth Ward** 18|
Zarletti | **Downtown** 22|

VIEWS

☑ Bacchus | **Downtown** 26|
Bayou | **E Side** 18|
Coast | **Downtown** 18|
Gilbert's | **Lake Geneva** -|
Golden Mast | **Okauchee** 21|
Knick | **Downtown** 21|
☑ Lake Park | **E Side** 26|
☑ Riversite, The | **Mequon** 28|
Roots | **Brewers Hill** 26|
Sebastian's | **Caledonia** -|

VISITORS ON EXPENSE ACCOUNT

Coquette Cafe | **Third Ward** 24|
Cubanitas | **Downtown** 21|
Eagan's | **Downtown** 20|
Edwardo's Pizza | **W Side** 20|

WINE BARS

WINNING WINE LISTS

WORTH A TRIP

MILWAUKEE

SPECIAL FEATURES

Wine Vintage Chart

This chart, based on our 0 to 30 scale, is designed to help you select wine. The ratings (by **Howard Stravitz,** a law professor at the University of South Carolina) reflect the vintage quality and the wine's readiness to drink. We exclude the 1991–1993 vintages because they are not that good. A dash indicates the wine is either past its peak or too young to rate. Loire ratings are for dry white wines.

Whites	88	89	90	94	95	96	97	98	99	00	01	02	03	04	05	06
French:																
Alsace	-	25	25	24	23	23	22	25	23	25	27	25	22	24	25	-
Burgundy	-	23	22	-	28	27	24	22	26	25	24	27	23	27	26	24
Loire Valley	-	-	-	-	-	-	-	-	-	24	25	26	23	24	27	24
Champagne	24	26	29	-	26	27	24	23	24	24	22	26	-	-	-	-
Sauternes	29	25	28	-	21	23	25	23	24	24	28	25	26	21	26	23
California:																
Chardonnay	-	-	-	-	-	-	-	-	24	23	26	26	25	27	29	25
Sauvignon Blanc	-	-	-	-	-	-	-	-	-	-	27	28	26	27	26	27
Austrian:																
Grüner Velt./ Riesling	-	-	-	-	25	21	26	26	25	22	23	25	26	25	26	-
German:	25	26	27	24	23	26	25	26	23	21	29	27	24	26	28	-

Reds	88	89	90	94	95	96	97	98	99	00	01	02	03	04	05	06
French:																
Bordeaux	23	25	29	22	26	25	23	25	24	29	26	24	25	24	27	25
Burgundy	-	24	26	-	26	27	25	22	27	22	24	27	25	25	27	25
Rhône	26	28	28	24	26	22	25	27	26	27	26	-	25	24	25	-
Beaujolais	-	-	-	-	-	-	-	-	-	24	-	23	25	22	28	26
California:																
Cab./Merlot	-	-	28	29	27	25	28	23	26	22	27	26	25	24	24	23
Pinot Noir	-	-	-	-	-	-	24	23	24	23	27	28	26	25	24	-
Zinfandel	-	-	-	-	-	-	-	-	-	-	25	23	27	24	23	-
Oregon:																
Pinot Noir	-	-	-	-	-	-	-	-	-	-	-	27	25	26	27	-
Italian:																
Tuscany	-	-	25	22	24	20	29	24	27	24	27	20	25	25	22	24
Piedmont	-	27	27	-	23	26	27	26	25	28	27	20	24	25	26	-
Spanish:																
Rioja	-	-	-	26	26	24	25	22	25	24	27	20	24	25	26	24
Ribera del Duero/Priorat	-	-	-	26	26	27	25	24	25	24	27	20	24	26	26	24
Australian:																
Shiraz/Cab.	-	-	-	24	26	23	26	28	24	24	27	27	25	26	24	-
Chilean:	-	-	-	-	-	-	24	-	25	23	26	24	25	24	26	-

ON THE GO.
IN THE KNOW.

ZAGAT TO GO℠

Unlimited access
to Zagat dining &
travel content
in hundreds of
major cities.

Search by name,
location, ratings,
cuisine, special
features & Top Lists.

For BlackBerry,® Palm,®
Windows Mobile®
and mobile phones.

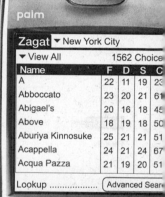

Get it now at **mobile.zagat.com**
or text* **ZAGAT** to **78247**

Zagat Products

RESTAURANTS & MAPS

America's Top Restaurants
Atlanta
Beijing
Boston
Brooklyn
California Wine Country
Cape Cod & The Islands
Chicago
Connecticut
Europe's Top Restaurants
Hamptons (incl. wineries)
Hong Kong
Las Vegas
London
Long Island (incl. wineries)
Los Angeles I So. California
(guide & map)
Miami Beach
Miami I So. Florida
Montréal
New Jersey
New Jersey Shore
New Orleans
New York City (guide & map)
Palm Beach
Paris
Philadelphia
San Diego
San Francisco (guide & map)
Seattle
Shanghai
Texas
Tokyo
Toronto
Vancouver
Washington, DC I Baltimore
Westchester I Hudson Valley
World's Top Restaurants

LIFESTYLE GUIDES

America's Top Golf Courses
Movie Guide
Music Guide
NYC Gourmet Shop./Entertaining
NYC Shopping

NIGHTLIFE GUIDES

Los Angeles
New York City
San Francisco

HOTEL & TRAVEL GUIDES

Beijing
Hong Kong
Las Vegas
London
New Orleans
Montréal
Shanghai
Top U.S. Hotels, Resorts & Spas
Toronto
U.S. Family Travel
Vancouver
Walt Disney World Insider's Guide
World's Top Hotels, Resorts & Spas

WEB & WIRELESS SERVICES

ZAGAT TO GO℠ for handhelds
ZAGAT.com℠ • ZAGAT.mobi℠

**Available wherever books are sold or at ZAGAT.com. To customize
Zagat guides as gifts or marketing tools, call 800-540-9609.**